AF496454

# A New History of the
# ROMAN EMPERORS

# A New History of the
# ROMAN EMPERORS

### Roger Michael Kean

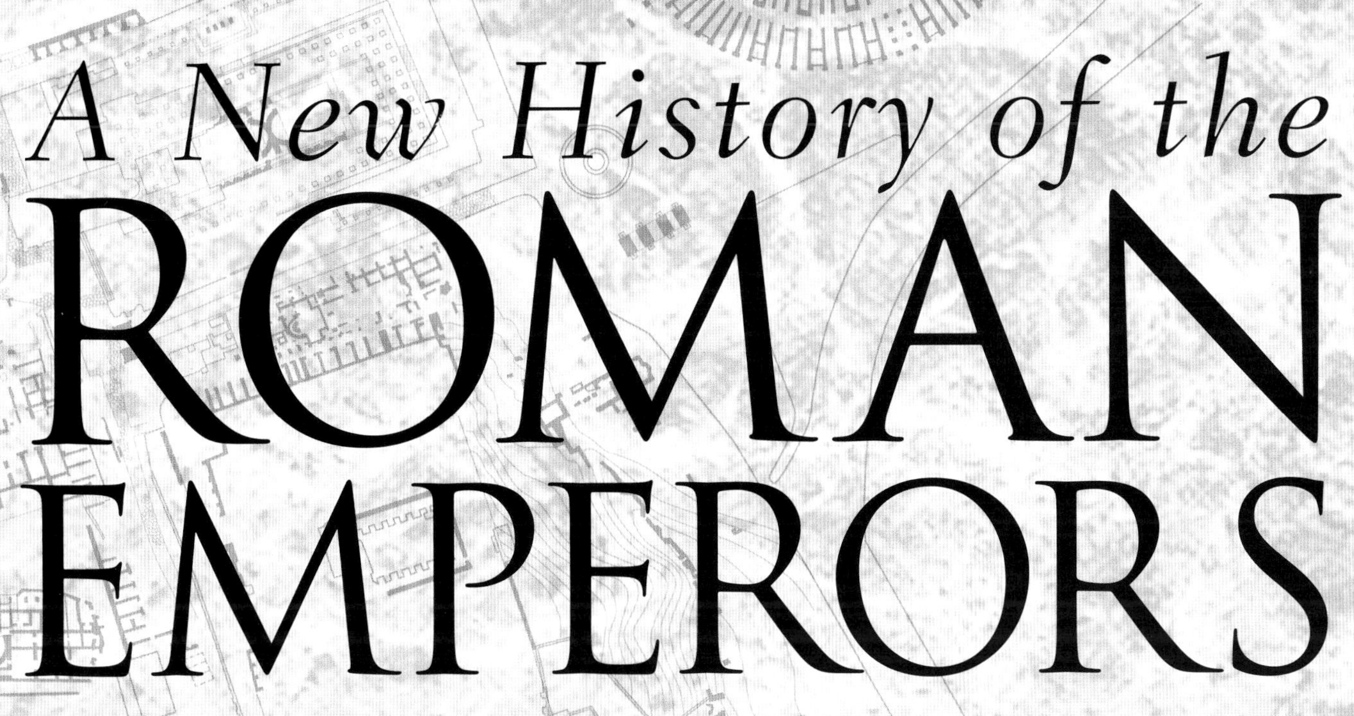

THALAMUS

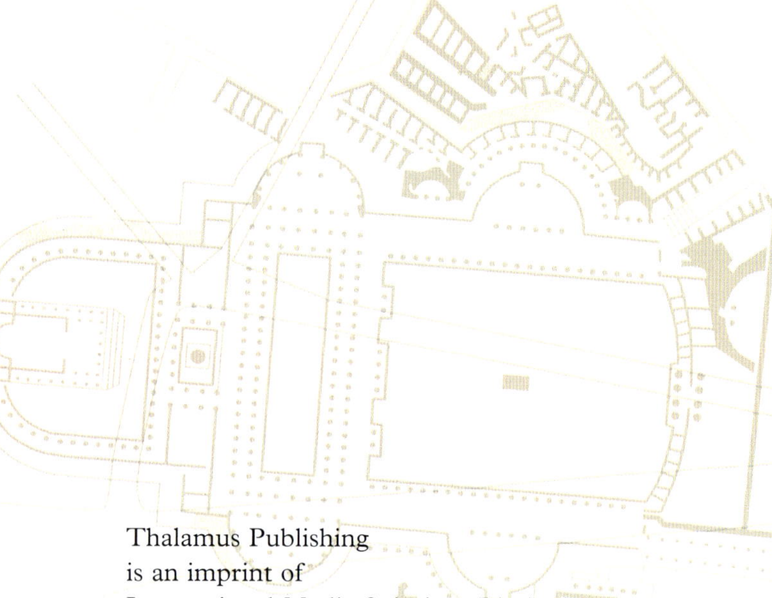

Thalamus Publishing
is an imprint of
International Media Solutions Limited
4 Attorney's Walk, Bull Ring,
Ludlow, Shropshire SY8 1AA
England
01584 874977



British Library Cataloguing in Publication Data
A CIP Data Record for this book
is available from the British Library
ISBN 1-902886-36-7

Project editor: Warren Lapworth
Maps and design: Roger Kean
Illustrations: Oliver Frey

Typeset in Plantin and Helvetica Neue Condensed

Printed and bound in China
This book is printed on acid-free paper

10 9 8 7 6 5 4 3 2 1

Picture acknowledgements
All photographs by the author

# CONTENTS

# End of the Republic

[157–44 BC]

There are as many theories behind the fall of the Roman empire as there are historians to put them forward. Its rise, however – and the concurrent collapse of the Roman Republic – is somewhat easier to understand. By the middle of the first century BC the Roman state had become a victim of its own success. Conquests to the west in Spain, to the east beyond Macedonia into Asia Minor and across the Mediterranean in North Africa had made the senatorial governing system unsustainable. In addition, the senate – the body of three hundred most senior Romans – had grown complacent and fractious, riven with factional conflicts that often centred on the ambitions of the ancient aristocratic families on the one hand and those of the 'new men', politicians arising from the rural Italian provinces, on the other. These two social groups broadly divided themselves between the *optimates*, conservatives who put the rule of the senate first, and the *populares*, reformers who worked through the *tribuni plebis*, people's tribunes, rather than the senate. The division of opinion was almost exclusively concerned with the benefits of the city of Rome and its Latin hinterland, not with the greater matter of empire. Rome might have been the centre of the world, but its plutocrats acted more like parochial land-owners than the governors of an empire.

Rome itself had also swelled to bursting point, filled with a mass of indolent citizens who paid no taxes, thanks to recent conquests. The mob was bored and happily exchanged yesterday's allegiance for today's, swayed by the next clever orator to come along. Street violence and open rioting was symptomatic of the crisis facing the Republic, which only a strong man could quell. And a strong man needed the power of the army behind him, but this was no easy matter. Constitutionally, the senate elected two consuls for each year to draw up legislation and command the legions when required. Neither was allowed to serve a second term, but was given a province to govern for a further proconsular year – usually a time to make a deal of money. However, periods of extended conflict, such as the Punic Wars, had meant that consuls had their terms prolonged to provide military continuity – soon enough some men found good reasons to prolong their term or repeat their consulship.

Gaius Marius (157–86 BC) was the first. He had himself elected consul first in 108 BC, again in 104, and then every year – first warring against the Numidian Jugurtha in Africa, and then against Germans invading Italy – until his sixth consulship in 100. Marius used this period to reform the army – an unprofessional institution, manned by civilian conscripts who gave their time on an annual basis as part of the duty expected of every Roman citizen. The men were dismissed at the end of each campaigning year only to be recruited again in the following season. Marius scorned this inefficient system. Wars were lasting longer – Jugurtha took the field for four years – and farmer-citizen warriors were no longer up to the task. Marius abandoned the practice of raising troops from among the land-owning farmers and instead enlisted volunteers from the proletariat. But men of the mob needed proper pay, not the regular military stipend, to afford arms and armour, and they expected to be kept in service to the end of their useful lives and then settled on a smallholding for their old age. In effect, the legion became a permanent organisation into which new recruits could be added. It was also one that owed allegiance to its commander,

Bust of Gaius Marius, the man credited with founding the professional Roman army – one loyal to its *legatus* or general before the state.

*Opposite:* Lucius Cornelius Sulla Felix ('Lucky') made apparent how a ruthless man could wield the Roman army as a personal weapon.

a man now more than likely to lead them for much longer than the traditional year. The legions, first under Marius and then his ambitious successors, effectively became their general's private force.

If Marius's extended consulships were contrary to all precedent, his erstwhile lieutenant, Lucius Cornelius Sulla (138–78 BC), outdid him. After a civil war between the supporters of the two former colleagues, Sulla marched on Rome and declared himself dictator in 81. Allowed for in times of grave national danger, the role gave whoever held it absolute power until the crisis had passed and then an indemnity against the results of their actions after standing down. Sulla's unilateral assumption was unprecedented too. Sulla ruled Rome without limitation to the term of his office and without recourse to the law – thousands died in paranoid purges, including senators and men of the equestrian order, Rome's middle class businessmen. When, to everyone's surprise, he laid down the dictatorship at the end of the year he left behind a power vacuum into which stepped ambitious young lieutenants like Gnaeus Pompey, Marcus Crassus and Caesar.

**GENIUS MILITARY COMMANDER,** gifted orator, prolific writer and law-maker, Gaius Julius Caesar (12/13 July 100–15 March 44 BC) was a man of many parts. He spoke the language of the common legionary but moved among Rome's elite on equal terms – at least as regards his patrician status; the *optimates* feared his popularist stance. From the ancient patrician gens Julii, young Julius was parted from wealth when he was fifteen and his father became a victim of political scheming and fell from grace. Caesar was raised in Rome's poor Subura quarter and, until his middle adult years, he remained immured in poverty, always scheming to win the patronage of the monied or the politically powerful.

## The Roman empire at the birth of Julius Caesar, 100 BC

He pursued a typically military career with great success, earning honours along the way and coming to the notice of the fabulously wealthy Marcus Licinius Crassus (115–53 BC), who acted to find Caesar gainful employment. Caesar's first senior administrative posting was as propraetor of Hispania Citerior (Nearer Spain), recently subdued by Pompey after the rebellion of its governor Quintus Sertorius, for which action the upstart general became known as Magnus, the 'Great'. Here, Caesar distinguished himself sufficiently to stand for the consular elections on his return to Rome. He needed a consulship to earn a proconsular governorship afterwards – his only chance of accumulating wealth. Crassus supplied the election finance and Pompey was induced to assist by Caesar's offer of his daughter Julia's hand in marriage; the Magnus was greatly enamoured of her. With their joint support, Caesar became one of the consuls for 59, and their partnership was later known as the First Triumvirate. In this, Caesar's status as the junior partner was one he barely tolerated. The triumvirate was not legally constituted, the private agreement assured its members of co-operation, each acting in the interests of the others to secure increased power and wealth.

The arrangement served them well. Pompey returned to successes in Spain and was given a greater hand in the senate's affairs on his return. Crassus dashed off to command armies in search of the Orient's fabled riches. Unfortunately his generalship didn't match his business acumen and he was killed in 55 while fighting the Parthians at Carrhae (Harran) in Mesopotamia. Julia's death the year before broke the bond between Caesar and Pompey, who was unnerved by the extraordinary success his junior partner had achieved in subduing the vast tracts of Gallia Comata (Gaul of the Long Hairs). This task kept Caesar away from Rome between 58–51, in which time he overran most of Gaul and Belgica, subdued the German tribes living in the north of the region and pushed them back across the Rhine. He even crossed to the island of Britain, but gave up his limited invasion when fresh trouble broke out behind him in Gaul under the leadership of the charismatic Vercingetorix. Through brilliant strategic planning, the legions finally cornered the Avernian prince at Alesia, and by 58 all of Gaul was under Roman rule. Of more importance to him personally, Caesar now had a large, highly trained force of seven legions, whose soldiers adored him without reservation.

He now looked to Rome for his reward, demanding a consulship while he was still propraetor of Gaul, thus continuing his *imperium* and its automatic immunity to legal prosecution for any illegal acts he may have carried out in his province – of which, according to his political enemies, there were plenty. Like a slap, the senate awarded Pompey his third consulship but without a colleague to hinder him, while insisting that Caesar enter Rome as a private citizen to canvas for the election. Furious, Caesar wasted no time in bringing the power of his willing legions to bear, invading north Italy early in 49. He strove for a peaceful situation, if one was possible on his own terms, but refused to lose the initiative through caution. Pompey chose to withdraw across the Adriatic to begin marshalling an army in the Balkans.

Rome fell to Caesar with scarcely any fighting, but loyalty in Spain to the Pompeian cause sent him hot-foot there to defeat Pompey's legions before he had time to raise a second army in the Balkans. In his brief absence Marcus Antonius (Mark Antony) was appointed to the most senior military post, *magister equitum* (master of the horse), and left in charge of Italy, where he ensured that the compliant senate named Caesar dictator. Victory in Spain was swift and at the end of a very hectic 49 BC, he set off to confront the Republicans, which clash came at Pharsalus in northern Greece in the summer of 48. Despite being outnumbered, Caesar's foot broke the massed Pompeian cavalry and then routed the infantry.

The democratic governor of Spain, Quintus Sertorius (*top*) rebelled against the tyrannical rule of Sulla in 80 BC and successfully held out against the senate for seven years until Pompey (*above*), one of Sulla's most devoted officers, wore down the rebels. Sertorius committed suicide and young Pompey claimed the glory.

Coin of Vercingetorix, a prince of the Celtic Averni tribe who opposed Caesar. The Averni were to become the staunchest of Romanised citizens.

Pompey fled to the coast and took ship to Alexandria in the hope that the children of Ptolemy XII Auletes, Cleopatra and Ptolemy XIII, would remember that when their father lived he owed his Egyptian throne to Pompey's political clout. They did not – when he landed, Pompey the Great was treacherously murdered on the beach, and his pickled head handed as a peace offering to a horrified Caesar on his arrival in Alexandria early in 47.

Now undisputed ruler of the Roman world, he mediated between the squabbling factions at the Alexandrian court, eventually siding with Cleopatra (making her his mistress and giving her a son, Caesarion), and then returned to Rome. The sojourn was brief; in 46, he went to Africa and defeated Pompey's remaining Republican forces at Thapsus. Among those there, Pompey's sons Gnaeus and Sextus fled to Spain. Caesar pursued them and ended the war at the battle of Munda in 45. Gnaeus died there but Sextus made good his escape, eventually ending up in Sicily. Although the refugee was unable to do much while Caesar lived, he became a serious trouble-maker later.

**HAVING LABOURED LONG AND HARD** for his cherished position of power, Caesar set about enjoying the rewards, reforming the government, legislation and society. In 46 his dictatorship was renewed again, for ten years, but two years later he was given the office for life. Honours were heaped on him. His birthday became a public holiday. The month of his birth was renamed 'Julius' after him. There seemed no end to his exaltation. He refused the title *rex* (king) and rejected the crown Antony offered him in 44 at the Lupercalia festival, but Caesar adopted many kingly trappings. When Cleopatra came to reside outside Rome's walls, bringing Caesarion with her, patrician, senatorial and equestrian disquiet turned to open rebellion. Rome did not take kindly to foreign monarchs or princes with a hereditary right.

According to Cicero, the conspiracy was contrived by people with 'the courage of men but the understanding of boys' – in other words, they were naïve if they believed killing Caesar would restore the Republic. On the agreed day, the Ides (15th) of March 44, Caesar went to the senate at its appointed place for that day, the Porticoes of Pompey. There, at the foot of Pompey's oversize statue (which Caesar had allowed to remain), the large group of conspirators murdered him. Cleopatra fled back to Egypt, vituperatively declaiming that the conspirators were traitors. Although there were certainly lofty as well as less noble motives for the assassination, the act unleashed a civil war that ensured the end of the Republic. So many Italian soldiers who took part venerated their former commander almost as a god and the Julian bloodline as holy, that as far into the future as the accession of Vespasian in AD 70, Roman soldiers would only  accept a new emperor who had a hereditary link to the Julii, and would-be emperors for two hundred years would cite their hereditary ties to the first Caesar, which soon ceased to be a name and became a title. Caesar himself had not become an emperor, but he had made it possible – even inevitable – that his successor Octavian would.

For some years senators held meetings in various venues after the destruction of the original Curia Hostilia. Caesar built the new senate house (*above*) on the edge of the Forum (it was partly rebuilt by Diocletian in the fourth century).

Three re-erected columns of Julius Caesar's temple to Venus Genetrix stand at the end of his forum (*left*), which Augustus completed, built in the old market place behind the Basilica Aemilia.

Statues of the iconic 'Dying Gaul' were popular with Romans of the late Republican and eraly imperial periods. Capitoline Museum, Rome.

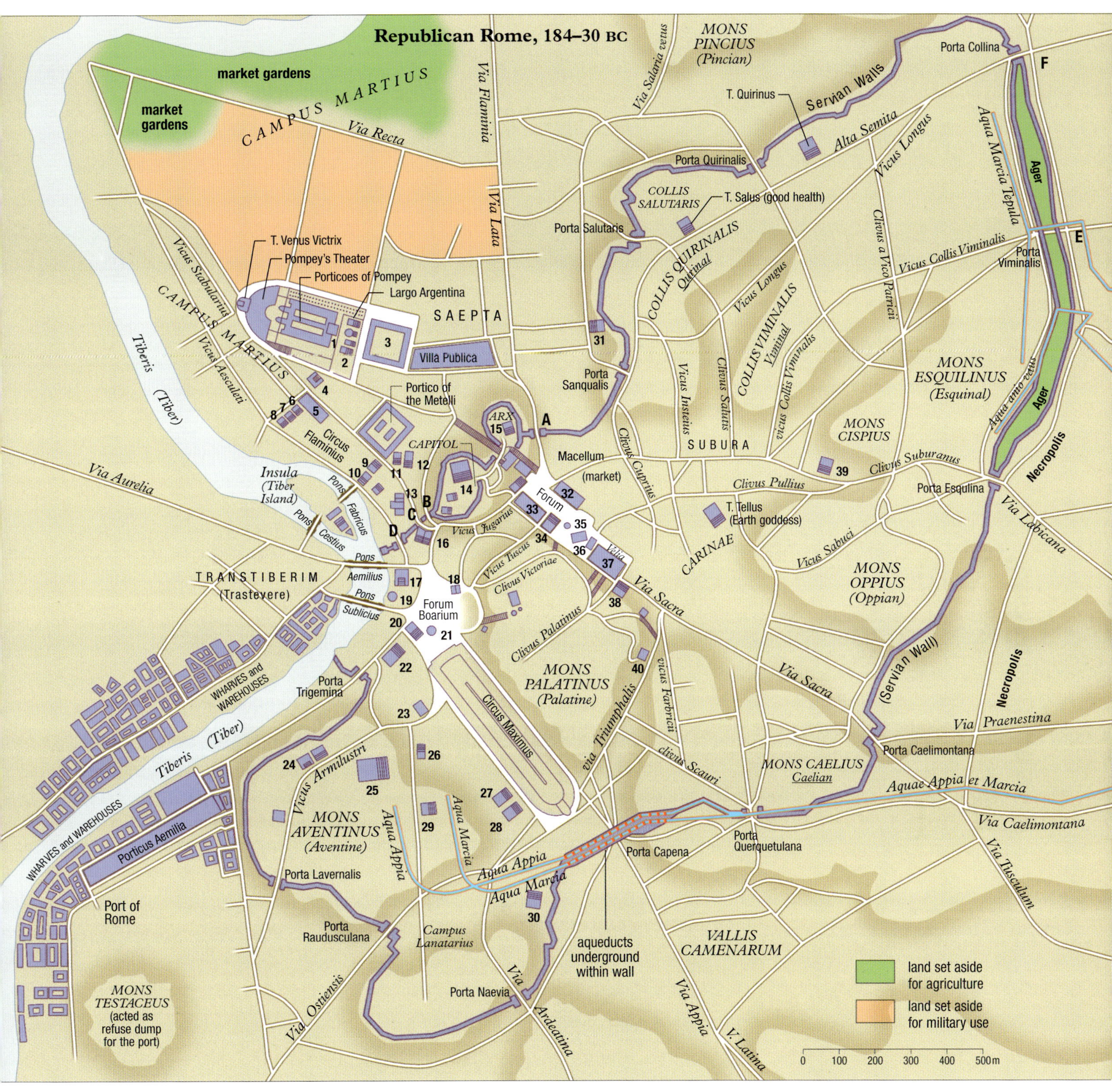




1  Pompey's meeting house, site of Caesar's murder
2  four temples, part of Pompey's complex
3  possible site of Pompey's villa
4  T. Herculis Musarum
5  Porticus Minucia
6  T. Vulcan
7  T. Hercules Custos
8  T. Mars Invictus
9  T. Juno Regina
10  T. Jupiter Stator
11  T. Apollo Sosianus (healing)
12  T. Bellona (foreign war)
13  temples to Pietas, Janus, Spes (hope), Juno Sospita
14  T. Jupiter Optimus Maximus
15  T. Juno Moneta
16  T. Fortuna & T. Mater Matuta
17  T. Portunus (god of the harbor)
18  T. Janus
19  T. Hercules Olivarius (olives)
20  Ara Maxima Herculis (great altar of Hercules)
21  T. Hercules Invictus
22  T. Ceres (headquarters of the Plebeian Aediles)
23  T. Flora (vegetation)
24  two temples for the cult of Free Citizens
25  T. Diana (looks after slaves)
26  T. Luna (moon)
27  T. Mercury (headquarters of Guild of Merchants)
28  T. Venus Obaequens (protects prostitutes & adulterers)
29  T. Juventas (coming of age for boys)
30  T. Bona Dea (protects women)
31  T. Semo Sancus Dius Fidius (oaths and treaties)
32  Basilica Aemilia
33  Basilica Julia
34  T. Castor & Pollux
35  T. Vesta
36  Domus Publicus (home of the Vestal Virgins & Pontifex Maximus)
37  Porticus Margaritaria (jewelers, perfumiers, and luxury shops)
38  the hut of Romulus
39  T. Juno Lucina (registry of Roman citizen births)
40  Curiae Veteres (ancient meeting halls)

# ONE

# The Julio–Claudian Dynasty

[63 BC–AD 68]

Octavius, the boy, had a long way to go to become Augustus, above. His seminal influence was Julius Caesar, coin below, minted in 44 BC.

## Augustus  Gaius (Julius Caesar) Octavianus - Imperator Caesar Augustus
[ 16/1/27 BC–AD 19/8/14 ]

The future Augustus was born on 23 September 63 BC, probably at the family estate in Velitrae. The historian Suetonius said the Octavians were famous only in ancient Velitrae, but Octavius escaped rural obscurity because he was the grandson of Julius Caesar's younger sister. At twelve, he made his first oration at the funeral of Julia, Caesar's daughter and wife of Pompey the Great. At his triumph over Pompey Caesar awarded Octavius military decorations, even though at sixteen he was too young to have seen military service, but two years later he followed Caesar to Spain to fight Pompey's sons, Gnaeus and Sextus. It was in Gallia Narbonensis that Octavius first met Marcus Vipsanius Agrippa, one of Caesar's junior tribunes, who remained Octavius's companion and supporter for the rest of his life.

Gnaeus Pompey was killed at the battle of Munda in 45 BC and Sextus escaped to Sicily where he made a nuisance of himself. Caesar sent Octavius to Apollonia in Epirus to begin planning a war against the Parthian empire and the nineteen-year-old was there when he heard of Caesar's assassination. Since – to almost everyone's surprise – Caesar named him as his heir, Octavius ignored his mother's pleas to stay away from politically dangerous Rome. Caesar left the bulk of his fortune to his posthumously adopted son. For Mark Antony, Caesar's colleague in the consulship, there was nothing. He'd been certain of Caesar naming him and this was not only a blow to his pride but also to his purse; his dissolute, profligate lifestyle and political ambitions required the support of Caesar's fortune. Not surprisingly, Antony gave 'the boy' a cool reception when Octavius arrived in Rome and accused him of dithering in the matter of arresting Caesar's assassins, particularly the ringleaders Marcus Junius Brutus and Gaius Cassius Longinus. All had been allowed to leave Rome free men, and they had fled to Macedonia and Syria to raise a Republican army. The problem for both the senate and Octavius was that much of Caesar's treasury and his legions' loyalty were in Antony's consular hands, and he had the support of the current *magister equitum*, Marcus Aemilius Lepidus, in return for gifting him the office of *pontifex maximus* left vacant by Caesar's death. When Antony signalled his intention of assuming the role of dictator, senators reacted with horror.

The underlying motive in all of Octavius's actions was to avenge Caesar's murder and to keep his laws and decrees in force. To this end he sought election as a plebeian tribune to give him the authority to carry out his intentions. Antony used his consular powers to oppose Octavius on the ironic grounds that although a plebeian by birth he was now an adoptive Julian, therefore a patrician and ineligible to be a tribune. Antony's attitude drove Octavius into the hands of the *optimates* who – seeking any advantage – wanted to use his name against Antony's naked ambition. Cicero – so opposed to Caesar's faction – now gathered Caesar's young heir into his Republican camp, and Octavius agreed to be guided in all things by the great rhetorician. For his own part, Octavius needed Cicero's powerful voice as a weapon against Antony, but never believed that Cicero held him in high esteem, wisely since the great man said in private 'praise [Octavius], honour him, then get rid of him'.

In 43 BC Antony, feeling a cold wind blowing, left Rome for the proconsular command of Gallia Cisalpina, which he'd awarded himself by overturning Caesar's appointment of Decimus Junius Brutus to the province. Cisalpina lay outside Italy, but close enough to be in touch with Rome. However, already ensconced at Mutina (Modena), Brutus refused to give up his command and Antony's legions besieged the city. Cicero then began a series of impassioned speeches against Antony, and in one called him one of 'the very blackest and foulest monsters that have ever lived since the birth of man'. The consuls for 43, Aulus Hirtius and Gaius Vibius Pansa, took an army north to aid Brutus, to which Octavius attached himself. Lepidus also marched. Antony attempted to expel Brutus but he lost two battles near Mutina and withdrew to the safety of Lepidus's camp. Both consuls died in the action, which prompted Octavius to request one of the vacancies. He already knew that Caesar's legions would follow him, so when the senate refused, Octavius marched on Rome and secured the office by threat. He now styled himself Gaius Julius Caesar Octavianus (Octavian), and basked in his unparalleled popularity among the Italian armies and the plebs as Caesar's true heir.

Personal ambition had undone Rome's last opportunity to restore the Republic, and Cicero's heroic efforts to revive it had turned into little more than hot air. However, at twenty-one Octavian still had much to achieve, and his first steps revealed a shrewd grasp of politics. Correctly fearing that the senate would disperse his legions to avoid paying the veterans, he laid aside his differences with Antony and Lepidus, and the three most powerful Romans met at Bononia Felsina (Bologna) in 43. The result, intended to present a united front against the senate and the assassins, was the *triumviri reipublicae constituendae* (Triumvirs for the Regulation of the Republic). Unlike the First Triumvirate, the Second was set up by law, and was effectively a joint dictatorship. Virtually at sword point, the senate granted the triumvirs draconian powers to hunt down Caesar's killers. In the ensuing purge, more than 2,000 were executed, including the too-voluble Cicero who was of no further use to Octavian and whom Antony wanted gagged forever. But the real enemy was massing to the east under the banners of Brutus and Cassius.

The triumvirs crossed the sea in 42 and slaughtered the seventeen rebel legions at Philippi in Macedonia. Rather than risk capture, Brutus and Cassius committed suicide. Antony and Octavian now redistributed the empire between them, Antony grabbing the east and graciously letting Octavian take the troublesome western provinces and Italy, which included the command against Sextus Pompey. Lepidus was sidelined in Africa – yet to deliver its future promise. When Octavian began settling his Philippi veterans on appropriated Italian land he ignited the Perusine War. Mark Antony's wife Fulvia and his brother Lucius took up arms on behalf of the

Marcus Junius Brutus struck this coin bearing his portrait to mark the assassination of the 'tyrant' Julius Caesar on the Ides of March, 44 BC.

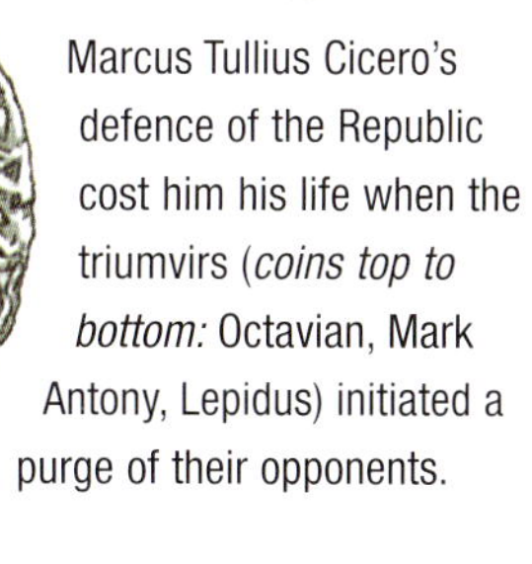

Marcus Tullius Cicero's defence of the Republic cost him his life when the triumvirs (*coins top to bottom:* Octavian, Mark Antony, Lepidus) initiated a purge of their opponents.

Sextus Pompey honoured his dead father and brother Gnaeus on the reverse of a coin issued in 42 BC.

dispossessed Italians. After months of desultory skirmishing, Lucius surrendered at Perusia (Perugia) and Fulvia died shortly after. The conflict might have spiralled into full-scale civil war when Antony hurried back from the Orient and landed at Brundisium in 40, but both armies – all from Caesar's old legions – forced the two men to make peace. The triumvirate was re-established and to secure it, Octavian married his sister Octavia to Antony.

Having occupied Sicily in 45 BC, Sextus Pompey had created a pirate navy and blockaded Rome's essential grain supplies from the island. The threatened famine brought the triumvirs to the table in 39. As a part of the complex peace overtures Octavius married a relative of Sextus's named Scribonia, by whom he had a daughter, Julia. The talks dragged on for two years until bored Antony left again for the east, leaving the matter in Octavian's hands. In the meantime, Agrippa was busy secretly building his friend a massive navy so he was almost ready when Octavian divorced his ill-matched wife and called off all bets with Sextus.

Under somewhat scandalous circumstances, Octavian immediately forced the divorce of Livia Drusilla from her cousin-husband Tiberius Claudius Nero and married her. A member of the patrician Claudii, Livia had married her cousin when she was sixteen and bore him one son, Tiberius; she was pregnant with Drusus when Octavian swept her away. Although she gave Octavian no children – an ommission that led to endless succession problems – the marriage lasted, spanning fifty-two turbulent years until Augustus's death.

In 36 BC Octavian felt ready to tackle Sextus and amphibiously invaded Sicily. Agrippa's fleet swung the balance by annihilating the Pompeians at Naulochus in September. Sextus fled to Antony (where he was soon executed on conspiracy charges), while Octavian confronted Lepidus. His fellow triumvir had brought his army from Africa for the campaign and now claimed Sicily for himself. Octavian gambled that the Caesarian legionaries had little love for Lepidus and went among them, persuading the soldiers to desert. He was right; they did. He deposed Lepidus from the triumvirate and exiled him, while allowing him to remain *pontifex maximus*.

In the same year, Caesar's planned campaign against the Parthians ended in failure due to Antony's incompetence, and he returned in misery to Alexandria and his

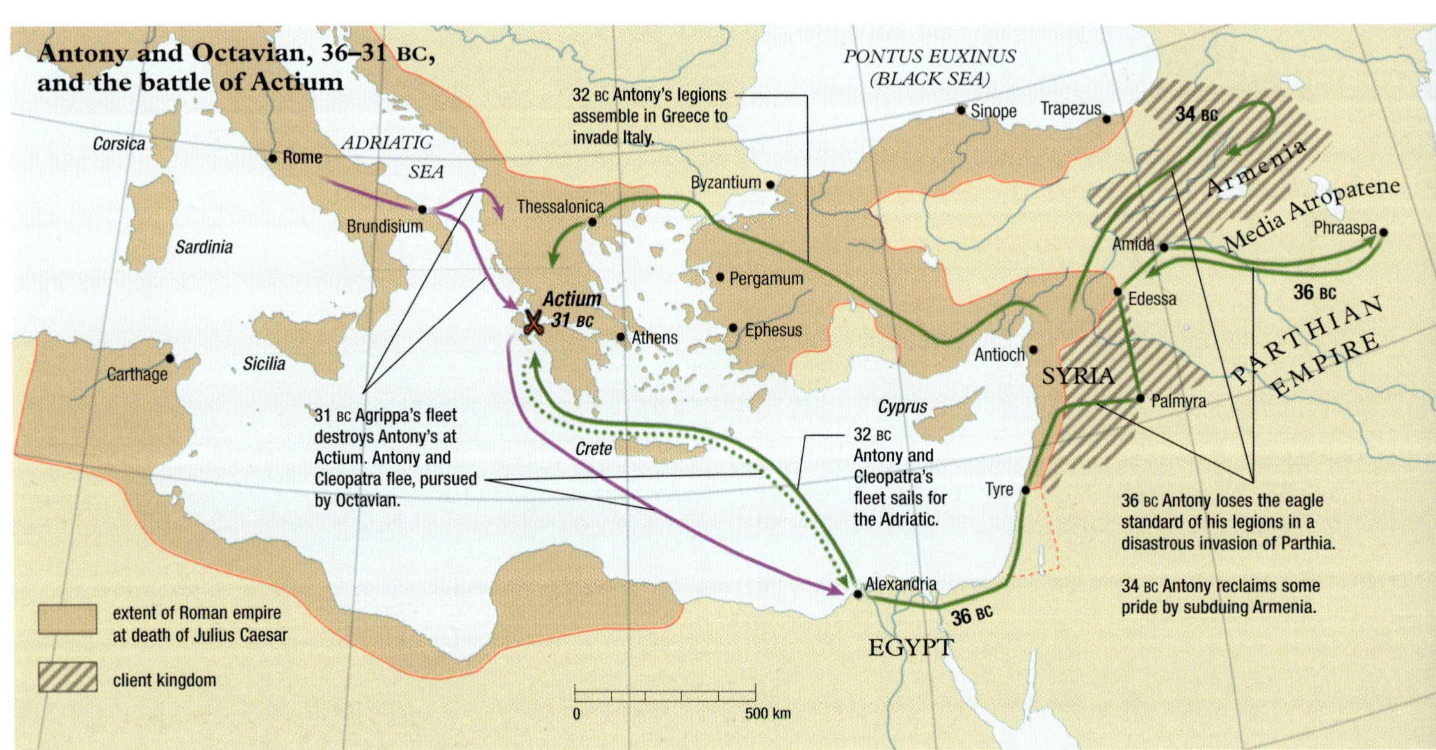

mistress, Queen Cleopatra Ptolemy VII. This affair had started in 41 BC, when Antony had summoned her to Tarsus to explain her actions since Caesar's death. Her effect on Antony may have been erotic, but politics lay in her heart. Rome had conquered the traditional recruiting grounds of Greek mercenaries by which Ptolemaic power in Egypt was maintained. Using her charms first on Julius Caesar and then on Antony was a sensible way of getting back some influence over those lost regions. At some point after 37 BC Antony put aside Octavia and married Cleopatra, a wedding that most Romans refused to recognise, but to Egyptians it consecrated Mark Antony as their king.

Antony's treatment of Octavia precluded any return route to Rome with Octavian in the way. His options were to found an oriental Roman empire with Cleopatra or invade Italy and deal with his rival. Whatever affection he enjoyed as Caesar's protégé had vanished in unlawfully marrying a reigning monarch and declaring Caesar and Cleopatra's son Ptolemy XV Caesarion to be the empire's true heir. In Rome, Octavian easily cleared the senate of the small Antonian faction and found little difficulty in talking up war, which was officially declared late in 32 BC. After much manoeuvering on land and sea the rival fleets finally clashed at Actium in the Ionian Sea on 2 September 31. Under Agrippa's increasingly skilled naval command, his fleet was swiftly triumphant. Immediately, Octavian established his control over Antonine Achaea and Asia, then invaded Egypt. Cornered in 30, Antony and Cleopatra committed suicide, and Egypt became a Roman province. Although he sent Antony's two children by Cleopatra to Rome where they were raised and educated by his sister Octavia as their rank deserved, he had Caesarion killed, thereby removing a legitimate contender for Roman rule.

Octavian's sister Octavia was thrust out of the way by Mark Antony so he could marry Cleopatra, the queen of Egypt (seen here on a coin that suggests she was not the famous beauty of popular imagination).

**THE INVENTION OF AUGUSTUS**, first emperor of Rome, was a gradual process. Drawing a halt to his momentum after Actium, Octavian graciously offered the power that lay in his grasp to the senate, and in doing so appeared benign and bountiful. He avoided the overt dictatorship of Caesar and instead ruled in the guise of a constitutional *princeps* or first citizen. The senate responded just as he'd hoped by offering him more authority than ever before; he was granted a continuous seven-year consulship that lasted from 29 to 23 BC (Romans counted inclusively).

Although he was backed by the power of the legions, which made him Rome's *de facto* ruler, in a law-obsessed society his position was arbitrary and he had no legal warrant. He remedied the seeming impasse in two so-called Constitutional Settlements, of 27 and 23 BC. At the first, he announced his intention of returning to private life and was only 'persuaded' otherwise amid clamours from the senators (and his own planted clique of supporters). In return for 'handing the state back to the senate', Octavian received the proconsular command of Gaul, Spain (except Baetica), Syria, Cyprus and Egypt. After a show of reluctance, Octavian graciously accepted. These provinces – which in effect he had placed at the disposal of the senate and people – were already governed by his legates. And he could point to legal precedents – the extended commands granted to Pompey and Caesar, for instance – which appealed to his desire to appear to be maintaining traditions while doing nothing alarmingly new or innovative. This *imperium proconsulare* was granted for a period of ten years, but as with many term-condition privileges given him, no one attempted to take it back when it expired.

In a continuing modest manner which personified parsimony and moderation, he courted the senate, reiterating all the while that its main function was to advise rather than rule. More honours were forthcoming. On 16 January, Octavian was named Augustus, a word ringing with religious significance and social meaning but falling

Marcus Vipsanius Agrippa, soldier, admiral, governor, administrator and Octavian's close friend was the second man in Rome.

Octavian, now Caesar Augustus, an early coin from c.27–23 BC.

*Opposite:* Augustus in full military regalia; throughout his life he was shown in the full vigour of youth.

well short of suggesting overt political dominance. 'Augustus' was only a cognomen, but he came to be known by it, and after his death it was granted the status of a title. The Romans had no word for 'emperor', which is derived from *imperator*, the title given by his soldiers to a successful general after a victory but who has yet to celebrate a triumph. In time, since the power of the army made its *imperator* Rome's sole ruler, the word came to be associated with 'emperor'. Augustus preferred the title of *princeps*, which leads to the use of the word 'principate' to describe the rule of the early Roman emperors. It was a nicely modest attribute, familiar to Roman ears for centuries, which suited his subtle but relentless method of gaining total control by stealth.

Only one major hurdle remained – perpetuation of his dynasty. Never since the time of the kings had Rome considered a hereditary succession to a head of state. Since Augustus only held his special commission from the people and senate, he couldn't will his powers to anyone else. He needed a solution that not only retained his 'legal' powers but also made them transferable to a chosen successor. His solution was ingenious – the absorption of the tribunes' powers which enabled them to transact business with both the senate and the people, and to enact or veto legislation. Gathered in the princeps' hands and his to also bestow an another, the *tribunicia potestas* (tribunician power) rendered his nomination of a successor more feasible. Conferral on another man would designate him as the princep's successor because he would be the equal of Augustus. On 26 June 23 BC the senate conferred on Augustus the *tribunicia potestas*, which was ratified by the people through a special assembly (the last time ordinary Romans would have this authority).

With both his tribunician and proconsular powers, Augustus now had the ability to direct affairs in every wing of domestic and foreign administration. These two powers were long to remain the twin pillars of the Roman emperors' lawful position. That a people drilled in the rewards of republicanism should permit a takeover, even one carried out by stealth, is not such a mystery. Ordinary Romans had seen a century of unprecedented domestic violence. As more men were recruited into the army, vast tracts of land lay untended, causing economic hardship and shortages. The Republic had offered no comfort in difficult times, while the reign of Augustus heralded peace and stability. Under his auspices there came a new era of enhanced personal safety and recourse to law. Further, Augustus did not make Caesar's mistake of alienating the senatorial order and Rome's aristocracy. Indeed, by courting the senate he effectively hid from view the degree to which he pulled the strings of government.

He increased its powers in a way Caesar would have never permitted. The senate became one of the two high courts from whose verdict there was no appeal, and it possessed legislative powers that had once belonged to three public committees. The transfer to Augustus of the traditional powers of veto of the plebeian tribunes meant their virtual removal from the legislative process, which further enhanced the senate's illusory authority. Augustus also endeared himself to the equestrian order by filling newly created magistracies from among their ranks. More significantly, he formed an inner cabinet or *concilium* from the two presiding consuls, a representation of minor magistrates and fifteen senators chosen by lot. Nevertheless, as the historian Cassius Dio wrote 'nothing was done that did not please Caesar'.

Octavian's second wife, Livia Drusilla, had two sons by a previous marriage, Tiberius and Drusus, but bore Augustus no children.

**AS THE REAL BASE OF AUGUSTAN POWER,** ensuring the army's loyalty was a primary concern. Augustus continued the professionalisation begun under Marius by establishing a standing field army comprised of twenty-eight legions, made up of volunteers who received standard wages over a prescribed period, and with fixed rewards on discharge. At their induction, recruits once swore an oath of loyalty to the state; Augustus now altered the oath to one of loyalty to the princeps (as the 'state'), to be renewed each New Year. With this the troops recognised Augustus as their sole paymaster and guarantor of their discharge rewards.

Increasingly, hand-picked *equites* filled senior military posts traditionally reserved for sons of the nobility; and men from Augustus's own family wielded the general's baton. Another innovation dramatically changed tradition. Under the new order, military glory was Augustus's own; no longer would a victorious general celebrate a triumph as *imperator*. During his reign more than thirty triumphators rode behind Augustus in procession as the princep's companion in glory, and inevitably they were one of the imperial circle.

The Augustan foreign policy was one of consolidation, although he kept the army busy with many tasks. Diplomacy and rule through 'allies' or client kings replaced naked aggression. Augustus regarded haste and recklessness as sins in his military commanders, and was fond of quoting proverbs such as 'More haste, less speed', and homilies like 'Give me a safe commander, not a rash one'. It was a principle that he never fought a battle unless more could be gained by victory than lost by defeat.

The concentration of the praetorian guards was perhaps the most significant innovation. In 133 BC Scipio Aemilianus – the man who destroyed Carthage in the Third Punic War – named his personal bodyguard after the *praetorium*, the area of a Roman military camp in which the consul-general pitched his tent. Thereafter legates in the field formed a personal guard for the campaign's duration. After Actium, Augustus combined his and Antony's guards and formed them into a permanent unit of nine cohorts, about 4,500 men, stationed in towns around Rome. The praetorian

guards enjoyed shorter terms of service and treble the wages of regular legionaries. It's little surprise that the praetorians soon recognised the strength of their bargaining position. At first Augustus was their commander, but in 2 BC he appointed two equestrian praetorian prefects to take joint control.

**'I FOUND ROME BUILT OF SUN-DRIED BRICKS;** I leave her cloathed in marble,' Augustus boasted, justifiably, for he certainly transformed the capital's appearance. New white marble from Luna (Carrara) in northern Italy and coloured marbles from all over the provinces added lustre to new and old structures. No less than 82 temples received repair during 28 BC alone. He repaired Pompey's Theatre and two new ones were built, the theatres of Marcellus and Balbus. The Temple of Apollo on the Palatine, and the Temple of Mars Ultor (Avenging Mars) were only the most obvious of his prestige buildings, the latter a part of his Forum, built to cope with the recent great increase in the number of law-suits caused by a corresponding increase in population. Agrippa too built Rome's first great public baths, raised the original Pantheon, repaired temples and built aqueducts. There were even attempts to control the unruly elements of Rome's unplanned and teeming streets. These were lined with tenement blocks called *insulae* (*lit.* islands). Built around a courtyard, with shops fronting the street, they sometimes reached a height of seven storeys. Fire from cooking was a continual hazard. Insulae – constructed of timber frames and perishable mud bricks – burned easily, and their height made them prone to collapse, burying the hapless victims of lower floors under burning debris. Augustus limited the height of apartments to five floors or a maximum height of 20 metres. He also instigated the *vigiles* or firefighters. The city was divided into fourteen districts under the control of magistrates elected annually by lot. Each district had its own administrative and technical services including *vigiles*; the total for the whole city numbered 7,000.

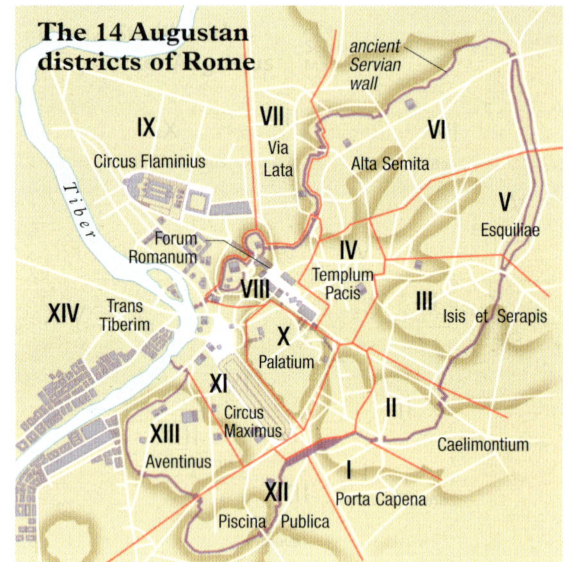


Augustus was assiduous in the administration of justice, often remaining in court until nightfall. The existing laws that he revised and the new ones he enacted dealt largely with public extravagance, adultery, licentious behaviour, bribery and the encouragement of marriage in the senatorial and equestrian orders. The latter grew into an obsession. In 18 and 17 BC he imposed penalties on the plebs and especially the *equites* for remaining unmarried. There were rewards for those couples who produced children. These marriage laws helped to counter a worrying drop in the birth rate, but they also regulated the decadent aristocratic lifestyle. Augustus's concern with a return to older Roman morals and virtues sponsored a religious revival, which he promoted from the office of *pontifex maximus* after its holder, the ex-triumvir Marcus Lepidus, died in 12 BC. This combined all his secular powers with that of Rome's most senior religious figure. The invention of the principate was now complete and formed the basis of absolute power for all subsequent Roman emperors.

Despite his position, Augustus was modest in his habits. He lived in a small house on the Palatine until it disappeared under the Temple of Apollo and the senate voted him a new 'palace' beside the temple. However, the compact rooms were unadorned by either the marble he was so fond of or tessellated floors and the furnishings were unpretentious, couches and tables 'hardly considered fit for a private citizen'. Augustus liked to give traditional dinner parties, but ate and drank sparingly himself. His favourite food was that of the common people: coarse bread, whitebait fish, fresh hand-pressed cheese, and green figs ('of the second crop'). The dinners were, however, jolly affairs because of his talent for bringing the shy into the conversation, and his own natural good humour. He enjoyed cheerful people and often sought the company of

Augustus as *pontifex maximus*.

small boys with whom he could enjoy a game of marbles. He particularly liked Moors and Syrians for their happy appearance, and loathed people who were in any way deformed, regarding them as bringers of bad luck. This prejudice explains the unease he felt whenever in the presence of his grandnephew, the future emperor Claudius, who of all his handsome family was the most ill-favoured in stance and appearance.

Augustus presided over a flowering of the arts, particularly literature – he was a noted author himself. Among others, he supported the careers of Livy, Virgil, Horace, Tibullus and Ovid, although irreverent Ovid affronted the new Augustan morality with his poem *Ars Amorata* (Art of Love) and ended up being banished. It was obviously easy to overstep the mark with bluff but dangerous Augustus – Cassius Dio's comment is as apt for poets as for senators: 'nothing was done that did not please Caesar'.

**A CLUMSY AND EASILY FOILED ATTEMPT** on his life in 23 BC did not please, and prompted concerns as to the future. Having provided himself with the legal precedent of a succession, the question arose as to whom this honour should go, since he only had his stepsons Tiberius and Drusus, disqualified as Claudians. The army wanted Julian blood, which also ruled out Agrippa (but who would have to be regent should he die). So he turned to his nephew Marcellus (technically a Claudian, but as grandson of Julius Caesar's sister also a Julian). In marking out Marcellus Augustus established the central strategy for the perpetuation of the principate: a series of stepping stones that indicated the princeps' preference. These consisted of allying the chosen to the imperial family through marriage and promoting the would-be successor through the *cursus honorum* at a pace far in advance of the traditional age requirements. And so in 25 BC Marcellus married fourteen-year-old Julia, Augustus's only child. Alas, it was in vain. Marcellus succumbed to an illness and died at the end of 23. With Marcellus gone, Augustus appointed Agrippa – who was recalled from his position in the Orient – to act as regent with a share of the *imperium proconsulare* until another Julian should appear. Augustus tied his friend to the imperial family by obliging him to marry widowed Julia. After the wedding, Agrippa returned to the east, and then in 18 Augustus made him his colleague in the *tribunicia potestas*. Julia bore Agrippa three sons, Gaius in 20, Lucius in 17 and Agrippa Postumus in 12 BC. There were also two daughters – Julia the Younger, and Agrippina. Julian blood was again in the ascendancy and Augustus adopted Gaius and Lucius as 'Caesars'. This honour for Agrippa made him at the very least the father of the next emperor. Augustus involved his stepsons by appointing them as legal guardians of the infant Caesars. This demotion probably didn't bother easy-going Drusus, but Tiberius was clearly disgruntled at being passed over, and his relations with the children were never good.

When Agrippa suddenly died in the spring of 12 BC he robbed Augustus of a trusted friend and regent. Agrippa's sons were still too young to be heirs (the third still unborn at his father's death, hence his nickname Postumus). Augustus now forced Tiberius to divorce the wife he loved and marry the twice-widowed Julia. This clear signal showed that Tiberius was replacing Agrippa as the regent-guardian to the two young Caesars. Tiberius was now unhappily palace-bound by his duties, so much so that he astonished everyone by suddenly retiring from public life and exiling himself on the island of Rhodes in 6 BC. Augustus, infuriated by the defection, had to rely on his own still-robust health to see his adopted sons to their maturity. But again fate intervened: Lucius died of an illness at Massilia in AD 2 and Gaius two years later of a wound received during a siege in Armenia. Augustus bowed to the inevitable and recalled Tiberius to Rome after Lucius's death as the only family member with the experience to help him.

Titus Livius (Livy, c.59 BC–AD 17) wrote the most detailed history of Rome up to the time of Augustus.

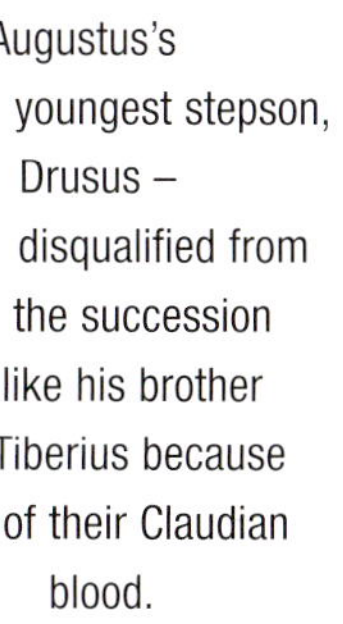

Augustus's youngest stepson, Drusus – disqualified from the succession like his brother Tiberius because of their Claudian blood.

Augustus married Marcellus, his 19-year-old nephew, to his daughter Julia (coin portrait), but his unexpected death wrecked the succession plans.

# The Julio-Claudian Dynasty

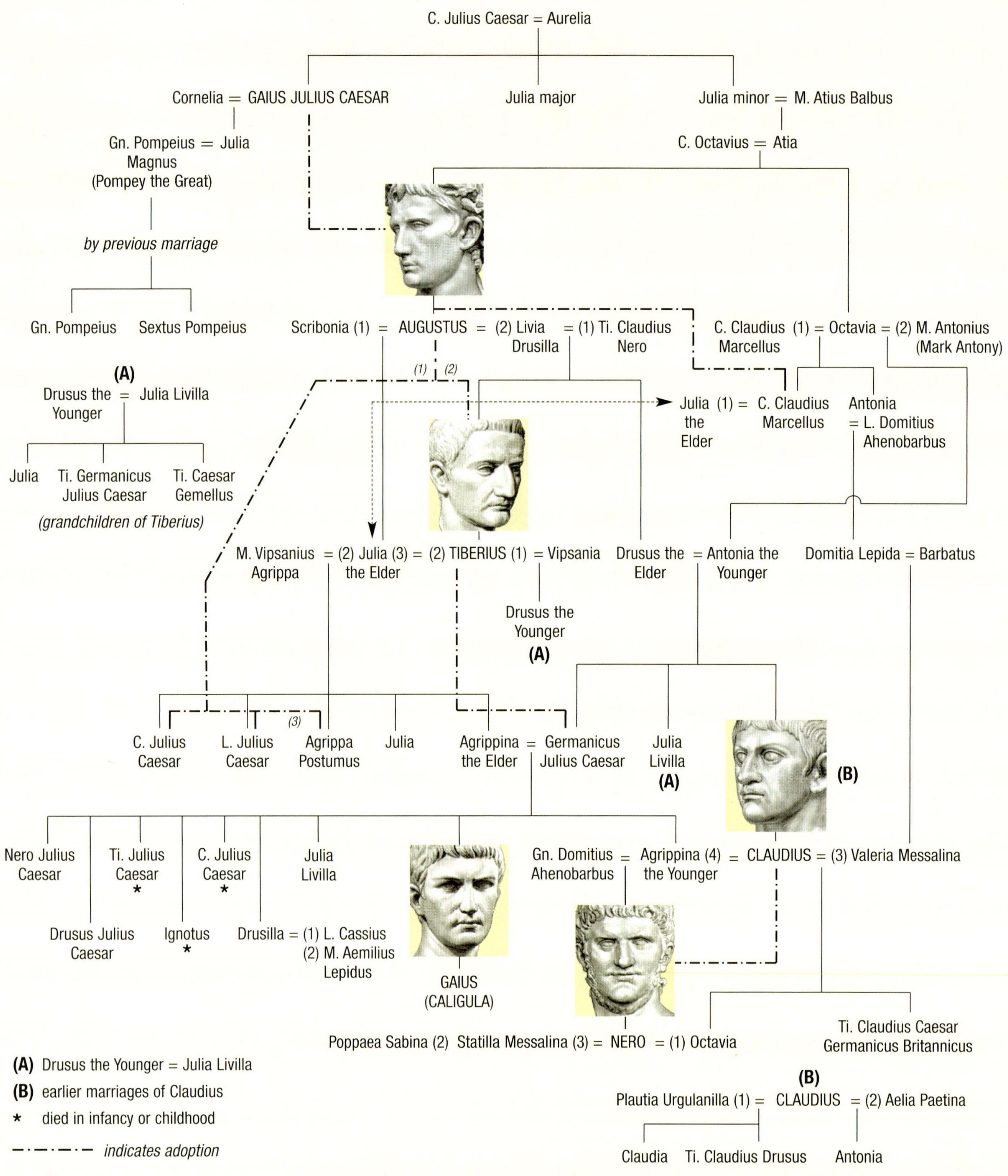


However, help was all Augustus had in mind as he maintained Tiberius in the regent's role by adopting his surviving grandson, the young Agrippa Postumus, and obliging Tiberius to adopt his dead brother Drusus's son, his nephew Julius Caesar Germanicus. This pushed Tiberius's own son, Drusus the Younger, to the position of second choice. Although he was also a Claudian, Germanicus had Julian blood on his mother's side and moreover had married Agrippina, Agrippa's daughter, Augustus's granddaughter. Unfortunately, the teenaged Postumus was a brutal lout, who was banished to the small coastal island of Planasia in AD 7. Whether he liked it or not, up to the time of his death Augustus came to rely more on dour, grumbling Tiberius.

Despite the family's internal strains, Augustus, who stood for a return to old Roman moral virtues, was keen to present a united image of the imperial house to the populace. He left a superb example of this family-values propaganda in the southern frieze of the *ara pacis augustae* (Altar of the Augustan Peace), dedicated in January 9 BC. It depicts the imperial family parading as a dignified and corporate entity. The message is one of dynastic harmony and the promise of future stability. The reality, clearly, was rather different.

Augustus passed away at his country villa at Nola in the afternoon of 19 August AD 14 at the age of seventy-five. In his long life he had totally transformed the Roman state and secured a hereditary succession. In his funeral oration, Tiberius compared Augustus to the hero Hercules; and in September – his birth month – he was voted the status of a god, *Divus Augustus*. His testament named his stepson Tiberius and his wife Livia as his heirs. It directed that Tiberius should take two-thirds of his estate and adopt the title Augustus, while Livia should take the balance as Augusta. Tiberius was bequeathed an empire that enjoyed external security, internal peace, a constitution that Romans found acceptable but an army wedded to the sacred Julian bloodline.

## Tiberius  Tiberius Claudius Nero Caesar
[ AD 19/8/14–16/3/37 ]

The Claudians had an ancient lineage dating back, according to one legend, to the time of Romulus, but at least to the expulsion of the kings in 509 BC. At the time of Tiberius, who was born in Rome on 16 November 41 BC, the Claudians had amassed twenty-eight consulships, six triumphs and two ovations. Although the Claudians used several nicknames, the most popular were the Sabine word 'Nero', meaning 'strong and energetic', and 'Drusus', dating from 283 BC, when its first holder killed an enemy chieftain called Drausus in single combat. As a quaestor, Tiberius's father, Tiberius Claudius Nero, commanded Julius Caesar's fleet in 48 BC. Unfortunately he picked the wrong side in the Perusine War but avoided the slaughter that followed and escaped to Sicily, where Sextus Pompey spurned Nero as an ex-Caesarean. So he joined Mark Antony, and when peace came, returned to Rome in Antony's company. Octavian's forgiveness of his former enemy almost certainly carried a price. With Nero came his wife Livia Drusilla, who Octavian determined to marry, and it seems that Nero – not exactly in any position to argue – surrendered her and the children to him, and apparently died soon after.

The constant flight from Octavian's forces provided Tiberus with a tumultuous childhood, dragged from town to town, his young life almost snuffed out on several occasions. However, as Octavian's stepson things looked up. At fourteen he took part in Octavian's triumph of 29 BC after Actium. He rode on the left of the triumphator's chariot, while Augustus's favourite Marcellus sat astride the more auspicious right-hand horse (Marcellus was soon dead, so not such a good omen after all).

Enigmatic and darkly complex, intelligent and cunning, Tiberius was given to bouts of severe depression and grim moods. In this, he was the opposite of Augustus, and his repressed Republican sentiments hardly helped their relationship. When he was about eighteen he married Vipsania, Marcus Agrippa's daughter by a previous marriage to Pomponia, daughter of Cicero's friend Pomponius Atticus. The couple loved each other passionately – a rare occurrence in a world of arranged marriages and they named their son Drusus. Vipsania had good reason to be proud of her husband

Gaius and Lucius Caesar (top), Agrippa's sons adopted by Augustus, both died young. Their youngest brother Postumus was banishd in AD 7.

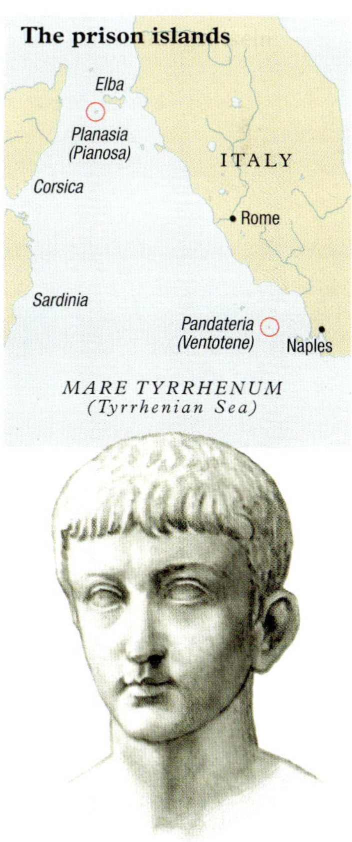


Bust of Tiberius in early adolescence.

The balance in Tiberius's early life – his beloved first wife, Vipsania Agrippa, from the Ara Pacis, and his brother Drusus, from a coin, before 9 BC.

Tiberius bust and coin from the time of his accession, aged 53.

whose military career – while not inspired – was certainly solid. Among his achievements, one stands out: in 20 BC Tiberius evicted the Parthians from Armenia, restoring the Roman client king Tigranes to his throne and, as importantly, recovering the eagles of the legions lost in the failed campaigns of Marcus Crassus (53 BC), Decidius Saxa (40 BC), and Mark Antony (36 BC). Augustus was said to have wept in public when his stepson handed over the sacred standards.

For Tiberius, the death of Agrippa was a double tragedy. Augustus coerced him into divorcing Vipsania to marry Julia. As Augustus's daughter, Julia was also Tiberius's stepsister (not to say also his recent stepmother-in-law) – the kind of tangled web so typical of the dynastic Roman families. After a short honeymoon period of mutual, if distant, contempt, they came to loathe each other bitterly, and Julia made little attempt to hide her ridicule of him as a man. Julia soon began a series of scandalous sex affairs that eventually led to her downfall. To get his mind off Vipsania, Augustus put Tiberius back to work by giving him important military commissions in Pannonia and Germany. He was consul for the second time in 7 BC together with Gnaeus Calpurnius Piso, and granted the *tribunicia potestas* in the following year, the year he fled to Rhodes.

Several factors contributed to this clearly dangerous move. His mother Livia's constant bullying – she considered him weak for not aspiring to the succession – Julia's scandalous behaviour and her contempt for him, the Caesar-brats to whom he was the unwilling stepfather and the loss of comfort from his brother Drusus – killed in 9 BC after a fall from his horse during a brilliant campaign that had taken his legions as far north as the river Elbe. Lost and depressed, Tiberius retired to Rhodes with a small retinue and his personal astrologer Thrasyllus. Tiberius soon came to regret this hasty decision but received only the Augustan cold shoulder when he asked if he might return to active life. He was left in the wilderness for over four years.

**THE NEW REIGN GOT OFF TO A POOR START** with a murder, a confused senate, a suicide and an army mutiny. The exiled young Agrippa Postumus posed a dynastic threat and was executed on the island of his banishment. The historian Tacitus makes Tiberius responsible, without specifically blaming him. Suetonius allows that Tiberius or Augustus or even Livia in his name might have written the order. Tiberius threatened to make the responisble guard answerable for the unauthorised killing; on the other hand he shelved the inquiry – the matter forgotten, so perhaps he did have a hand in it. As for Augustus, he may have feared that leaving the loutish Postumus alive would create instability. And Livia? Some sources go so far as to suggest she was behind the unfortunate deaths of so many Augustan favourites as far back as Marcellus. If so, it was all to see her weak son Tiberius on the throne – Postumus was simply the last obstacle standing. Tiberius's disgraced wife Julia, despairing that her banishment would never be revoked now her last son was dead, committed suicide on the island of Pandateria to which Augustus had exiled her after discovering her disgusting behaviour.

The senate convened on 18 September to inaugurate the new reign. Such a transfer of power had never happened before and nobody, including Tiberius, knew what to do. Tiberius professed reluctance to assume the office and the confused and probably alarmed senators lost their patience. Most thought him a dissembling hypocrite, and one senator cried out: 'Some people are slow to do what they promise; you are slow to promise what you have already done.' Tiberius may have been genuinely reluctant. He'd never enjoyed the cloying offices of Roman administration over the freedom of military life. In any case, wasn't he just following Augustus's precedent when he had to be 'persuaded' to accept the imperial powers? Unfortunately, where Augustus used tact, Tiberius came across as obdurate. Throughout his reign, Tiberius was to confuse and frighten the senators. His actions and edicts seem to suggest that he wanted the senate to act on his implicit desires rather than on his explicit requests. And Tiberius held no high opinion of his senatorial colleagues: 'Men fit only to be slaves,' he said of them.

The long reign of Augustus had accustomed people to the concept of a sole ruler, but there had never been a succession, and the change of emperors prompted the soldiers to demand their unpaid back wages and a pay rise. Mutinies broke out in Germania and Pannonia. Tiberius put his popular nephew and adopted son Germanicus in command of the German legions and his son Drusus went to Pannonia. In Moguntiacum (Mainz) the troops begged Germanicus – a man of Julian blood – to seize the throne, which he flatly refused to do. Both young legates finally brought the situation under control, first Drusus then Germanicus, who put his legions to work in an unauthorised conquest of territory across the Rhine.

Tiberius's early years were generally good. He remained true to plans for the succession by favouring Germanicus over his son Drusus. He behaved with discretion in his dealings with magistrates and the senate as a whole. He rejected any overtly sycophantic honours, such as setting the title *princeps* before his name or *pater patriae* after; and he even refrained from adding the name Augustus to his own. His notorious parsimony resulted in legislation to cut down waste, slashing the expense of public entertainment by setting limits on the number of gladiatorial combats at many festivals. He introduced price controls on household furniture, set an annual regulation on market values and restricted the wasteful amount of food offered for sale in cook-shops. To set an example, he frequently served guests half-eaten dishes left over from the day before – which rendered an invitation to dinner a dubious treat. Tiberius also adhered to Augustus's foreign policy, refusing to extend the frontiers in spite of Germanicus's defiance in a series of trans-Rhenic campaigns in AD 14–16. Germanicus and his extensive family were popular with his troops, the *equites* and the Roman mob, so he wasn't easy to control. Tiberius finally brought his nephew to book by awarding him a triumph on 26 May 17. Then, as soon as possible in the following year, he packed him off to the eastern provinces with a *maius imperium* on a sort of fact-finding mission and one piece of tricky diplomacy.

Tiberius felt that the diplomatic task – installing a Roman appointee in Armenia without damaging friendly relations with the Parthian empire – was beyond the heir-apparent's abilities but knew sending someone of lesser rank would have been an affront to Germanicus. As insurance he sent his trusted former consular colleague Gnaeus Calpurnius Piso as governor of Syria with instructions to restrain Germanicus from any serious indiscretions. As Germanicus's inferior, Piso should have contented himself with offering advice. Unfortunately, he meddled in arrangements already made by Germanicus and refused him military aid when it was requested. Piso may have thought he was acting rationally – and with the support of Tiberius. Furious, Germanicus ordered Piso to leave Syria, but a few days after Piso had taken ship, Germanicus fell sick and died on 10 October 19. With his last words he accused Piso of having poisoned him.

Germanicus's widow Agrippina brought back her publicly adored husband's ashes, loudly declaring Piso guilty of murder and hinting at Tiberius and Livia's involvement, claiming that they wanted his natural son Drusus to succeed to the throne. The senate put Piso on trial, where he cleared himself of poisoning Germanicus, but failed to get an acquittal on the charge of misconduct in his province and inciting the Syrian troops against his superior. In this, not even Tiberius could help him. Unable to see a way out, Piso committed suicide together with his wife Plancina. Tiberius had always acted properly towards Germanicus, and if he had reservations about his headstrong but affable nephew, son – after all – of his own beloved brother Drusus, it seems unlikely that they extended to assassination. Unfortunately, Piso's suicide convinced many that Tiberius was guilty. He remained

Born Nero Claudius Drusus on 24 May 15 BC, he became Julius Caesar Germanicus on his adoption by his uncle, Tiberius.

Publicly adored, Germanicus and his wife Agrippina (the Elder)

aloof from the proceedings, as did Livia although she was close to Plancina. It was an absence that was also interpreted as the action of guilty parties.

At some point after the episode, Tiberius elevated his son Drusus. His wife Julia Livilla, daughter of Antonia and Tiberius's deceased brother Drusus the Elder, gave birth to twin sons to him AD 19, Tiberius Germanicus Caesar and Tiberius Caesar Gemellus. Although the boys had some Julian blood, Tiberius stood by the prior right of Germanicus and Agrippina's sons because his own grandhildren were only distantly descended from Julius Caesar through Antonia. Tiberius – now in his early sixties – began absenting himself from Rome, leaving the administration in the hands of Drusus and the praetorian prefect Sejanus. In a long catalogue of rapacious men, Lucius Aelius Sejanus certainly qualifies as a nasty piece of work. He'd been appointed as the colleague of his father Lucius Seius Strabo, a wealthy equestrian, but had held the prefecture on his own after Tiberius promoted Strabo to the prefecture of Egypt in AD 15. Through a combination of energetic efficiency, fawning sycophancy and outward displays of loyalty, he gained the position of Tiberius's closest friend and advisor. Tiberius openly praised him as 'the partner of my labours'. Drusus, however, suspicious of the prefect's ambitions, did not find co-operation easy. Tensions were resolved when Drusus died under mysterious circumstances on 14 September 23, quickly followed by one of his sons, Tiberius Germanicus. Sejanus's wife Apicata later asserted that her husband had seduced Drusus's wife Livilla and persuaded her to poison her husband. The seduction story, at least, seems true, for within two years Sejanus had divorced Apicata and requested Livilla's hand. Tiberius refused this last step in allying Sejanus to the imperial family, but in every other respect the prefect had a free hand.

Sejanus concentrated the cohorts of the praetorian guards that Augustus had stationed separately around the city into a single camp – the *castra praetoria* just beyond the old Servian wall, which gave him 9,000 troops stationed on the city's edge. After Tiberius left Rome for the last time in 26 to retire on his island retreat of Capri, Sejanus was the most powerful man in Rome. Livia was one cause for the retirement. Always the dominant force in his life, Tiberius resented her treating him as if he were still a child. She vexed him by meddling in the administration, which she saw as her right not only as the Augusta but by virtue of being the brains of the imperial family; and there was no denying that it was her house that was the centre of life in the court, with her many young favourites such as Servius Sulpicius Galba. When, angered by his obduracy, Livia produced some of Augustus's old letters and read out his unflattering comments on Tiberius's sour and stubborn character, the two parted in bitterness. Tiberius only saw her once more in the last three years of her life. He refused to attend her funeral in 29, withheld the bequests of her will and vetoed her deification on the untrue grounds that she had forbidden it.

Livia's death left Sejanus unchecked. He became the emperor's voice and any senator who dared question him had only to glance at the menace of the praetorian guard or at his flock of *delatores*. Under Tiberius the role of these professional informers had expanded as a result of a

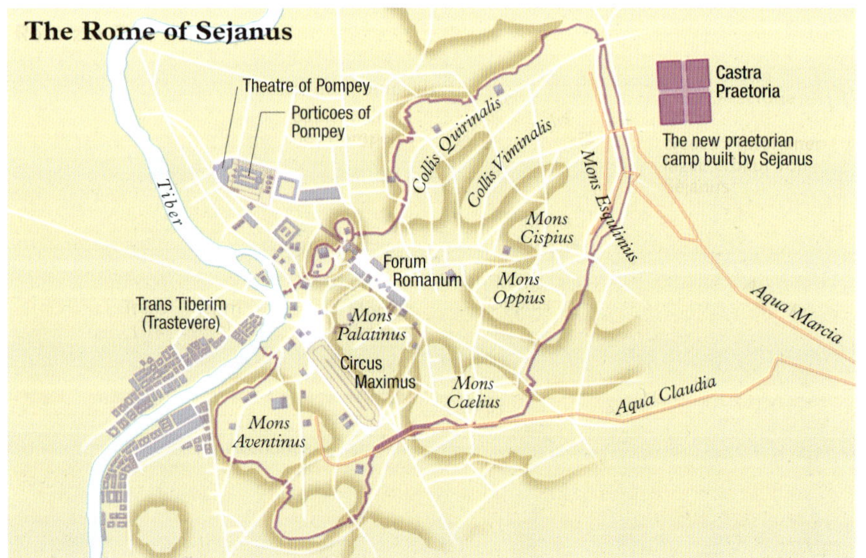

Tiberius's son Drusus and his faithless wife Julia Livilla, sister of Germanicus and Claudius, whom Sejanus, *right*, seduced into poisoning her husband.

revision to the law of treason, although Tiberius quashed many cases brought before him. Sejanus, however, increasingly found them useful in pursuing his ends, and what amounted to a reign of terror developed. An informer's reward for a successful prosecution was at least a quarter of his 'treasonous' victim's property. Naturally, such easy gains attracted the most unscrupulous men to invent charges against the wealthy.

Sejanus began a regular persecution of Agrippina, whose never-ending fulminations against Tiberius gave him plenty of excuses. Tiberius seems to have approved; he too was tired of Agrippina's waspish tongue and fed up of the adulation the senate and people heaped on her sons, the two eldest of whom – the Caesars Nero and Drusus – were the heirs apparent until Tiberius's remaining grandson Gemellus grew up. In rapid succession Nero and Agrippina were arrested in 27 and imprisoned on the island of Pandateria, and Drusus was in turn arrested and imprisoned in the gloomy Palatine palace. Nero and Agrippina died in captivity in 31, and Drusus only survived them by two years; apparently expiring from deliberate starvation.

By the end of 27 only two obstacles to ultimate power stood in Sejanus's path – other than the ageing empror – the young imperial princes, Tiberius's grandson, Gemellus, and Germanicus's surviving son Gaius Caligula. Events now moved quickly. The voice of reason belonged to elderly Antonia, daughter of Mark Antony and Octavia, the emperor's sister-in-law and mother of Germanicus, with whom Tiberius had remained on good terms. When the stately matron told him of Sejanus's plotting Tiberius believed her, and acted. Tricking the prefect into thinking he was about to receive a share in the *tribunicia potestas*, Sejanus attended the senate on 18 October 31. But in an unexpected turn of events, the letter sent by Tiberius initially praised Sejanus, and then suddenly denounced him as a traitor and demanded his arrest. Chaos ensued. Supporters of Sejanus headed for the exit, others were confused, fearing that this was another Tiberian test of their loyalty.

In setting the trap, Tiberius had called on the strength of Naevius Sutorius Macro, prefect of the new *cohortes urbanae* (urban chorts or police), to suborn the praetorians and replace the usual guard at the senate house with his own men of the vigiles. Macro conveyed Sejanus to prison and shortly after executed him. Sejanus's family was arrested and put to death in the witch-hunt that followed; followers and friends of Sejanus were denounced and imprisoned, or tried and executed. Livilla's end came when her mother imprisoned her in a room without food; noble Antonia paid her own penance by listening as her daughter died of starvation.

**FOR HIS REMAINING YEARS** Tiberius remained on Capri. The stories of his depravity and appalling cruelty were almost certainly inventions of Suetonius and Tacitus, historians living in a later age, whose autocratic rulers aspired to a high moral tone by playing up the excesses of their predecessors. The accounts of the roué emperor's sexual antics with youths and young children of either sex seem at variance with the certainty that Capri was filled with scholars. Nor are they consistent with the extraordinary amount of hard work that Tiberius put in right up until his death – even unloved Rome was well cared for. Under Tiberius the city prefect of Rome became a permanent and important official, responsible for maintaining law and order with the cohortes urbanae, who policed the streets. Tiberius created an efficient administration of the provinces through a series of prudent appointments. He extended the terms of governors, which lessened the temptation to get rich quick that had bedevilled the Republican period when governors only held the office for a year.

Despite his aversion to spending, Tiberius provided large subsidies in 19 so that the price of grain could be lowered. When a financial crisis arose in 33 because of a shortage of coinage in circulation, he lent the treasury a million sesterces, interest free, and spent a similar sum in 36 to repair the damage caused by a massive fire on the Aventine. In contrast, there was almost no spending on new public buildings apart

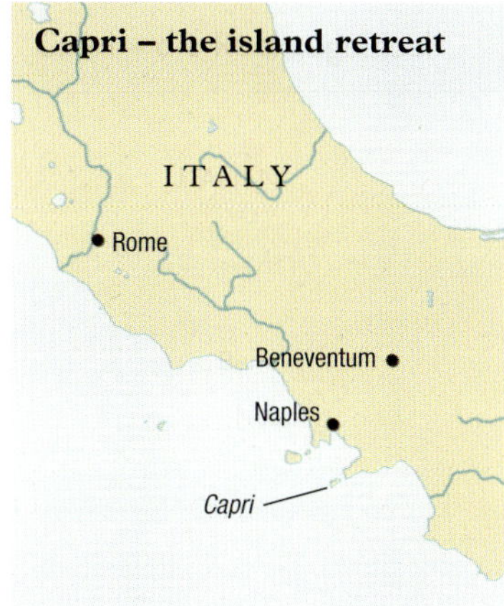

from completing the restoration of Pompey's Theatre, and a new temple to the Deified Augustus that went so slowly it remained unfinished at his death. He erected a huge palace on the Palatine, even though he spent almost no time in it and its fabric soon fell into disrepair.

In the matter of the succession, Tiberius had a choice between his grandson Tiberius Gemellus, who at sixteen was too young, and his grandnephew Gaius, Germanicus's son. At twenty-three he was also young, but Gaius was of the Julian blood line. Tiberius, who held suspicions that Gemellus was actually the illegitimate offspring of Sejanus, solved the question by appointing both as his co-heirs. There are indications that he would have liked to pass over Gaius, whom he knew suffered from serious character flaws, but being a Julian made it unwise to do so. Tiberius gave Gaius no responsible offices and kept him at Capri under his watchful eye. Thus it was that, in 37, when Tiberius fell ill and feared his death was imminent, Gaius was in his company. The court left Capri for the mainland but had only reached Misenum when, at 78, Tiberius died on 16 March, and Gaius profited from being the heir on the spot.

## Gaius Caligula  Gaius Julius Caesar Germanicus
[ AD 18/3/37–24/1/41 ]

Gaius was born on 31 August AD 12, either at Antium (Anzio) or Augusta Treverorum (Trier). His father Germanicus was constantly on the move, which explains the confusion over his birthplace. As a child on campaign with Germanicus, Gaius was nicknamed Caligula (Bootikin), which is how history knows him, because he wore the miniature uniform of a private soldier, including the *caliga*, or half-boot, of the infantryman. He was the youngest of the six boys born to Augustus's adopted grandson, and Augustus's granddaughter, Agrippina. His childhood was not a happy one, spent amid an atmosphere of paranoia, suspicion and murder.

After his father's mysterious death in Syria, Agrippina had returned to Rome and Gaius lived with her until her arrest by Sejanus. His great-grandmother Livia took in the adolescent in AD 27 and then, following her death two years later, Gaius went to live with his other grandmother Antonia. Shortly before the fall of Sejanus in 31 Tiberius summoned him to Capri as his brothers and mother suffered their violent deaths. By the time of his accession, Gaius Caligula had only held two minor offices.

Inevitably, there were rumours that he was involved in Tiberius's death – or at least helped him on the way. The newly promoted praetorian prefect Macro was said to have connived, and this may have been true, although the allegations gained currency with the appalling events of Caligula's reign. Certainly, due largely to Macro's efforts, Gaius's succession went smoothly and the senate voted him the imperial prerogatives on 18 March 37. Gaius entered Rome on 28 March amid scenes of extravagant rejoicing at the reality of having a true Julian as the head of state. And his first acts as princeps were generous. He honoured the bequests of Tiberius and those of Livia (which Tiberius had held up), ended the activities of the *delatores*, quashed pending treason trials, publicly destroyed the personal papers of Tiberius, which may have implicated the elite in the destruction of the Agrippina faction, and he gave Tiberius a splendid funeral. Finally, recalled exiles received compensation and those who had been wronged by the imperial tax system were reimbursed.

If the senatorial order was concerned about his inexperience, they kept quiet – but there were worrying signs. Gaius gave the praetorian guard a huge donative, which hinted at dark doings in Misenum. He had Tiberius's will annulled on the grounds of insanity, which was not difficult in the light of the senate's dislike of reclusive Tiberius, which had the benefit of disinheriting his co-ruler Gemellus. Gaius then adopted Gemellus and made him *princeps iuventutis*, a move which established that he alone

Contemporary portraits of Gaius Caligula depict a handsome youth, but with a hint of the latent bully.

and not the will of Tiberius could elevate the youth; and it also implied that he could remove the office if it pleased him. Young, generous and Julian, Gaius basked in the love of his people. Yet within four years he lay dead in a palace corridor, murdered by the very men entrusted to protect him.

Suetonius describes Gaius as being tall, with a pallid complexion and a badly built, hairy body. His forehead was broad and forbidding and, despite his youth, he was almost bald on top, about which he was so self-conscious that he later made it a capital offence for anyone to look down on him from above. With sunken eyes, hollow temples, a thin neck and spindly legs, Suetonius gives a splendidly vituperative portrait. Given the propensity for Graeco-Roman sculpture of the period to favour accuracy, the statues depict a young man of more general appeal. The best, however, wonderfully suggests the latent teenage bully, coupled with a grim determination. Perhaps Suetonius's description dates from the last year of his reign, when dissolute living and the ravages of Julian-inherited epilepsy that frequently struck him down had taken their toll.

The ancient histories are unanimously hostile towards Gaius Caligula, perhaps most eloquently summed up by a line from Suetonius: 'So much for Caligula the Emperor; the rest of this history must needs deal with Caligula the Monster.' It's difficult to distinguish between fictional invective, histrionic lampooning and possibly factual writing. It seems that within months of his accession in 37, Gaius fell seriously ill – probably a nervous breakdown of some kind – and emerged from it changed. He insisted on being treated as a god, he stood beside the shrine of Castor and Pollux in the Forum Romanum to be worshipped by all visitors, and established his own shrine nearby. He had a life-sized golden image displayed, dressed in clothes identical with those he happened to be wearing. It was his habit to commit incest with each of his three sisters in turn, his favourite being Drusilla. When she suddenly died – he may have had a hand in it – Gaius had her deified. He used his two other sisters, Agrippina the Younger and Julia (usually known as Livilla), as prostitutes for his courtiers, and then had the nerve to banish the girls for committing immoral acts – although they were also accused of conspiring against him.

Too much may have been made of his illness, but within weeks he had come to ignore the senate and its powers, he enjoyed humiliating senators and *equites* alike and did away with the *concilium*. He removed the senate's right to issue bronze coinage, and even made senators prostrate themselves before him as if he were an oriental potentate. By early 38 there was much uneasiness among the aristocracy at the way Gaius was establishing an absolute monarchy. Men who traditionally had a share in the government could no longer even offer advice and those that presumed to do so were invariably executed on the flimsiest of excuses. This even included Macro, who found himself increasingly divorced from the affections of the emperor he had helped create. Gaius suspected everyone of fomenting rebellion around Tiberius Gemellus. In one anecdote, suspecting that Gemellus had been taking precautionary emetics against the poison Gaius intended to administer, he scoffed: 'Can there really be an antidote against Caesar?' Evidently not; Gemellus was executed in May 38.

Late in 39 Gaius went to the Rhine to deal with a plot instigated by Marcus Aemilius Lepidus (a twice-removed nephew of the triumvir), widower of Drusilla and lover of her sister Agrippina the Younger. Gaius's third sister, Livilla was also implicated. Lepidus had gained the support of the *legatus legionis* of Germania Superior, Lentulus Gaetulicus, but in an unusually well timed move, Gaius arrived on the frontier before the two could join up. The appeal of the Julian Gaius worked its magic and the mass of legionaries rallied to him under the command of two praetors, Livia's protegé and stern disciplinarian Servius Sulpicius Galba and the inspired thirty-year-old strategist Titus Flavius Vespasianus (Vespasian).

Co-heir, grandson of Tiberius, Gemellus was quickly sidelined by Caligula (*seen in an accession coin*), who had the youth executed.

Caligula's sisters, Agrippina the Younger (Agrippinilla), Drusilla and Julia Livilla were all rumoured to have had incestuous relations with him.

Coin of Herod Agrippa I, whose oriental manners influenced Gaius, who favoured him with power in Judaea.

From the Rhine, Gaius announced an invasion of Britain, which began in the spring of 40 and turned into a ludicrous farce. Having gathered his forces on the Gallic coast, Gaius had the legions drawn up in battle array on the beach facing the sea. No one had any idea what his intentions were, when he suddenly ordered the men to gather up shells in their helmets – the 'plunder from the sea and Neptune'. He sent the resulting hoard to Rome to be presented in his triumph. This absurd incident has taxed historians, but if it is more than a scurrilous chronicler's anecdote of the time, one modern theory is that it represented a colourful and humiliating punishment for the Roman troops – ever fearful of the sea – who simply refused to board the waiting galleys. The same thing was to happen to Claudius two years later.

On his return to Rome, to raise money the loathed *delatores* and treason trials became the order of the day – forty months of extravagance had squandered Tiberius's fortune and the invasion fiasco had bankrupted the state. The praetorian guard turned tax enforcers; Gaius held auctions of theatrical props, for which senators were forced to bid ludicrous prices; he taxed foodstuffs, porters and prostitutes. Making wealthy men priests of Gaius's own godhead and then charging them an exorbitant fee for the honour was a favourite scam. Failure to comply resulted in execution and the confiscation of property. Gaius enjoyed inflicting physical and mental pain on those he intended to execute. He was particularly fond of inviting parents to witness their sons' executions, and when one father excused himself on grounds of ill-health, kindly provided a litter for him.

Apart from the fanatic loyalty of the captured German tribesmen, captained by Thracian officers, he'd selected as a personal bodyguard (who apparently held his madness as divine), only the praetorian soldiers held him in any sort of affection because of the donative and subsequent extra benefits. But their officers felt marginalised by the German bodyguards and it was from this direction that the end came. No one had stepped into Macro's post, and the acting commander, a veteran named Cassius Chaerea, had good reason to hate his master. Chaerea was the victim of Gaius's insults, teases that implied the tough old soldier was effeminate. Gaius would give him obscene phrases as the password for the day, and force him to kneel and kiss the suggestively wiggled imperial finger.

On 24 January 41, just past midday, as the emperor left a theatre performance for luncheon, friends guided him into a rarely used side passage leading to the palace and Gaius became momentarily separated from his Germans. At this moment Cassius Chaerea stepped out and struck him down with a sword thrust to the neck, while another guards officer, Sabinus, stabbed him in the breast. Having ruled for only three years and ten months, at the age of twenty-eight Gaius Caligula died in a pool of his own blood. Frenzied praetorians then seized the empress Milonia Caesonia, whom Gaius had married (his fourth wife) in 39, killed her and snatched her infant girl child, and swung her by her little ankles to bash her brains out against a column.

The senate he had so humiliated repealed all his acts. Gaius's reign established that his autocratic will was the Roman law, and the more ludicrous of his actions – even if exaggerated by later historians – were little more than the petulant whims of a callow youth demonstrating that he could do whatever he liked. The claim that he made his race horse Incitatus a consul smacks more of an adolescent prank aimed to prick senatorial pomposity than a really determined intention. But the bridge of ships he built across the bay at Baiae in 39 was real. Dressed in Alexander the Great's breastplate, Gaius rode across the bay like a god, an extravagantly theatrical advertisement of his divine power. What the reign makes most clear is the degree to which the senate had come to depend on the emperor and the level of tyranny that was inherent in the Augustan model of the principate. After Gaius Caligula the empire's fortunes would wax and wane as a direct consequence of the qualities of a single man.

## Claudius  Tiberius Claudius Caesar Drusus Germanicus
[ 26/1/41–13/10/54 ]

The tale of Tiberius Claudius Drusus quivering behind a curtain following the death of Caligula is told by Suetonius. When a praetorian stalking the palace corridors discovered him, the son of Drusus, nephew of Tiberius, and grandson of both Mark Antony and Livia Drusilla fell at his feet pleading for his life. Not the best start for an imperial ruler, but Claudius had good reason to be fearful after the murder of his nephew Caligula resulted in a wave of reprisal killings carried out by the loyal Germans. As luck would have it, his discoverer was among the ranks of the those opposed to senatorial ambitions to redeem the Republic. The reluctant noble was propelled by the soldier's fellow guardsmen to the safety of the *castra praetoria*, where – since their existence had no meaning without an imperial ruler and regardless of his dismal reputation – they raised Claudius up and proclaimed him emperor on 25 January, the day after Gaius Caligula's death. The basic fact of the principate – implicit in the Augustan settlement but always carefully disguised – was now made plain: the emperor's position ultimately rested on the sword and not on the consensus of the senate and people. Within the senatorial order – powerless to prevent the accession – there were a few who knew of his hidden accomplishments as a liberal historian and anticipated his rule to be favourable to their cause. Although he had some Julian blood from his grandmother Octavia's side, he'd never been adopted into the Julian house, and remained a Claudian, also better favoured by the senate. However, this did not prevent him adopting the populist name of Caesar. Since he had no legal claim, the adoption of 'Caesar' marks the first step in the word's transmutation from a nickname to a title meaning ruler.

On the face of it, Claudius was not an ideal candidate to rule the civilised world. Born at Lugdunum (Lyons) on 1 August 10 BC, an attack of childhood paralysis had left him with an unattractive appearance. He is said to have drooled, had a runny nose, stammered and habitually trembled. His handsome family did everything to keep him out of the public eye. His mother Antonia called him a monster and accused others of stupidity by exclaiming: 'He's a bigger fool than even my son Claudius!' Livia scorned him and Augustus worried whether he would reflect badly on the imperial family: 'The question is whether he has – shall I say it? – full command of his five senses,' he wrote to Antonia, '…should he prove physically and mentally deficient, the public must not be given a chance to laugh at him and us.' However, Augustus suspected there might be more to his 'idiot' grandson than met the eye. He told Livia, 'How on earth anyone who talks so confusedly can nevertheless speak so well in public – with such clearness, saying all that needs to be said – I simply do not understand.' Nevertheless, Augustus cautiously kept Claudius away from any important offices, so he spent his youth in almost complete isolation. This seclusion afforded Claudius ample opportunity to study. He became an accomplished historian, producing books on Etruscan, Augustan and Carthaginian history. None has survived.

In his first imperial acts, he had his nephew's murderers executed, but acted generously towards those senators implicated in the plot. He stopped the treason trials, recalled exiles, including Gaius's two sisters Agrippina and Livilla, abolished absurd taxes and provided spectacles in the Circus Maximus. There were, however, at least six plots during his reign and he executed thirty-five senators and between 200 to 300 *equites* in the process of suppressing them. He probably survived these through a wise policy of courting the praetorian guard. Nor were the legions ignored. Early on Claudius pursued a bold foreign policy: in his first months he suppressed a revolt in Mauretania; in 43 he conquered the south of Britain, extended Roman influence in the state of

There was more to Augustus's 'idiot' grandson than met the eye: an unflattering likeness of Claudius, based on a statue fragment found in England, now at the British Museum.

Palmyra, situated between Syria and the Euphrates, and annexed Lycia. He annexed the client kingdoms of Judaea in 44, Thrace in 46 and Ituraea (an area between the north of Judaea and the plains of Damascus) in 49, which was incorporated into Syria. This military activity provided the soldiers more opportunities for booty.

Preparations for Britain's conquest were complete in 42 but delays occasioned by the troops' reluctance to embark – a replay of the problem faced by Gaius two years earlier – meant that the crossing took place in the spring of 43. Under the command of Aulus Plautius Silvanus, four legions of experienced troops and auxiliaries numbering some 50,000 men landed at Rutupiae (Richborough, Kent). The legions fought their way north, halting at the Thames to await the carefully stage-managed arrival of Claudius. During the eight-week wait for the imperial bandwagon, complete with war elephants, all immediate resistance was crushed. Claudius continued unchallenged to Camulodunum (Colchester). He left the new province sixteen days later in the hands of Plautius. The conquest resumed in the spring of 44, in which the legate Vespasian, who had supported Caligula in 39, won most of the glory. Claudius celebrated his triumph in 44, his military credentials firmly established.

Claudius was a surprisingly effective emperor, with a steady hand on the administrative, fiscal and legal tiller. The tenor of his rule was one of steady, unalarming growth. He continued the reforming programmes of Caesar and Augustus, particularly in founding colonies in the imperial domains, which were lagging behind the senatorial provinces. Claudius also started a Romanisation process destined to be a contentious, that of granting Latin rights to Gallic tribes deemed ready for the benefits and the tax obligations. His ruling made wealthy Gallic nobles eligible for senate membership as long as they were Roman citizens.

Mounted warrior of the Atrebates on a coin minted by Roman client king Verica, whose eviction from Britain provided Claudius with an excuse to invade.

Tasks once performed by annually elected magistrates were now undertaken by a growing group of permanent civil servants, generally recruited from among the ranks of the *equites* but his own freedmen held the most important posts. His closest advisors were Greeks: Pallas, financial secretary; Narcissus, secretary-general; Callistus, legal secretary (who had gained prominence under Gaius); and Polybius, the privy seal. These freedmen even sat in for him at senatorial sessions on occasions. Claudius appreciated the native intelligence and experience of the slaves with which he had earlier surrounded himself, and rated their abilities more highly than those of any aristocrat. This type of secretariat had existed before, but centralisation meant that freedmen now wielded more power than they would have done under Augustus or Tiberius. The most noticeable changes came in the area of public finance. The various financial bureaux were now united under one central *fiscus* or imperial treasury; even the ancient *aerarium saturnii* (public treasury, stored under the temple of Saturn) was removed from the control of senatorial propraetors and placed under equestrian quaestors in 44.

This increasing centralisation of bureaucracy was only hastened by several famines due to wheat shortage, which were largely the result of peculation among responsible *equites*. Claudius overhauled the food-providing institutions and went to lengths to improve agricultural productivity. He completed two aqueducts, Aqua Claudia and

Aqua Anio Novus, begun in the time of his predecessor, and constructed a deep-water harbour at Portus, near Ostia. Food transportation benefited from new roads, the Via Claudia Valeria to the Adriatic coast, and roads over the western and Julian (eastern) Alps. He also had the bed of Lacus Fucinus (Fucine) drained to provide farming land, although this doomed project failed after eleven years.

Socially, Claudius was clumsy and coarse, and had an unhealthy fascination with the death throes of gladiators at the many games he sponsored. His attitude to religion was reactionary, yet his foreign policy was forward-thinking and successful. The contradictions in his nature are summed up in his attitude towards Jews. While guilty of banishing them from Rome, possibly in response to unrest stirred up by the new sect of Christians, he confirmed their rights in other locations. He also appealed for Jews and non-Jews in Egypt to stop the 'destructive enmity' that existed between them. In contrast to his reign Claudius's domestic life was a disaster. One bride-to-be, Livia Medullina, died on her wedding day. Claudius divorced his first two wives, Plautia Urgulanilla and Aelia Paetina (the sister of Sejanus). Valeria Messalina, his third wife, was forced on him by mischievous Gaius Caligula, who enjoyed the joke of Rome's greatest beauty shackled to Rome's ugliest old man. Claudius executed her after she cuckolded him. His fourth wife poisoned him.

Messalina gave Claudius a daughter, Octavia, in 39 and a son, Tiberius Claudius Caesar Germanicus, in 41, later renamed Britannicus to commemorate Britain's conquest. Messalina's lax sexual reputation was well known, but her Julian stock made the marriage politically useful and he no doubt tolerated dissolute behaviour for that reason – at least until she took advantage of his absence at Ostia in 48, to play-act a marriage ceremony with a lover, the consul-elect Gaius Silius. This was treason, similar to Marcus Aemilius Lepidus and Agrippina the Younger's conspiracy against Gaius. Claudius ordered their immediate executions. There followed a scramble among the civil servants to place their preferred candidates at Claudius's side. His intimate friend Lucius Vitellius argued for Agrippina the Younger, forcefully backed by Pallas (she was his mistress so the union would strengthen his position). Claudius's infatuation for Agrippina suggested by Suetonius seems improbable – she was his niece, she'd been one of her brother's court prostitutes, and there was the affair with Lepidus. Additionally, by a former marriage to Gnaeus Domitius Ahenobarbus, scion of a powerful but dissolute Roman family, some thirty years her senior, she had an eleven-year-old son, Lucius Domitius Ahenobarbus. In spite of the glaring disadvantages, in 48 Claudius was finally persuaded to accept a union that brought to him a direct descendant of Augustus with strong Julian connections.

Agrippina's powerful personality dominated the emperor's last years. Her simple aim was to see her son on the throne in place of the younger Britannicus, but more than that to rule the empire through him. With the active help of Pallas she soon became influential; her image soon appeared on coins and the senate voted her the title Augusta. The extent of her power can be seen in the naming of Colonia Agrippina, the new town in Germania Inferior. Shortly after the wedding Agrippina contrived the betrothal of her son Lucius Domitius to Claudius's daughter Octavia, and in 50 his adoption by Claudius over Britannicus, who was five years the junior. Lucius took the name Nero Claudius Caesar Drusus Germanicus, and in 53 he married Octavia. Claudius took the precaution – as Tiberius had done – of appointing a loyal man, Sextus Afranius Burrus, as praetorian prefect to safeguard Nero's succession when the time came.

Agrippina's ambitions drove her impatience. At sixty-three Claudius was fit and well. Were he to live for much longer he might well alter the priority of the succession (which Narcissus was urging Claudius to do). Also, at sixteen Nero showed signs of

Coin of King Antiochus IV of the Seleucid dynasty. In 44 Claudius gave him Comagene to rule as a 'legate of the Augustus', effectively qualifying his royal status as that of an imperial bureaucrat.

Claudius's last two wives, dissolute Messalina (*top*) and murdering Agrippina the Younger, Nero's mother.

Nero and Agrippina, the mother intent on ruling the empire.



intractability – if she waited much longer for him to become emperor he would no longer need his mother's advice and Agrippina would lose her hold over him. On 13 October 54, Claudius died as a result of poisoning. According to Pliny the Elder, Agrippina paid a notorious poisoner called Locusta to doctor a dish of mushrooms. He vomited this up and was poisoned a second time with another poison administered both orally and as an enema. And then, just to make sure, he was smothered.

The reign of Claudius was graced by stability and good government at home and in the provinces, and the successful management of client kingdoms. He was careful, intelligent, aware and respectful of tradition, but given to bouts of rage and cruelty. He was willing to sacrifice precedent to expediency, while using precedent to justify his actions. And, despite an apparently amiable disposition, he was utterly ruthless in his treatment of those who crossed him. Augustus's suspicion that there was more to his 'idiot' step-grandson than met the eye was more than fully borne out by the events of his unexpected reign.

## Nero  Lucius Domitius Ahenobarbus/Nero Claudius Caesar Drusus Germanicus
[ 13/10/54–9/6/68 ]

More than any imperial reign, Nero's provides the most fertile ground for dramatisation. Characterised by extravagance, despotism, promiscuity and madness, it ended the Julio-Claudian dynasty and plunged the Roman world into a vicious civil war. In the areas of government and economy little of merit was achieved and much damage done: insurrection in the provinces, rampant inflation, devaluation, the mass murder of Christians to mention a few evils of the reign. Appropriately, history has left us with the image of the insane emperor, playing his harp while watching Rome burn.

Many of Nero's vices were probably inherited, although as a self-acclaimed artist-performer, he was more than capable of presenting them on a broad stage. Lucius Domitius Ahenobarbus was born at Antium (Anzio) on 15 December AD 37. Acknowledging the predicted nature of his newborn son, Gnaeus Domitius Ahenobarbus told a companion that any child born to him and Agrippina the Younger was bound to have a detestable nature and become a danger to the public.

Following his mother's banishment, his aunt Domitia Lepida raised him and, according to Suetonius, she chose a dancer and a barber to be his tutors, which goes some way to explaining his obsession with performing music and dance, not to say with his appearance. In his adolescent years this unsuitable education was rectified when Claudius revived the family fortunes by rescinding Agrippina's exile. She appointed the stoic philosopher Seneca to be his tutor. Nero's accession went smoothly, thanks to the praetorian prefect Burrus, and a compliant senate voted the seventeen-year-old the imperial powers. The armies were not expected to contest a great-great-grandson of Augustus, and none did. The praetorians were duly thanked with a donative. Nero then spoke to the senate, promising to restore the Augustan principle of the division of powers between princeps and senate. Seneca, of course, wrote the speech for him.

Augusta Agrippina styled herself as co-ruler alongside her son. The first coins minted during the era show their heads side by side. Her first actions were the elimination of the Claudian secretaries, and the few remaining Augustan descendants who may have posed a threat, including poor Aunt Lepida. However, Nero's tutors Seneca and Burrus were opposed to the idea of a woman ruling Rome, and persuaded him against his mother. As her power waned, Agrippina played her trump card and switched her allegiance to her stepson Britannicus. But it was a poor hand, in 55 Britannicus died of poisoning – Nero claimed an epileptic fit was to blame. At the same time Agrippina was accused of treason but brazened it out, although Nero made his mother remove herself from Rome, leaving the government effectively in the hands of Seneca and Burrus. For a period of five years after Agrippina's banishment, these two ran the empire's affairs well while the emperor ignored the boring matters of state.

Besides his passion for all things aesthetic, he enjoyed the pleasures of alcohol and promiscuous sex. A thuggish thrill-seeker, Nero prowled the streets of Rome in darkness with friends – Annaeus Serenus, prefect of the vigiles, and Marcus Salvius Otho, a young noble destined briefly for the purple – beating up revellers. When the joys of this pastime dried up, he turned his attentions to racing, scandalising Roman aristocrats by becoming a chariot racer. Charioteers were generally trained slaves and Nero was the only noble-born among them. His passion for Hellenistic sports resulted

The face of Nero, *above*, last of the Julio-Claudians, shaped by vice, cruelty and despotism.

in the Neronian Games of AD 60, inspired by the Olympian Games in Greece. His unseemly predilection for athletics – contrary to popular belief, he was not interested in Roman gladiatorial contests – was accompanied by a growing zeal for the performing arts. Actors of the age were considered lowly, vulgar types, but Nero seized any opportunity to perform, prohibiting anyone to doze or leave the theatre on pain of death.

However, among his unsuitable companions two stand out. Poppaea Sabina, Othos's wife, became Nero's lover in 58 after he sent her husband to govern Lusitania in Spain. Gaius Ofonius Tigellinus, exiled in 39 by Gaius Caligula for adultery with Agrippina, had returned to find preferment with Nero. The beautiful Poppaea urged Nero to get rid of his mother, in whom she rightly perceived a dangerous rival. Seneca and Burrus had been busy hinting at the same end for some time, and Nero had developed a virulent hatred of Agrippina. After a foiled attempt to drown her – rather absurdly on a ship designed to fall apart in the sea (a good swimmer, she was rescued by a fishing vessel) – the prefect of the Misenum fleet had her executed.

Nero now shook off all restraints. Having grown impatient with Seneca and Burrus, at Poppaea's urging he forced Seneca into retirement when Burrus died in 61. The emperor tired of Octavia and divorced her on the grounds that she was barren, which may have been true, and adulterous, which was unlikely, then exiled her. Octavia was executed shortly after and Nero married Poppaea. He then appointed his counsellor of the past months, Tigellinus, to the joint command of the praetorians from which position he exerted a further degenerate influence on Nero. Licentiousness, unbridled extravagance, and sensuality became court features. Not content with girls, he seduced free-born boys and raped a Vestal Virgin. He tied men and women to stakes and attacked their genitals while dressed as a wild beast, and went through a sham wedding with a boy named Sporus, who was castrated to make him into a 'girl' for the event.

Historically, the most famous event of Nero's reign is the great fire of Rome. Nero was cast as the villain, after he unguardedly suggested that the conflagration – which started on the night of 13 July 64 and burned for seven days, destroying three of Rome's fourteen regions and badly damaging a further seven – was a godsend, since it provided space for his new palace, the Domus Aurea (Golden House). In fact Nero, who was miles away at Antium when the fire started, took energetic measures to bring the fire under control and provide relief for the victims. He was responsible for a host of new building and fire regulations to help prevent what was a common hazard in Rome. Nevertheless, the mob howled and, seeking a scapegoat, lit on the burgeoning but marginalised sect of Christians. Thousands died in punishment for a crime they had not committed.

**THANKS TO NERO'S LAVISH SPENDING** on the Domus Aurea, the *fiscus* emptied and inflation increased. When devaluation of the gold *aureus* failed to ameliorate the situation Nero resorted to murdering wealthy men. Tigellinus organised cohorts of the detested *delatores* to hasten charges and convictions. In 65 a plot to replace Nero with the wealthy, charming senator Gaius Calpurnius Piso was uncovered, thanks to the efforts of a praetor-designate named Marcus Cocceius Nerva. Nero's readiness to eliminate opposition through murder created an atmosphere of paranoia. In the reign of terror that followed the conspiracy many popular figures died either by execution or forced suicide, including the poet Lucan, Nero's ex-tutor Seneca and Gaius Petronius, author of the *Satyricon*, whose louche description of *Trimalchio's*

Too young to pose a threat, Claudius's son Britannicus survived a few years into his brother-in-law Nero's reign; bust and commemorative coin.

Octavia (top), Claudius's daughter, Nero's first wife, divorced and executed so Nero could marry the devious Poppaea Sabina.

*Dinner* perfectly sums up the greedy, sexually lax atmosphere of Nero's court. Poppaea Sabina also died in 65 after receiving a bad-tempered kick in the stomach from Nero while she was pregnant; but this was obviously an accident.

Unwisely, Nero also chose to attack the celebrated general, Domitius Corbulo. For his sweeping successes in almost every theatre of the empire, Corbulo had become a hero among his own troops, and his victories made him the most famous general of his day with the public. He was forced to commit suicide and this senseless act caused the soldiers of legions on every front to raise their voices in outright hostility. Tigellinus continued suppressing Nero's enemies, unhindered by his new colleague, Gaius Nymphidius Sabinus, who was appointed in the same year. In the reign of terror that followed the Piso conspiracy, virtually all of Rome's remaining patrician nobility was wiped out.

By September 66 Nero's unpopularity had driven him to Achaea, where his artistically Greek heart lay, blissfully unaware that days after his departure Tigellinus had fled Rome in advance of a lynch mob. In Greece Nero involved himself in a whirl of musical diversions and athletic competitions, in which he always won the first prize – he even won prizes in competitions he never attended. His adoring reception so overwhelmed the emperor that, on 28 November 67, Nero proclaimed Achaea liberated – not exactly free, but independent of Macedonia and released from taxation. This liberation had consequences in the west where – thanks to Claudius's reforms – the Gauls considered theirs the empire's senior provinces. The affront to Gallic pride was sufficient for the standard of rebellion to be raised, and the insurgency soon spread to Spain and Africa, where the rebellious proconsul of Africa, Clodius Macer, furious at Nero's tyranny, cut off the grain supply to Rome. Famine soon set in, compounded by a combination of fraud and incompetent administration.

A serious revolt among the Jews in Judaea and the deteriorating situation at home halted Nero's plans to visit Egypt. He returned to Rome at the start of 68. Abandoned by Tigellinus, odious to the mob for the innumerable executions and quite unable to disentangle the administrative chaos, Nero had run out of options. His only hope lay in the praetorian guards, but in this he was cheated. In the final act Sabinus, the remaining prefect, promised the guards a massive donative in the name of Livia's old friend Servius Sulpicius Galba, the govenor of Hispania Tarraconensis. With the populace set firmly against him and open mutiny among the legions, on 8 June 68 the senate declared Nero a public enemy and declared for Galba. The shamed emperor fled to the suburbs where on the following day, lacking the courage to take his own life, he ordered his loyal freedman Epaphroditus to stab him. The Julio-Claudian dynasty ended as Nero fell, uttering the words, 'What an artist I die.' His long-suffering but faithful mistress Acte buried him anonymously in the Ahenobari mausoleum, just outside the Servian Wall on the side of the quiet Pincian Hill.

Eliminated: Lucius Annaeus Seneca (*top*) tutored young Nero but later accused of conspiracy, he committed suicide, as did the celebrated general, Gnaeus Domitius Corbulo.

This coin makes no attempt at flattery, Nero's excessive lifestyle is all too apparent.

# TWO

# Year of the Four Emperors

[AD 68–70]

### Galba  Servius Sulpicius Galba
[ declared 6/4/68; princeps 8/6/68–15/1/69 ]

Galba's greed knew no bounds. When the people of Tarraco offered him a golden crown said to weigh 6.8kg, he had it melted down and made them supply the 85gm needed to tip the scales to the advertised weight.

In the spring of 68, the governor of Gallia Lugdunensis, Gaius Julius Vindex, raised the standard for a nationalist movement, aiming to win for the Gallic provinces what Nero had bestowed on Greek Achaea. As a Romanised Gaul, his was also a cry for freedom from tyranny. Vindex canvassed provincial legates to join him in open rebellion and his appeal found support with the governor of Hispania Tarraconensis, seventy-year-old Galba. This was hardly surprising, for wealthy Galba had just heard that Nero wanted him dead.

Born on 24 December 3 BC between Tarracina and Fundi some 100 kilometres south of Rome, Galba owed his advancement to the patronage of Augustus's wife Livia. Galba outlived both his wife Lepida and their two sons and he remained a widower. He had governed Aquitania, Germania Superior (39–40), Africa (45–46) and now Hispania Tarraconensis, starting in 61. On 6 April Galba pronounced himself 'Legate of the Senate and Roman People', although his troops saluted him as princeps. Backing came from Aulus Caecina Alienus, proconsular governor of Baetica, Marcus Salvius Otho, Nero's ex-friend and quaestor of Lusitania, and his senior legate Aulus Vitellius.

The governor of Germania Superior, Lucius Verginius Rufus, refused to join the cause and marched to Vesontio (Besançon) on 7 May, where he overwhelmed Vindex in battle. Despite the experience and strength of his forces, Verginius made no attempt to proclaim himself emperor, but he did put his army at the senate's disposal, further weakening Nero's position. Since he needed no rivals on his flanks, Galba ordered the assassination of rebellious Clodius Macer at his base in Africa and ensured the restoration of the grain supply. Then, with the Spanish army and two newly recruited legions, Galba set off for Italy in the late summer, with Otho as his second in command.

Tacitus wrote: 'the secret of empire was revealed: an emperor could be made elsewhere than at Rome.' Now anyone with a provincial army to back him could aspire to the principate. By October 68, Galba was in Rome; however, chaos greeted his arrival. Resolute when he set his mind to solving problems, not even his grasping years governing four provinces had prepared Galba for the deplorable state of the *fiscus*. Since economies had to be made, everyone's pocket was hit: public shows were banned and promised donatives witheld – even from the praetorian guard. Stories of Galba's notorious inflexibility had preceded him to Rome, and they were soon confirmed as he had men of all ranks sentenced to death without trial on the scantiest evidence that they disapproved of his administration. His popularity plunged.

Described by Tacitus as a 'mediocre genius' and 'capable of being emperor had he never ruled', Galba unwisely interfered in the commands of the already disaffected German legions, and in Germania Inferior the troops became mutinous when Fabius Valens, legate of Legio I Germana, executed the governor Fonteius Capito. Galba sent his creature Aulus Vitellius to replace Fonteius, who promptly made boastful promises to the men. At the start of 69, the soldiers of Germania Superior refused to take the annual oath to the emperor, and two days later joined the legions of Germania Inferior in proclaiming Vitellius as emperor. Valens supported Vitellius, as did Galba's treacherous former associate Caecina, the governor of Baetica, whom Galba had sent to command another legion in Germania Superior.

Galba may still have held on to power, even though his parsimony had made his position insecure with the praetorian guard. But fatally he adopted the callow and inexperienced Lucius Calpurnius Piso Frugi Licinianus – a descendant of Sextus Pompey – as the man to succeed him. This act of imperial ingratitude spurred Otho, who wanted the adoption himself, to action. With promises of paying Galba's withheld donative, Otho won over the praetorians, who proclaimed him emperor on 15 January 69. They seized Galba in the Forum, murdered him and paraded his head on a pole around the city. The senate hastily ratified Otho's accession.

## Otho  Marcus Salvius Otho
[ 15/1/69–16/4/69 ]

Born at Ferentium in April AD 32, Otho's family traced its roots to an ancient Etruscan royal house. His father was a consul and a trusted administrator under Tiberius, Gaius and Claudius. Plutarch relates that young Otho was so extravagant he even teased Nero about the young emperor's meanness. Otho married the greatest beauty of her time, Poppaea Sabina, only to lose her to Nero after his 'banishment' to govern Lusitania.

Otho immediately adopted the name Caesar to emphasise his (bogus) status as the heir of the Julii. It was not, however, enough for the Rhine troops, to whom he was a part of the hated Vindex-Galba axis. The nine legions had declared Vitellius emperor on 3 January 69, and advance forces under Valens and Caecina were moving south at the month's end, while Vitellius brought the main army behind them. Otho could count on the legions of Pannonia, Dalmatia and Moesia. But the Illyrian army needed time to reach Italy, and until it did he only had his imperial retinue of about 9,000. Any other support Otho could hope for was too distant to count – Gaius Licinius Mucianus in Syria and Vespasian in rebellious Judaea. Vitellius's combined forces numbered some 70,000.

On 14 March, Otho moved north to hold the line along the Po valley and keep open communications with the Illyrian troops. He was barely in time. Caecina had crossed the Alps and by the second week of March sat beside the Po near Cremona, soon to be joined by Valens, who had swelled his force by some 40,000. The two commanders were eager to win a victory before Vitellius could arrive with the main force, and in this they succeeded. Concerned by the bridge the Vitellians were constructing across the Po, Otho ordered the larger part of his main force to advance from Bedriacum to interrupt its completion. As his men became strung out along the Via Postumia, Caecina and Valens attacked near Cremona on 14 April. The battle of Bedriacum resulted in the defeat of Otho's small army. Otho, who was at Brixellum with a force of infantry and cavalry to impede any Vitellian units that managed to cross the Po, realised that his strategy had proven too risky. To avoid a protracted and bloody conflict, two weeks short of his thiry-seventh birthday, on 16 April 69, Otho fell on his sword at dawn, ending a three-month rule.

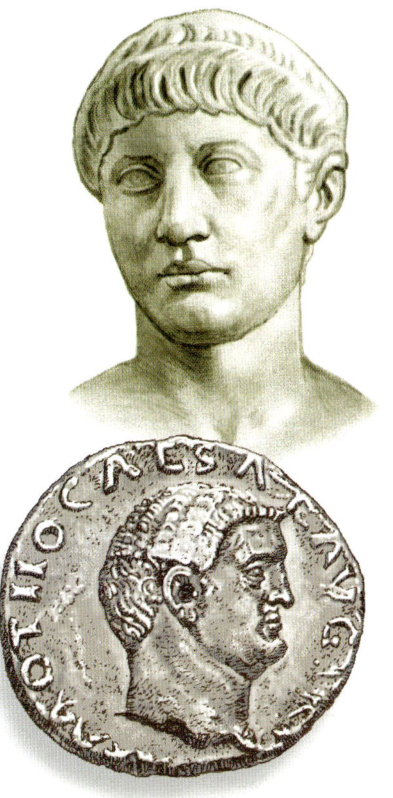

Bust and coin of Otho: an early friend and confidant of Nero, the emperor's theft of his wife Poppaea Sabina made Otho a willing conspirator in Nero's downfall.

## Vitellius  Aulus Vitellius
[ declared 3/1/69; princeps 19/4/69–20/12/69 ]

Vitellius, born in September AD 15, was the son of Lucius Vitellius, the confidant who persuaded Claudius to marry Agrippina. The younger Vitellius seems to have been equally at ease in aristocratic circles, successively winning the attention of the emperors Gaius, Claudius and Nero through flattery and political skill. When Galba appointed him governor of Germania Inferior late in 68, no one was probably more

Bust of Marcus Antonius Primus, a native of Toulouse. He rallied the Flavian troops for an advance attack on Vitellian Italy.

surprised than Vitellius, for he had almost no military skills. Perhaps wily Galba thought there would be little to fear in the way of treachery from a man whose reputation for flummery and gambling was notorious. If so, he was wrong. In the event, after his proclamation, Vitellius wisely relied on the superior skills of his generals Valens and Caecina, while following behind with the reserves.

Unhindered, Vitellius now proceeded to Rome at the head of his troops, Roman and mercenary, plundering Gaul and Italy in a drunken orgy, to arrive in late June. He dispersed Otho's legions to their respective provinces and disbanded the existing praetorian guard, replacing them with cohorts of his own German troops. However, he made no move against the three Illyrian legions, now sitting on Italy's northeastern border. There followed the familiar round of revenge killings with which Vitellius hoped to secure his position. He was too lazy to be brutal himself, but allowed Caecina and Valens to do the wet work. He assumed his powers gradually, participated in senate meetings, and put on games for the Roman mob. But no public display of either strength or modesty could mask the fact that he lacked talent. His highest achievements lay in gluttony, in which he was said to be unmatched;

**Progress and key events of the civil war, 68–70**

Vitellius claimed he was Nero's chosen successor. Caligula admired his skill as a charioteer; Claudius, his skill at dice; Nero his sycophancy. In turn, Vitellius adopted Nero's greed, Caligula's cruelty and none of Claudius's common sense.

and his days were numbered. By mid-July news arrived that the legions across the Adriatic had raised the popular Vespasian, governor of Judaea, to the purple.

At some point in his career, almost every soldier in the Roman army had served under Flavius Vespasian, or knew someone who had. It was little surprise, therefore, that when the news of Otho's death reached Illyria, the legions stationed there declared themselves Flavians to a man; the Egyptian and Syrian legions soon followed suit. Marcus Antonius Primus, in charge of Galba's recently raised Legion VII Galbiana (recruiting in Pannonia), took overall command of the Illyrian legions under the Flavian banner and marched quickly to seize the Julian Alpine passes before the Vitellians could reach them. Although his forces were barely half of those available to Vitellius, Antonius struck first, through the Po line as soon as the two arriving Pannonian legions met him at Padua. Near Verona they were joined by the three legions from Moesia. This massing of the enemy forced the Vitellians to retreat towards Cremona and a race developed between the two sides to reach the city. In the ensuing battle the Flavians were triumphant and Cremona was brutally sacked by the victors. It is thought that as many as 50,000 souls were slain in the four-day orgy of violence.

Vitellius had lost the north, but still held onto the peninsula with the praetorians, a newly raised legion and the urban cohort. Nevertheless, at the Flavian approach, many of his troops deserted and he was forced back on Rome. Since Antonius did not expect further reinforcements from his nearest ally, Mucianus, who was held up repelling a Dacian invasion of Moesia, he pressed on to the very walls of the city with his five legions.

Oddly, Vitellius had never replaced the urban prefect appointed by Otho, who was none less than Vespasian's older brother, Flavius Sabinus. Now, the desperate emperor negotiated terms with Sabinus, and on 18 October 69 agreed to abdicate. But the besieged troops, furious at their leader's desertion, attacked Sabinus, who retreated to the Capitol with units of the urban cohort and Vespasian's youngest son, the eighteen-year-old Domitian. A fierce battle broke out, during which the Temple of Jupiter Optimus Maximus was destroyed. Domitian managed to escape, but Sabinus was cut down, and the Vitellians once more held Rome – for the day only. On the following morning of 20 December, the Flavian army assaulted Rome and fought its way into the city. Vitellius disguised himself in dirty clothing and hid in the imperial doorkeeper's quarters, leaning a couch and a mattress against the door for protection. Dragged from his hiding place by the Flavians, he was hauled off to the Forum, where he was tortured, executed and his body tossed unceremoniously into the Tiber.

On 22 December, the anxious senate recognised Vespasian, and voted him all the principate's powers and prerogatives. It was hoped that this would stop the Flavian army from sacking Rome, but neither Antonius nor Domitian – hailed as a Caesar to Vespasian's Augustus – could halt the disorder. The victorious soldiers continued the rampage until Mucianus arrived in January 70 and took the office of regent in Vespasian's name. Rome now awaited its new Augustus, who finally arrived in October. The civil wars were at an end and a new dynasty ruled the Roman empire.

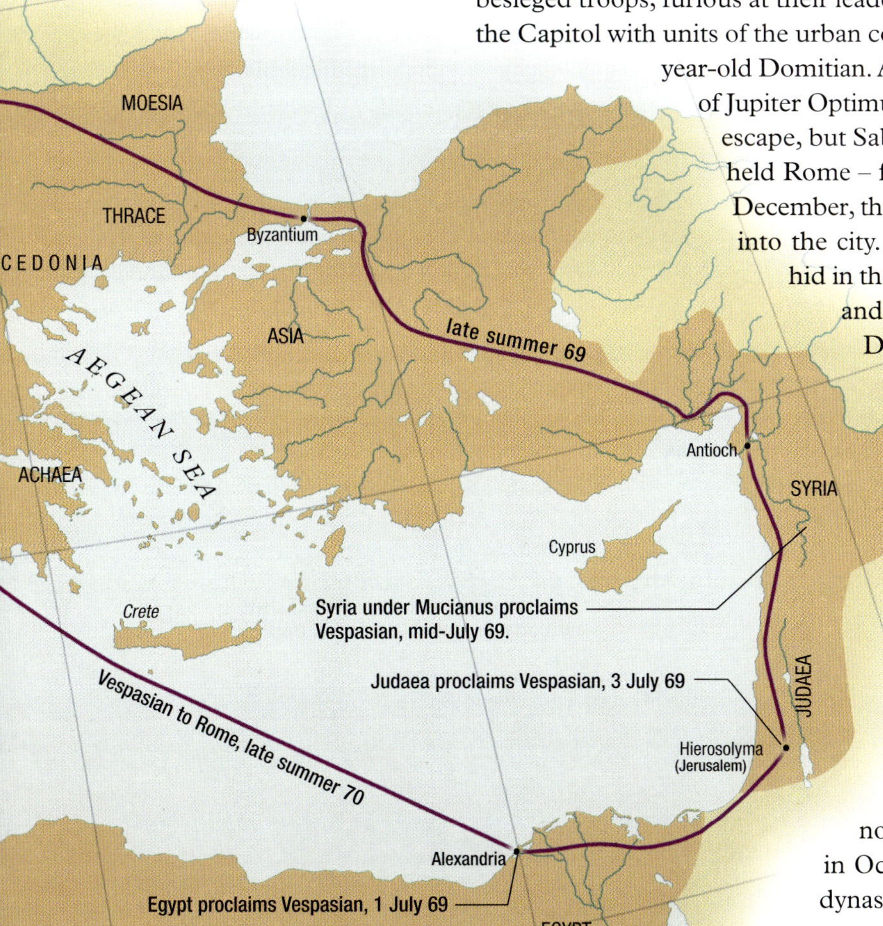

# THREE
## The Flavian Dynasty
[AD 70–96]

### Vespasian  Titus Flavius Vespasianus
[ declared 1/7/69; princeps 22/12/69–23/6/79 ]

The Flavians were not Roman aristocracy. Vespasian's father, Titus Flavius Petro, a mule breeder from Reate (Rieti), is first recorded as a centurion in Pompey's doomed army facing Caesar's at Pharsalus in 48 BC. On his discharge he went to Asia as a tax gatherer – a rare one according to statues raised to him there inscribed 'To an Honest Tax-gatherer'. Titus became a money-lender and then retired appropriately to Raetia (a banker in what is modern Switzerland), where he died, leaving his wife and two sons, Sabinus and Vespasian.

Vespasian came into the world on 17 November AD 9 in Sabine Falcrina, near Reate, a hamlet far detached from Rome. He had a good education and his mother Vespasia Polla's brother, a quaestor, started him on the *cursus honorum*. He was a military tribune in Thrace, held a quaestorship in Creta-Cyrenaica and the offices of aedile and praetor, the latter in Germania where he helped Gaius Caligula in 39. Narcissus became Vepasian's patron at Claudius's court, to whom he owed his Rhine command and a conquering army in Britain in 44, where his brilliant record made him a popular figure. The historian Suetonius said of him: 'He went to Britannia, where he fought 30 battles, subjugated two tribes and took more than 20 *oppida* [Celtic hill forts], Vectis Insula [Isle of Wight] besides.' With one quarter of the invasion force, his Legion II Augusta conquered three-quarters of the Romans' target territory. Vespasian was awarded triumphal insignia, as well as a consulship for the last two months of AD 51.

However, the accession of Nero – and specifically his mother Agrippina – cast Vespasian into the wilderness for some fifteen years. Vespasian served on the empire's periphery and in the process, he acquired a wife, Flavia Domitilla, who bore him two sons, Titus and Domitian, and a daughter, Domitilla. When Flavia died before his accession Vespasian returned to his former mistress, Caenis. Born a palace slave, Caenis had risen to become the Augusta Antonia's secretary and was later given her freedom, but the law that forbade senators to marry freedwomen meant she could never become his wife. Caenis, an intelligent, clear-headed person, exerted a beneficial influence over Vespasian. In 66 came a reversal of fortunes when Nero included Vespasian on his tour of Greece. Vespasian was, therefore, the man on hand when a revolt broke out in Judaea, and Nero sent him to deal with the problem.

Starting spring of 67, with 60,000 legionaries, auxiliaries and allies under his command, in the company of his eldest son Titus, Vespasian subdued Galilee by October and surrounded Jerusalem. It was fighting in Judaea, he was to recall, that he came close to death for the second time, when he was narrowly rescued after being cornered by Jewish resistance fighters; the first time had been in Athens, when he fell asleep during one of Nero's interminable musical recitals. And it was from Judaea that Vespasian surveyed the fast-moving situation in Italy. The events in Rome of December 70 meant that he could no longer tarry waiting for the fall of Jerusalem, so he left the task in his son's hands. Vespasian went to Egypt to deny Vitellius any grain while Marcus Antonius Primus and Mucianus battled their way into Italy. By the time he reached Rome news of Jerusalem's fall had arrived, so the senate was able to decree their new Augustus a suitable triumph to greet him. At the age of sixty-one,

Bust of Vespasian as the down-to-earth country type he really was.

Vespasian was now at the helm of an empire shattered by a year of anarchy. There had been an enormous loss of public confidence in the principate's power, which he needed to heal. In this he enjoyed a natural advantage: a rustic, common-sense upbringing combined with a sterling military career.

Vespasian had learned the value of providing housing, sanitation and an efficient tax-collecting system during his overseas service and he brought to Rome the native shrewdness of an Italian farmer, rather than the intellectual brilliance of the city-dweller. He notoriously loathed any form of affectation – all too prevalent among the new nobility arising from Nero's depradations. When a young man, reeking of perfume, approached him to give thanks for a promotion in rank, Vespasian turned away in disgust and cancelled the order, adding: 'I should not have minded so much if it had been garlic.'

Gallic nationalism sparked by Vindex was still prevalent and an auxiliary commander, Julius Civilis, led a revolt. Although swiftly suppressed, it underlined the need for military reform. It was clear that the revolt of Civilis had succeeded due to the widespread support he found among the troops quartered in Gaul and along the Rhine. Although called 'Roman', most were natives of their region and commanded by native officers. Vespasian issued orders that in future auxiliaries were to serve away from their own regions to avoid nationalistic sympathies colouring their loyalty to the state, nor were they allowed any longer to serve under native officers. Vespasian was well aware that an idle army is a dangerous beast, so in 73 he gave the soldiers a new task under Gnaeus Cornelius Clemens, legate of Germania Superior, to straighten out the frontier by pacifying and fortifying the triangular area known as the Agri Decumates – the modern Black Forest – lying between the upper Rhine and Danube.

Vespasian also recognised another lesson in the revolts of Vindex and Civilis. Many provinces, especially those of Gaul, had attained such a level of Romanised development that they wanted to play a greater part in the cultural and political life of the empire. Claudius had opened up the senatorial order to Gallic nobles, but little else had been done in this direction. Denied participation, Vespasian feared that provincial energies would be diverted towards nationalism and separatism. In 73 he

Vespasian (*above*) had little truck with religion or the trappings of imperial protocol but he was politically astute in allowing the senate to honour his wife Domitilla with divinity; she died before his accession.

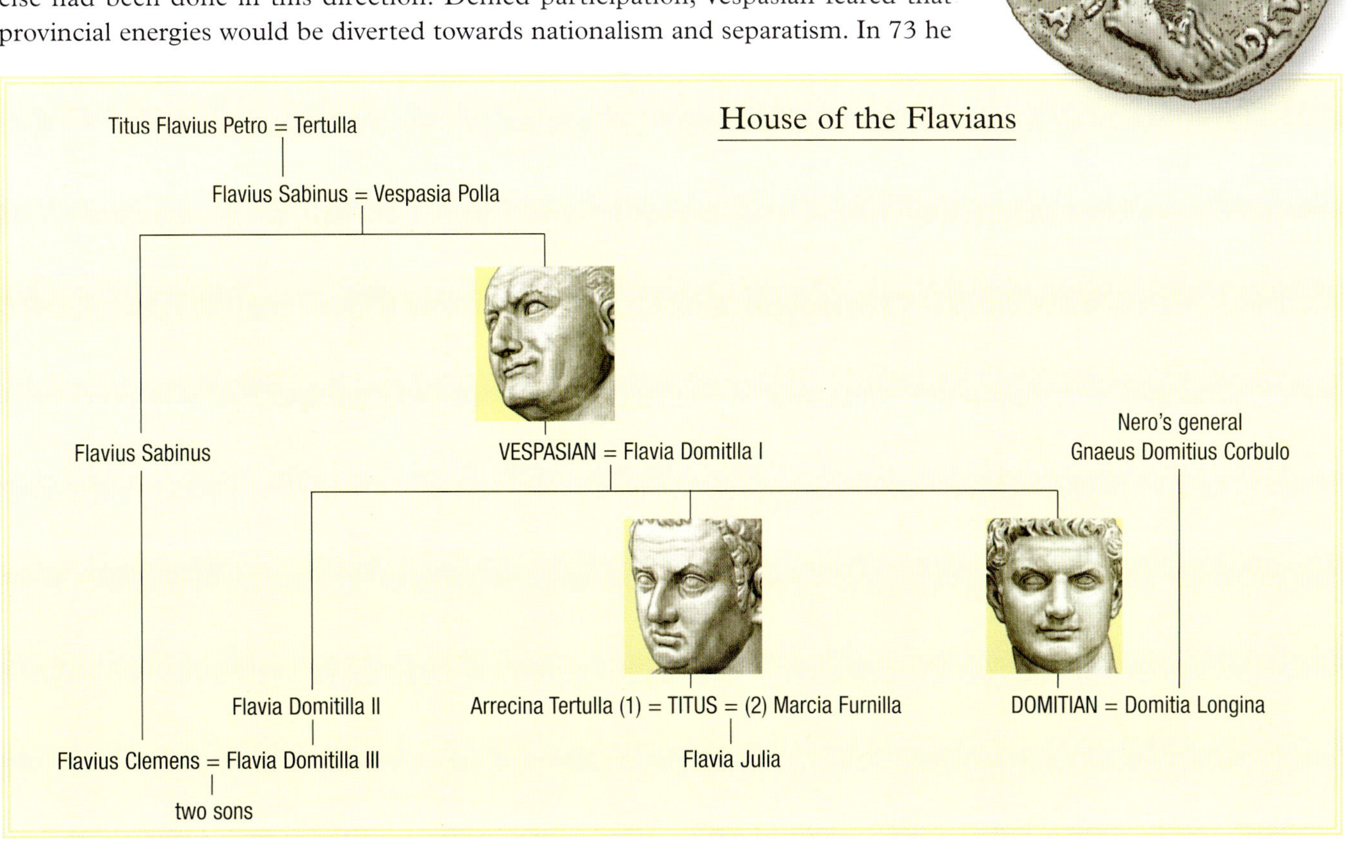

assumed the office of censor and filled gaps in the senate with a new aristocracy drawn from the Italian *municipia*. He then conferred Latin rights on Baetica and granted municipal charters to provincial towns. Between 74–84 no fewer than 350 Spanish towns received their charter. He also founded numerous *coloniae* (colonies of usually veteran soldiers) elsewhere in the empire. Once made a Latin *municipium*, its local elite automatically acquired Roman citizenship and became eligible for high positions within the principate. In this, Vespasian was quite open that, like Augustus, he intended to have a senate amenable to his actions – in gratitude, they should obey rather than just be co-operative. However, even those naturally opposed to him wanted no return to the spendthrift years of Caligula or Nero; Vespasian was famous for his parsimony. He made it the business of his reign to restore the moral foundation of the state and its economic stability before turning to artistic embellishment.

Among Vespasian's many achievements, a few stand out. In Rome, he expanded the city's sacred boundary to help relieve overcrowding and restored the Capitol and the Temple of Jupiter Optimus Maximus destroyed in 69. Work began on three massive new monuments. On the Caelian Hill he raised a temple in honour of the deified Claudius, a project cannily designed to identify Vespasian as the legitimate heir to the Julio-Claudians, while distancing himself from Nero, who had built the platform as a raised palace garden. To celebrate the new tranquility, the Templum Pacis (Temple of Peace) appeared beside the Forum Romanum. On the Palatine, Vespasian pulled down Nero's palace and began construction of the extensive Domus Flavia that his younger son Domitian would complete. But above all, he started on a massive amphitheatre on the site of the lake of Nero's Domus Aurea, known as the Amphitheatrum Flavium. It's better known today as the Colosseum.

Restoring the economy was a monumental task, but by the end of his ten-year reign it was accomplished by often unpopular means. Cities freed from paying tax in the past – Rhodes, Byzantium and Samos – now had to pay again. Achaea, freed by Nero, was returned to provincial status and had to pay, as did Trachian (coastal) Cilicia and Comagene. No part of daily life escaped Vespasian's taxes, including the most basic production of human urine, which was collected for use by fullers in cleaning woollens. Titus – more fastidious than his gruff father – was said to have complained that taxing the contents of the public latrines was unsavoury. Vespasian held out a coin taxed on the first day and asked him to sniff it. When Titus said he smelled only its metallic odour, his father laughed and exclaimed that was odd, because it had come directly from a urinal.

Unlike the majority of his predecessors, Vespasian died unmolested in his bed on 23 June 79, after contracting a brief illness; perhaps fortunate that his two ambitious sons Titus and Domitian were prepared to let nature take its course. At the age of 78, his life finished on an ironic note when Vespasian, who never mustered much faith in Roman religion or superstition, uttered, 'Woe is me, I think I am turning into a god.'

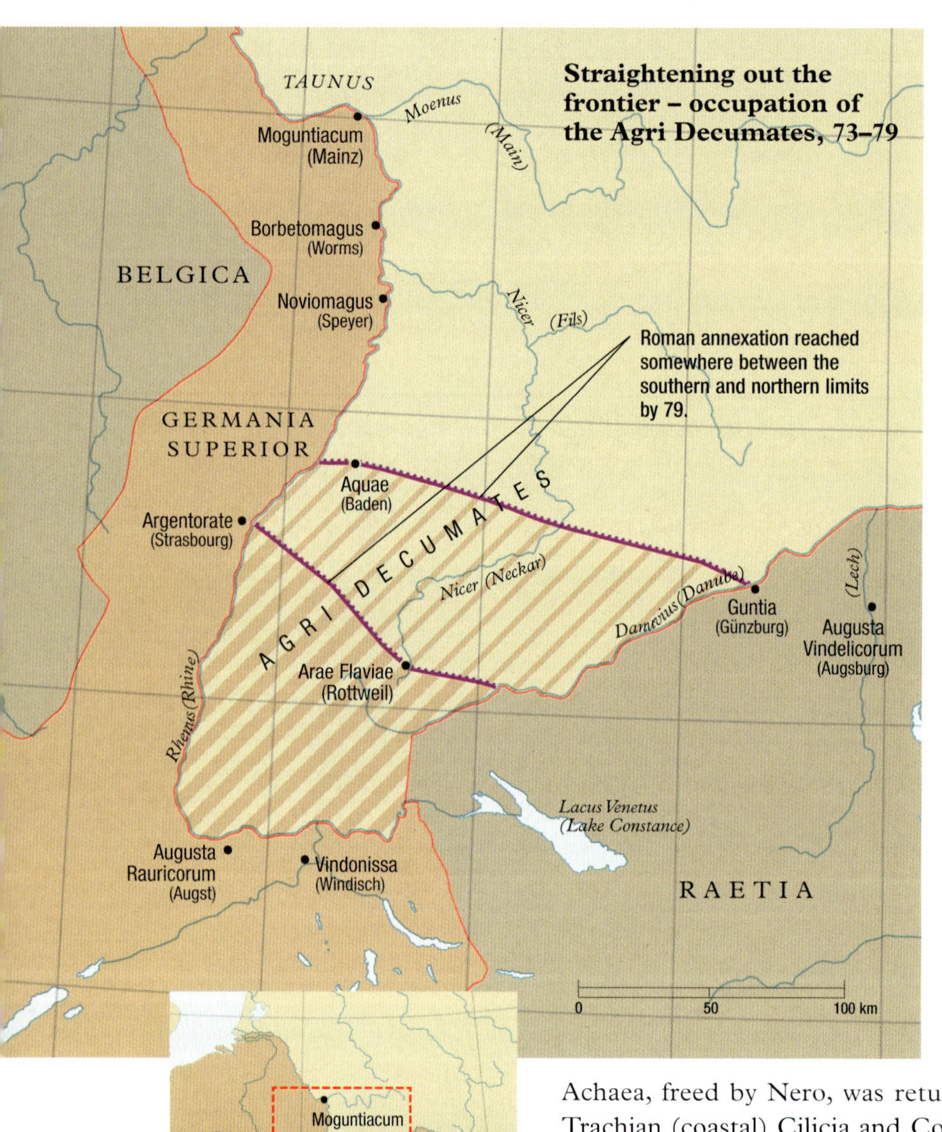

## Titus  Titus Flavius Vespasianus
[ 23/6/79–13/9/81 ]

Such was the care with which Vespasian had prepared for the succession, there was no question about the immediate elevation of Titus, who was in his fortieth year. There was, however, a great deal of unease. Titus had a reputation for extravagance and ruthlessness, and the senate – never entirely well disposed towards the humbly-born Flavians – feared he might be another Nero. It turned out differently.

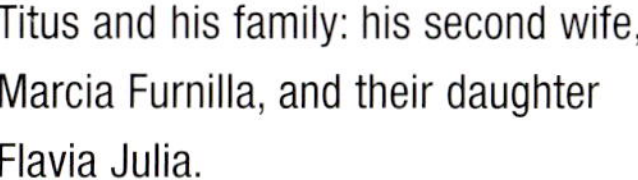
Titus and his family: his second wife, Marcia Furnilla, and their daughter Flavia Julia.

Titus was born on 30 December AD 39 in a small bedroom in a Rome slum tenement block. But Vespasian's political ascent under Claudius meant that young Titus became a close companion to the emperor's son Britannicus, and the two studied together in the palace. Suetonius tells a story of how Narcissus called in a physiognomist to examine Britannicus's features and predict his future. The seer was emphatic that Britannicus would never become princeps, but that Titus would.

Nero agreed to his appointment in 66 as *legatus legionis* of XV Apollinaris to help Vespasian deal with the revolt in Judaea, even though he had not yet been a praetor, the post normally held by a senator before becoming a legionary commander. Joseph ben Mattathias (c.37–100), known to history as Josephus, wrote a glowing account of Titus's contribution in the Jewish Wars, but as a close confidant of Vespasian, Josephus had a strong Flavian bias. With four legions under his command, Titus began the assault on Jerusalem in the spring of 70. The investment of the formidable fortifications was a lengthy and bitter business in which typical Roman discipline and sheer doggedness won the day. By August, the outer Temple court had been breached and, in the ensuing attack, the Temple burned to the ground and all the captives were slaughtered. His troops hailed Titus *imperator* and he earned his reputation as a cruel butcher in subduing those he'd conquered and the ruthless treatment of the eastern provinces his army marched through while returning to Rome. He celebrated a lavish double-triumph with Vespasian (who would not waste the money on two separate events) for the fall of Jerusalem.

Titus demonstrated his administrative skills as his father's partner, politely attending senate meetings and asking advice of his elders. On the other hand Suetonius claims that he was an adept forger who created evidence to win convictions. Titus was doing the regime's necessary dirty work, while leaving Vespasian on high moral ground. Set against this impression, Suetonius says that Titus was naturally kind-hearted and he began dispersing fears about his nature the moment he became princeps. The better qualities noted by Suetonius came to the fore in an unbroken succession of lavish public spectacles, the giving of gifts and gestures of open-handedness to any who petitioned him. He poured vast amounts of capital into extensive building schemes in Rome, including Rome's largest yet and most luxurious baths. He also started construction of his triumphal arch astride the Via Sacra where it tops the hill before descending into the Forum, widely admired today as the most perfect of all Roman monumental arches. Titus dedicated the unfinished Colosseum with games that lasted for a staggering hundred days.

Titus's joyous reign was marred by two calamities. In 79, Vesuvius sensationally erupted, smothering the towns of Pompeii and Herculaneum on the wealthy Roman holiday coast of the Bay of Naples. Even as Titus was visiting the disaster zone a huge fire broke out in Rome and damaged the new Capitol, Agrippa's Pantheon and Baths, and a sizeable residential area. Titus responded by pouring money and resources into the stricken regions, even selling some of his own furniture to raise relief funds.

His death at Reate after reigning for only two years, two months and twenty days followed a short illness. Malaria was the probable cause, but because there was little love between Titus and his younger brother, suspicion also fell on Domitian. Childless, Titus was heard to say that he appointed Domitian as his successor, but he never conferred the *imperium proconsulare* or *tribunicia potestas* on his brother. Fortunately for the empire, no one wanted a return to civil war, and when the praetorians proclaimed Domitian emperor, the senate didn't demur. Gaius Caligula began a bright reign and turned sour when the funds ran out; would Titus have been similar had he lived longer? But bright, handsome Titus died before his star could fade, so that after his unexpectedly short reign he came to be regarded as Rome's most beloved emperor.

## Domitian  Titus Flavius Domitianus
[ 13/9/81–18/9/96 ]

By contrast, at his death Domitian's memory was damned. Unlike Titus, thirty-year-old Domitian had no administrative experience to speak of. Neither his father nor his brother had seen fit to promote him to any offices, apart from some minor consulships, one as Vespasian's colleague. He had been styled *princeps iuventutis* and Caesar, but these were empty titles without sensible duties to go with them. However, Domitian's reign turned out to be a successful one by any standards. And yet the ancient histories vilified him as one of the cruellest and most despotic of tyrants.

Suetonius claimed that one of his favourite pastimes was catching flies and then stabbing them with a sharp stylus, and that he regularly scorched prisoners' testicles to make them reveal information. While there undoubtedly was a streak of Flavian cruelty in Domitian, the calumnies attributed to him are largely exaggerations of later writers who viewed the Flavians as jumped-up rustics. A new dynasty succeeded Domitian and, anxious to portray itself in a good light, highlighted any wickedness of the previous. However, he was touchy about any perceived affront to his dignity and later his desire for deification during his lifetime was clearly apparent – a refusal to worship him was taken as a sign of atheism, a sin that ended the careers and even lives of many.

Born in Rome on 24 October 51, ten years after Titus, Domitian was not educated in the palace, yet he received sound training in Rome in the same way as any member of his class. He gave public recitals of his works, conversed elegantly and was remembered for sound arguments in debate. With his mother dead in his infant years, a father constantly away in the provinces and a brother avoiding the hindrance of a younger sibling, Domitian's adolescence was marked by isolation. This bred within him a preference for seclusion similar to Tiberius; a need for self-reliance combined with tactlessness and an easily injured dignity characterised his autocratic reign. Tellingly, the writings of Tiberius were his favourite reading.

Domitian was in Rome with his elderly uncle Flavius Sabinus during the upheavals of 68–70, and narrowly escaped with his life. In late 70 he married Domitia Longina, daughter of the legendary general, Gnaeus Domitius Corbulo, whose name was synonymous with the military achievement Domitian craved. Better still, the marriage brought with it the general's substantial base of clients, which improved Domitian's status. However, the marriage was troubled. An only child died young, and he exiled Domitia in 83. He later recalled her to the palace, where she lived with him in some

Coin of Domitian: his brother Titus was a hard act to follow and later historians vilified Domitian by picking on his negative traits to the exclusion of his positive achievements.

tumult until his death.

Domitian made it clear immediately that he wanted servants and not partners in the government. He held consulships for the first eight years and a total of seventeen times in all, and only gave it up because he came to scorn such a lowly senatorial rank. After first attending senate meetings he soon stopped, ignoring the body altogether and taking decisions in the style of an old dictator. Instead, he relied more on the aid of *equites* and gave the order increased importance, and by placing knights in positions previously reserved for senators, he further earned the aristocracy's odium.

Domitian's ambitious and spectacular building programme was unmatched by any other emperor since Augustus. After the great fire of 64, the civil wars of 68–69, and the devastating fire of 80, Rome was badly in need of repair. He began to erect, repair or complete some fifty structures, including the restored Temple of Jupiter Optimus Maximus on the Capitol. He finished the Colosseum. On the Campus Martius he erected an odeum, a new circus (still visible today as the Piazza Navona) and a stadium for his *ludi capitolini* (Capitoline Games). Domitian closely identified himself with the ancient Roman gods Minerva and Jupiter, publicly linking the latter divinity to his regime through the *ludi capitolini* founded in 86. These were held every four years in the early summer, and consisted of chariot races, athletics, gymnastics, music, oratory and poetry. Contestants came from many nations, and no expense was spared. On the Forum face of the Capitol he built a temple to his deified father and brother, and completed the Arch of Titus that celebrated the capture of Jerusalem. He raised a new shopping centre in the Saepta, and built granaries and water works. His most spectacular edifice was the vast palace on the Palatine, larger by far, in substance if not extent, than the Domus Aurea. Adjacent to Vespasian's Domus Flavia, the Augustana was a continuation that fully covered Nero's extension on the Palatine as well as a considerable part of the palace of Tiberius, and stretched from the ramparts above the Forum to the Circus Maximus, towering like a cliff above it.

The huge building programme and the expense of several costly wars had a predictable economic effect. Free-giving Titus had not left the *fiscus* in a particularly healthy state. However, Domitian left a healthy *fiscus* through a variety of means that did much to blacken his memory. The rigorous collection of taxes soon sparked a short-lived rebellion in Africa and rumblings elsewhere. Inevitably, confiscation and murder returned to the menu of money-raising methods, along with the reappearance of the hated *delatores*.

While the military abilities of Vespasian and Titus were genuine, those of Domitian were not. And yet during his reign there were more wars and military campaigns against the empire's enemies than at any time since the late Republican period. This was clearly due to necessity – German and Dacian tribes were putting pressure on the frontiers. He claimed a triumph in 83 for subduing the Chatti, a warlike German tribe of the Taunus mountains that threatened Germania Superior in the region of Moguntiacum (Mainz). Historians disagree on the outcome, many preferring the view of Tacitus that the campaign was illusory, even a joke. Grumpy Tacitus, however, had a declared interest – Domitian's need for British troops in Pannonia and Moesia curtailed the operations of the historian's admired father-in-law, the British governor Gnaeus Julius Agricola. During his tenure (76–84) Agricola cherished the ambition of conquering all of the British Isles, including Hibernia (Ireland). Agricola had subjugated Wales (to a degree) and pressed far north in Scotland to rout the last Celtic army in Britain at Mons Graupius (probably the mountain of Bennachie, near Inverurie) when Domitian wanted the reinforcements and recalled Agricola.

Historians who disagree with Tacitus's judgement on Domitian's campaign, which ruthlessly drove the Chatti out of the Main valley and away from the Rhine to

Bust of Domitian, bust and coin of his wife Domitia Longina, daughter of the famous general Corbulo; she plotted her husband's assassination.

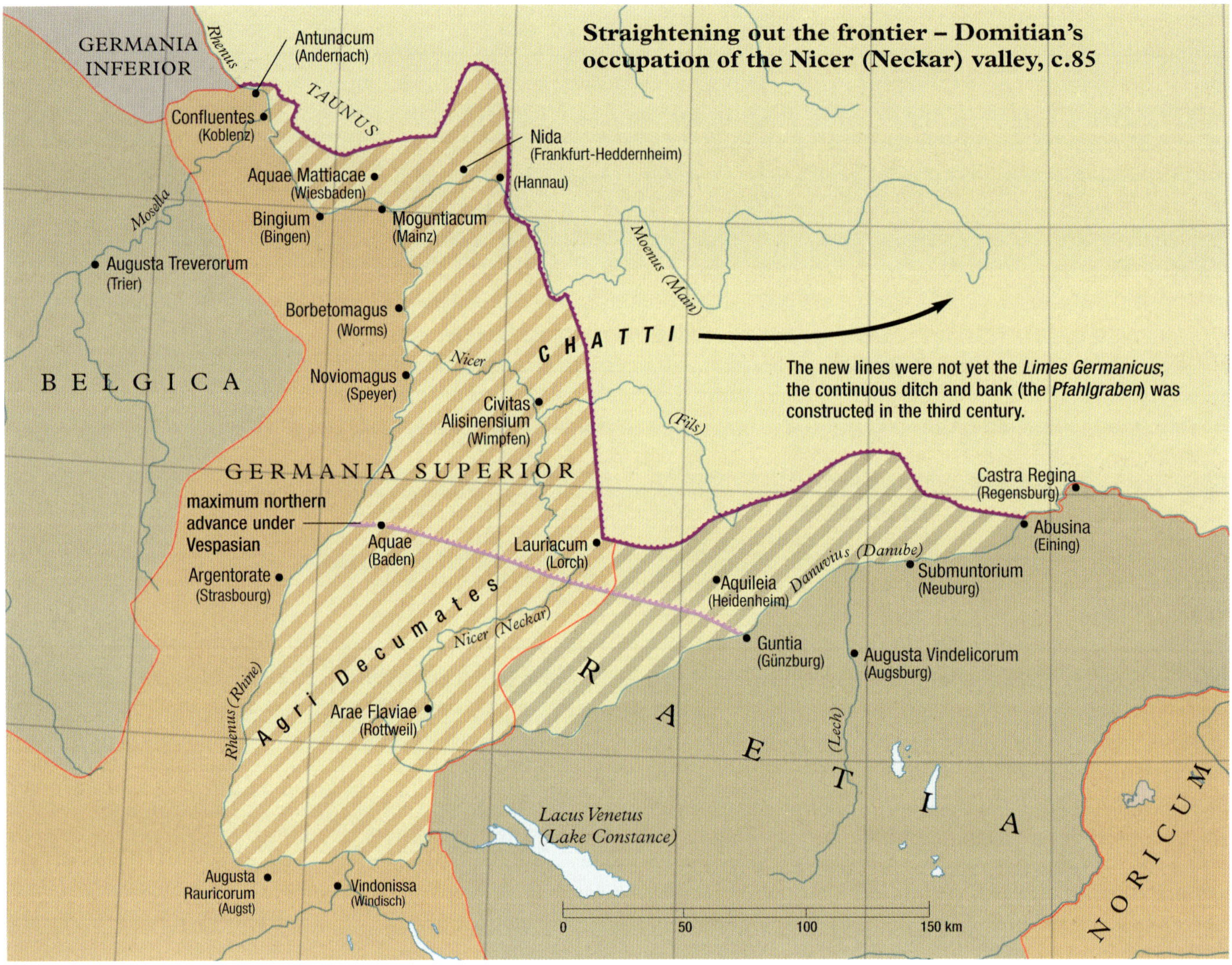

disappear in the wild German forests, point to the archaeological evidence of the fortifications erected along a 193-kilometre line stretching from north of the Taunus around the western Main valley. This then incorporated the Neckar valley and joined Vespasian's northernmost line of the Agri Decumates. Domitian was also responsible for strengthening the north bank of the upper Danube, from his new German line, east to Abusina (Eining). The peace these new defences brought to the enlarged Germania Superior was last until the third century.

Moesia suffered a massive invasion by Dacian tribes living north of the lower Danube in 85 – the First Dacian War – but were driven back, only to return the following year when Domitian's praetorian prefect Cornelius Fuscus was lost with all the men of Legion V Alaudae. The Romans returned in 88 – The Second Dacian War – which was far from settled when, in the same year, the legate of the two legions stationed at Moguntiacum, Lucius Antonius Saturninus, raised his standard. The reason is unclear, but perhaps he coveted the purple for himself and felt the time was ripe. In any event, Domitian's courting of his troops paid off. By the time he arrived in January 89, the other six Rhine legions had declared their loyalty and Saturninus had died in a skirmish. However, the insurrection shook Domitian so badly it became the root of the terror that he unleashed soon after.

Domitian's last years were a period of tyranny and cruelty. The *delatores*, already at work filling the *fiscus*, were kept busy uncovering imagined plots. Any charge, no matter how slight – failing to toast the emperor's health, for instance – resulted in confiscation of the man's estate and secured his execution. The Roman mob, not

Dacian king Decebalus; from Trajan's Column. His aggressive stance led to two wars against Domitian.

much affected, was treated to circuses and lavish shows in the arenas, but the senatorial order suffered heavily. Sensible men retired from any form of public life and hid away on their country estates. Pliny the Younger, Juvenal, Suetonius and Tacitus all record the prevailing atmosphere of terror. Christian writers later referred to Domitian as the 'second great persecutor' (the first being Nero). Given his devotion to Roman pagan religion, it's easy to see how such stories evolved, but hard evidence of his antipathy – other than considering Christians atheists from the Roman point of view – is lacking. Christians may have been banished or executed during the Terror, but no organised persecution is evident. Whereas there is clear evidence that the Jews were made to feel uneasy under Domitian, who scrupulously collected the Jewish tax and harassed Jewish tax dodgers during much of his reign.

When Domitian executed his harmless cousin Flavius Clemens in 95 on a charge of atheism (probably a failure to salute the emperor speedily), and then exiled Clemens' wife Domitilla, his own niece no less, no one felt safe from his paranoia. A palace plot to assassinate Domitian was formulated between his wife Domitia, his chamberlain and the praetorian prefect. The plan for his murder was simple enough. Domitian was persuaded to give an interview on 18 September 96 to exiled Domitilla's disgruntled and jobless steward, who came before his emperor with an injured arm. Concealed in the bandages was a knife with which he fatally stabbed Domitian, who was just a month short of his forty-fifth birthday.

Domitian had no son to follow him, and he had not entirely ignored the question of who should succeed him, having named the sons of his cousin Clemens. However, after having their father executed, they were dropped as being unsuitable, and if he had other arrangements in mind, the assassin put an end to them. The conspirators, however, were prepared. They had secured a candidate for the principate, the old and respected senator Marcus Cocceius Nerva.

This coin shows a defeated German warrior kneeling before triumphant Domitian.

# FOUR
## The Nervo-Trajanic Dynasty

[AD 96–138]

### Nerva  Marcus Cocceius Nerva
[ 18/9/96–27/1/98 ]

Bust and coin of Marcus Cocceius Nerva: his adoption of Trajan to be his successor was a significant first for imperial Rome.

When Nerva – on the early stages of the *cursus honorum* – uncovered the Piso conspiracy against Nero in 65, the grateful emperor rewarded his praetor-designate with triumphal insignia and placed his statue prominently in the palace. On his father's side there had been five consuls starting with his great-grandfather in 36 BC; his grandfather, a distinguished jurist, accompanied Tiberius on his retirement to Capri in AD 26. On his mother's side an aunt was Tiberius's great-granddaughter. Born on 8 November 30, his name does not appear on any legionary rolls suggesting that he didn't pursue the traditional aristocratic military path; neither was he a public speaker nor a legal advocate.

Nerva shared a consulship with Vespasian in 71 and with Domitian in 90 – Nerva, clearly an adept at foiling conspiracies, had alerted the emperor to the revolt of Antonius Saturninus in 89, a factor which may have preserved him against the Terror. At sixty-six Nerva was really too old for the job and his support of the Flavians, particularly Domitian, should have disqualified him in senatorial eyes; his distant relationship to the Julio-Claudians on his mother's side should have doubly damned him with the aristocracy. On the other hand, he was a prudent and capable senator who demonstrated his tact by quickly taking an oath as princeps not to execute any senator.

It was politically expedient for Nerva to distance himself from Domitian and channel popular resentment against the Flavians and away from his principate. An officially encouraged damnation of Domitian began, and in a shrewd move Nerva opened the Domus Augustana to the public, renamed Domus Populi. He moved to a modest house in the Horti Sallustiani, the garden district Vespasian had preferred. Exiles were allowed back, and confiscates had their estates returned. Nerva won over the senate without giving it any real power, retaining that for the principate, but he re-established the tradition of senatorial co-operation with the emperor, which would endure throughout most of the next century.

In a reign of only sixteen months, Nerva undertook little public building. He appropriated Domitian's uncompleted forum that linked that of Augustus to the Templum Pax and dedicated it in 98, which is why it's known today as the Forum of Nerva. His greatest monument, however, was not a building but the institution of the *alimenta*. Under this scheme small farmers pledged their land as security and were allowed to borrow up to a 12th of its value from the *fiscus*. The five per cent interest on the loan was repaid not to the *fiscus* but to their *municipium*, which used the money to support the children of poor parents. The *alimenta* was a great success, since it not only alleviated Italian poverty to some extent, but also caused a regeneration of Italian farming. Wealthy nobles followed the example and founded similar schemes of their own, so that soon several thousand children were being provided for in Italy, and more in the provinces as the concept spread. The *alimenta* was to remain in place until the time of Diocletian.

These were popular measures, but not everyone was content. Dissatisfied that Nerva had refused Domitian's deification, the praetorian guard mutinied in October 97 under their prefect Casperius Aelianus – Domitian's appointee. They took Nerva hostage and demanded he hand over Domitian's murderers. With little option he did so and was then forced before the Roman mob to give a humiliating speech of thanks

to the mutineers for their 'public-spirited' action. This event, coupled with growing unrest among the provincial troops, convinced Nerva that he required a successor who could not only keep order among the soldiers, but would also appeal to them. For this reason he passed over his male relatives and chose Marcus Ulpius Traianus (Trajan), announcing his appointment in late October 97. Trajan was immediately acclaimed as Caesar *imperator*, granted the *tribunicia potestas* and named as Nerva's consular colleague for the following year.

The adoption of Trajan by Nerva is one of the more significant moments in Roman history, not because he was adopting outside his immediate family – the Julio-Claudians had done that– and not because his successor was popular with the army. That, after all, was essential. What is extraordinary is that Trajan was not even an Italian. Now a man from the provinces could aspire to the purple. Trajan was based on the Rhine at the time of his adoption and he was at Moguntiacum when Nerva suffered a stroke on 1 January 98. Three weeks later Nerva died at his villa in the Gardens of Sallust. From his headquarters Trajan insisted that Nerva's ashes be placed in the mausoleum of Augustus and asked the senate to vote on his deification.

## Trajan  Marcus Ulpius Nerva Traianus
[ nominated October 97; princeps 28/1/98–9/8/117 ]

'During a happy period of more than fourscore years, the public administration was conducted by the virtue and abilities of Nerva, Trajan, Hadrian and the two Antonines.' So said Gibbon in his massive work *The Decline and Fall of the Roman Empire* of the period he rightly considered to be ancient Rome's apogee. Of these five, Trajan – undoubtedly one of the greatest warrior-emperors of all time – was one of Roman history's most admirable figures, a man who by his actions deserved the renown that he enjoyed in his lifetime and in subsequent generations.

The Ulpii came from Italica, a Latin colony in Baetica (close to modern Seville), and Trajan was born there on 18 September 53, five years behind his sister, Ulpia Marciana. The Ulpii settled in the region late in the third century BC, but Trajan's father – also Marcus – was the first Ulpius to pursue a senatorial career. He had served under Corbulo and Vespasian in the Jewish War and received a propraetorship and then a consulship in 70. At the end of his term he returned to Baetica as its governor. He probably died before 100, having seen his son become emperor, and was deified in 113 as *divus traianus pater*.

The young Trajan, then, was supported by his father's sparkling career, and determined not to let him down. He married Pompeia Plotina, from Nemausus (Nîmes) in Gallia Narbonensis, a woman much younger than himself. He was a quaestor in 78 and praetor in 84. In 86, he was made guardian to young Publius Aelius Hadrianus (Hadrian), another native of Italica, whose father had recently died. As the legate of VII Gemina, Trajan took the legion to the Rhine in 89 to help crush the uprising of Antonius Saturninus. He next fought in the Dacian wars, and was rewarded with a consulship in 91. There followed the governorship of Moesia Inferior and then that of Germania Superior. And it was in his headquarters at Moguntiacum that the young Hadrian, now a tribune, brought Trajan the news that he had been adopted by Nerva and nominated co-emperor and heir-designate.

Technically, Trajan was already emperor before Nerva's death. Evidently, he felt no pressing need to go to Rome because after despatching a solemn oath to never execute a senator, he proceeded to Pannonia. Being away from Rome at such a time would have been the undoing of any previous princeps but at forty-four conscientious, sober

Spanish Trajan and his younger virtuous wife Pompeia Plotina.

The reverse of Trajan's coin honours his natural father on the right and his adoptive father Nerva.

Decebalus slits his own throat rather than fall into Roman hands; from the frieze on Trajan's Column, Rome.

Trajan had the charisma to take command of the empire simultaneously with finishing a distant military campaign and only reached Rome in the spring of 99. His modest entry on foot indicated a common touch from the first, instantly healing the rifts Domitian had created. Plotina was equally modest. On entering the palace she said, 'I enter here such a woman as I would hope to be when I depart.' Trajan spent two years winning over all the classes of Rome. Yet he was no less absolute master of the state than Domitian, but his good nature and respect for those who had until recently been his superiors won him great acclaim. He was unofficially styled *optimus princeps* (the best first man) by the people.

Trajan found military life more enjoyable than the comforts and trappings of the imperial palace – he had spent more than ten years as a tribune, and it was in his nature to want to push Rome's frontiers beyond those of the Flavians. And like Claudius, he might also have considered that a successful campaign of conquest would bolster his new reign. He had already signalled in 98–99 that the wily rogue Decebalus of Dacia would be the first target. Preparations for a great campaign began, with the transfer of western legions and the enrolment of two new legions: II Traiana and XXX Ulpia. This brought the empire's total strength to thirty legions.

The aggressive stance of Decebalus was the political pretext for an invasion of Dacia, but traders claimed that the land north of the Danube was rich in gold, silver and essential minerals, and a fat profit from conquest would be extremely useful at the start of the reign. In 101 the emperor took the field with an army estimated at about 100,000 men. The war required all the military technology, engineering and discipline for which the Roman army was renowned. The old road of Tiberius on the Roman bank of the Danube through the Porta Ferea (Iron Gates) was completely rebuilt by the brilliant civil engineer Apollodorus of Damascus. Apollodorus converted the old narrow path in the spectacular gorge into a breathtaking highway by cantilevering the road out from the sheer face of the rock so that the legionaries felt as though they were marching on water.

Despite a Roman victory at Tapae, where Domitian's general Tettius Julianus had defeated the Dacians in 89, the campaign was inconclusive by the time winter set in. The break in hostilities was not wasted: the troops trained and engineers built more portable war engines. In the early spring Trajan moved with great speed, crossing into Dacia at Drobeta and then driving through the Carpathian passes into the heart of Transylvania. In 102 Decebalus was forced to a humiliating peace, and Roman garrisons were stationed in Banat and Transylvania. Trajan then returned to Rome, celebrated a triumph, and added the title Dacicus to his titles. Decebalus, however, once left to his own devices, undertook to challenge Rome again. Having secretly rearmed, in 105 the Dacians overwhelmed the garrisons north of the Danube and began raiding across the river in Moesia. Trajan responded immediately by gathering an even larger army, which crossed the Danube again at Drobreta early in 106. This time all of Transylvania was annexed. Decebalus, driven from his capital of Sarmizegethusa, chose to commit suicide rather than be paraded in a Roman triumph to be ritually strangled afterwards.

Over the next three years the new province was treated to a rapid process of Romanisation, with road building and the planting of *coloniae* inhabited by citizens drawn mostly from the eastern provinces. Even as this was happening, Roman forces annexed Arabia Petraea on the death of Dabel, the Nabataean king, with its wealthy mercantile cities such as Petra. The smaller northern part was joined to Syria, while the southern region became the new province of Arabia, with its capital at Bostra.

The vast wealth of the Dacian mines that now came to Rome as war booty enabled Trajan to support an extensive building programme. Under the care of tireless Apollodorus, Trajan set about transforming the capital. He had already commenced a new forum next to that of Augustus, but the remaining room under the rising Quirinal

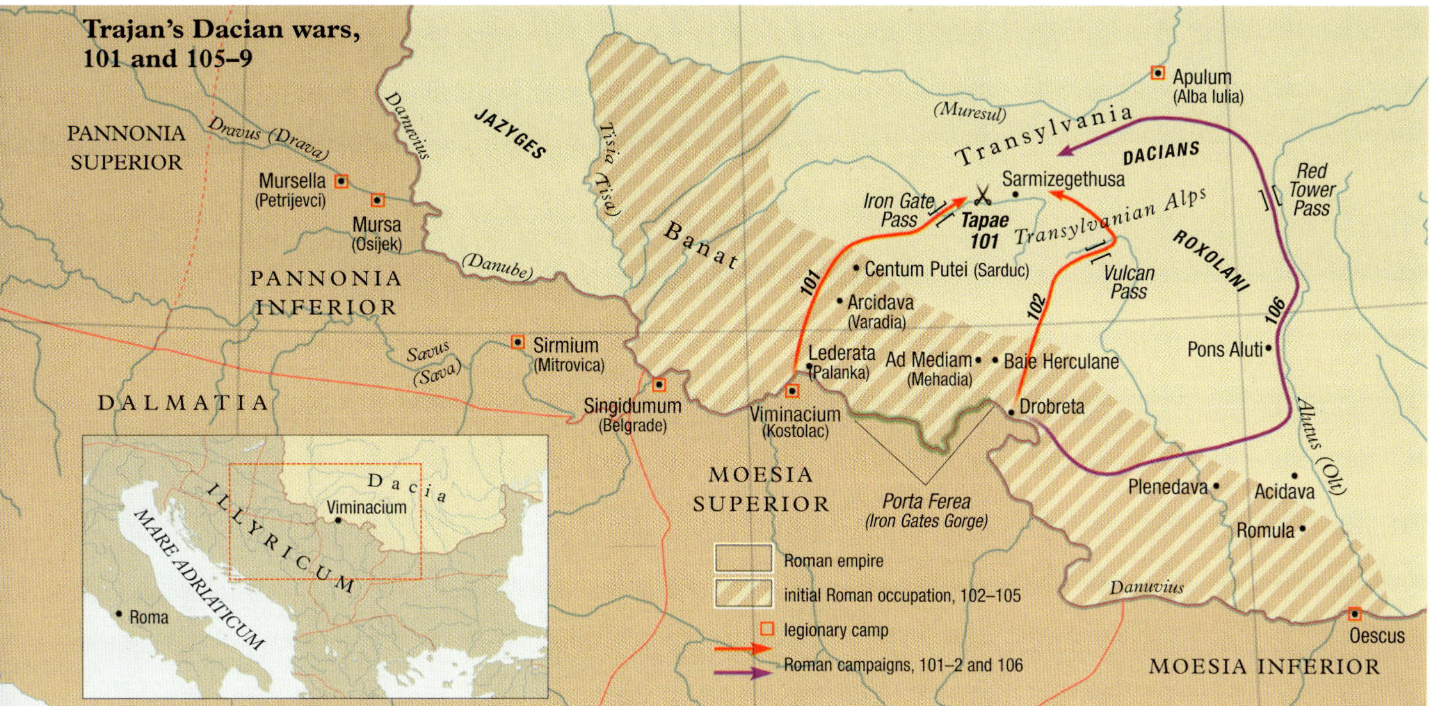


was insufficient for his enlarged scheme. Accordingly, Apollodorus had a massive swathe cut into the hillside and completely removed the low col joining the Capitol to the Quirinal. The rise of the Quirinal was then cleverly used to create a massive, tiered shopping centre, much of it still visible today. The Forum of Trajan – largest of all the Roman imperial forums – comprised the Basilica Ulpia, which served as a law-court, and two libraries, one Greek, one Latin. Between them rose Trajan's Column, sculpted with twenty-three spiral bands filled with 2,500 figures, depicting the history of both Dacian wars. Unusually, Trajan did not construct a temple in its precincts, a matter later rectified by Hadrian.

To the northeast of the Colosseum, using a great part of Nero's Domus Aurea as the foundation, he built the largest baths complex in Rome, which would be

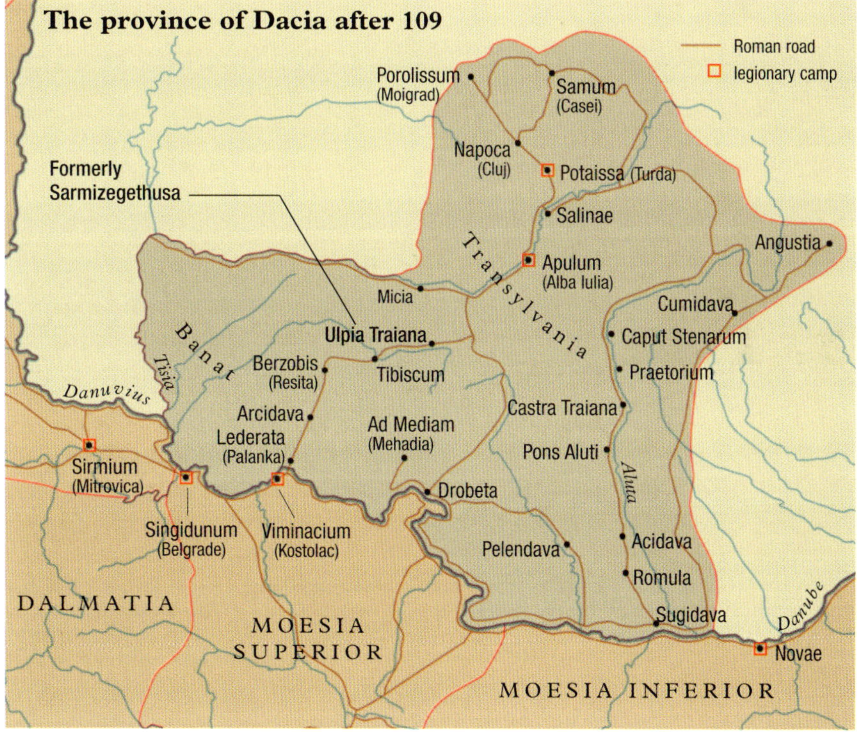


exceeded in scale only by those of Caracalla and Diocletian. This required a new aqueduct, the Aqua Paola, which still supplies water to modern Rome. He involved himself in extensive civil projects all over Italy – roads, aqueducts and new harbours on the Tyrrhenian and Adriatic seas. When old Ostia silted up, Claudius had built a new harbour two kilometres to the north (Portus). Now, Trajan enlarged the facilities and dug a canal to bypass the lower Tiber and link Portus to Rome for barge traffic.

Trajan was as passionate about games as anyone and outdid Titus, celebrating his return to Rome in 107 with combats that ran for a 123 consecutive days, and in which more than 11,000 gladiators took part. These were just the first of many such lavish spectacles. Not only the Colosseum, but also the Circus Maximus was kept busy. It

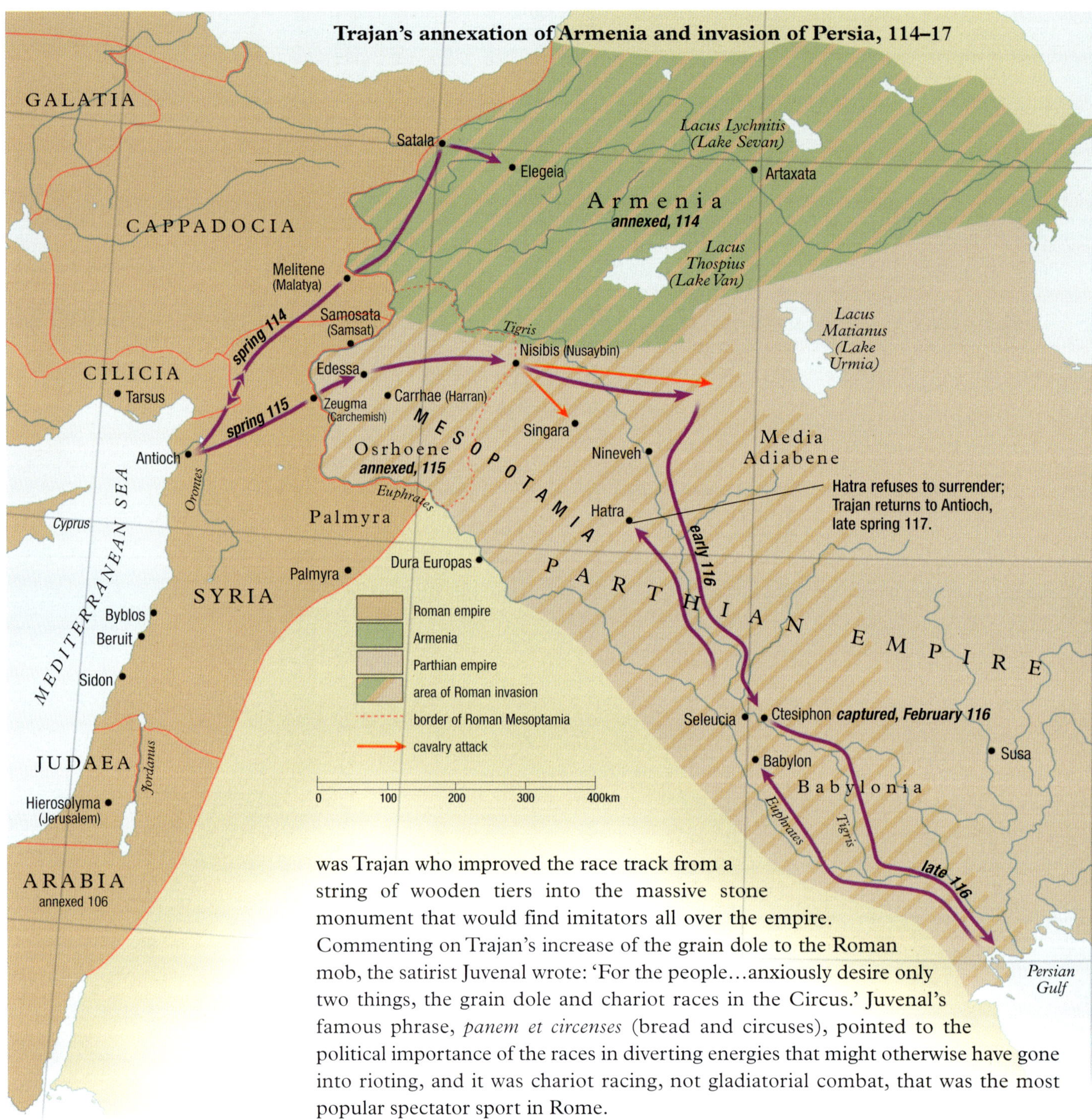



was Trajan who improved the race track from a
string of wooden tiers into the massive stone
monument that would find imitators all over the empire.
Commenting on Trajan's increase of the grain dole to the Roman
mob, the satirist Juvenal wrote: 'For the people…anxiously desire only
two things, the grain dole and chariot races in the Circus.' Juvenal's
famous phrase, *panem et circenses* (bread and circuses), pointed to the
political importance of the races in diverting energies that might otherwise have gone
into rioting, and it was chariot racing, not gladiatorial combat, that was the most
popular spectator sport in Rome.

To this point, the relationship between princeps and senate had characterised the
empire's politics; whether they more – or less – conformed to Augustus's fiction of a
determining senate with the guidance of the emperor. Trajan's rule was as autocratic
as any, but his good relations with the senate allowed him to accomplish whatever he
wished without much opposition. Claudius had controlled the Imperial Civil Service
through his personal freedmen, rarely allowing senators to interfere, but Trajan
formed a professional elite from among senators to order and control the state's
functions. He also promoted the careers of several of his military colleagues and
principal legates in the Dacian wars. He trusted them and, more importantly, they
trusted the emperor. They were all of proven ability, energetic, used to strict
organisation and decisive action, and happy to take orders. In this, they combined
the best of Republican government's military nobility, but without the wastage of

experience caused by the Republic's annual rotation of senior offices.

Trajan had no close male relatives, but the women in his life played important roles. His virtuous wife Pompeia Plotina, named Augusta in 105, was instrumental in Hadrian's accession. She survived Trajan, dying probably in 121, and was honoured with a temple shared with her husband that Hadrian built in Trajan's Forum. Trajan was close to his older sister Marciana. She too received the title Augusta in 105 and was deified on her death in 112. Her daughter Matidia became Augusta on her mother's death, and was in her turn deified in 119. Trajan's women travelled with him on public business and were frequently involved in major decisions. His grandniece Vibia Sabina, daughter of Matidia, married Hadrian in 100, and this is the only indication that Trajan considered Hadrian a potential successor.

The annexation of Dacia had secured the Danube frontier, but Rome's eastern boundary was less certain. The great semi-circle stretching from Syria to the Black Sea had few natural obstacles to mark a secure frontier and was vulnerable to Parthian attack from Mesopotamia. The pact signed with Nero gave Rome the right to maintain a client king on the Armenian throne, but with the approval of the Parthian king. In 113 Chosroes I appointed Exedares, the son of his brother and predecessor, to the throne of Armenia in breach of the treaty. Trajan promptly declared war. He sailed to Antioch in October and mobilised the Syrian army. As the preparations for an advance into Armenia progressed, Chosroes – who was suffering dynastic problems at home – attempted a compromise. He offered to remove Exedares and replace him with his other nephew, Parthamisiris. It's not clear how this was intended to placate Trajan, who in any event refused to give a clear response, even though Exedares was deposed.

In the spring of 114 Trajan crossed the upper Euphrates and advanced into Armenia. At Elegeia near Erzerum, Parthamisiris laid down his crown and Trajan pronounced Armenia a Roman province. In the following year the Romans struck into Parthia, eventually capturing Ctesiphon in February 116. Having advanced as far as the Persian Gulf, garrisoning wherever possible, Trajan wintered in Babylon, dreaming of equipping a fleet to attack India. However, from this point on events turned against him. Roman communications were long and the forts spread thin on the ground. Uprisings all along the line threatened the precarious Roman hold. Trajan was forced to give up his newest province of Parthia and begin a gradual retreat to Mesopotamia. The weary Roman army reached Antioch early in 117, the men to be dispersed to different regions where rebellions had broken out, some started as early as 115.

After the Temple of Solomon's destruction in Jerusalem by Titus, the Jews had been dispersed from Judaea and large numbers had settled in Mesopotamia, Egypt, Cyprus and Africa. Their passionate hatred of Roman rule sparked insurrections in Mesopotamia that rapidly spread to the other Jewish settlements. An estimated million were slaughtered on both sides of the divide by 117. Trajan left for Rome, intending to direct operations from there; but he never completed the journey. Pausing briefly at Selinus in Cilicia, the emperor suffered a stroke and died within a few days on 9 August 117 – a little over a month short of his sixty-fourth birthday – with his wife Plotina and his loyal praetorian prefect Acilius Attianus at his bedside.

Trajan's reign was one of the best periods in Roman history, the moment when it reached its greatest extent, embracing the Mediterranean with openings on the Atlantic, the Black, Caspian, and Red seas, and – very briefly – the Persian Gulf. He richly deserved his title of *optimus princeps*, not only for his very real achievements, but also for the quality of his mercy (at least towards Roman citizens) and the modesty of his principate. Eschewing any notions of divinity, the soldier-emperor preferred to see himself portrayed as a *civilis*, an ordinary man. Time only increased Trajan's aura. In the late fourth century, when the empire had dramatically changed in character, each new emperor was hailed with the prayer, *felicior augusto, melior traiano!* (More fortunate than Augustus, better than Trajan).

Trajan's wife Plotina (*top*) and his beloved sister Marciana. The women played crucial roles in his life, including his sister's daughter Matidia, (*below*).

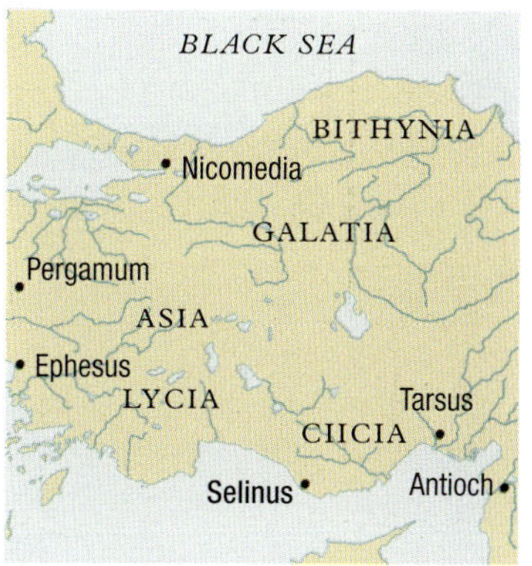

### Hadrian  Publius Aelius Hadrianus / Caesar Traianus Hadrianus Augustus
[11/8/117–10/7/138 ]

Hadrian's Aelian ancestors moved from Hadria, a small town in Picentine Italy, to Italica in Baetica at the conclusion of the Second Punic War, generations before his birth. The histories are divided on whether Italica was his birthplace – on 24 January 76 – or Rome, but if the former it seems he only spent a brief period in Italica before returning to the capital. His mother, Domitia Paulina, came from a distinguished family of Gades (Cadiz), one of the empire's wealthiest provincial cities. His father, Publius Aelius Afer, had attained the ranks of praetor by the time of his death.

Hadrian was a second cousin to Trajan (Hadrian's grandmother and Trajan's father were brother and sister), and when Hadrian, aged nine, lost his father in 85 Trajan became one his guardians; the other was Acilius Attianus, another eminent man of Italica, who became Trajan's praetorian prefect.

At eighteen Hadrian began a rapid rise up the *cursus honorum*. After a junior magistracy he was a military tribune for three consecutive years between 95 and 97 in Pannonia, Moesia Inferior and Germania Superior. In 101 he became a quaestor and a praetor in 106. In the same year Trajan appointed him *legatus legionis* of I Minerviae in Germania Inferior. In the following year he was *legatus pro praetore* of Pannonia Inferior, and in 108 consul, ten years before the traditional age for the office. This meteoric career was clearly unusual, but at the point in 117 when he was *legatus syriae* and Trajan died, there was no indication from the princeps that Hadrian would succeed. Some of the Augustan signs were there: accelerated appointments; a family relation to Trajan – marriage to the emperor's grandniece Vibia Sabina.

On the day after Trajan's death his wife Plotina and Acilius Attianus, Hadrian's surviving guardian, announced that Trajan had adopted Hadrian. Plotina, Attianus and Hadrian's mother-in-law Matidia set off immediately for Rome to ensure the succession. Popular scandal accused Plotina of forging the adoption papers because she was Hadrian's secret lover. Since they were almost the same age, this might have been true – although, given his sexual preferences, it seems hardly likely – but Rome was ever a hotbed of gossip. On 11 August 117 the troops of Syria hailed forty-one-year-old Hadrian as their emperor. He remained in Syria, but wrote to the senate to request divine honours for Trajan and to confirm his accession to the principate. He added the usual promise that he would never execute a senator. The senate's acquiescence was a mere formality in the face of the Syrian army's proclamation. Extraordinary permission was given for the burial of Trajan's ashes within the city's sacred *pomerium*, eventually to be interred at the base of his column in his own forum.

From Antioch, Hadrian proceeded with a policy in marked contrast to Trajan's. Retrenchment and consolidation characterised his reign, convinced as he was that the empire had reached the limits of its resources. He began immediately by recalling the troops from the lower Euphrates and abandoning Trajan's new provinces to client kings. This abrupt reversal of foreign policy proved unpopular among the Roman elite, and unrest broke out in Rome, even as Hadrian's mollifying tactics were calming the Jewish unrest. When a plot against his life was uncovered, Hadrian hastened to Rome, arriving on 9 July 118. He was too late, however, to prevent the executions of the four alleged ringleaders, senators and consulars who had been close associates of Trajan's and probably resented Hadrian's adoption and his pacific policies. Hadrian always maintained that they were executed without his consent. True or not, their deaths made the new emperor's course easier and silenced opposition among the nobility to his frontier policy. But the

Rome's most cultured emperor, Hadrian left statues and busts of himself in every corner of his realm, sporting the new-look beard and curled hair.

The great stand-off: Hadrian and his wife Vibia Sabina (*opposite*) had an unhappy union, not helped by the emperor's homosexual nature.

## The Nervo-Trajanic House and the Adoptive Antonines

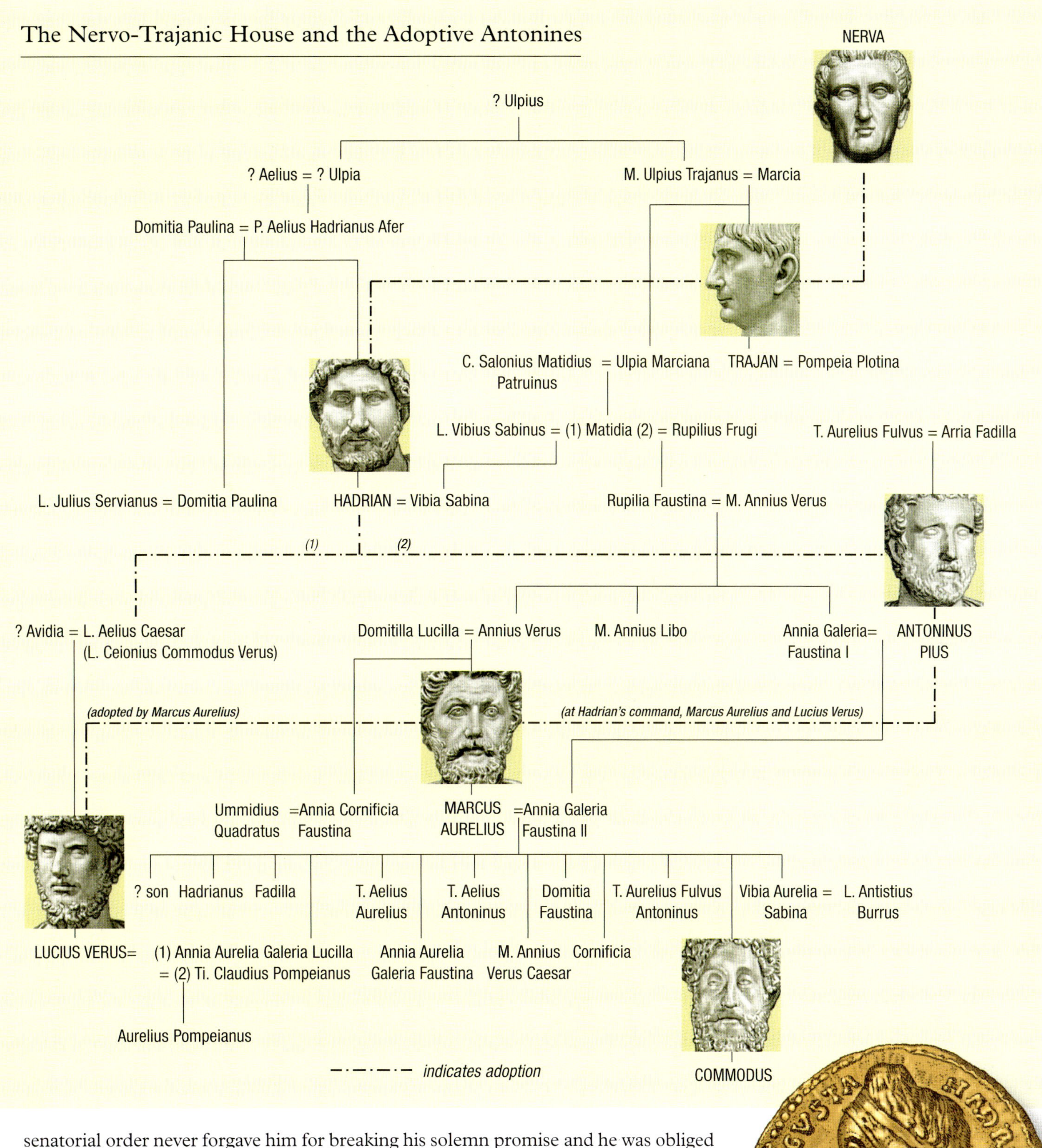


senatorial order never forgave him for breaking his solemn promise and he was obliged to swear in person never again to mete out punishment to any senator unless the senatorial court decreed otherwise.

Almost certainly cowed by Trajan's ferocity, the barbarian tribes maintained a low profile throughout Hadrian's reign, playing to the emperor's non-aggressive stance. To the obvious corrolary – that a static army loses its edge, grows demoralised and becomes a potential cause of trouble – Hadrian answered with continual tours of inspection to keep the legions and garrisons up to scratch. As a result, he spent barely half his reign in Rome. He introduced a greater degree of equality by increasing the rankers' comforts and levelling those of the officers. He was strict in ensuring that promotions were earned for merit, not favour, and earned the soldiers' devotion for his efforts. Hadrian also placed a greater reliance on the use of native auxiliary cavalry than had been the case previously, and reversed Vespasian's practice of only allowing them to serve under Roman officers. In fact, by this time it was rare to find Italian officers, except at the highest level, most being enrolled from among the provincials.

While the frontiers remained calm, Hadrian knew that this might not always be the case. To this point the Roman frontiers had relied on traditional army camps and mobile garrisons, but now Hadrian erected many major and permanent structures. The British garrisons, thinly dispersed in a line that stretched north from the Tyne valley to a small camp at modern Inchtuthil, near Perth, were vulnerable – attested to by the disappearance of Legion IX Hispania, wiped out during a tribal uprising at about the time of Hadrian's accession.

The decision was taken to pull back and establish a firm frontier along the line of Agricola's original boundary between Luguvalium (Carlisle) and Segedunum (Wallsend, Gateshead). Stretching between the Solway Firth and Tyne estuary, it was 117 kilometres long. Construction began in 122, the work carried out by legionaries (not slaves as often thought), and was completed by 128. The core of lime concrete was faced with dressed stone. It averaged 4.6m in height and 3m thick at the base. Small forts with sally-ports were built at a regular distance of one Roman mile, and over time 16 main forts were attached to the wall. Immediately to its north a V-shaped ditch was dug out to a depth of 3m and with a width at ground level of 8m.

The ditch and wall would not have kept out a determined attack – and indeed in future years there would be several serious incursions south of Hadrian's Wall – but the sheer scale of this undertaking demonstrated Roman might and was

intended to deter insurrection rather than act as an impregnable defensive barrier. It also served an economic purpose by defining Roman boundaries, allowing the tithing of goods passing in either direction, since the wall was open to authorised north-south trade. The 15,000 auxiliaries who manned the wall, drawn from various parts of the empire, were a further bar to Caledonian marauders, and it's a testament to the project's success that it enabled the Romans to maintain a presence as far north as this for almost three centuries after its construction.

Hadrian's other great fortification can be found on the 322km section stretching between the upper reaches of the Rhine and Danube known as the *limes germanicus*.

Unlike the British wall, the *limes* were constructed of split-oak trunks embedded in a ditch and fastened on the inside by cross-planking. This explains why they have suffered far more over the centuries than Hadrian's Wall. Of similar construction, the 166 km long palisade on the Raetian frontier followed the line established by Domitian between Lauriacum (Lorch) and the Danube near Abusina (Eining). No defences of this kind have been found along the lower Danube frontier; this is not really surprising since Dacia provided substantial protection and was well garrisoned.

**THE PROVINCES BENEFITED** from Hadrian's imperial perambulations, although in the first instance the cost of receiving the emperor's retinue fell on the towns no matter how modestly Hadrian comported himself. In almost all cases, however, the provincials received far more than they had to give since Hadrian undertook public works wherever he went – he was Rome's greatest town-planner. New cities sprang up all over the empire, perhaps the most famous being Hadrianopolis (Adrianople) in Thrace, renamed Edirne in the 15th century by the Ottoman Turks. Wherever he went, Hadrian and his architects met with approval – except in Jerusalem where his plans caused a dangerous rebellion.

Despite prolonged absences from the capital, Rome was not ignored. Hadrian was almost certainly the most artistically gifted emperor that Rome ever produced. A fine public speaker and student of philosophy, he held his own with luminaries in their fields; he wrote poetry and an autobiography and he was a fine architect in his own right. He completed Trajan's Forum with a large temple dedicated to Trajan and Plotina, and then in 121, when he was about forty-five, began construction of the temple of Venus and Rome overlooking the Colosseum. It was massive, at more than 91m in length, and housed giant seated statues of Venus and Roma, which caused Trajan's jealous architect Apollodorus to sneer, saying that if they stood up their heads would bang on the ceiling. Hadrian dedicated the complex on 21 April 135.

The Hadrianeum or temple of Neptune exhibited sculpted representations of the provinces, indicating the blurring of the distinction between Italy and the provinces that was taking place during his reign. Nearby, on the right bank of the Tiber above the Vatican, he commenced his mausoleum, larger than that of Augustus. Approached by a new bridge, the Pons Aelius, the mausoleum was still unfinished at the time of his death. Some 40km east of Rome at Tibur (Tivoli), Hadrian built his stupendously big palace. More a small city than a 'villa', it covered 285ha and contained some hundred individual buildings in a multitude of architectural styles. Reflecting his life of travel, the adornment was superbly eclectic, although Greek styles predominated. Here Hadrian reconstructed many of the places he had visited, such as the Canopus of Alexandria and the Vale of Tempe.

The Pantheon, Hadrian's crowning glory, built between 118 and 125, sat on the site of Agrippa's original in the Campus Martius. This extraordinary feat of engineering provided a dome with a height exactly equal to its diameter – a perfect half-sphere. The dome's span remained unsurpassed until modern times, and is greater than that of St Peter's in Rome. As was his modest custom, Hadrian inscribed the architrave with the original dedication of Agrippa; he seldom put his own name on a monument. The Pantheon was devoted to all the Roman gods, but its survival is down to the Byzantine emperor Phocas, who gave the building to Pope Boniface IV

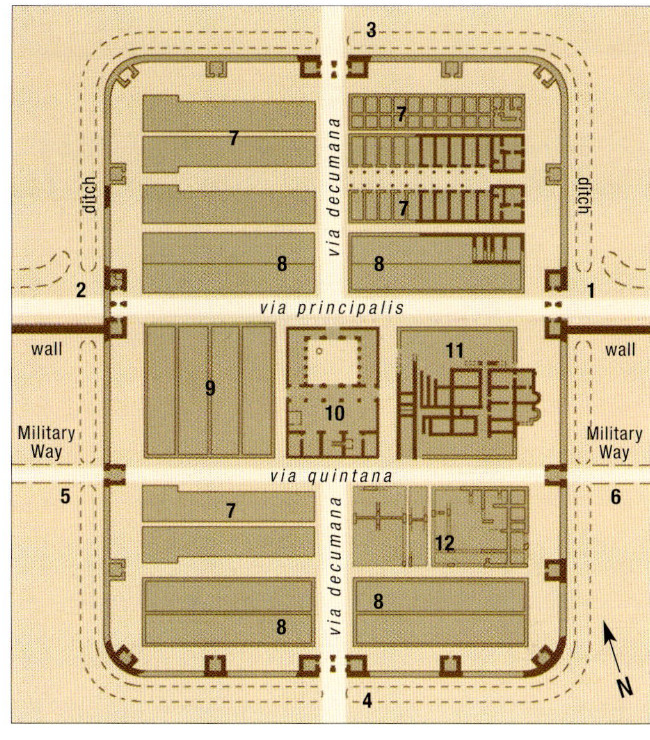


**Hadrian's Wall – plan of Cilurnum (Chesters) fort**

1 *Porta principalis dextra* (main east gate), with twin towers and double portals. The gateway doors would have been of oak reinforced with iron straps. The three other main gates were of similar construction.

2 *Porta pincipalis sinistra* (main west gate).

3 *Porta Praetoria* (north gate).

4 *Porta decumana* (main gate), connecting to Corstopitum 12 km away.

5 *Porta quintana sinistra* (smaller west gate).

6 *Porta quintana dextra* (smaller east gate).

7 Barracks.

8 Stables.

9 Granaries and workshops, including a forge and armoury.

10 *Principia*, the regimental headquarters.

11 Quarters for the *praefectus equitum*, adjacent to the fort's luxurious bath-house.

12 Building which probably contained the hospital.

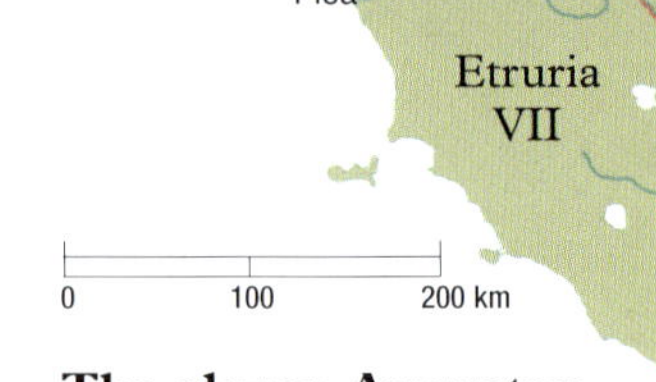



**The eleven Augustan regions of Italy**

Vibia Sabina could not compete with Hadrian's predilection for handsome boys, like the Bithynian youth Antinoüs, and their marriage remained barren.

in 608 to convert it into the church of Santa Maria ad Martyres.

Hadrian's attention to detail is also found in his codification of Roman law, known as the Codification of the Praetor's Edict. In one respect, this brought within the principate's autocratic control an element of Roman life that had so far escaped it. On the other hand, it benefited citizens by providing a standard interpretation of the complex judicial processes that had grown up over centuries. An urban praetor in the mid-Republic issued a statement of the legal procedure and interpretation that he proposed to follow during his annual term of office. In theory this fixed how the laws would be interpreted from that point on. However, his successor was not bound by this *edictum perpetuum*, in fact it was only when the Cornelian Law of 67 BC was passed that a praetor was even obliged to honour his own edict, let alone that of his predecessors. Nevertheless, situations would arise in which, to suit the circumstances, the praetor needed to add to the body of law or modify an existing law; not a state of affairs that recommends itself to autocratic rule.

Therefore, Hadrian decided to codify all the accretions to the body of statute law in the form of his own *edictum perpetuum*, which would have binding force thereafter. If any additions or further modifications were to be necessary, it would be the emperor in future who would determine them.

For this monumental task Hadrian appointed a famous jurist, Salvius Julianus, who completed the work by 129, bringing together in a straightforward and modern document centuries of praetorian edicts. Hadrian's Edict has been lost, but many excerpts made by commentators survived in Justinian's Digest of the sixth century. To improve legal administration, Hadrian appointed four men of consular rank, each of whom toured two to three districts of Italy as circuit judges. This innovation reduced the crippling costs of bringing an appeal to Rome – previously the only place cases could be heard – and relieved pressure on the emperor and urban praetor's overcrowded courts.

To handle the demands of new legislation and extensive reformation of the state's financial matters, Hadrian continued the advancement of *equites* begun by Augustus, Claudius and the Flavians, but went further in creating an Imperial Civil Service that was finally removed from the imperial household. Thus its members were public servants – although under the emperor's control – rather than his personal agents. In doing so, he regularised the Service's composition, throwing out the freedmen, and making a civil career a proper part of the *cursus honorum* for the equestrian class. The most radically changed office was that of the highest equestrian, the praetorian prefect. His ceased to be a military function and he became a legal officer presiding over the emperor's judicial *concilium*.

**WHILE HADRIAN'S TRAVELS** were primarily motivated by military matters, he was probably Rome's most curious emperor, interested in a wide spectrum of his world: sport, science, architecture, literature, art, nature and especially Greek culture – he was sufficiently vain to curl his hair with tongs in the Greek manner. The third-century writer Tertullian called Hadrian '*omnium curiositatum explorator*' – a tourist who visited all the sites and monuments, climbing mountains to admire views of the sunset. It was during his trip to Bithynia in 123 that he met the handsome Antinoüs, when the boy would have been about twelve. His father may have been a provincial stone mason. Hadrian's pederasty was widely known, his preference – in strict accordance with the Greek manner – being for boys above the age of thirteen. Accordingly, Hadrian had Antinoüs sent to Rome, to enter the imperial *paedagogium*. This institution, painted by some of the ancient histories as an infamous boy harem for the emperor, provided an education for future palace or civil service administrators. Its beginnings probably date from as early as the reign of Caligula, who housed his favourite charioteers there. As Antinoüs went to Rome, Hadrian travelled on and so they did not meet again until Hadrian returned to the capital in 125. By all accounts, Hadrian's infatuation with Antinoüs far exceeded his interest in any other youth. From this point on until his untimely death Antinoüs remained constantly in Hadrian's company. The relationship was not likely to please Vibia Sabina. In a male-dominated Roman world, the barreness of their marriage was blamed on Hadrian's wife, but his sexual preferences can hardly be excluded from fault.

Disaster struck in October 130. During a visit to Egypt the imperial court had reached a point on the mid-Nile when Antinoüs drowned in the river; accident, suicide or something more sinister? It has been a fruitful source for speculation ever since. In his extravagant grief Hadrian raised a new city on the Nile's east bank named Antinöopolis, and he peopled it with Graeco-Egyptian army veterans. The city became the centre of a new cult to Antinoüs the god. He entered the Egyptian pantheon and soon after that of the Romans. In his beloved Greece Hadrian further encouraged the cult's growth, and traces survived in Achaea for another two centuries. Hadrian erected numerous statues of Antinoüs at his Tivoli villa and almost everywhere he went thereafter. Indeed, his obsession with three-dimensional representation was responsible for a vigorous revival of classical Greek sculpture.

Having seen to the rites for Antinoüs, Hadrian moved to Judaea, where exceptional ineptness tripped up his normally benign care; perhaps the recent bereavement warped his judgement. Jerusalem still lay in ruins and he determined to rebuild it as the colony Aelia Capitolina, with a temple of Jupiter erected on the site of Solomon's temple. There was uproar from the outraged Jews and in response Hadrian threw them out and forbade them ever to live in Jerusalem again. The resulting uprising flared into open war by 132 under the leadership of the Jewish prince Simon Bar Kokhba. The Jews registered some initial successes but were eventually ground down by the size and strength of the Roman forces pitched against them. At least six legions became involved and, after three years of fighting, the Jewish force was cornered at Bethar fortress, west of Jerusalem, in 135 and cut down. Vengeance belonged to Hadrian, who killed or enslaved any Jews who had not already fled the region in the great diaspora. Jerusalem was entirely Romanised, Judaism banned, and the name Judaea erased from the map by renaming it Palaestina. The Jews were now entirely without a homeland, and would remain so until the twentieth century.

At the conclusion of the Jewish rebellion Hadrian, now in his sixtieth year, was assailed by an illness that made him irritable, testy and suddenly aware of his mortality. In 136 he adopted his long-time companion, Lucius Aelius, and elevated him to the rank of Caesar. The selection was unpopular. Aelius had little to recommend him other than his powerful connection. His health was poor, he'd no military experience and it turned out to be an unhappy choice because he died of tuberculosis on 1 January 138. Hadrian turned to another and within six weeks adopted the fifty-one-year-old senator Titus Aurelius Fulvus Boionius Arrius Antoninus on 25 February. Antoninus, who may have been related to Trajan's wife Plotina, had a blameless reputation. With an eye to the future, Hadrian obliged Antoninus to adopt two sons to secure the succession beyond him: Antoninus's seventeen-year-old nephew Marcus Annius Verus and deceased Lucius Aelius Caesar's seven-year-old boy, Lucius Ceionius Commodus. The former choice was a fortunate

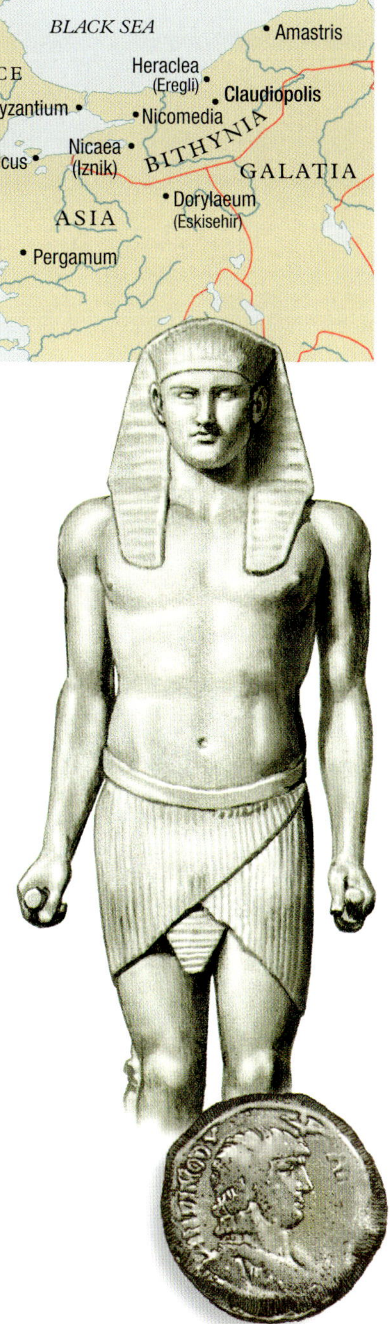



Deified in death: Antinoüs entered the pantheon of Egyptian and Roman gods. Coins were minted and his cult was to last for more than two centuries.

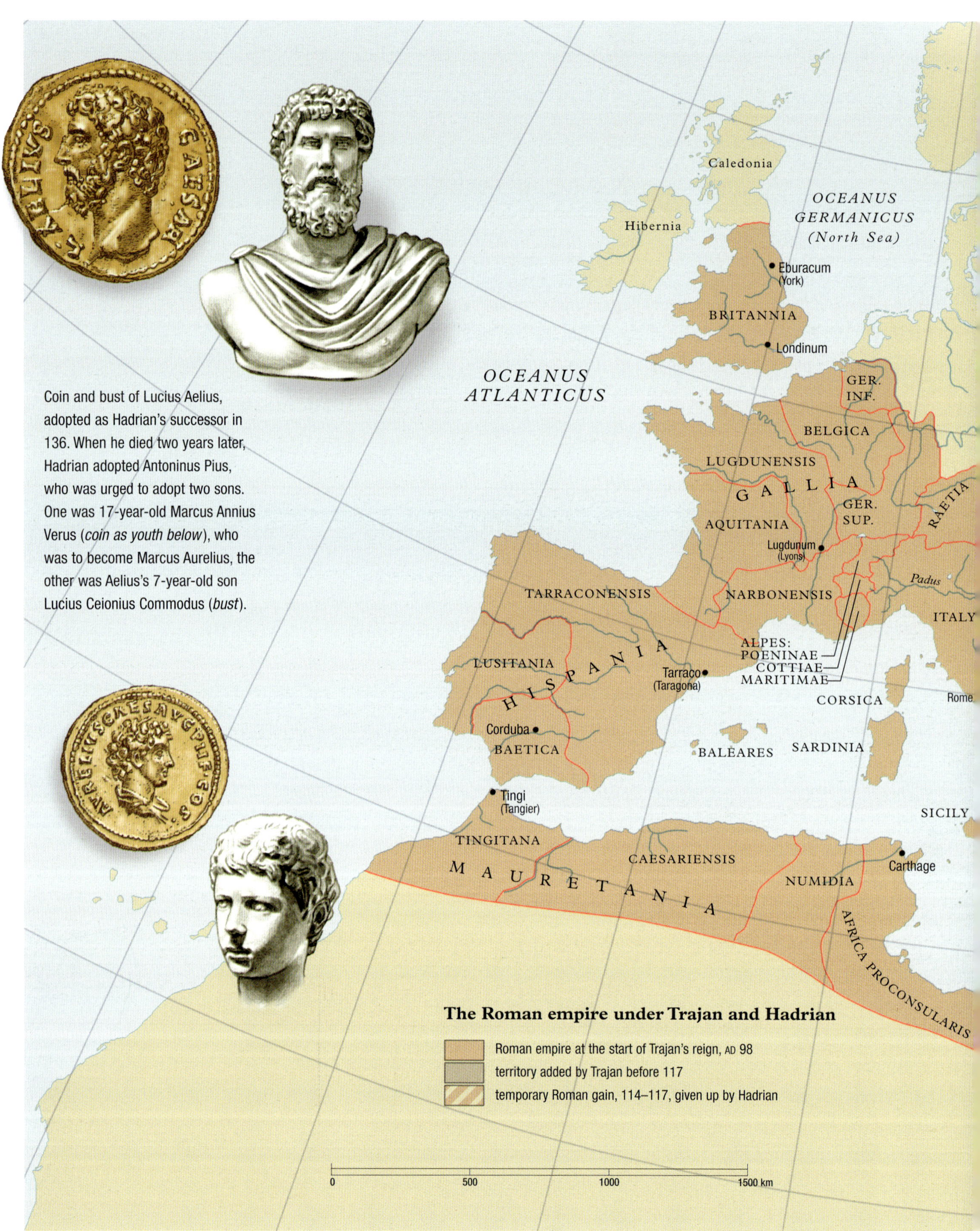



Coin and bust of Lucius Aelius, adopted as Hadrian's successor in 136. When he died two years later, Hadrian adopted Antoninus Pius, who was urged to adopt two sons. One was 17-year-old Marcus Annius Verus (*coin as youth below*), who was to become Marcus Aurelius, the other was Aelius's 7-year-old son Lucius Ceionius Commodus (*bust*).

### The Roman empire under Trajan and Hadrian

one, for he would become Marcus Aurelius, last of the great Roman emperors of the period; the latter was less successful.

On 10 July 138, aged sixty-two, Hadrian died of his illness (probably also tuberculosis) at Baiae, on the Bay of Naples. Having spent almost half of his reign away from Rome, and much time in Tivoli when he was in Italy, he had become a distant and unpopular character. Hadrian played a significant role both in developing the foreign policies of the empire and in its continuing centralisation of the administration. Augustus was his proclaimed role model, but the real echoes are those of Claudius for his care of the empire, Nero for his interest in the arts, Vespasian for the supervision of the finances and Trajan for his grasp of the empire itself. Few today would disagree that he was one of the most remarkable men Rome ever produced, and yet his passion for organisation meant that he introduced reforms into the principate that resulted in the growth of the bureaucratic machine that would soon restrict initiative and ultimately destroy the empire.

A coin minted on the occasion of Hadrian's visit to Jerusalem shows a Jewish mother making a peace offering to the emperor. It clearly didn't work, his actions led to a bloody uprising.

**Left:** The Arch of Septimius Severus stands at the western edge of the Roman Forum. The inscriptions on the upper register were altered by Caracalla to erase his brother Geta's name. Unlike Rome's other triumphal arches, which were designed for soldiers to pass through, this arch was raised on a podium well above the forum's ground level.

**Right:** Detail of the spiral relief from Trajan's Column depicting legionaries marching along the cantilevered road built by Apollodorus in the Iron Gates gorge of the Danube, on their way to defeat the Dacian king Decebalus.

**Below:** Detail from the south frieze of the Ara Pacis, Rome. It shows flamines, priests and augurs – almost all family members of Augustus – processing in ceremony.

# FIVE
## The Antonine Dynasty

[AD 138–192]

### Antoninus Pius  Titus Aurelius Fulvus Boionius Arrius Hadrianus Antoninus Pius
[ 10/7/138–7/3/161 ]

Antoninus was born on 19 September 86 at Lanuvium, an old Latin city some 32km southeast of Rome. His father's family, originally from Nemausus (Nîmes) in Gallia Narbonensis, had established itself firmly in the senatorial and consular class. Most of Antoninus's youth was spent at Lorium, only 20km from Rome, to which he later retreated from the cares of the empire. He entered public life as a quaestor in 112, made praetor in 117 and consul at the age of thirty-four. Antoninus married Annia Galeria Faustina, the daughter of Marcus Annius Verus (whose nephew of the same name he later adopted). He became one of Hadrian's new circuit judges and in 133–36 served as proconsul of Asia – the only recorded time that Antoninus spent outside Italy – where his remarkable administrative qualities reccommended him for a position on Hadrian's *concilium*, where he remained until the emperor's death.

The succession was already secured by Antoninus's adoption of Marcus Annius Verus, his nephew by marriage, who became Marcus Aurelius Antoninus, and the younger Lucius Ceionius Commodus. His twenty-three-year reign, one unequalled in Roman history for its peace and prosperity, showed such devotion to the wellbeing of his subjects that the title Pius was deserved. In everything Antoninus did, modesty was his watchword – which is why his reign is so easily overlooked. He continued Hadrian's pacific policy and consequently trade and commerce flourished as never before. The high quality of municipal life, bolstered by continuing operation of the *alimenta*, is revealed in the numerous inscriptions throughout the provinces that record the generosity of wealthy patrons or the charitable activities of a growing citizen-middle class. Antoninus had no intention of draining this prosperity by burdening the provinces with expensive imperial visits and remained at or around Rome where he could receive messages from all parts of the empire equally quickly. He only left the capital to visit his nearby estate at Lorium. He was equally restrained in respect of building programmes. In Carthage a grand baths complex bore his name, he completed Hadrian's mausoleum and the Hadrianaeum, built the modest temple in the Forum of Antoninus and Faustina (dedicated to his wife, who died in 141) and made repairs to the ancient Sublican bridge and the Colosseum.

Antoninus applied himself to the awakened interest in the law that Hadrian's Edict had promoted. He appointed expert jurists to advise him on additions to the statutes that introduced a new spirit of leniency and humanitarianism, which went so far as to legislate against abuse of slaves. In religion Antoninus lacked Hadrian's skepticism, and was devoted to the traditions of virtuous Roman worship. This meant that he was remarkably tolerant, and during his reign the adoption of new eastern deities increased, although he maintained Trajan's ambivalent policies towards the Christians.

Antoninus Pius died at the age of seventy-four on 7 March 161 at his beloved Lorium. So the story goes, he passed away peacefully after giving his praetorian prefect the password for the day, 'equanimity'. It summed

Probably the most underrated emperor of the period, Antoninus Pius reigned over the last period of complete peace the empire would enjoy.

One of a series of coins struck in 147 to celebrate Rome's 900th birthday. It depicts Aeneas fleeing Troy, eventually to become Rome's ancient founder.

up his reign. 'Probity' would have been equally appropriate; he left his adopted sons a reported surplus in the *fiscus* of 675 million sesterces. In many histories Antoninus Pius merits only a small mention because no matters of import occurred in his long reign and perhaps because extravagance and cruelty are more exciting historical subjects than loving care of government. In his *Meditations*, Marcus Aurelius wrote of his adoptive father: 'Think of his constancy in every act rationally undertaken, his invariable equability, his piety, his serenity of countenance, his sweetness of disposition, his contempt for the bubble of fame, and his zeal for getting a true grasp of affairs.'

**Marcus Aurelius** Marcus Annius Verus / Marcus Aurelius Antoninus Augustus
[ Caesar 139; r.7/3/161–17/3/180 ]
**Lucius Verus** Lucius Ceionius Commodus / Lucius Aurelius Verus Augustus
[ 7/3/161–1 January-February 169 ]

Marcus Aurelius, born Marcus Annius Verus at Rome on 26 April 121, came from a distinguished family originally of Ucubi, near Cordoba, Baetica, whose members revolved in Hadrian's orbit. His father died when Marcus was only three, and the emperor took an interest in the boy's welfare. A serious youngster who enjoyed intellectual pursuits and embraced the teachings of rhetoric and philosophy, Hadrian punned on his name Verus, calling the boy 'Verissimus' (most truthful). In 136 Hadrian betrothed him to Ceionia Fabia, daughter of Hadrian's designated successor Lucius Aelius.

Antoninus Pius and his wife Annia Galeria Faustina, remembered as model rulers who cared for Rome's wellbeing.

Like his older sister Fabia, Lucius Ceionius Commodus was also born at Rome, on 15 December 130. In making his succession plans, Hadrian betrothed the young boy to Annia Galeria Faustina (the Younger), daughter of the newly adopted Antoninus Pius, thus cementing a complex interdependent web of marriages to underpin the strength of the principate into the future. At the adoption ceremony held on 25 February 138 Marcus was one month off his seventeenth birthday and his adoptive brother Lucius was seven. Marcus took the names of Marcus Aelius Aurelius Verus, but was usually known as Marcus Aurelius. The younger heir-apparent became Lucius Aelius Aurelius Commodus and then later – to emphasise his relationship to his adoptive brother Marcus – simply Lucius Verus.

Antoninus Pius later altered Hadrian's succession plan by breaking off Marcus's prior betrothal to Ceionia Fabia, engaging him instead to his own daughter Faustina the Younger. This naturally meant breaking off Lucius's earlier engagement to her, and the implied greater favour shown Marcus. While Marcus Aurelius continued to live by and espouse stoicism, Lucius Verus was altogether a more lightweight figure, although when Antoninus died in 161 he was sharing the consulship with forty-year-old Marcus. As Hadrian had planned, Marcus immediately accepted Lucius as his co-princeps, and betrothed him to his daughter Annia Aurelia Galeria Lucilla. For the first time the empire was jointly ruled by consent, but being the younger brother, partner, and proposed son-in-law to Marcus Aurelius could not have been easy for Lucius – Marcus the sober, thoughtful philosopher; Lucius a handsome,

Bust and coin of Marcus Aurelius as Caesar, a studious pupil who immersed himself in stoic philosophy.

vain man who highlighted his blond hair with gold dust. Early in 162, the two emperors were temporarily separated.

A revived Parthian empire had again challenged Roman control of Armenia. Vologeses III seized the opportunity of Antoninus's death to depose and replace the Roman puppet with his own. Roman forces sent to oppose him suffered severe setbacks. Marcus Aurelius argued that an imperial presence would underscore the seriousness of the empire's response and Lucius consented to go, marrying Lucilla at Ephesus en route. With no military experience Lucius left strategy in the capable hands of Gaius Avidius Cassius, the legate most respected by the Aurelian *concilium*. Cassius prosecuted a successful campaign in 163–66, storming and destroying most of Parthia's major cities and strongholds, including Seleucia and Ctesiphon. Parthian resistance collapsed, Armenia was reoccupied, Mesopotomia annexed to the empire again and a joint-triumph of the Augusti celebrated in October 166, during which Marcus's five-year-old son Commodus was named Caesar.

Lucius pursued a self-indulgent lifestyle in Rome, gambling, drinking, racing and consorting with whores and actors (the same thing in the eyes of the respectable). Marcus disapproved of Lucius's ways and after his return from Syria Lucius showed far less deference to his adoptive brother, whose conscientiousness he found stuffy Serious strife between them probably lay in the near future. Fate, however, decided differently.

**BEYOND THE DANUBE AND UPPER RHINE,** German tribes, increasingly pressed against the frontier by other tribes in central Europe, were greedily eyeing Roman territory. In particular, the Quadi and the Marcomanni, both ruthlessly suppressed by Domitian and Trajan, were determined to move into the richer territories that lay within the Roman borders. In 166–67, they poured across the Danube into Raetia, Noricum, Pannonia and through Dacia into Moesia. The fighting was more serious than anything the Roman army had ever experienced; one barbarian force attacked cities in the Po valley and besieged Aquileia and the Roman army was in no state to retaliate. The triumph of 166 had been overshadowed by a plague brought back from Syria by the returning legions. Possibly smallpox, perhaps typhus, the epidemic wiped out entire populations. Incapacitated by illness, it took the under-strength army time to regain control of the situation, largely due to the efforts of three generals: Tiberius Claudius Pompeianus in Pannonia Inferior, Publius Helvius Pertinax in Raetia, and Marcus Claudius Fronto in Moesia Superior. By 168, the initial success of Pertinax in Raetia had discouraged the barbarians surrounding Aquileia and they withdrew as Marcus and Lucius brought reinforcements to relieve the city. With the situation apparently under control, Lucius pressed Marcus for a return to Rome, and it was as they travelled south in the spring of 169 that Lucius fell ill of the plague near Altinum (Altino), and died three days later, aged thirty-eight.

Marcus remained in Rome until the autumn, when a fresh German invasion necessitated his presence at the frontier. The Jazyges, having been thwarted in Pannonia, turned their attention towards Dacia. Marcus added the province to Fronto's command, but the campaign was unsuccessful and Fronto was killed in battle. Marcus decided to take command himself. Before departing he married his widowed daughter Lucilla to Tiberius Claudius Pompeianus and left him in charge of Rome. In effect, Marcus Aurelius was never to return, spending the last fourteen years of his reign in continual warfare.

His strategy of defeating each tribe in detail to maximise the Roman army's superior tactics while mitigating its weakness in numbers proved successful. However, he settled numbers of tribesmen within the empire as farmer-auxiliaries. This had

The joint-rulers were theoretically equals, but Marcus Aurelius (*top*) dominated Lucius Verus by both age and dedication.

been done before, but Marcus Aurelius tied the settlers to their land by law. In this way he hoped to alleviate some of the pressure on the borders as well as repopulating parts of Illyricum. Based at Carnuntum, he won a victory over the Marcomanni in late 171 and over their neighbours the Quadi in 174, before transferring to Sirmium from where, in the following year, he inflicted a defeat on the Jazyges – a proper revenge for their killing of Fronto in 169. Marcus soon emerged as a second Trajan, raising new legions, constructing new camps and refurbishing frontier fortifications. His only break from the wild northern frontier came in 175, when the redoubtable warrior Gaius Avidius Cassius, now Syrian proconsul, claimed the throne for himself. However, by the time Marcus reached Antioch soldiers loyal to him had already killed Cassius. He then spent time travelling and settling eastern affairs, even indulging himself with an extended stay in Athens. However, the northern war still raged and he returned there in 177, taking with him sixteen-year-old Commodus, who had been elevated to co-Augustus and given the *tribunicia potestas* and *imperium proconsulare*. This broke with Nerva's tradition of adopting a man of merit from outside the immediate family, and as events turned out, it was the emperor's worst decision.

Marcus Aurelius continued the conscientious and careful administration of his four predecessors, and despite the ruinous war he left his successor an adequately filled *fiscus*. Despite his adherence to stoic philosophy, he paid tribute to the ancient state cults, and showed great tolerance to all the new religions emanating from eastern mysteries, with the exception of the Christians. Although official policy avoided persecution, their usefulness as scapegoats for local crises made Christians subject to abuse. During the worst depredations of the plague in 167, violence erupted in many parts of the empire and in Lugdunum the atrocities amounted to a pogrom. Tertullian

Faustina the Younger, Marcus Aurelius's wife for 30 years, was tainted by promiscuity and political intrigue.

Coins of Marcus Aurelius and Faustina the Younger.

later called Marcus Aurelius a 'friend of Christianity', and indeed he wasn't the cause of the persecution, but neither did he do anything to prevent what is the worst stain on his principate.

His unhappy marriage to Faustina the Younger endured for thirty years, during which time she bore him thirteen children. The two with the most bearing on history were the daughter Annia Aurelia Galeria Lucilla, who first married Lucius Verus and then Tiberius Claudius Pompeianus, and the son Commodus. Faustina was accused of employing poison and of murdering people, as well as being free with her favours to gladiators, sailors and also men of rank, particularly Gaius Avidius Cassius, with whom she was suspected of conspiring to bring Marcus down in 175. And yet Marcus trusted Faustina and defended her reputation. She died in the same year as a result of an accident while staying with him in camp in southern Cappadocia.

Given the nature of his difficult reign, Marcus Aurelius left few monuments behind. The best known, which stands today in Rome's Piazza Colonna, is a column similar to Trajan's, with spiral reliefs depicting Marcus's Marcomanni campaigns of 172–75. Begun in the last half of the decade, Septimius Severus completed it in 193. There are important differences between the two columns. Whereas Trajan's imagery is an aggrandisement of conquest, Marcus's shows the defence of an empire under threat. Three arches commemorating his military achievements were lost, although eight reliefs on the Arch of Constantine came from one of them, and three other reliefs displayed today in the Capitoline Museum came from another.

No bricks and mortar, then, but Marcus Aurelius is best remembered from his writing. In his *Meditations* he used Greek to set down his innermost thoughts in a simple manner, as they occurred to him and without literary artifice, and they are in extraordinary contrast to the continual slaughter in the muddy northern forests. They were written in breaks between the almost continual fighting on the frontier, probably at his alternate headquarters of Vindobona (Vienna) and Sirmium (Mitrovica), and it was at the latter where he died of natural causes on 17 March 180 at the age of 59 – the last emperor of the period now known as Pax Romana.

## Commodus  Lucius Aelius Aurelius Commodus /
## Marcus Aurelius Commodus Antoninus
[ Caesar 166; joint 177–17/3/180; sole to 31/12/192 ]

Commodus succeeded to all power without opposition, the first emperor since Domitian to follow his natural father. History praises Marcus Aurelius, 'that philosophic monarch', as Gibbon called him, except in elevating his son he bequeathed Rome its worst tyrant since Gaius Caligula, arguably one of the worst ever. Commodus, the first prince to be born to a ruling emperor, came into the world at Lanuvium on 31 August 161. The tenth of Marcus's children, he was named Commodus after the co-emperor Lucius Ceionius Commodus [Verus]. Styled Caesar at the age of five, Marcus groomed Commodus to succeed and he became co-Augustus in 177, after the revolt of Avidius Cassius. He was an innocent looking, handsome adolescent with curly blond hair. But he allowed himself to be easily influenced by others, especially if they possessed a poor character, which seemed to appeal to Commodus.

Although the eighteen-year-old emperor promised the army he would prosecute the war against the Germans, Commodus had no intention of doing so. He hankered after the luxuries of Rome and his favourite pastime: gladiatorial combat. Treaties with the Quadi and Marcomanni were rapidly concluded, which the soldiers ever after viewed as a betrayal of his father's name. However, the move proved successful in pacifying the barbarians, and obliged them to accept various conditions in return for allowing some further German settlement in those areas Marcus Aurelius had offered in 169–70. On 22 October 180, Commodus arrived in Rome to a hero's welcome, after which his father's ashes were interred in Hadrian's mausoleum. Coins issued in 181 display the youthful, triumphant warrior bringing the booty of victory to the citizens of Rome. But tensions between emperor and senate sprang from his special taxation to fund the splendid games he held and the massive hand-out to the mob that went with them. Nothing recommends the relatively long and inglorious reign; Commodus built nothing and didn't concern himself with the empire's administration, leaving that in the hands of his various successive praetorian prefects.

**THE ANTONINES WERE TRADITIONALLY ASSOCIATED** with the cult of Hercules and, as statues of him attest, Commodus began to dress like the god, wearing lion skins and carrying the deity's famous club. And it was not long before he insisted on being worshipped as Hercules. He changed the names of the months to accord with all his titles: Lucius, Aelius, Aurelius, Commodus, Augustus, Herculeus, Romanus, Exsuperatorius, Amazonius, Invictus, Felix, Pius. If a further sign of his unbalance were required, his continual public appearances in the arena supplied it. Commodus defeated the most skilled gladiators and killed ferocious beasts. The sham must have been obvious – his human opponents were only supplied with wooden swords… and some limped, as did many of the drugged animals. The first plot occurred as early as 182, when a senator named Quintianus attempted to stab Commodus and was overpowered by praetorian guards. Those implicated included the emperor's older sister Lucilla and her cousin the ex-consul Marcus Ummidius Quadratus. The men, including one of the prefects, Tarrutenius Paternus, were executed and Lucilla banished to Capri, where shortly after she too was put to death. The remaining prefect, Sextus Tigidius Perennis, was left in sole charge of the empire, the first man in possession of such power since Sejanus during the reign of Tiberius.

While Commodus concerned himself with the complexities of running his palace harem, comprised of 300 each of young girls and boys, and organising ever more bizarre gladiatorial games, Perennis handled all the

Commodus was an attractive youth and Caesar, but as an adult his identification with the god Hercules became a mania as the emperor demanded appropriate worship.

Bruttia Crispina married Commodus when he was 16. Ten years later he banished her and she was later executed.

Annia Aurelia Galeria Lucilla (*bust and coin above*), whose first husband had been Lucius Verus, had a stormy relationship with her brother Commodus (*coin right*).

affairs of state, but the court's essential instability continually undermined him – and those who followed. The egregious chamberlain Cleander manoeuvred Perennis to his execution in 185 and took his place. In 190 Cleander sold twenty-five consulships, making a complete mockery of the venerable institution, and in the same year the mob tore him limb from limb during food riots. A string of short-lived prefects followed until in 192 the last, Quintus Aemilius Laetus, determined to end the mad emperor's reign. Commodus announced in November his intention to rename Rome Colonia Commodiana and become consul in the New Year.

Laetus, an *eques* from Hadrumetum (Sousse) in the province of Africa, was careful in his choice of conspirators, first placing fellow African provincials in key posts about the empire: the able generals Septimius Severus and Clodius Albinus were given the governorships of Pannonia Superior and Britain respectively. Another ally, Pescennius Niger, was sent to take charge of Syria. The senatorial order loathed Commodus and even within the palace courtiers terrified of the unhinged emperor were willing to join, among them the chamberlain Eclectus and Commodus's favourite concubine Marcia. And after some debate the future emperor was selected: the defender of Raetia and now urban prefect, Publius Helvius Pertinax.

The assassination called for Marcia to administer a fatal dose of poison, which she did on the evening of 31 December 192. Commodus became ill and vomited up his food… and the toxin. But the conspirators had a reserve plan. Narcissus, a courtier and the emperor's sparring partner, overpowered and strangled the nauseated Commodus in his bed on the same night. The body was later taken out, cremated and the ashes ignominiously buried in a civic cemetery. It seems inconceivable that the insanity of Commodus should have been allowed to bring the Roman empire almost to its knees, but it is a reflection on the one hand of the weakness of a debilitated senate and the abhorrent behaviour of the praetorian guards on the other. Pampered by the emperor, who invited gangs of the younger soldiers to his pansexual orgies and lavish feasts, and continually in receipt of extra donatives, the guard had descended into little better than enforcers for a regime of thuggery. The death of Commodus brought the Antonine dynasty to a close. It also spelled the end of the period of constitutional principates and heralded the long, weary fall of the Roman empire into despotic autocracy.

# SIX
# Emperors of the Civil War

[AD 192–197]

## Pertinax  Publius Helvius Pertinax
[ 1/1/193–28/3/193 ]

In many respects, the elevation of Pertinax resembles that of Nerva: in his sixties, relatively old to be emperor; chosen by conspirators to replace an assassinated despot; respected by senators for his commendable service to the empire. He even revived the Republican title of *princeps senatus* (first man of the senate) with which to style himself, in deference to the aristocracy, with whom he had little in common, for he was the son of a freedman, Helvius Successus, who had prospered in the clothing trade. Pertinax hailed from the Ligurian town of Alba Pompeia (Alba), some 56km southeast of Augusta Taurinorum (Turin), where he was born

The rule of Publius Helvius Pertinax was speedily terminated by praetorian guards angry at the exacting disciplinarian's economies.

on 1 August 126. Pertinax studied in Rome and became a teacher of grammar. At some point in his mid-thirties, he sought a more financially rewarding career in the army and served in Syria, Britain, Mesopotamia and against the German invasions of Raetia in 166–68. Humble Pertinax married into the aristocracy, gaining the daughter of the ex-consul Flavius Sulpicianus. In the early 170s he was adlected into the senate and named consular colleague in 175 to the man who would succeed him, Didius Julianus.

At dawn on the first of January 193 Laetus awakened Pertinax escorted him to the *castra praetoria*, where the prefect promised a donative of 12,000 sesterces for each man. This sum persuaded the reluctant guards to acclaim Pertinax. The senate gave him a standing ovation – occasioned by sheer relief – and declared Commodus *damnatio memoriae*. Pertinax immediately set about restoring the shattered government. He reduced Commodus's exorbitant taxes and reimplemented the suspended *alimenta*. The senate was allowed to participate fully again in political life – all good omens to inaugurate another reign like that of Nerva. But it was all an illusion. An exacting disciplinarian and inflexible once he'd decided on a course of action, Pertinax dealt firmly with the defiant, almost unmanageable, praetorian guard by taking a position similar to Galba's – he refused to pay the donative promised by Laetus. Like Galba's, it was an unwise stand to take. His argument that stringent economies were necessary failed to impress. When violence threatened, Pertinax backed down and paid up with money raised from selling off Commodus's chattels. The gift silenced the rumblings, but only for a short time. When Pertinax pressed on with revisions of praetorian privileges, the guards' anger boiled over.

Pertinax was in Ostia overseeing the regulation of the interrupted grain supply when news reached him that a planned coup would place the consul Sosius Falco on the throne. Pertinax hurriedly rode back to the city to defuse the situation. By now even Laetus was unable to hold back the soldiers under his command, and a few days later on 28 March 193 a gang of praetorians entered the palace. With a bravado typical of him, Pertinax confronted the troops and was killed in the unequal fight. His reign had lasted just eighty-seven days.

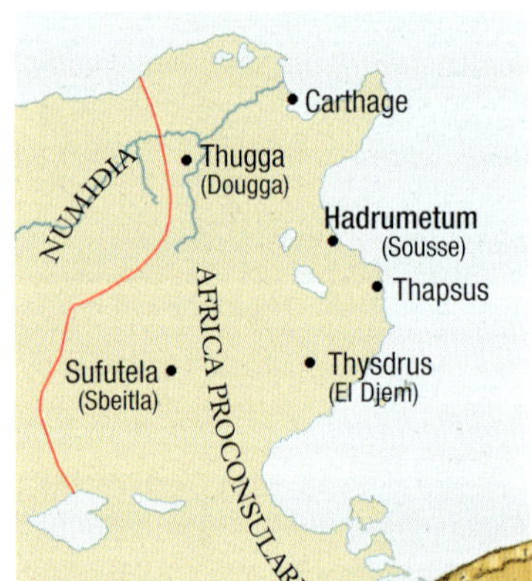

Didius Julianus 'reigned' for 66 days after buying the empire in an auction.

Coins depicting Manlia Scantilla, wife of Didius Julianus, and their daughter Didia Clara. They survived his fall thanks to the celemency of Septimius Severus.

## Didianus Julianus  Marcus Didius Severus Julianus
[ 29/3/193–1/6/193 ]

The grandson on his mother's side of Hadrian's celebrated jurist Salvius Julianus, Didius Julianus was born at Mediolanum (Milan) at some point between 133–37. He was typical of the provincial elite who had enjoyed greater social status during the reigns of Trajan and the Antonines. His father was of a provincial Italian family, while his mother originally came from Hadrumetum. The connection to his celebrated grandfather meant that Didius Julianus was educated in the household of Domitia Lucilla, mother of the emperor Marcus Aurelius, and enjoyed both her patronage and that of her son. On the face of it, Julianus had a distinguished military and political career in Asia, Africa and on the Rhine. He was a consul with Pertinax in 175 at the traditional age of forty-two, and proconsul of Dalmatia in 176. By 180 he was back on the Rhine, governing Germania Inferior, followed by proconsular spells in Bithynia and, in 189, Africa again before his return to Rome.

It appears to be an illustrious career and yet in almost all cases Julianus was placed in positions of control where nothing of vital military importance was occurring. Was his military capability in doubt? And the prestige he acquired from his offices did not translate into respect from his fellow senators. He had the reputation of a sensualist and spendthrift. This was not the stuff of leadership; and events revealed him to be an opportunist.

With no clear succession, the man in charge during an *interregnum* was the urban prefect, Flavius Sulpicianus, who was also Pertinax's father-in-law. But aware that he needed praetorian support, Sulpicianus hurried to the *castra praetoria* where the guards had barricaded themselves against mob revenge for the murder of Pertinax. There, Sulpicianus promised the soldiers a large donative if they would proclaim him emperor. The praetorians were unconvinced and Didius Julianus seized his opportunity. Almost tripping over his toga with indecent haste he rushed to the camp and claimed that, as close career colleagues, he had been Pertinax's choice. He made an improved offer over his rival's and an ignoble auction began. Naturally, the praetorians wanted as much as they could get, and egged on the two men. Each continued to up his bid until Sulpicianus reached the figure of 20,000 sesterces per man, equivalent to about eight years' pay. Didius Julianus went for broke and offered 25,000. At this last bid, the praetorians agreed and the Roman empire was sold. The camp gates opened to welcome Didius Julianus and the soldiers invested him with the purple. For Julianus, the shameful deal sealed his bitter end.

In his only effective act, he put Laetus to the sword. The senate confirmed his elevation, but the mob erupted, screaming for Pescennius Niger, governor of Syria, to return to Rome as their ruler. All classes of the city were fed up with the situation and each faction championed its own strongman. Popular Niger was not the only favourite, there were also Clodius Albinus in Britain and Septimius Severus in Pannonia Superior. Severus – the nearest of the three – was in command of two highly trained legions, with a call on the two stationed in Pannonia Inferior. At Carnuntum on 9 April 193, the Pannonian troops declared for their general only twelve days after Pertinax's death.

Didius Julianus attempted to negotiate as Severus marched unopposed into Italy, but his envoys kept defecting. At the end of May

Severan forces reached Interamna (Terni), 80km north of Rome. On the last day of May the praetorians switched allegiance. The senate promptly revoked Didius Julianus's imperial powers and recognised Severus as emperor. Didius Julianus was put to death the following day. His reign had lasted sixty-six days. Severus entered Rome on 9 June 193. The civil war, however, was not over. A few weeks prior to these events Clodius Albinus had assumed the purple in Britain, as had Pescennius Niger in Syria.

## Pescennius Niger  Gaius Pescennius Niger Justus

[ April 193–autumn 194 ]

Pescennius Niger was born into a central Italian equestrian family at some point between 135–40, but only held the rank of centurion in his early military career in Egypt. Commodus adlected him into the rank of praetorian senators, and he campaigned successfully alongside Clodius Albinus against the Sarmatae in Dacia in 183. His reward for good service was a consulship in the late 180s and again in 190. In the following year he was sent by Laetus to govern Syria. Niger was tall although quite fat and, it was said, if the wind was in the right direction his troops could hear his booming voice from 1,500m away. His military reputation and stern discipline earned him his men's respect. The only other known personal details are that he was over-fond of wine and that he only ever had sex with children.

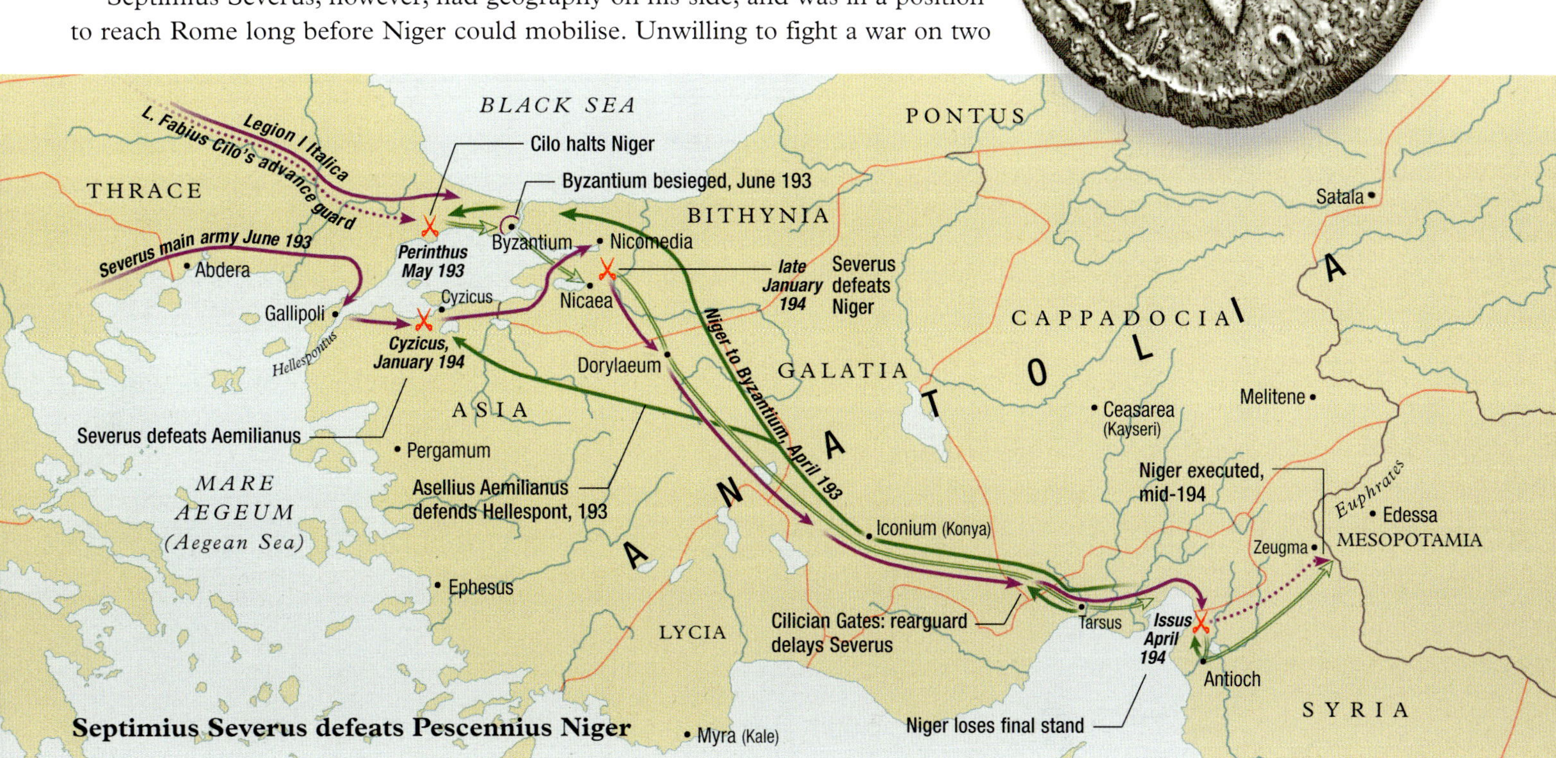

Many of the Roman mob backed Pescennius Niger's bid for the purple.

His faction in Rome was the largest of the three contenders and, based in Antioch, dispatches informed Niger that rioters in the Circus Maximus had shouted for him to seize the throne. He enjoyed several advantages: the equestrian governor of Egypt approved of his cause; Asellius Aemilianus, Asia's governor, was a close ally; and crucially Byzantium offered him open gates, giving the Nigerians a toehold on the European coast. Within days all nine of the eastern legions proclaimed him emperor, which gave him the strongest force of all – at least on paper. Further, he was encouraged in his cause by a message from Vologeses V of Parthia, offering his (doubtless dubious) support.

Septimius Severus, however, had geography on his side, and was in a position to reach Rome long before Niger could mobilise. Unwilling to fight a war on two

Vologeses V, king of Parthia, prommised support to Niger.

fronts, Severus offered his other rival, Albinus in Britain, the title of Caesar, which effectively pronounced him heir to the throne. Having conciliated the potential western threat, Severus set out to deal with the more dangerous contender to his east. Niger's strategy was to occupy Byzantium and then advance to Perinthus, which straddled the two main roads from Europe to Asia, but the Severan legate Lucius Fabius Cilo beat him to it. His Moesian legions denied Niger entry to Perinthus early in May 193, who then fell back on Byzantium. A siege of the city began at the start of June.

Severus reached Perinthus towards the end of the summer. With besieged Byzantium guarding the Bosphorus crossing, Severus crossed the Hellespont at Gallipoli. The first battle took place at Cyzicus early in January 194, where the Severans proved superior to those under the command of the Asian governor Aemilianus. With Severan forces on the Asian coast, Byzantium was vulnerable and no longer a tenable stronghold. Niger retreated to Nicaea, while Severus slipped behind him to occupy Nicomedia, effectively blocking the way back to Byzantium. On the plain near Nicaea Niger's troops suffered a severe defeat – only nightfall saved them from utter destruction. In disarray, the remnant fled across Anatolia to Antioch. Here, Niger learned that Legion II Traiana had defected to Severus and turned Egypt over to the Severan cause. In quick order, the other eastern governors also switched sides and Niger even faced revolts in Syria. When Severus pushed through the Taurus barrier to threaten Antioch, Niger marched out with the Syrian army and again suffered a debacle at Issus. Abandoned by all but his most loyal men, Niger fled to Parthia, but never got there: short of the Euphrates he was captured and killed in mid-194. His decapitated head was parcelled up and carried to Severus.

Severus divided Syria into two provinces, Syria Coele and Phoenicia. His purpose was to prevent any future eastern governor gaining military power as great as Niger's. Having personally confiscated the estates of Niger's adherents, Septimius Severus made himself extremely wealthy, a useful adjunct to his victory. Vologeses was spared an immediate Roman conquest because Severus still had obstinate Byzantium to knock out and, more vitally, treasonable correspondence between Clodius Albinus and the senate had been detected. Severus declared Clodius Albinus a public enemy and prepared to relocate the European legions to Viminacium on the Danube in preparation for a war in the west.

## Clodius Albinus  Decimus Clodius (Septimius) Albinus
[ April 193–19/2/197 ]

Coin of Clodius Albinus, claiming the title Imperator Caesar.

Clodius Albinus had the most prestigious pedigree of all three contenders. His was a branch of one of Rome's most ancient families. By virtue of an earlier arrival in Rome, the Claudians became patrician, while their tardier cousins the Clodians missed the opportunity to reach the noblest level of the ancient aristocracy and only achieved plebeian rank. They were, however, quick to seize aristocratic status when wealthy plebeians were permitted to become senatorial and consular in the mid-fourth century BC. Albinus was born at some point between 140–50 into a wealthy family of Hadrumetum. He enjoyed writing erotic stories, was a womaniser, a stern disciplinarian and ruthless commander. After a successful early military career, he entered the senate during the reign of Marcus Aurelius. Later, while governing Bithynia in 175, Clodius remained loyal to the emperor when the revolt of Avidius Cassius took place in Syria. In common with his rivals for the throne, he distinguished himself in the Illyrian campaigns early in Commodus's reign and served as a consul at some point in the mid-180s. In 189 he was made governor of Germania Inferior and, at the instigation of fellow-Hadrumetan Laetus, went to govern Britain in mid-192.

His three legions proclaimed him emperor in April 193, and he received the military support of the governors of Hispania Tarraconensis and Africa. However, when Severus offered to adopt Clodius and make him Caesar in preference to his own two sons, the deal was accepted. This is confirmed by an issue of coins in 194 portraying him as IMP.CÆSAR.D.CLODIVS.SEPTIMIVS.ALBINVS. It's unlikely that Clodius trusted this arrangement, and indeed the adoption was merely a ruse to keep him out of the way until the defeat of Pescennius Niger. Early in 195 Severus named his seven-year-old son Caracalla as Caesar and his heir. While this was a sound means of securing the succession, it was also a calculated insult designed to draw Clodius away from the safety of his island fortress and force a battle where Severus thought he could win it: in Gaul.

Clodius took the bait, crossing to Gaul in 196 with some 40,000 troops, and marched to Lugdunum (Lyons) to set up a headquarters there. Clodius faced an opponent who could draw on the overwhelming forces of the Illyrian legions, and – critically – the four German legions also declared for Severus. This forced Clodius to strike a tactical blow early in his campaign against the enemy closest to his lines of communication, commanded by the governor of Germania Inferior. They met near Augusta Treverorum and Clodius won, but insufficient resources prevented a follow up, and the province remained in the Severan camp. Septimius Severus and his army left Viminacium for Gaul late in October 196. Severus, who had learned of growing senatorial hostility to his cause, diverted to Rome with a detachment under Cilo and compelled the senators to declare Clodius Albinus a public enemy. He also appeased some tempers by showing clemency towards those senators who had supported Niger. He left for Gaul towards the end of the year.

Clodius Albinus's fine pedigree was no match for the cunning viciousness of Septimius Severus.

The German delaying tactics had robbed Clodius of the initiative in invading Italy because the Severans had used the time to block the Alpine passes. But if Severus thought it would be an easy war, he underestimated his rival. Morale among the British and Spanish troops was good after their recent victory in the north, and although the Gallic provinces had few soldiers, many of the *municipia* backed Clodius and provided him with a large auxiliary force. The first battle took place at Tinurtium (Tournos) on the Arar (Saône), 105km north of Lugdunum and ended in a draw. Clodius retired to Lugdunum.

According to the ancient sources the battle of Lugdunum, which was fought over two days from 19 February 197, was one of the fiercest ever between Roman adversaries. While both camps possessed large numbers of men, the claim of Dio Cassisus that each side fielded a 150,000 men should probably be discounted; perhaps only a third of that figure actually took part. In the early stages of the bitter fighting the Severans were pushed into retreat, but in the end the superb discipline of the war-hardened Illyrian legionaries told and the Clodian legions were broken, leaving the battlefield strewn with thousands of bodies. Clodius became trapped in a house beside the Rhône, where he committed suicide, leaving the Roman empire in the undisputed hands of Septimius Severus.

Clodius Albinus might have made a good emperor. He had the breeding and qualities of an administrator-aristocrat, enjoyed the patronage of the senate and showed a flair for soldiering. His misfortune was to be pitched against a rival who was his superior in cunning, daring and sheer viciousness in battle. His death finally brought to an end a period of instability in the empire that rivalled that of the civil war that brought Vespasian to the throne in 70. This one, however, had dragged on for several years, done immense damage to the fabric of Roman society and weakened the frontiers at a time when barbarian enemies surrounded it.

# SEVEN
# The Severan Dynasty

[AD 193–235]

### Septimius Severus  Lucius Septimius Severus
[ 9/4/193–4/2/211 ]

Dynasty founder Septimius Severus introduced sweeping changes to the army which made it more democratic.

Julia Domna, the second wife of Septimius Severus, remained a power for a quarter of a century.

Septimius Severus showed no sentiment to the memory of his rivals or their supporters. Byzantium – which held out, even after Niger's head was paraded before the walls as an example to its citizens of what to expect for their continued defiance – capitulated after eighteen months in 196, the defenders put to the sword, the city razed and its walls pulled down. Niger's family, clients, supporters and cities that had aided his cause were punished without mercy. As for Clodius Albinus, Severus laid his corpse out on the ground and trampled it mounted on his horse before beheading the body. The head went to Rome as a warning to any supporters and the corpse was tossed in the Rhône, along with the bodies of his executed wife and sons.

His unbridled cruelty earned Severus the quietly whispered nickname of the 'Punic Sulla', a reference to his African origin and the notorious dictator of the late Republic. But his vicious acts should not be likened to the opportunistic violence of a coward like Commodus. As Dio Cassius wrote: 'He ruled with vigour and, when he found it useful, a calculated cruelty.' Septimius Severus was born 11 April 146 in Leptis Magna, on the coast of Tripolitania, a region of the province of Africa. Wealthy since Punic times, Leptis Magna was an important commercial centre by the end of the second century. His father Publius Septimius Geta, most likely of Punic descent, was an equestrian living in Rome with consular cousins. Depending on the sources, Severus was educated either well in Latin and Greek literature, or he was not very well educated at all. He was small of stature but powerfully built, although in old age he became very weak and ridden with gout.

Severus went to Rome after his eighteenth birthday and received the invaluable help of his cousins, who arranged his entry into the senate and gained him the attention of Marcus Aurelius. Surprisingly, for the warrior-emperor he would become, Severus was never a military tribune and yet swiftly became a quaestor with a posting to Sardinia where frankly there was little to do. Next, he took the post of legate to the proconsul of Africa, before returning to Rome where, in 175, he married Paccia Marciana, who seems also to have been of African origin. The marriage, which remained childless, lasted a decade until her death. In that same year, aged only twenty-nine, Marcus Aurelius adlected him into the senate. Severus's career continued to flourish as the empire passed to Commodus. He served as governor in Hispania Tarraconensis, commanded Legion IV Scythica in Syria and held the governorships of Gallia Lugdunensis, Sicily and Pannonia Superior.

While at Lugdunum in 187, the now-widowed Severus married Julia Domna, a woman from a prominent family of Emesa in Syria. Being skilled in astrology, Severus investigated the horoscopes of potential brides from every corner of the empire; Julia Domna's forecast claimed she would marry a king. Severus married her as soon as she set foot in Gaul and in a trice Julia made him the father of two sons, Bassianus (Caracalla) in April of 188, and Geta in May 189. Severus served as a consul for the first time in 190, but since this was the year Cleander sold twenty-five consulships the office's prestige was hardly significant. His appointment by Laetus to command the Pannonian legions was, however, and placed Septimius Severus in the advantageous position in which he found himself in 193.

The large Clodian party in Rome trembled at his return. Coolly breaking the senatorial oath he had given four years before on his first triumphal entry to the city, countless numbers were put to death, consulars, those of praetorian rank, nobles and many distinguished women; and their property confiscated to swell the *fiscus*. But once the cleansing was finished, a degree of peace descended as Severus turned his vengeance on the Parthian empire. He needed no pretext – Vologeses' lukewarm support for Pescennius Niger more than provided the *casus belli*. In 197–99, in a swift repeat of the campaigns of 115–17 and 163–66, the Roman army captured the Parthian capital of Ctesiphon and reasserted the claim to Mesopotamia. Of the estimated 100,000 inhabitants of Ctesiphon, all the men were killed and the women and children sold into slavery. The already tottering state of Parthia was dealt a blow from which it never recovered – as Rome later had reason to regret. On 28 January 198 Severus added the victorious title Parthicus Maximus to his nomenclature and elevated his sons: Caracalla to co-Augustus and Geta to the rank of Caesar.

The companion of his efforts was one of the two praetorian prefects, another native of Leptis Magna, perhaps even a distant relative, named Gaius Fulvius Plautianus. By the time the imperial cortège returned to Rome in 202, Plautianus was the emperor's closest confidant and advisor, as well as being the sole prefect, having arranged from a distance the murder of his colleague. The comparison between Plautianus and Sejanus is telling, but Plautianus achieved a further status than Tiberius allowed Sejanus, by marrying his daughter Plautilla to the heir-apparent Caracalla. In the following year lavish games celebrated Severus's *decennalia*, after which the imperial family visited Leptis Magna, where Severus embellished his home city with splendid new civic monuments.

It seems strange that such an extremely purposeful man as Severus should leave so much of the administraton to Plautianus, who abused his position of power in numerous ways. But the emperor's Syrian wife Julia Domna, an intelligent woman who surrounded herself with a retinue of scholars and writers, disliked and mistrusted him. By 204, unhappily married to Plautilla, Caracalla, had come to loathe his father-in-law. Severus was also tiring of Plautianus's ostentation, which at times seemed to surpass that of his own. Matters came to a head in January 205 when Caracalla informed Severus that Plautianus was plotting to have them both assassinated. Whether true or a fabrication, Severus acted swiftly and Plautianus was taken and executed. His children were exiled, and Caracalla divorced Plautilla, gleefully banishing her to the Lipari Islands.

**ONE OF THE TWO MEN SEVERUS APPOINTED** to the vacant praetorian posts points to an admirable aspect of his interests, for he was the eminent jurist Aemilius Papinianus (Papinian). A conscientious judge, Severus appreciated legal reasoning and advanced the development of Hadrian's codification of the law. However, his position as ultimate appeals judge had brought an ever-increasing legal workload to his desk, and he came to rely heavily on his *concilium*, which was largely comprised of experienced jurists. His reign ushered in the golden age of Roman jurisprudence, and his court employed the talents of the three greatest Roman lawyers: Domitius Ulpianus (Ulpian), Papinian, and Julius Paulus. All prolific writers, their works later formed the primary source for the sixth-century codification of Roman law by Justinian.

The impression given that Severus was one of the outstanding imperial builders, is misleading. In the main his reputation rests on the restoration of a very large number of ancient buildings – on which he had

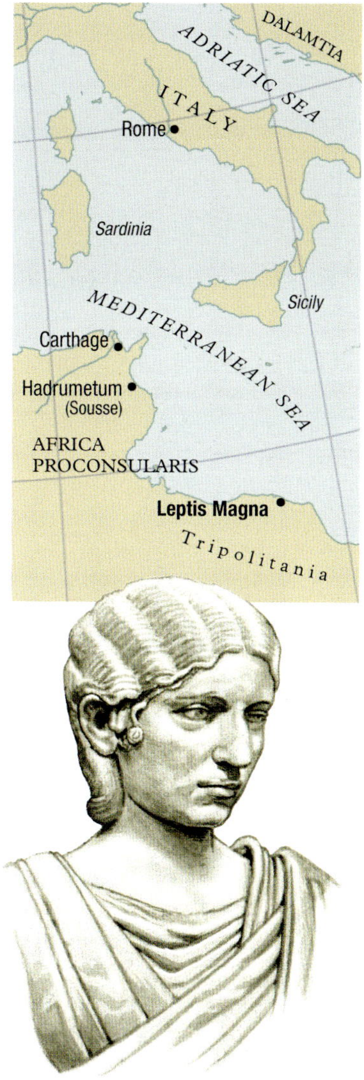


The innocent victim: Plautilla, the praetorian prefect's daughter, married Caracalla, who loathed her. When her father fell from grace, so did she.

This coin features Septimius Severus on the obverse and Julia Domna with their two sons Caracalla and Geta on the reverse.

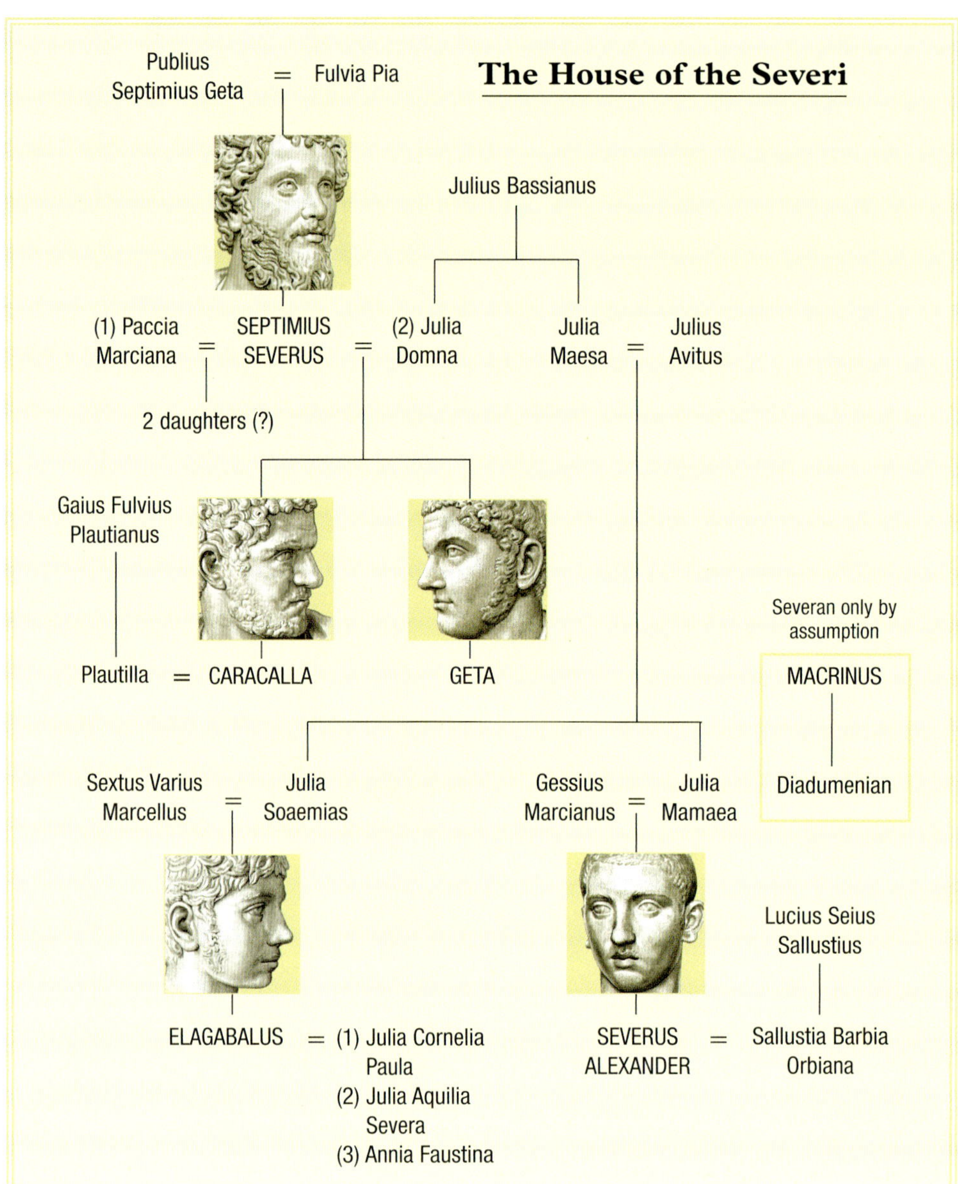

A denarius of Geta struck when he was about four styling him as PONT.PRINC. IVVENTVTIS (pontifex, princeps iuventutis – priest and junior prince).

his own name inscribed, as though he'd erected them. However, he did rebuild Byzantium, Caracalla having persuaded him of its strategic importance, on a larger scale and surrounded with a circuit of defensive walls. At 400 by 118m the Hippodrome was one of the largest monuments erected by Septimius Severus. It occupied the area of what is now the park in front of the Blue Mosque and had an estimated capacity of a 100,000 spectators. His most famous monument is his own arch in the Forum. Dedicated in 203, the year of his *decennalia*, it departed from the customary single accessible arch by having three openings set on a high plinth above the Republican level of the Forum. In its original state statues of the emperor and his two sons standing in a chariot, flanked by further equestrian statues, crowned the top. On the Palatine Severus made additions to the imperial palace which enclosed the eastern end of the hill above the Circus Maximus, and he constructed the massive cliff-like loggia that rationalised parts of Tiberius's palace and the additions made by Domitian above the Forum.

Severus was responsible for substantial reforms of the financial administration. There were still two treasuries: the imperial *fiscus* and the *patrimonium principis* which consisted of the many domains administered by the emperor's procurators. Severus now diverted the revenues of the imperial and senatorial provinces as well as the *patrimonium* to his *fiscus*. The initial funds received from the confiscated estates of Niger, Clodius and their supporters went into a new treasury called the *res privata principis*. Since this was then to receive any new 'acquisitions' made by the emperor, it rapidly grew and outstripped the old *patrimonium*.

Severus also reorganised the army. To non-commissioned officers, and even rankers, he opened up entry to the officer-elite, previously the exclusive preserve of the aristocracy and *equites*. He increased soldiers' pay by a half, and – in recognition of the extensions of the service periods made by previous emperors – they were allowed to marry (or cohabit under the common-law of *contubernium*). He also raised three new legions, I, II and III Parthica, stationing II Parthica just outside Rome at Albanum (Albano). This – the first imperial legion stationed in Italy – formed a central reserve which could be sent quickly to wherever it was most needed. These additions brought the Roman army's strength to thirty-three legions. However, the burden of paying a much larger number of troops their better salaries fell on the taxpayers, a development that eventually led to increased hardship, inflation and, throughout many areas of the empire, virtually wiped out the middle class of Roman society.

The order Severus imposed on his subjects failed to extend to his adolescent sons, whose sibling rivalry sometimes resulted in physical injury. The elevation of Geta to co-Augustus alongside Caracalla heightened their mutual antipathy. Convinced that strict military discipline would instill some sort of imperial responsibility in his squabbling sons, despite his deteriorating health, the sixty-two-year-old warrior-emperor took them with him to Britain in 208. Events in the province had taken a nasty turn. After Clodius's depletion of troops in 197, the Caledonian Maiatae tribe had taken advantage and overrun a great part of northern Britain. Hadrian's Wall was badly damaged, and military and urban centres as far south as Deva (Chester) and Eburacum (York) were overthrown. The governor, Virius Lupus, eventually restored some order by bribing the Maiatae to return home, but Severus wanted a permanent solution.

The emperor, his sons and the admirable prefect Papinian, arrived with reinforcements and established themselves at Eburacum, from where Severus planned to take the war into Caledonia. As Geta took over the province's adminstration, Severus and Caracalla led the army. In 209 and 210, the Romans penetrated deep into the north. But there was to be no repeat of Agricola's great victory of Mons Graupius. The tribes, refusing open battle, adopted guerrilla tactics instead, harassing the Romans at every opportunity. Losses were tremendous; Dio Cassius put the figure at no less than 50,000. In 211 the Maiatae revolted again and Severus ordered the massacre of every tribe member, but he was unable to lead the expedition. Weak from illness and fearing his time was near, Septimius Severus remained at Eburacum, where he died on 4 February 211. His final words to Caracalla and Geta were reported as being: 'Agree with each other, give money to the soldiers, and scorn all other men.' They took notice of the last two points, but ignored the first.

## Geta  Lucius Publius Septimius Geta
[ joint 4/2/211–February 212 ]

Named after his paternal grandfather, Geta was the younger son by eleven months, but it is expedient to recount his history first simply because he lasted the least time. Born on 27 May 189 at Mediolanum, where Severus was resident in between his governorships of Gallia Lugdunensis and Sicily, during Commodus's reign, history reveals little about his upbringing and his early elevation to high state rendered the *cursus honorum* irrelevant.

Geta claimed an equal authority with Caracalla when Severus died. The two were barely on speaking terms during the return journey to Rome from Britain. Once in

Two busts of Geta show him as a boy of about nine and the young prince who found favour with the army.

Obverse of a coin depicting Geta as GETA PIVS AVGVSTVS BRITANNICVS, issued shortly after the campaign in Britain of 211.

Coin portrait of Caracalla as the young Caesar.

Busts of Caracalla as a young boy and the emperor who believed he was Alexander the Great.

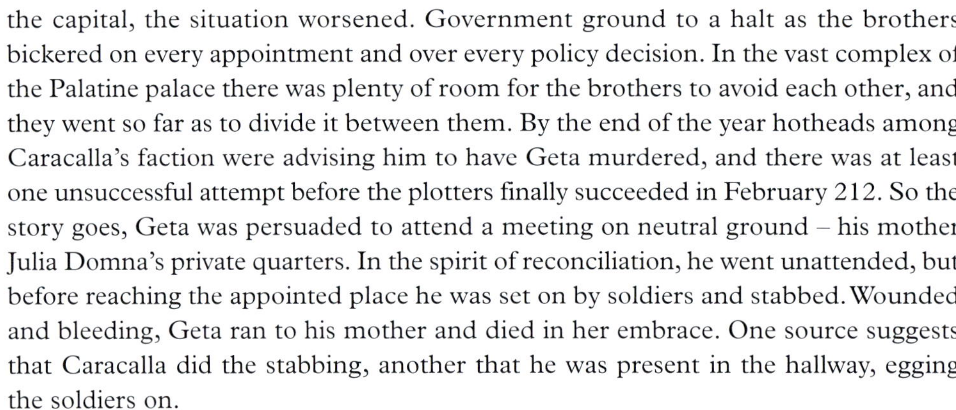

the capital, the situation worsened. Government ground to a halt as the brothers bickered on every appointment and over every policy decision. In the vast complex of the Palatine palace there was plenty of room for the brothers to avoid each other, and they went so far as to divide it between them. By the end of the year hotheads among Caracalla's faction were advising him to have Geta murdered, and there was at least one unsuccessful attempt before the plotters finally succeeded in February 212. So the story goes, Geta was persuaded to attend a meeting on neutral ground – his mother Julia Domna's private quarters. In the spirit of reconciliation, he went unattended, but before reaching the appointed place he was set on by soldiers and stabbed. Wounded and bleeding, Geta ran to his mother and died in her embrace. One source suggests that Caracalla did the stabbing, another that he was present in the hallway, egging the soldiers on.

Caracalla claimed the murder came in response to a plot, and Geta's death started a wholesale slaughter of his supporters. The looting and bloodshed lasted for many days, during which it is said as many as 20,000 died. While this is almost certainly an exaggeration promoted by those who hated Caracalla, he did go to extreme – if clumsy – lengths to expunge his brother's hated memory from the Severan monuments. There is an easily viewed example in the fourth line of the inscription on the Arch of Septimius Severus: Geta's name has been blotted out and replaced with additional honorifics for his murderer. Inevitably, popular feelings were strong for Geta and tradition soon idealised him as a kind and gentle prince, taken by treachery far too soon. This, too, is an exaggeration, since there is no evidence that Geta was substantially better than his brother. His ashes were buried in the palace gounds, where they remained until the accession of Elagabalus in 219, who transferred them to the Mausoleum of Hadrian to join those of his father and brother.

## Caracalla  Septimius Bassianus / Marcus Aurelius Antoninus
[ joint 4/2/211–February 212; sole to 8/4/217 ]

Caracalla was born in Lugdunum on 4 April 188. The name Bassianus commemorated the Syrian family of his mother Julia Domna. The nickname by which history knows him, Caracallus (Caracalla), which derived from his favourite dress, the *caracallus* or long, hooded Celtic cloak, was never used officially or in his presence. He was only ten when Severus elevated him to co-Augustus, and to establish the dynastic link Septimius Bassianus Caracalla became known as Marcus Aurelius Antoninus. Caracalla is another of Roman history's mysteries. He may have been mentally unstable, but was clearly no Commodus, despite an obsession with becoming an oriental conqueror like Alexander the Great. Christian writers cited his cruelty, immorality, avarice and treachery, but this is attributable to his indifference to the continuing plight of the expanding sect. On the credit side Caracalla was a brave soldier, reasonable administrator and did much to consolidate the empire's security. As indicated by his adoption of barbarian dress, he had little sympathy with traditional Roman virtues or customs.

Herodian claims that Caracalla, driven by impatience, begged the physicians to 'to do him [Severus] some mischief' as he lay on his sickbed in Eburacum. His first action as joint-emperor was to make peace with the Caledonians. The Romans abandoned the Antonine line and withdrew behind the greatly strengthened Hadrian's Wall. His second act was the removal of any of his father's supporters who might be expected to enforce Severus's dictat that his sons should rule jointly. The praetorian prefect Papinian was deposed and later executed, his old tutor and his father's counsellor were both put to death, as was his divorced wife Plautilla. Papinian was replaced by Marcus Opellius Macrinus, a native of Africa who had attracted the attention of Plautianus and risen to a high office in the imperial service. Geta might well have been a victim at this point but for the army's intervention; the soldiers viewed the younger brother with greater affection, since he more resembled his father in character and appearance. Thus the Severan brothers returned to Rome, discord, murder and massacre.

Once the terror of early 212 subsided, Caracalla undertook a series of administrative reforms. In keeping with his father's military policies, the troops received further increases in pay and in legal rights. His most significant innovation, however, was the granting of citizenship to every single free man within the bounds of the empire, thus completing a process begun by Claudius 150 years earlier. This *constitutio antoniniana* was designed to achieve greater standardisation in the increasingly bureaucratic Roman state, but cynics point to the increase in taxable persons as the real reason. At the same time, he handed jurisdictional rights over citizens to the provincial governors. This was consistent with Hadrian's reform that reduced the necessity in Italy of bringing appeals to Rome for hearing, but extended it to the empire as a whole. However, in the legal sphere Caracalla was content to leave court matters to others.

He also reintroduced the hated *delatores* and his secret agents exercised a tyranny over all classes, including the senatorial order, to which he showed only disdain. The *constitutio antoniniana* failed to bring in sufficient revenue to cover the increased costs of Caracalla's lavish spending on the army, so he followed Nero's precedent of debasing the currency, a practice that was to continue and bring the empire to the brink of bankruptcy within another forty years.

The money wasn't spent on architecture, since Caracalla began no concerted construction programme beyond some refurbishment of old Ostia's public buildings, with the exception of the magnificent *thermae antoninianae*, which today bear his name as the Baths of Caracalla. Into this grandiose project went greater sums than many of his more illustrious predecessors had spent on several buildings. When completed after his death, it accommodated up to 1,600 bathers in utmost luxury. The baths were sited amid gardens surrounding two libraries, two temples, a stadium built on the vast cistern and ranges of shops. The water was supplied by the Aqua Antoniniana, a newly built extension of the Aqua Marcia. Although the main building seems to have been completed just before Caracalla's death, Severus Alexander finished the complex.

After divorcing his wife Plautilla, Caracalla banished her to the Lipari Islands, off the north coast of Sicily, and then had her executed when he came to the throne.

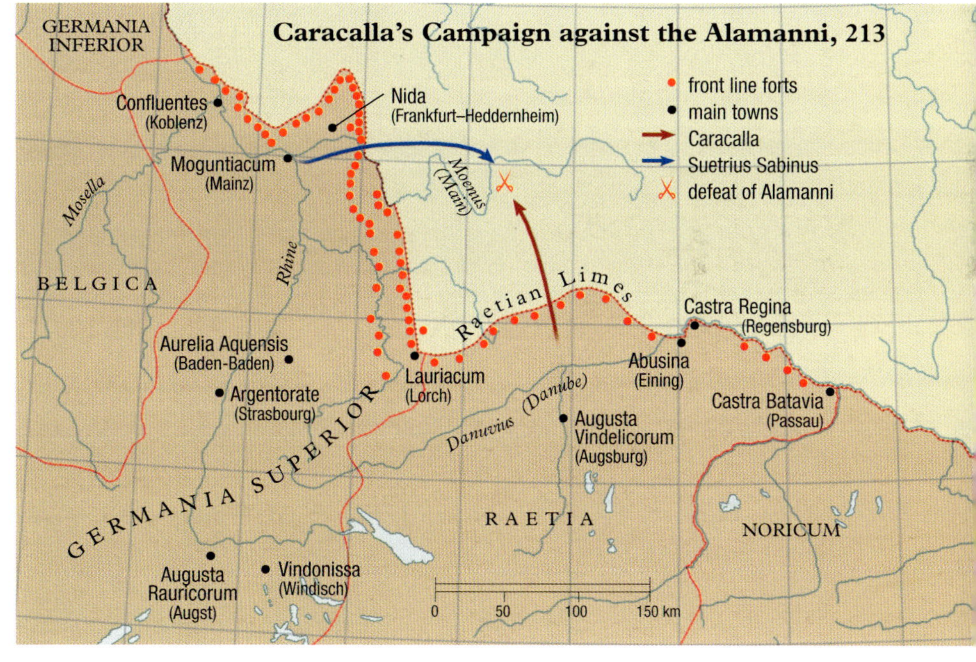


Caracalla spent little time in Rome. Early in 213 he left the city in the hands of his cousin by marriage, Sextus Varius Marcellus, as both urban and praetorian prefect, and set out for Gaul and a campaign in Germania Superior and Raetia. He was only to return to Rome once for a brief duration. The reason for military activity in the north was the arrival of a tribe new to the Romans, the Alamanni. Many of the Roman forts originally constructed of wood were remade of stone, and new ones built. On 11 August Caracalla crossed the Raetian frontier and Suetrius Sabinus, governor of Germania Superior, set out from Moguntiacum (Mainz) in a pincer movement. The strategy was a success, and the Alamanni were soundly defeated on the banks of the Main.

His next major campaign was designed to exploit a civil war between the brothers

A Parthian coin shows Vologeses VI, who lost out to Artabanus V, and a denarius of Caracalla depicts the emperor with brutal realism, suffering from the illness that plagued his last three years.

Vologeses VI and Artabanus V of Parthia. He proceeded to Edessa (Urfa) in 216 and annexed the buffer state of Osrhoene, then advanced into Parthia – where Artabanus had defeated Vologeses – sacking several fortresses. But on hearing that the enemy had retired to consolidate for a more effective resistance, Caracalla did likewise, returning to Edessa for the winter. The ancient sources mention the zeal with which he visited temples during his travels, but this hardly fits with his secular character – another factor better accounts for his apparent religiosity. During the Alamanni campaign, Caracalla had become afflicted with a chronic illness that no physician seemed able to cure. Wherever he went, he attended temples famous for their connection to healing. After subduing the Alamanni, he visited the shrine of a Celtic god called Grannus – Romanised as Apollo Grannus – at Aurelia Aquensis, which was renowned then, as it is today as Baden-Baden, for its healing waters. In Pergamum the emperor spent a whole night sleeping in the temple of Asclepius, the Greek god of healing. At Alexandria the exercise was repeated in the Serapeum, built by Ptolemy III in honour of the syncretic Graeco-Egyptian deity Isis-Serapis, who was associated with death and healing.

On 8 April 217 Caracalla set out from Edessa on a similar mission to visit Carrhae, where stood the ancient temple of Sin, the Syrian moon god. During a pause to evacuate his bowels, he was attacked and killed by a centurion called Julius Martialis. It seemed a fittingly ignoble end for a fratricide. After his divorce from Plautilla, Caracalla had been content to remain single, and there were no children. Whether he had made any plans for the succession is not known, but since he was only 29 when he died and certainly lacked any Antonine prudence, it's unlikely to have yet occurred to him. When the Syrian troops hailed the praetorian prefect Marcus Opellius Macrinus as the new emperor, the relief felt universally in Rome at the tyrant's death ensured that the senate eventually recognised the army's choice.

**Macrinus**  Marcus Opellius Severus Macrinus
[ 11/4/217–8/6/218 ]
**Diadumenian**  Marcus Opellius Diadumenianus Antoninus
[ Caesar 11/4/217, co-Augustus in 218 ]

Macrinus was not remotely related to the Severi, although for historical convenience he is usually included in the dynasty. He also had the unique distinction of being the first Roman emperor who didn't belong to the senatorial order and the only legitimate ruler of the undivided empire to never put foot in Rome during his reign. There is, however, little else to recommend him. Born in Caesarea, Mauretania Caesariensis, in about 165, Plautianus appointed him to imperial service. Macrinus rose rapidly through the ranks of the civil service to become comptroller of the *res privata principis*. At some point he married and a son, Diadumenianus, was born. When Caracalla replaced Papinian with Macrinus, he shared the command with Oclatinius Adventus, but the real power belonged to Macrinus since Adventus was an uneducated and ageing man who had risen from the ranks, a beneficiary of Severus's democratisation of the army. They both accompanied Caracalla on the eastern journey in 213 and the subsequent campaign.

Macrinus seems to have entertained suspicions that Caracalla was concerned about his loyalty, and the motive for the emperor's murder was the prefect's fear for his own safety. When an astrologer advised Caracalla's viceroy in Rome, his cousin Marcellus, that the emperor was in danger from Macrinus and his son, Marcellus wrote a warning letter. The missive arrived while Caracalla watched a chariot race, so rather than interrupt the notoriously intemperate emperor the courier gave the packet to the prefect. On reading its contents, Macrinus felt bound to make the astrologer's prediction come true. His chosen assassin was Martialis, a disgruntled centurion who wanted to avenge his brother's execution on a trumped up charge. Macrinus had no intention of Martialis surviving to tell any tales and made sure of his death at the hands of Caracalla's German bodyguard as soon as possible after the deed was accomplished.

The troops proclaimed Macrinus on 11 April 217 after a delay of three days and he immediately identified himself with the Severi by taking the name Severus. He elevated Diadumenian to Caesar and named him as his heir. Macrinus attempted to raise sympathy by the tried and tested policy of reversing the worst of his predecessor's taxes and announcing an amnesty for political exiles. However, events prevented him from going to Rome, and the senators, while acquiescing to the eastern army's choice, were unhappy that Macrinus had assumed the imperial powers and titles before they had been conferred by the senate's customary decree. Recent history had shown that poor relations between ruler and senate needn't seriously handicap the emperor, but losing the army's loyalty was inevitably fatal.

The Parthians, having regrouped, returned in strength and invaded Mesopotamia. Macrinus hoped to avoid a battle with Artabanus, but fighting took place near Nisibis. Neither side gained much advantage, but as soon winter approached a peace was patched up that didn't favour Rome. Macrinus returned all the Parthian prisoners, paid Artabanus a large indemnity, and handed control of Armenia to Parthia. None of this instilled confidence among the soldiers. Worse, when Dacian tribes crossed the lower Danube to attack the garrisons weakened to support the Parthian campaign, the Moesian commanders were ordered to sign an ignominious treaty with the barbarians. Macrinus's return to the Severan rates of pay for recruits to economise fostered further unrest. With the recruits grumbling and the European legions clamouring for either a fight to the death with Parthia or an immediate return to their Moesian homelands, Macrinus's position was looking decidedly shaky.

At this point the Severi struck back through the women – the indefatigable Julias. At moments in Roman history, women as much as men became prominent; few periods, however, were as dominated by the actions of women as that of the Severan dynasty, during which time four luminaries – all named Julia – worked with, behind, or against the emperors. They were the Julias Domna, Maesa, Soaemias and Mamaea.

As the wife of Septimius Severus, Julia Domna exercised influence in the empire for more than twenty years. She was the younger daughter of Julius Bassianus, a member of the local Syrian aristocracy of Emesa and hereditary high-priest of the sun-god El-Gabal. Her older sister, Julia Maesa, married the wealthy Emesene equestrian Julius Avitus and bore him two daughters, Julia Soaemias and Julia Mamaea. Maesa spent many years in Rome with her sister, during which time she accumulated a great fortune. Soaemias was born in about 180. She married Sextus Varius Marcellus, a native of Apamea in Syria with a successful equestrian career before being adlected into the senate. They had numerous children, of whom Avitus became the emperor Elagabalus, but her morals were always in question and she was accused of prostituting herself as part of the divine mysteries of El-Gabal. Julia Mamaea was quite different to her sister Soaemias. Not of the branch that drew benefit from the family's association with El-Gabal, she avoided contact with the oriental religion that characterised the reign of her nephew. She married an *eques* called Gessius Marcianus and in 208 bore him Alexianus, who later became the emperor Severus Alexander. Mamaea was said to have been converted to Christianity by Origen (185–c.253), one of the greatest of the early theologians of the eastern Church, and was recognised as *religiosissima*.

To Macrinus's discomfort Julia Domna and Julia Maesa had accompanied Caracalla to Antioch, and these two indomitable women voiced aloud their suspicions that Macrinus was responsible for the death of their son and nephew. Julia Domna chose to starve herself to death as a public protest, while Julia Maesa retired to Emesa and the palatial family home, shared with her widowed daughters and their sons.

After usurping the Severan crown, Macrinus failed to win the support of the senate and people. When his army lost faith in him, his fate was sealed.

Diadumenian's age is unknown, but the coin below struck in 217–18 depicts him as little more than an adolescent

Power of the Severan Julias: This bust of Julia Mamaea portrays the determined set of a ruler whose guiding hand made her son Severus Alexander's reign wise and just.

The coins below, top to bottom: Julia Domna, Julia Maesa, Julia Soaemias and Julia Mamaea.

Soaemias's boy Varius Avitus Bassianus was the eldest, and although he was only fourteen he'd just become the chief priest of El-Gabal, a Syrian form of the Phoenician god Ba'al. When she overheard some soldiers of Legion III Gallicia on leave from nearby Raphaneae remark on how like Caracalla Avitus looked, Julia Maesa conceived of a plot to place her grandson on the throne. With the help of her chief eunuch, Gannys, she and Soaemias put about the story that Avitus was the illegitimate but only son of Caracalla, and that Macrinus had usurped his birthright. Since Soaemias was known in Rome as a notorious adultress, the fiction was credible.

Usefully, her current lover was the Raphaneae camp commander, Publius Valerius Comazon. Soaemias worked on Comazon, who agreed to smuggle Avitus into the legion's camp on the night of 15 May 218, and at dawn the next day presented the fourteen-year-old to the troops. The soldiers were promised a large donative and they accepted Avitus as Caracalla's rightful successor with the name Marcus Aurelius Antoninus. The boy-priest was proclaimed emperor in May 218. Macrinus sent a force of cavalry against Emesa, but the troops deserted to Antoninus, killed their commander and sent his head back to Macrinus. The Antonine force at Emesa was now considerably enlarged, news of which, together with the 'discovery' of Caracalla's son, created further disaffection as it spread. Macrinus went to II Parthica's headquarters at Apamea to restore confidence by rescinding the pay reduction. He raised nine-year old Diadumenian to the rank of co-Augustus and offered a donative to all the men. While the restored pay was welcome, their emperor's military reputation lay in tatters, so his actions only appeased the soldiers temporarily. When Macrinus set out with II Parthica and cohorts of the praetorian guard to attack Antoninus, the legion deserted in the ensuing skirmish. Macrinus fled to Antioch.

With a severely reduced army, he met the Antonine force in battle on 8 June 218 outside Antioch, where the outcome was never really in any doubt. Macrinus left the battlefield disguised by having shaved his hair and beard and attempted to reach Europe. He was recognised by a centurion at Chalcedon on the Bosphorus and arrested, taken back to Antioch and put to death, along with his son.

## Elagabalus
### Varius Avitus Bassianus / Marcus Aurelius Antoninus Elagabalus
[ 8/6/218–6/3/222 ]

Antoninus counted as his *dies imperii* the date of the victory, after which he became known as Elagabalus, in keeping with the oriental custom of identifying a priest with the god whom he served. Good looking, effeminate and a moral pervert, Elagabalus brought to Rome a profligacy that outdid even the worst excesses of Commodus. Varius Avitus Bassianus was born at some time between the autumn of 203 and the spring of 204. By the time of the events in 217–18, Elagabalus was consecrated to the honourable ministry of high priest of El-Gabal in his temple of Sol Invictus (the Unconquered Sun). In the resulting battle with Macrinus, both Elegabalus and Gannys played their martial parts. As Gibbon wrote:

> *Antoninus himself, who, in the rest of his life, never acted like a man, in this important crisis of his fate approved himself a hero, mounted his horse, and, at the head of his rallied troops, charged sword in hand among the thickest of the enemy; whilst the eunuch Gannys, whose occupations had been confined to female cares and the soft luxury of Asia, displayed the talents of an able and experienced general.*

From Antioch, Elagabalus wrote to the senate claiming the imperial insignia, an assumption that did nothing to endear the unknown boy-emperor to the Roman nobility. According to his wishes, his grandmother and his mother were each proclaimed Augusta. Julia Maesa sensibly wanted to reach the capital as quickly as possible, but Elagabalus ignored her pleas, dallying along the way to indulge in the fantastic rites of his religion. He also ignored his grandmother's suggestion that he should send ahead to Rome a sober portrait wearing a toga. According to the now-contemporary Dio Cassius:

> *He was drawn in his sacredotal robes of silk and gold, after the loose flowing fashion of the Medes and Phoenicians; his head was covered with a lofty tiara, his numerous collars and bracelets were adorned with gems of an inestimable value. His eyebrows were tinged with black, and his cheeks painted with an artificial red and white.*

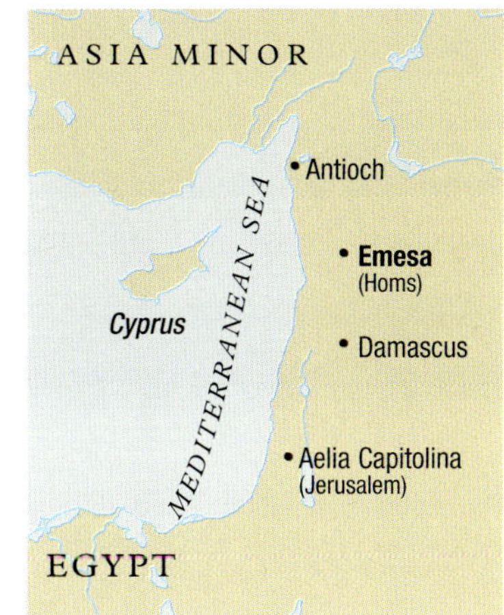


This extravagant image of decadent barbarity appalled equestrian and senatorial orders alike. However, it was simply a warning. Elagabalus entered Rome in the spring of 219 in a great procession through the streets over which gold dust had been strewn. The god, a black conical stone believed to have fallen to earth from heaven and which Elagabalus had brought to Rome, rested on a bed of precious gems on a chariot drawn by six milk-white horses. Elagabalus didn't ride with it, but holding the reins walked slowly backwards supported by his ministers, staring up in rapture at the divine presence. This procession was to be repeated on many occasions, eventually culminating in the magnificent new temple built on the Palatine, where the god dwelt. When it was completed, it rivalled Hadrian's Venus et Roma in area. It was the largest single structure on the Palatine and completed the hill's covering of imperial architecture.

In the temple precinct – suffused by rare aromatics, the incense of sacrifices, the fumes of rich wines, surrounded by troupes of Syrian girls performing lascivious dances to the sound of barbaric music – leading members of the administration and army, clothed in long Phoenician tunics, officiated with carefully concealed disgust. The emperor was officially styled Priest of the Unconquered Sun-God Elagabalus, and this title took precedence over all the other imperial titles. Among his imperial entourage came many low-born Syrians, who were now granted positions of high office, Publius Valerius Comazon foremost among them. He was appointed praetorian prefect and shortly after given the post of urban prefect, which made him the most powerful man in the administration.

Elagabalus was a treacherous youth. While some were raised, others were killed – among them Gannys – and Comazon was his willing executioner. Moral depravity was a required characteristic for preferment. The care of the grain supply was given to a hairdresser and a favoured charioteer received command of the *vigiles*. The translation of this grotesque oriental cult into the heart of Rome filled the nobility with detestation. In 219 Julia Maesa married Elagabalus off to the nobly born Julia Cornelia Paula. But in the following year he divorced her to marry Julia Aquilia Severa. All of Rome was scandalised, for Severa was a Vestal Virgin. He threw Severa aside a year later and, having executed her husband only a short time before, married Annia Faustina, who counted Marcus Aurelius among her ancestors. He married no less than five wives during his brief reign.

If this flurry of marital activity suggests the antics of a youthful stud, it's misleading – Elagabalus had little desire for any of his wives and no emperor before him – not even Hadrian – had flaunted his homosexuality so openly. As he entered his adolescence Elagabalus had the hairs plucked from his body in order to appear more feminine, and delighted in appearing before his subjects wearing female clothes and cosmetics. A blond-haired Carian slave named Hierocles acted as the emperor's 'husband', and was sometimes employed to 'capture' Elagabalus when he offered himself to passers by as a prostitute and then administer a sound beating as a 'punishment'.

Bust of Elagabalus: behind the wistul innocent appearance lurked a moral pervert and a wastrel.

Everywhere in the empire there was unrest. Julia Maesa, increasingly concerned that the emperor's growing unpopularity threatened her control of the government (she had been given the unprecedented right of a seat in the senate), determined that her other grandson Alexianus should be given official standing. She tricked Elagabalus into adopting his cousin – a straight-laced and likeable youngster of thirteen – on the grounds he could shortly hand over to him the boring matters of government – the few tasks Elagabalus bothered with – and devote more time to his priestly duties. Alexianus was adopted on 10 July 221 with the name of Marcus Aurelius Severus Alexander and received a share in the imperial powers and prerogatives.

Alexander's friendly disposition soon endeared him to the mob, the upper classes and the army, and sparked Elagabaline jealousy. By the beginning of 222, the processes of government were grinding to a halt as officials struggled to understand where the real authority lay – Elagabalus no longer spoke to his grandmother and she clearly preferred Alexander. Elagabalus launched a programme to corrupt his cousin by enticing him with all manner of perversions in a ridiculous attempt to damage his reputation, and when this failed, to kill him. But Alexander was well protected, thanks to his mother Julia Mamaea's prudence. Moreover, Alexander had become the praetorians' firm favourite; they saw little of Elagabalus, since he had no interest in military matters.

A trail of wives: Elagabalus went through as many as five wives, but the three women known are, left to right: Julia Cornelia Paula, the Vestal Virgin Julia Aquilla Severa and Annia Fausta.

Furious at failure, Elagabalus demoted Alexander from the rank and privileges of Caesar, but this roused the ire of a chilly senate and a furious *castra praetoria*. The guard swore to protect Alexander's life and keep a close watch on the emperor's conduct. The unstable situation could not last, and it may have been Maesa and Mamaea who conspired to leak a rumour to the praetorians that another attempt to assassinate Alexander had been barely foiled. The natural suspicion that they were too late and that their darling had already been murdered inflamed praetorian passions. The soldiers demanded that Elagabalus produce his cousin to prove that he was safe. The emperor responded by attempting to punish the ringleaders of what he considered to be a mutiny. The indignant praetorians rose up on 6 March 222 and massacred the minions of Elagabalus, his mother Julia Soaemias and the young emperor himself. They mutilated his corpse and then dragged it through the streets to the Tiber and tossed it in.

The reign of Elagabalus recalls that of Caligula, a callow youth raised in luxury who was then handed all the power in the world and fundamentally went off the rails. The failure of the Elagabaline reign is less to do with religious tensions, as generally claimed, as with sheer capricious incompetence. Even though Elagabalus's promotion of the Emesene sun-god was certainly ridiculed by contemporary observers, this cult was popular among soldiers, who associated it with that of Mithras, and it would remain so. Indeed, many succeeding emperors – and not all of Syrian origin – would come to regard Sol Invictus as the primary – but not necessarily exclusive – deity of the Roman pantheon. Elevated beyond his abilities and lacking discipline, Elagabalus's reign tragically highlights the failure of despotic government without even the dubious safeguards that were implicit in the fabrication of the Augustan principate.

## Severus Alexander  Marcus Julius Gessius Bassianus / Marcus Aurelius Severus Alexander

[ Caesar from 10/7/221, 6/3/222–March 235 ]

Alexianus was born in Arca Caesarea in Phoenicia on the first day of October 208. At his mother's insistence he was raised quietly and educated well, and had little if anything to do with the worship of the Emesene sun-god. When he was raised to the purple in March 222 Severus Alexander became Rome's youngest emperor, aged barely fourteen, and so the reins of government were in his mother Julia Mamaea's hands, his grandmother Julia Maesa living for only a short time after his elevation.

Herodian portrays the reign of Severus Alexander as a reaction not only against the profligate excesses of his cousin, but also as a rejection of the militaristic principles of Septimius Severus and Caracalla. In the Herodian picture, the ruler returns to something recognisable as an Augustan princeps, restoring to the senatorial order its ancient privileges, and favouring senators and the nobility over the *equites* and army. However, Herodian was the emperor's biographer and his assessment is clearly flattering. Unfortunately, the work of his contempary, Dio Cassius, is largely missing for this period, so sensible comparison is not possible.

Mamaea established a sixteen-man *concilium* of senators which, although it included the eminent jurists Ulpian and Paulus, and marked a return to sane government after Elagabalus, hardly indicates a restoration of government by consent of the senate. Alexander, under his mother's tutelage, restored prestige to the senate and respected its members, but despite his biographer's claims, he did not hand back any powers that had been gradually removed or break with the Severan principle of administration through a *concilium* and centrally controlled civil service. If anything, Alexander's regulation of some political offices tightened the autocratic power of the emperor. So vanished the offices of *tribunus plebis* and curule aedile. However, such offices had become honorary as their real functions were absorbed by the imperial bureaucracy, so this reform can be seen as more of an orderly tidying up of ancient Republican loose ends than an overt act of despotism.

That Ulpian, as a senator, was appointed to the office of praetorian prefect argues a new precedence of senators over equestrians, the class that had usually filled the post. Under Alexander, the traditional incompatibility between the prefecture and membership of the senate was removed and henceforth the prefect could be *vir clarissimus* (most distinguished gentleman) or *vir eminentissimus* (eminent gentleman). Nevertheless, equestrian prefects did not automatically become adlected into the senate as a result of the reform and indeed for the next fifty years the majority of prefects still belonged to the equestrian order.

The first nine years of Alexander's reign were peaceful, as the realm recovered from the excesses of Elagabalus through Mamaea's careful government. In this she was aided by her son's complete devotion, which prevented the discord that had marked earlier regencies. Two incidents marred the new order. Ulpian earned the displeasure of the praetorian guard for his unyieldingly strict command and, after an argument, some troops killed him in the emperor's palace. The other affected Alexander directly. In 225 Mamaea chose for him a bride named Sallustia Barbia Orbiana. She was from one of the few remaining genuinely patrician families, and her father Lucius Seius Sallustius was raised to the rank of Caesar. But Mamaea soon became jealous of the hold his new wife had over her son and forced him to divorce and banish her in 227. At the same time Sallustius was accused of an attempt on Alexander's life and executed. There is no record that Alexander resented this interference in his married life and thereafter he remained single, and Mamaea returned to her supreme position.

Bust of Severus Alexander as an adolescent and coin as the young emperor. He married Sallustia Orbiana but she was later banished.

Had his reign remained peaceful, Alexander Severus might have developed into a significant emperor, certainly in comparison with his immediate predecessors. But it was not to be, and in the following five years Alexander proved unequal to the major challenges. The first appeared from Persia. Since the days of Alexander the Great the Parthians had been the dominant Persian power. However, the debilitating wars with Rome weakened the ruling dynasty, which ended with Artabanus V. Opportunist Ardashir (Artaxerxes), king of the neigbouring tribe of Fars, who had subdued an area from the Persian Gulf to Isfahan, rebelled and proclaimed himself the restorer of the ancient Achaemenid empire and true Zoroastrian faith. In 227 he attacked and overthrew Artabanus in battle on 28 April. He assumed the title King of Kings, founding the Sassanian dynasty, named after his grandfather Sassan. The Sassanians were far more aggressive than the Parthians, who had only aspired to include Armenia within their boundaries. Ardashir's aims were to annex all of Asia Minor and eradicate Hellenistic culture from the



**The Roman empire in 235 at the end of the Severan dynasty**

region. It took three years for him to consolidate his position, so it was in 230 that news reached Rome that the Sassanians had overrun Mesopotamia, were threatening Syria and had laid claim to all the land that had belonged to Darius as far west as the Aegean. Alexander and Mamaea left Rome for Antioch early in 231. A last attempt to negotiate with Ardashir resulted in a curt response that Rome should immediately evacuate the territories that rightfully belonged to the Persian empire. The events of the campaign that followed remain unclear, although the presence of the emperor leant additional weight to Roman policy, because early Sassanid successes were reversed. While the Romans met with severe losses, they also inflicted heavy casualties. The result was an acceptance of the status quo rather than any settlement. Mesopotamia was recovered, Ardashir made no further moves for four years, and Alexander returned to Rome in 233 to celebrate a triumph.

On the northern frontiers Germans had crossed the Rhine and Danube to take advantage of the troop reductions made for the Persian campaign. Indeed, this serious incursion may well have been another reason for concluding the war against Ardashir. Accordingly, Alexander and Mamaea left Rome for Moguntiacum early in 234 to meet advance detachments of the Illyrian legions returning hurriedly from Syria. Their haste was understandable. Alexander had followed Marcus Aurelius's policy of granting the officers and soldiers on the frontier parcels of land, on condition that they and their sons continued to serve in the legions. The German invasion, therefore, was threatening more than the empire; it was a personal threat to the soldiers' families and homes. This also goes a long way to explaining the troops' fury with Alexander when, as was customary with him, he preferred to negotiate with the barbarian invaders. Viewing his pacific policy at best as cowardice and at worst as outright betrayal, the troops began to seek a general who was not afraid to fight the invaders.

The common Illyrian soldiery also despised the power that Mamaea exercised over her son, and her well-known favouritism towards the eastern legions. They wanted an emperor who was a western compatriot and chose Gaius Julius Verus Maximinus. A peasant of Thracian origin who commanded some Pannonian levies. In March 235, his soldiers invested him with the purple, and a few days later Alexander and Mamaea were murdered by their own soldiers near Moguntiacum. Thus came to an end the Severan dynasty and anything remotely resembling the Pax Romana.

A coin of Ardashir I – founder of the Sassanid dynasty – brought a level of aggression to Roman-Persian politics that the Parthian empire had never managed.

# EIGHT
## Into Military Anarchy

[AD 235–268]

**Maximinus Thrax** Gaius Julius Verus Maximinus
[ March 235–c.April 238, Germany and Illyricum ]

Severus Alexander's death marks the start of a fifty-year period of disorder and the dismemberment of the empire, prompted by the intertwined rules of five emperors, of whom – at three years – Maximinus Thrax, the first barbarian to ascend the throne of the Caesars, was the longest reigning. Born in about 173 in a Thracian village (hence the derisory nickname Thrax) to a peasant family, he started work as a shepherd. Later, he served in the army under the Dacian governor Gaius Julius Maximinus, who granted him Roman citizenship in 208 and provided his Roman name. His enormous physical strength attracted the attention of Septimius Severus, who promoted Maximinus to the centuriate. By about 230 he had gained equestrian rank within the army and was training recently recruited levies of Pannonian troops. These young soldiers were fiercely loyal to Maximinus, whose four decades of harsh military service placed him in stark contrast to the young and indecisive Alexander. When matters came to a head, it was their commander – who had never been a legate, let alone held a civil post – they wanted for emperor, and within days contingents all along the Rhine said the same. The senate had become powerless to intervene in any such choice, and therefore bowed to the inevitable.

Maximinus – inclined for practical reasons to leave Severan appointees in place – immediately faced two mutinies, although in each case agents betrayed the plotters. In response Maximinus cleansed the ranks of any suspected Severans by the simple expedient of replacing all officers of senatorial rank with his own promoted men. From this point on, his reign was effectively a battle against the nobility. Maximinus successfully dispersed the German tribes across the Rhine, and in the following year unrest among the Danubian tribes forced a move to Sirmium. He was still there in the spring of 238 when a rebellion erupted in Africa. Maximinus's desperate need of money for the soldiers' pay meant bleeding wealthy provinces, and his procurator in Africa had been confiscating rich landowners' property. Infuriated at their treatment some young nobles ganged up and murdered the offending official at his residence in Thysdrus (El Djem). The rebels then went to the aged proconsul of Africa, Gordianus (Gordian), who lived in Thysdrus, and invited him to become emperor.

Coins of Maximinus, his wife Caecilia Diva Paulina and their son Gaius Julius Verus Maximus, who was elevated to Caesar in 236.

**Gordian I** Marcus Antonius Gordianus Sempronianus Romanus Africanus
**Gordian II** Marcus Antonius Gordianus
[ ruled jointly January 238, in Africa ]

Since the elder Gordian was about eighty at the time of his accession, he was probably born in 159. His father was descended from the Gracchi who had dominated Roman affairs towards the end of the Republic, and his mother from a relative of Trajan. Gordian had two children: a son of the same name and a daughter, whose own son was to become Gordian III.

At the beginning of January 238, Gordian consented to be emperor. He moved from Thysdrus to Carthage where, after elevating his son to be his colleague, he sent an embassy to Rome to explain his actions to the senate, which body gratefully recognised the eminent Gordian and his son as the new joint-Augusti, and particularly approved of the proposed programme of constitutional government which came complete with a massive financial hand-out (Gordian's wealth was immense). This included the abolition of Maximinus's hated informers and a promise of a donative to the army. The senate declared Thrax a public enemy and formed a special Commission of Twenty, men who were assigned different parts of Italy to prepare for the anticipated invasion.



The outcome looked hopeful, but revolt was in the air. Some years earlier, Gordian had attempted to remove the governor of Numidia, Capellianus, from office for embezzlement. Now Capellianus grabbed the opportunity, and since he commanded the only regular troops stationed in the African provinces, Legion III Augusta, this was a genuine threat. The Gordiani could only muster a local volunteer militia to counter the rebel's advance on Carthage and these hastily recruited levies, under Gordian II, were no match for Roman soldiers. They were soon overwhelmed and the younger Gordian killed in the battle. On hearing of his son's death, the father committed suicide after a reign of just twenty-two days.

**Pupienus**  Clodius Pupienus Maximus
**Balbinus**  Decimus Caelius Calvinus Balbinus
[ joint, ruled early February 238–early May 238, Italy ]

Despite this setback, the senate was determined to oppose Maximinus and found replacements from among the Commission of Twenty to be the next Augusti. Pupienus was probably about sixty at the time. Of humble origins, he'd risen swiftly through the army ranks to chief centurion, tribune, praetor and proconsul of Bithynia, Achaea, Gallia Narbonensis and Germania Superior. He had secured victories over the Sarmatae and the Germans, and held two consulships as well as the office of urban prefect. Balbinus – of similar age – was better-born than his colleague and a distinguished administrator. While the senators approved of Pupienus, his severity as urban prefect had made him deeply unpopular with the Roman mob. In addition, the creation of two emperors by the senate didn't please the military – especially the praetorian guard, which viewed any resurgence of senatorial prerogatives with deep mistrust. As news of the election spread, rioting broke out throughout Rome, in part a reaction against Pupienus, but also probably a sign of the disappointment felt by both soldiers and civilians at the loss of Gordian funding. Eventually the parties reached a compromise, and in March 238 the senate promoted Gordian's grandson Marcus Antonius Gordianus to the rank of Caesar.

Meanwhile, Maximinus had begun his advance on Italy, but things went badly. His haste of departure left the army poorly provisioned and by the time it reached Emona (Ljubljana) the men were starving. The deserted town had been stripped of

Gordian I (*top*) and his son Gordian II, made emperors by land-owning Romans in Africa angry at the theft of the estates by Maximinus Thrax.

Short-reigning rulers at loggerheads:
Pupienus (*left*) and Balbinus.

food and the troops fell to muttering among themselves. Maximinus pushed on towards Aquileia, anticipating an easy victory and supplies. But thanks to the Commission of Twenty the town was ready and Maximinus faced a long siege without engines. Pupienus, having raised more troops in Ravenna, stood in his line of advance, preventing Maximinus from simply going around Aquileia. His men were at the end of their tether, and finally soldiers of Legion II Parthica, who wanted to get home to their wives and children at Albanum near Rome, went to Maximinus's tent and murdered him and his son while they slept. Their heads were sent to Rome as proof of the deed. Maximinus's troops were happy to acclaim a senatorially appointed emperor so long as he relieved their hunger, and the German allies, who remembered Pupienus with affection from his German tenure, flocked to be his personal bodyguard.

The new constitutional experiment worked well for only a few days before mutual suspicion began to plague Balbinus and Pupienus. Their problems were exacerbated by continual popular unrest, especially among the praetorian guard, who hated the rule of emperors appointed by the nobility, and were fearful that the German bodyguard of Pupienus was intended to replace them. Within days the praetorians had worked up a head of steam and marched on the Palatine. Each emperor believed the other was behind a plot to assassinate him, and was thus flustered and easily taken. When his Germans rushed to rescue Pupienus, the captors murdered both emperors, left their bodies in the roadway, then fled to the *castra praetoria* taking thirteen-year-old Gordian, wrapped in the purple, with them. The army was once again in control of an emperor's election.

## Gordian III  Marcus Antonius Gordianus
[ May 238–25/2/244 ]

Gordian III was born in Rome on 20 January 225. His mother was a daughter of Gordian I, but his father's name is not known. History holds little detail of Gordian's five and a half-year reign. His administration was in the hands of relatives or advisers, quite likely men who rose to prominence under the Severan and even late Antonine dynasties, until 241 when the highly qualified Gaius Furius Sabinus Aquila Timesitheus became praetorian prefect. Another beneficiary of the Severan democratisation of the military, Timesitheus had risen through the ranks to the centuriate and the equestrian order. He'd held an astonishing number of senior posts from Asia to Germania and Arabia to Gaul, often as a propraetor or substitute for a senatorial governor. Timesitheus's proven abilities quickly made him the central figure in Gordian's administration, and his authority was further enhanced by the marriage of his daughter, Furia Sabinia Tranquillina, to the young emperor in the summer of the same year. This promotion made Timesitheus the *de facto* ruler of the empire. And he faced problems – a new threat from the steppes, a tribe of Goths, took almost three years to evict from Moesia Inferior, while the Sassanid Persian empire had attacked in the east. The ageing Ardashir I had captured Nisibis and Carrhae during the last months of Maximinus's reign, and now his son Shapur I invaded Syria and threatened to take Antioch. With young Gordian in his train, Timesitheus set out for Syria.

Coins of young Gordian III and his wife
Furia Sabinia Tranquillina, daughter of
his praetorian prefect, Timesitheus.

Fighting commenced in the spring of 243, and the Roman army swept the Persians back. Antioch was saved, Carrhae and Nisibis were retaken and the Romans won a decisive victory at Rhesaena. Plans to continue the push on to Ctesiphon faltered, however, when Timesitheus suddenly died of an illness during the winter of 243–44. The second prefect, Gaius Julius Priscus, persuaded Gordian to appoint his brother Marcus Julius Verus Philippus (Philip) as Timesitheus's successor. Timesitheus had been content to exercise his power as Gordian's adviser, but it was soon clear that Philip had set his ambition on the purple. Using the failure of grain supplies to arrive on time, Philip fomented a rebellion among the troops by blaming Gordian for their misfortune. The emperor pleaded, even offering to resign and serve as Philip's Caesar, but after the soldiers declared their desire to have a man and not 'a child' as ruler, Philip had Gordian murdered. This happened at Zaitha, near Circesium, where he built a cenotaph indicating that the emperor died of natural causes; which is what the senate was told. The official dispatch also informed the senate of Philip's own proclamation by his army, and requested that Gordian III be deified – a sure way of deflecting blame for the emperor's death from himself.

## Philip I the Arab  Marcus Julius Verus Philippus
[ 25/2/244–September 249 ]
## Philip II  Marcus Julius Severus Philippus
[ co-Augustus 247–September 249 ]

Philip was born early in the reign of Septimius Severus, possibly in 204, in a village some 88km south-southeast of Damascus in the Roman province of Arabia. Its modern name is Shahba' and he later endowed it as a colony named Philippopolis. How much Arabic blood Philip had is unclear, Romans had probably been inter-marrying in the region for many decades, but his origins were seized on by later historians for his nickname. Philip married Marcia Otacilia Severa and she bore him a son, Marcus, in about 238. The ancient sources paint a dim picture of Philip, and may have glorified young Gordian by comparison. It's therefore predictable that they attribute Gordian's death to Philip, and certainly it remained a popular rumour among the Roman nobility. But Philip's claim that Gordian died of natural causes – epidemics were rife among the troops in the east – may have been true; and certainly, he did *not* die of battle wounds as claimed by Shapur.

It's equally predictable that the histories describe Philip's quick peace treaty with the Sassanians as dishonourable to Rome. Yet the terms reveal a different picture. Mesopotamia and Armenia Inferior remained under Roman control, an indication that Shapur had won no great victory, since this settlement pushed him back from his earlier gains. Rome was disadvantaged in Armenia Superior only in that its client king was under Rome's nominal control, but this situation had prevailed before. Philip made his brother Priscus governor of Mesopotamia, and raised his own son – about seven at the time – to the rank of Caesar before setting out for Rome. He arrived in the capital no later than 23 July 244, the date given for the discharge of veterans of Legion II Parthica. His attitude towards the senate was polite and deferential, and he established relations that remained generally cordial throughout his reign.

He drew his closest advisers from among his own family. The command of Moesia and Macedonia went to his brother-in-law Severianus, and Priscus was promoted to *praefectus praetorio rectorque orientis* (rector of the Orient), which effectively made him commander-in-chief of all the eastern legions – a position he was to abuse to his and his brother's cost. In the provinces Philip's name appears on many milestones attesting

Statue of Gordian III, combining a realistic likeness with an idealised pose, proving that instability had not damaged Roman craftsmanship.

Master of spin: The second Sassanian king, Shapur I, ruled from 241 until his death in 272 and became a thorn in Rome's side and an emperor-killer.

to his maintenance of the roads and care for transportation, and grateful provincials erected numerous dedications to him. In Rome he kept the mob happy with three money hand-outs. On the other hand, the almost continual state of war on the northern frontiers meant an increasingly onerous tax burden fell on all other classes of the population.

In 245–46 the Carpi kept Philip occupied on the Danube, until at the end of 247 he beat them decisively in open battle and they sued for peace. He returned to Rome to celebrate a triumph and, on 21 April 248, commemorate Rome's thousandth birthday with extravagant games. It seemed as though peace and prosperity had returned. In the early summer the two Danubian legions IV Flavia Felix and XI Claudia Pia Fidelis proclaimed one of their officers, Pacatianus, emperor. At the same time, three more revolts erupted in the east and a fourth in the west. The eastern disturbances were largely the fault of the emperor's brother Priscus, whose harsh administration and bludgeoning taxation led to the proclamation by the soldiers in Cappadocia of a certain Iotapianus. In Syria the pretender was Lucius Uranius Antoninus, who was a great deal more successful than the others, since he maintained his power base until 253. The third eastern revolt by a certain Sponsianus is only indicated by coin inscriptions, which is also true of that in the west. Of Priscus, nothing more is heard after the outbreak of Iotapianus's revolt, meaning that either he died naturally or was rightly a victim of the uprising he had caused.

Philip was so troubled by these upheavals that he offered to abdicate. None of the senators had an answer until Gaius Messius Quintus Decius, a consul for 249, expressed the opinion that none of the pretenders was fit to rule Rome, and that in any case their own troops would solve the problem by killing them. In this Decius was quite correct, although why the rebelling soldiers turned on their choices is not known. Despite the removal of the chief usurpers, Philip remained uneasy at the level of disaffection among the Illyrian legions, so he proposed to send Decius to take over from Severianus. Decius, a gifted diplomat, appeared to be a sensible appointment, but for Philip it was a blunder. Through vigorous but fair discipline Decius soon had the mutinous troops back in line, ensured their loyalty by arranging for salary arrears to be paid up and led them successfully against the Goths on the lower Danube. What

Busts and coins of Philip I the Arab, his wife Marcia Otacilia Severa and their sone Marcus Julius Severus Philippus.

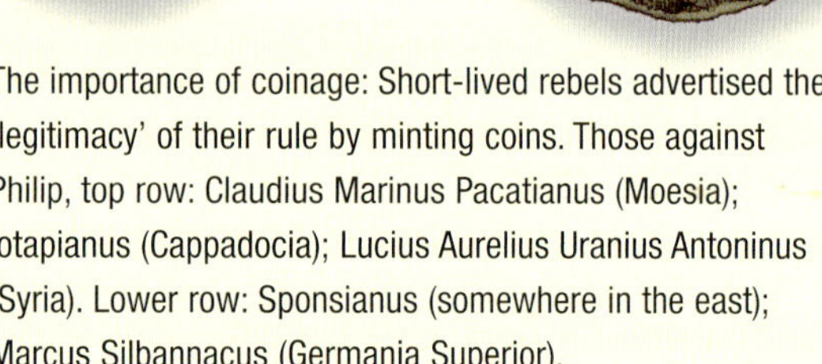

The importance of coinage: Short-lived rebels advertised the 'legitimacy' of their rule by minting coins. Those against Philip, top row: Claudius Marinus Pacatianus (Moesia); Iotapianus (Cappadocia); Lucius Aurelius Uranius Antoninus (Syria). Lower row: Sponsianus (somewhere in the east); Marcus Silbannacus (Germania Superior).

next occurred underlines how important it had become in this era for the legions to have their emperor in the field with them rather than in Rome. Impressed by their new commander, his soldiers acclaimed Decius.

Decius, who'd done nothing to create this situation, wrote to Philip expressing his concern and offering to give up the insignia his troops had imposed on him. But Philip, distrusting his sincerity, left Rome under arms at the end of June, compelling Decius to detach a sufficiently large force and march towards Italy. The two armies met outside Verona at the end of September 249 where a great battle was fought. Although outnumbered, the Illyrian soldiers were confident in the tactical superiority of Decius, and Philip was defeated. The emperor either died in battle or was later assassinated by his own troops. When news of the defeat reached Rome, the praetorian guard murdered Philip's young son.

## Decius  Gaius Messius Quintus Decius / Gaius Messius Quintus Traianus
[ September 249–1/7/251 ]

Philip's successor was born at the village of Budalia, near Sirmium in Pannonia Inferior to a provincial family, at some time between 190 and 201. His family may have been of Italian stock; his wife Herennia Cupressenia Etruscilla belonged to an ancient Italian family that had attained senatorial status. They had two sons, Herennius Etruscus and the younger known to history only as Hostilianus (Hostilian). His governorship of Moesia Inferior in 234–38 indicates that Decius achieved a senatorial rank early in his career. He was made urban prefect during Philip's reign, and he was a consul in 249 when the emperor charged him with the responsibility of restoring order among the Moesian legions.

Decius arrived in Rome in early October of 249. The senate confirmed his position and in turn Decius shrewdly assumed the name of Trajan. By this time Trajan's status as the greatest emperor since Augustus was firmly established, and his adopting the name endeared Decius to the troops – especially those of the Illyrian provinces Trajan had commanded. Decius formulated a traditionalist approach to government and during a peaceful first year undertook much restoration and reform. He instituted a vigorous programme of road-building throughout all the major provinces. Rome enjoyed the first burst of public building for almost twenty years – mostly extensive and necessary repairs.

Reasonable Decius was still an autocrat and he held the office of consul in every year of his reign. One of his more important administrative innovations – especially appealing to the senatorial order – was the creation of an office that superficially resembled that of the Republican censor. With his two sons still too young to take responsibility in his absence, this new office – given to the senator Publius Licinius Valerianus (Valerian) – provided Decius with a powerful representative to take care of Rome whenever he was called to the frontier. Valerian's functions included the revival of veneration for the state-religion in the face of increasing Christian communities. The Roman state was tolerant of other creeds so long as adherents gave suitable veneration to the state-religion, an adjunct of Roman politics, a condition the monotheistic Christians could not accept. Decius's intention was to have them return to the Roman fold through apostasy, for the state's part in the persecution was more passive than that of the people. In 248 popular fury against Christians erupted into a pogrom in Alexandria, in which several hundred perished. Decius decreed that Christians must make a public sacrifice to the Roman gods, after which each was given a *libellus* or a certificate. Those who refused were arrested and held without food or water in the hope that they would recant. Nevertheless, far more Christians died

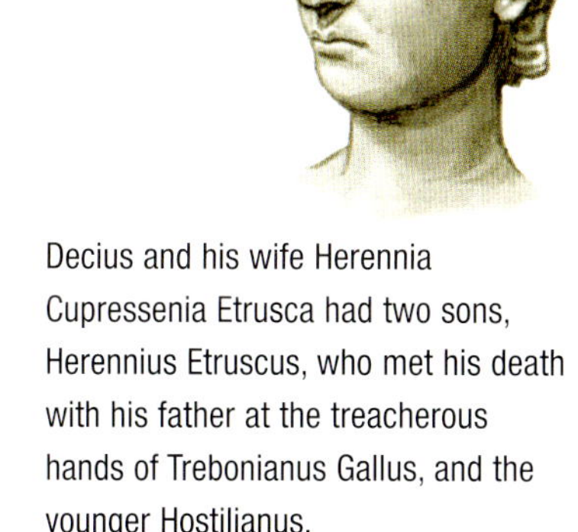

Decius and his wife Herennia Cupressenia Etrusca had two sons, Herennius Etruscus, who met his death with his father at the treacherous hands of Trebonianus Gallus, and the younger Hostilianus.

at the hands of citizens than by state execution.

In the summer of 250 barbarian activity on the Rhine and Danube involved Decius and Herennius. Successes in Raetia and Pannonia paled before another onslaught of two Gothic armies that crossed the frozen Danube over the fierce winter and entered Moesia. One force besieged Nicopolis, the other Philippopolis. Decius and Herennius relieved Nicopolis, but Philippopolis fell to the barbarians, who sacked it and massacred the inhabitants. Events now moved towards their tragic conclusion. The emperor, in company with Herennius and Trebonianus Gallus, governor of both Moesias, pursued the Goths around the region and finally engaged them on the first day of July 251 at Abrittus, some 96km north of Nicopolis. After initial successes in the battle, Decius was undone by the treachery of Trebonianus Gallus, who knowingly signalled the emperor forwards into marshy ground. His soldiers became bogged down and the enemy easily slaughtered them to the last man. The bodies of Decius and Herennius were never recovered. Of all the short-reigning emperors of the first half of the period of military anarchy, Decius had ruled best and most wisely; it was for later Christian writers to blacken his name. And Decius had the dubious distinction of being the first Roman emperor to be killed in battle fighting a foreign enemy.

**Trebonianus Gallus**  Gaius Vibius Trebonianus Gallus
[ 2/7/251–July 253 ]
**Gaius Vibius Volusianus (Volusian)**
[ co-Augustus November 251–July 253 ]
**Hostilianus (Hostilian)**
[ co-Augustus August 251–November 251 ]

His own troops readily hailed Gallus. Concerned with reaching Rome quickly to consolidate his rule, he signed a shameful treaty with the Goths. In return for their withdrawal they were permitted to keep their booty but – far worse – they were also allowed to take their Roman prisoners with them, many of noble rank; in addition he promised to pay an annual tribute. Gallus then went to Rome, where – to lend credence to his story that the Decii had died honourably – he raised Decius's younger son Hostilian to the rank of Augustus, and elevated his own son Volusian to that of Caesar. And so began a reign of barely two years, notable only for misfortune.

An outbreak of the plague that had wracked the empire for the past fifteen years carried off many, including Hostilian in November 251. The Sassanians attacked in 252 and overran Mesopotamia, defeated the Romans at Barbalissus (Mesken, Syria) and advanced as far as Antioch, which fell into Shapur's hands in the following year. Furious that the new governor of Moesia, Aemilius Aemilianus, had refused to pay the promised tribute, the Goths stormed back across the Danube, plundering the cities of the province and those of Thrace. A second band crossed from Europe into Asia and ravaged the country as far south as Ephesus. Gallus failed to react to any of these threats. Aemilianus organised relief for the sacked cities, rallied his legions, renewed his men's confidence and went on the offensive. His sudden attack took the satiated Goths off their guard. Their scattered forces were herded back towards the Danube and, amid a great slaughter, hurled across the frontier. This unexpected success ensured a temporary peace, and the recovery of Roman prestige so impressed the soldiers that spontaneously they raised up Aemilianus and made the governor their emperor on the spot.

Bust and coin of Trebonianus Gallus, former governor of Moesia turned traitor to his own emperor.

## Aemilian  Marcus Aemilius Aemilianus
[ c.May–early August 253 ]

The sources are contradictory on Aemilian: that he was born on a small island off the western coast of what is now Tunisia; that he was a 'Moor' or perhaps a 'Libyan'; that at the time of his death he was in his fortieth year and on the other that he was forty-seven, which puts his birth date somewhere between 207–14. One source reckoned he was from an insignificant family, while another claimed that Aemilianus used his distinguished ancestry to justify his seizure of the purple.

Aemilian advanced into Italy, hoping to catch Gallus and Volusian, promoted in Hostilian's place, before they had time to prepare. Gallus sent orders to Valerian, at this point commanding armies in Raetia and Noricum, to come to his assistance. But before Valerian could reach Italy, Aemilian had advanced to within 80km of Rome. Since his legions, fearing a Gothic counterattack against their undefended homes had prevented Aemilian stripping Moesia of soldiers, his force was not very large. This encouraged Gallus to take the field without Valerian's support, battle was joined at Interamna. His troops were not hardened fighters and they despised their emperor's apathy. When they realised the danger they were in, they murdered Gallus and Volusian, then swore their allegiance to Aemilianus.

There's little more of Aemilius Aemilianus to add. It's not even certain that he reached Rome, let alone made undertakings to the senate or received the imperial insignia. In Raetia, when Valerian's troops heard of Gallus's death, they raised up their man. News of the proclamation and the immediate arrival of Valerian at the head of a powerful and determined force prompted the Italian soldiers to rethink their position. According to the historian Zonaras, those who served with Aemilian were weary of civil war and recognised that they would be no match for Valerian's troops. They also judged their emperor unworthy of the realm and – sure that Valerian was better suited for rule because he would assume affairs in a more authoritative fashion – they killed Aemilian.

Volusian, son of Trebonianus Gallus, made first Caesar then co-Augustus with his father in 251.

Aemilius Aemilianus and his wife C. Cornelia Supra.

## Valerian  Publius Licinius Valerianus
[ c.July 253–June 260 ]
## Gallienus  Publius Licinius Egnatius Gallienus
[ co-Augustus c.September 253, sole ruler June 260–March 268 ]

The result relieved the senatorial order because in raising Valerian the army had avoided another civil war and elevated one of their own number to the purple. Valerian's son Gallienus was in Rome and to show goodwill, the senate made him Caesar. On his arrival in the capital in the autumn of 253, Valerian received the imperial powers from the senate and raised Gallienus to the rank of co-Augustus, making him a partner in the empire. In contrast with so many of his short-lived predecessors, Valerian came from an old Roman senatorial family. He was born during the reign of Septimius Severus, probably before 200, and is first mentioned in 238 as a consular negotiating with the embassy sent by Gordian I to Rome to secure senatorial approval of his rebellion against Maximinus Thrax. Valerian married Egnatia Mariniana and they had two sons, Gallienus – born in about 218 – and Publius Licinius Valerianus,

Valerian and his wife
Egnatia Mariniana.

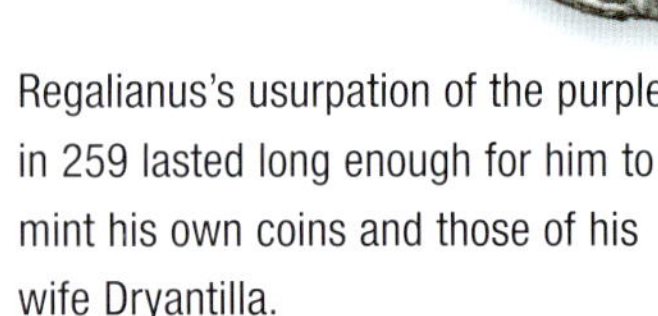

Regalianus's usurpation of the purple
in 259 lasted long enough for him to
mint his own coins and those of his
wife Dryantilla.

named after his father. In his turn, Gallienus married Julia Cornelia Salonina, and they had three sons: Publius Valerianus II, Saloninus, and Marinianus.

The two emperors enjoyed a few months of peace before insurrections along the Rhine demanded their attention. The wisdom in making his son of thirty-six years a partner soon became clear – while Valerian held the reins in Rome Gallienus took care of the frontier. He set out late in 254, and commemorative coins point to his considerable success during the first three years of his command. He secured victories on the right bank of the Rhine which prevented many German tribes from even reaching the river, while others were slaughtered as they attempted a crossing.

By 256 Valerian had concluded all the matters of state that had demanded his attention and determined to commence a campaign to regain Roman territory lost to the Sassanians by Trebonianus Gallus, leaving Gallienus as ruler of the western half of the empire. Gallienus may have envied his father's command of the east, for the pressures on him now mounted serially. The Franks, a ferocious German tribe from the northeast of central Europe, broke through the northern *limes*, devastating Germania Inferior and Belgica before advancing as far south as Hispania Tarraconensis, where they destroyed Tarraco (Tarragona). The Franks then pushed further south to the narrow strait with North Africa and pillaged the coast of Mauretania Tingitana. Along the Raetian *limes* the Alamanni broke through in 258, overran the Agri Decumates, sacked the city of Aventicum (Avenches, Switzerland) and extended their ravaging to the interior of Gaul, already reeling from the passing of the Franks. Either a second wave of Alamanni or the first force doubling back from Gaul then raided eastwards through Raetia and – greatest horror of all – attacked Italy through the Brenner Pass. The militarised provinces of Germania Superior and Raetia had failed to protect vulnerable Transpadane Italy, with its wealthy cities and light garrisons. Making a stupendous effort, Gallienus mounted a counterattack and won a victory over the Alamanni near Mediolanum. However, news of his son Valerian II's death on the Danube marred his triumph.

Gallienus then returned to the Rhine, but in the next year a revolt in Pannonia forced him to leave the defence of Gaul and Germania Superior in the hands of his second-in-command, Marcus Cassianus Latinius Postumus. He also left his younger son Saloninus at Colonia Agrippina under the care of the praetorian prefect Silvanus. Along the Danube Marcomanni, Sarmatae and Quadi attacked Pannonia, while the Goths and Carpi threatened Dacia and Moesia. In this confusion and uncertainty the Pannonian and Moesian legions had proclaimed their commander Ingenuus emperor. By prompt action and the aid of a large cavalry force commanded by the brilliant general Aureolus, Gallienus crushed Ingenuus in 259, but the remnants of his army continued in revolt by investing another officer, Regalianus, with the purple. Regalianus proved to be a tougher proposition than Ingenuus and it was not until 260 that Gallienus subdued the rebellion and restored unity in Illyricum.

Valerian faced his own problems in the east. He reached Antioch by 257, where advance detachments wrested control of the city from the Sassanian garrison. However, Valerian was unable to immediately prosecute a war against Shapur because Anatolia was suffering a series of barbarian assaults from a seaborne Scythian tribe called the Borani, who were attacking Bithynia, and the Goths, who had captured Chalcedon and were advancing on Nicomedia. Valerian divided his troops, sending one force towards Byzantium, while he marched to the relief of Bithynia. The army never reached its destination: in the region of Carrhae plague struck, killing many men. At this point Shapur attacked Syria again, threatening Antioch. Valerian turned back, but faced the reality that, lacking resources, he could no longer overcome his enemy.

Early in 260 he requested a treaty hearing. Assurances were given and, trusting in Shapur's good faith, Valerian set out with only a small retinue for Edessa where the Sassanian king held his court. Shapur arrested Valerian the minute he appeared and inflicted on him the ultimate humiliation by using the emperor of Rome as a human stepping-stool to assist him in mounting his horse. Valerian was treacherously led off to die in captivity. The exact date of his death is uknown, but he may have languished in prison for as much as two years. The Sassanians skinned his body and displayed the grisly trophy to demonstrate how Rome's prestige had been eclipsed. Decius was Rome's first emperor to be killed by foreigners; now Valerian was the first to be taken prisoner.

**THE SHOCK WAVES OF THIS DISASTER** were felt in every quarter of the empire, and sparked rebellions on a massive scale to which ultimately Gallienus had no effective answer, and which prevented any attempt to rescue or avenge his father. Even as he was subduing the Pannonian rebellion Gallienus was paying a higher price in Gaul, where the troops of Postumus revolted. This had its

A vigorous intensity emanates from this magnificent bust of Gallienus.

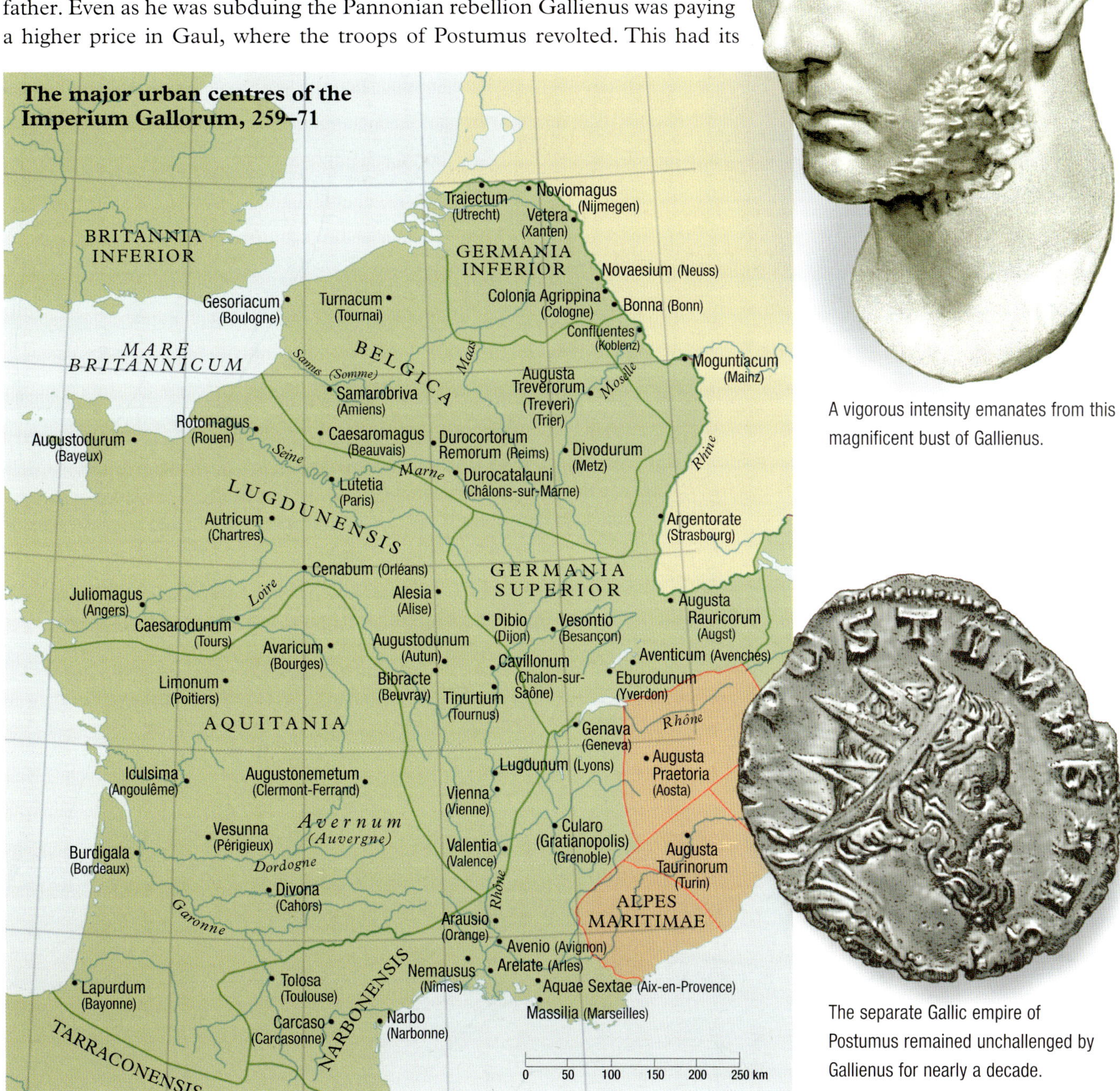


The separate Gallic empire of Postumus remained unchallenged by Gallienus for nearly a decade.

roots in the Gallic legions' perceived loss of the prestige they had enjoyed during the early imperial period, now eclipsed by that of the Illyrian armies. The soldiers, almost all provincial Gauls, felt exposed to the recent barbarian incursions and neglected by Rome. As Gallienus departed to deal with the Pannonian revolt, the Gallic legions turned to Postumus and demanded he take over. As usual, the political and military imperatives were driven by petty motives. A quarrel broke out over booty taken from barbarians by Postumus's soldiers. When Postumus distributed the spoils between his men, the praetorian prefect Silvanus ordered him to surrender everything to himself and Saloninus. The troops rioted, proclaimed Postumus emperor, and marched on Colonia Agrippina. At the threat of a siege, the town's garrison cravenly handed over Saloninus and Silvanus, and both were put to death immediately.

Within a year, Germania Superior and Inferior, Raetia, Gaul, Spain and Britain recognised the Imperium Gallorum of Postumus. For the next eighteen months Gallienus fought an indecisive war against his former second-in-command, but mounting pressures along the Danube became the more urgent problem. The eastern provinces were now at the Persians' mercy. In quick succession Antioch was retaken, Tarsus captured and then Caesarea (Kayseri) in Cappadocia. Since no help could be expected from Gallienus, one of Valerian's generals named Titus Fulvius Macrianus proposed his two sons to the dispirited Syrian garrisons and they were proclaimed joint-emperors by the troops. Anatolia, Syria and Egypt acknowledged this new Asian empire, but unlike the empire of Postumus, which remained independent for fourteen years, the Macriani empire did not survive long, falling no later than 262 to the new power in the east, Palmyra.

The state of Palmyra, lying between Roman Syria and the Euphrates, had grown wealthy on the lucrative trade route between Persia and the Mediterranean. Septimius Severus raised Palmyra to the status of a *colonia*, although it had retained a degree of autonomy while nevertheless gravitating into the Roman orbit. By 258, a certain Septimius Odaenathus (Odenath) is recorded as being a prince of Palmyra and accorded several Roman honorifics. In the crisis of 260 Odenath proclaimed himself king, gathered an army from Syria and Arabia, and attacked the Persians after their capture of Valerian at Edessa with such severity that Shapur was driven back across the Euphrates, leaving booty and prisoners in Odenath's hands. Recognising his inability to intervene, Gallienus wisely praised Odenath, entrusting him with the supreme command of all Roman forces in the east under the title *dux romanorum*. This move at least provided Gallienus with the semblance of maintaining 'Roman arms' in the face of Shapur; but the retaking of Asia Minor and Syria from the Macriani was the priority. Odenath didn't wait. By a mix of force and diplomacy, he detached most of the Syrian cities from the Macriani praetorian prefect Ballista, and then at the start of 262 attacked Emesa. Ballista was killed in the fighting, and the townspeople assassinated Titus Quietus, the surviving Macrianus, shortly after.

Four years later, the situation in the east was radically altered when Odenath and his elder son by a previous marriage fell to an assassin's knife in 266, possibly at Emesa. Since the government passed into the hands of his second wife Zenobia, whose infant son Vabalathus had been only second in line to the throne, it was inevitable she should be accused of plotting the murders. Zenobia was certainly the beneficiary of their deaths, and she had an entirely different agenda towards Rome. Over the next five years she set out to conquer all Rome's eastern possessions from Bithynia to Egypt, giving Gallienus's immediate successors a headache of imperial proportions.

Gallienus, his wife Salonina and two of their sons – Saloninus and Valerian II.

**IN HIS MILITARY REFORMS,** Gallienus went further than Septimius Severus by actually depriving senators of their ancient privilege of command. The final barriers separating lower from higher command were abolished, and any man who attained the centuriate could now rise to the very highest levels of command. Gallienus also placed a greater emphasis on cavalry – the new fluid situation required armies fleeter of movement, although recognition that cavalry could never win a battle alone safeguarded the infantry's pre-eminent position for the time being. By 258 Gallienus had formed an independent cavalry unit based in northern Italy under the command of the equestrian Aureolus. It was strategically positioned where it could be deployed to wherever it was needed in advance of the legions, and its importance can be seen in its equal standing with the praetorian guard.

In spite of his reforms, it is, perhaps, a tribute to Gallienus's realism, as well as an indication of his limited resources, that – as he had with Odenath – he understood Postumus was in a better position to keep the barbarians at bay in the west than a distant emperor, and so left him alone to get on with the job. In any event, a return of the plague in 262 kept Gallienus busy in Rome, followed by another incursion of Goths in the Balkans, which necessitated his presence in eastern Europe. The invaders raided Macedonia and Thrace, and pushed as far south into Achaea as Athens. It took until late July to evict them, and Gallienus returned to Rome in September 262. The emperor then spent the next five years in Rome, leaving the defence of Italy and Illyricum in the hands of his senior officers.

For the normally vigorous Gallienus, this uncharacteristic apathy points to a crisis of confidence, which is hardly surprising considering the palpable disintegration of the empire despite his every effort. His sabatical probably contributed to his own downfall, for the time he spent in Rome he luxuriated in culture, a pastime frowned on by his staff officers. Descended from ancient aristocratic stock, well educated, widely read and interested in Hellenistic art and philosophy, Gallienus together with his wife Salonina patronised a cultural movement referred to as the Gallienic Renaissance. The sculpture of this time indicates a revival of the classical Hellenistic form, with its echoes of other great artistic periods – Augustus and Hadrian, for instance.

This Hellenising influence so disturbed the Illyrian commanders who made up the bulk of his officer corps – in spite of a triumphant return to the battle front in 267, when Gallienus defeated a branch of the Goths called the Heruli on the banks of the Nessus – that a group of senior men plotted against him. In the same year came news of a revolt in Raetia and Italy. This was a personal blow, for the pretender was his stalwart cavalry general Aureolus, who had been entrusted with Italy's protection. Gallienus drove Aureolus into Mediolanum in the first months of 268, and laid siege to the city. But he was robbed of victory by the treachery of his own staff. These included the praetorian prefect Heraclianus, general Marcianus, the commander of the Dacian cavalry Crecropius and two high-ranking career officers, Lucius Domitius Aurelianus (Aurelian) and Marcus Aurelius Claudius. On the pretext of riding out with him to view some reported enemy movements, the conspirators fell on Gallienus and murdered him.

While ambition for power was an undoubted motive, the conspirators were all Illyrians, so in a sense this was not so much a dynastic change as a geopolitical one. In killing Gallienus, these stern Illyrians were substituting an Italian emperor of suspect Hellenistic sympathies for one who was first a soldier and second a native of the region from which Rome's best troops were now recruited. The winner of the throne was Marcus Aurelius Claudius. The senate meekly rubber-stamped the change. What could the once-august body do to reverse the trend of army decisions? The empire was in chaos; it was a time for strong-armed men to wield power, and despite his best intentions Gallienus had been unequal to the task. The plague had wiped out whole communities, with a consequential reduction of income from taxes.

A bust thought to be of the trusted and innovative cavalry commander Aureolus, who turned against his emperor.

Barbarian invasions, 250–57, and fragmentation of
the Roman empire at the death of Gallienus, 268

NORTH SEA
Britannia
Inferior
Eburacum
(York)
Britannia
Superior
Londinium
Gesoriacum
(Boulogne)
ATLANTIC
OCEAN
Germania
Inferior
Colonia Agrippina
(Cologne)
FRANKS
258, Alamanni occupy
the Agri Decumates
Augusta Treverorum
ALAMANNI
MARCOMANNI
Belgica
QUADI
Lutetia
(Paris)
Damube
Agri
Decumates
RAETIA
NORICUM
Carnuntum
SARMATAE
Lugdunensis
Germania
Superior
PANNONIA
SUP.  INF.
Rhine
Aventicum
(Avenches)
ALAMANNI
DACIA
Ulpia
Traiar
Aquitania
FRANKS
(Brenner Pass)
Aquileia
Mursa
259
Lugdunum
(Lyons)
Verona
Gallienus crushes
Ingenuus
Mediolanum
(Milan)
Burdigala
(Bordeaux)
Narbonensis
Genua
MOESIA
SUPERIOR
Tolosa
(Toulouse)
Narbo
(Narbonne)
258
Gallienus defeats
Alamanni
ADRIATIC
SEA
DALMATIA
Legio
(León)
ITALY
Rome
MACEDONIA
Caesaraugusta
(Zaragoza)
Tarraconensis
CORSICA
EPIRUS
Imperium
Lusitania
Toletum
(Toledo)
Tarraco
(Tarragona)
TYRRHENIAN
SEA
Olisipo
(Lisbon)
Emerita Augusta
(Mérida)
Baleares
SARDINIA
Corduba
FRANKS
SICILY
Baetica
Hippo Regius
(Annaba)
MEDITERRANEAN
Tinigi
(Tangier)
256–7 Franks raid
North African coast
Caesarea
(Cherchell)
Carthage
Hadrumetum
(Sousse)
MAURETANIA
TINGITANA
MAURETANIA
CAESARIENSIS
NUMIDIA
Leptis Magna
CYRENAICA
AFRICA
PROCONSULARIS

Roman empire of Gallienus
allegiance to Gallienus or doubtful allegiance
Raetia seized by Aureolus for Imperium Gallorum
Imperium Gallorium (Gallic empire)
empire of the Macriani
Palmyrene empire
Sassanian empire

barbarian pressure point
major barbarian raid
Sassanian campaign
city destroyed by barbarians
major battle
FRANKS  barbarian tribe

0  100  200  300  400 km

Postumus himself suffered rebellion, first from Ulpius Cornelius Laelianus (*left*) at Mainz in December 268 and then from Marcus Aurelius Marius (*below*) in the same month, who actually succeeded him for a few days.

To pay for the wars, he had debased the currency to such a point that his last mintings were only of *billon*. These coins, made from a high proportion of base metal such as copper with of tiny amounts of either gold or silver, were virtually worthless; the Roman state was bankrupt. And while Gallienus cannot be held to account for the ravages of plague, he certainly was blamed for the break-up of the provinces. By the end of his reign, the 'Roman empire' consisted only of Italy, Illyricum and the recently recovered Raetia, with a tentative hold on the provinces of Africa.

In time for Gallienus's *decennalia* celebrations of 262, a certain Marcus Aurelius Victor had a splendid triple arch erected in honour of the emperor, replacing the ancient Porta Esquilina in the Servian Wall. Today only the central arch remains, trapped between dilapidated Renaissance buildings – a sad metaphor for a man who might have been among Rome's greatest middle-period imperial rulers, but who found himself caught between insuperable odds on every side.

Titus Fulvius Macrianus seized the opportunity to promote his sons as joint-rulers of Asia Minor and Syria.

Titus Fulvius Iunius Macrianus (*top*) and his younger brother Titus Fulvius Iunius Quietus came up against the might of Palmyra, which brought an end to their short reigns.

# NINE

# Restoration of Imperial Unity

[AD 268–285]

### Claudius II Gothicus  Marcus Aurelius Claudius
[ March 268–January 270 ]

The officers who murdered Gallienus selected fifty-five-year-old Marcus Aurelius Claudius over his junior by only two years, Lucius Domitius Aurelianus (Aurelian), because the new emperor would need to calm the troops' uncertain temper and Aurelian was a noted disciplinarian – not that Claudius was a pushover. He's described as being tall with fiery eyes and strong enough to knock out the teeth of man or beast with a single punch. His sop to Gallienus's troops – apart from a small donative – was the execution of Aureolus, who had surrendered. Claudius then sent a firm dispatch to the senate to prevent the persecution of Gallienus's relatives and supporters. Unfortunately, over-eager sycophants murdered Gallienus's third son, Marinianus, one of the consuls for 268, together with Gallienus's brother, Publius Licinius Valerianus, before Claudius's edict reached Rome.

Claudius put aside the empire's restitution in order to concentrate on dire threats from the Alamanni and Goths. They were a greater danger than the Imperium Gallorum of Postumus, who in any case had made no threatening moves (he'd even refused Aureolus's invitation to join his revolt against Gallienus), a policy that brought about his downfall. The lack of expansionist policies meant less booty for the soldiers. When Postumus refused his troops permission to loot Moguntiacum after crushing a rebellion in 268, they rebelled, killed him and replaced him with Marius, a simple soldier. Apparently an armourer by trade, Marius was killed by a sword of his own manufacture some three days after his elevation. Into the vacuum stepped Marcus Piavonius Victorinus, a wealthy military commander elected by his garrison troops at Augusta Treverorum. Victorinus presided over a collapsing empire; the Spanish provinces had returned their allegiance to a Rome reinvigorated by Claudius, and the towns of south Gaul were wavering. With rebellious rumblings in Gaul, Claudius felt he could safely leave the rival state to self-destruct while he dealt with the barbarians.

Having invaded Raetia in the confusion following Aureolus's rebellion, the Alamanni had penetrated unopposed into Italy through the Brenner Pass earlier in the year. Claudius, with an army of 35,000 met the barbarian host of three times the size on the shore of Lacus Benacus (Garda) in November and the Romans were the supreme victors. More than half of the Alamanni were captured or slain and the remnant fled into the wilds. The Goths had attacked across the Black Sea in the summer of 268 in some 2,000 ships transporting a host of 320,000 men, attacking cities of the Moesian coast, then Byzantium, the Hellespont and the Aegean Sea, where they laid siege to Potidaea and Cassandria. As the Roman army approached, the Goths divided into two forces. The larger marched overland, intent on reaching the Danube and eventual safety in their own lands but Claudius inflicted such losses in a battle near Naissus (Nis) that the barbarians retreated into the Haemus mountains, harrassed every step by Aurelian's cavalry. For the success of this campaign, Claudius added Gothicus to his titles.

Military and economic factors prevented Claudius from accomplishing much in his administration. He made no alteration to Gallienus's policies and granted the senate no extra privileges. Nevertheless, he was courteous and maintained good relations with the senators throughout the twenty-two months of his reign. Even as

Claudius II's two-year tenure as emperor was spent waging war against the Goths, hence his nomeclature.

Claudius concluded the Gothic war, Vandals massing on the Danube opposite Pannonia and former allies of Rome, the Juthungi, were threatening Raetia. Leaving Aurelian to mop up in Haemus, Claudius went to Sirmium to take charge of the defences, and it was there in January 270 that he succumbed to the plague that had broken out among the defeated Goths and spread to the Roman troops. Genuinely mourned by soldiers and senate, he was deified, and the senate had his golden statue erected in front of the temple of Jupiter Optimus Maximus.

## Quintillus Marcus Aurelius Claudius Quintillus

[ c.February–c.May 270 ]

On leaving Italy, Claudius had left his brother Quintillus in command of the troops concentrated at Aquileia. When news of the emperor's death reached them there the men proclaimed Quintillus emperor. Eutropius describes Quintillus as 'a man of singular moderation and grace, and comparable or even preferable to his brother…' It's probable that the senate preferred Quintillus above Aurelian, the natural warrior-successor to Claudius, whose uncertain temper they feared. However, Quintillus was not an improvement over his brother in military matters. Aurelian swiftly finished the war against the remaining Goths attempting to escape Haemus to return to their homes, and then moved to Sirmium, where he was proclaimed emperor by the legions of Claudius. Clearly bewildered by this turn of events, Quintillus made no move to counter the usurpation of his imperial powers. Having heard the news and failed in an attempt to turn his soldiers against Aurelian, he found himself abandoned and committed suicide by opening his veins on the twentieth day of his reign. By far the better man was now sole ruler of the still-fragmented empire.

Claudius II's brother Quintillus replaced him, but lasted no longer than Aurelian's acclamation by the Danube legions.

## **Aurelian**  Lucius Domitius Aurelianus
[ c.May 270–c.October 275 ]

Aurelian and his wife Ulpia Severina. The emperor wears the crown of Sol Invictus, whom he promoted to head the Roman pantheon.

Aurelian was born on 9 September 214 or 215 in Sirmium (Mitrovica). His father was a tenant farmer of a senator named Aurelius, from who he took his name. Like his fellow Illyrian Claudius, Aurelian had a military career, probably rising to the rank of *dux equitum* (cavalry commander) under Aureolus. Aurelian married Ulpia Severina and she bore him a daughter.

Aurelian's legions made short work of the Juthungi, who had grown lazy on the booty of several Italian towns lying in the shade of the Alps. He then hastened to Rome in the winter of 270 where the senate conferred on him the imperial powers without delay. Although the question of what to do about the Imperium Gallorum and Zenobia of Palmyra was paramount, an army weary of continual warfare and in need of reorganisation obliged Aurelian to put any plans on temporary hold. As far as Gaul was concerned, Victorinus had just been murdered by his quartermaster in what appears to have been a matter of private revenge. Using the influence of her massive wealth, Victorinus's mother Victoria secured the succession for her nominee, the senatorial governor of Aquitania, Gaius Tetricus. But in spite of his best attempts, Tetricus and his son now ruled, at best, a distressed and fragmentary state. Aurelian followed Claudius's example and left it to its own disruption.

As for Zenobia, the Palmyran queen had occupied Antioch in the winter of 268–69, then marched south through the province of Arabia to attack Egypt, which she brought under her control. From Alexandria, she offered Aurelian an olive branch by minting coins with his head on one side and that of her son Vabalathus on the reverse. Buying time, Aurelian concluded the agreement and granted her son the titles Gallienus had given to his father Odenath. It was an expedient that in appearance maintained Rome's sovereigty in the east, but there was no doubt that it also enhanced the real power of Zenobia and Vabalathus.

Nearer to home Aurelian closed the Roman mint pending an investigation into its officials' peculation, then halted a Vandal invasion of Pannonia just in time to force march back to north Italy, where an alliance of the rebuffed Juthungi, Marcomanni and Alamanni had swept down through the Alps as far south as Placentia (Piacenza). Aurelian advanced to a position north of the barbarians, intending to cut off their line of retreat. Instead, the Romans fell into an ambush, and the emperor suffered his first defeat. In Rome mint labourers thrown out of work rebelled under the leadership of the procurator Felicissimus, encouraged by elements in the senate who saw Aurelian's defeat at Placentia as evidence that his authority was at an end.

This was far from true. The ill-disciplined barbarians failed to follow up on their victory and split into separate bands to plunder the rich countryside, where each band was easily defeated in detail. A furious Aurelian returned to the capital, rounded up those senators who had opposed him and either confiscated their estates or had them executed. The defiant mint-workers retreated to the Caelian hill and blockaded themselves inside the imperial mint. But it was a hopeless cause against the skill of Aurelian's soldiers. In the resulting skirmish, thousands were wounded or killed, and their leader Felicissimus executed on the spot. The surviving engravers were exiled to Serdica (Sofia), which no doubt accounts for the improved quality of minting there.

With peace restored, Aurelian began work on the monumental defensive wall for which history best knows his name. Building Rome's Aurelian Wall was tantamount to admitting the future inability of Roman forces to prevent barbarians raiding freely into Italy even as far south as the capital. Work started in 271 to enclose the city's fourteen Augustan districts, including the previously unfortified Transtiberim (Trastevere). Several other Italian cities also received new fortifications at this time or had older ones refurbished.

**BY THE START OF 270** Cappadocia and Galatia had fallen into Zenobia's hands. The queen, however, was determined to expand her boundaries to the Aegean and Black seas. But she was thwarted from taking much of Bithynia by the sterling efforts of its praetor, Vellius Macrinus, who fortified Nicaea, withstood the Palmyrene assault, and then retorted with a powerful counterattack that repelled Zenobia's army. Undeterred by this – as she thought – temporary setback, in the summer of 271 she assumed the title of Augusta and Vabalathus that of Augustus. This flagrantly advertised breach of the convention agreed with Aurelian was publicly flaunted on the coinage. The emperor was outraged – and ready.

In an expertly conducted campaign, Aurelian sent his trusted general Marcus Aurelius Probus to retake Egypt while he marched the army through Asia Minor, mopping up lukewarm resistance in Anatolia on the way to Antioch, where Zenobia had concentrated her forces under the command of Zabdas, her general. To do so, she had drained Egypt of Palmyrene troops, so Probus encountered little fighting to recapture Alexandria. Antioch was protected by heavy cavalry and infantry units posted along the banks of the Orontes to the north of the city. Aurelian now showed his flair for shrewd tactics by using his lightly armed Dalmatian horsemen to engage their heavily armoured opponents, but then to retire when attacked and wait for the heat of the sun to wear down the enemy. The repeated tactic worked, and the exhausted Palmyrene advance guard was completely defeated.

It was only a skirmish, but the outcome threatened to cut off Antioch from Palmyra, so Zenobia abandoned the city and withdrew first to Apamea and then to Emesa. In close pursuit, the Romans passed through Apamea, Larissa and Arethusa, which opened their gates to Aurelian, to face the Palmyrene army of some 70,000 outside Emesa. Here, the tactics that had worked so well for Aurelian at Antioch almost brought disaster, but seeing that his light cavalry was being overwhelmed, he sent in the heavy Roman legions against the Palmyrene light infantry. The power-shock of massed Roman foot had rarely been bested in open battle, and it was no different at Emesa. The enemy was routed and the legions wheeled around to attack the enemy's heavy cavalry in its rear. Caught between the legions behind them and the Dalmatian horsemen to the front, the Palmyrene casualties were enormous. Zenobia and Zabdas retreated across the Syrian desert to Palmyra and prepared for a siege while they anticipated reinforcements from the Sassanians, with whom she thought she had a deal.

However, Persian aid was unforthcoming, and after a brutal siege under the burning sun Zenobia made a breakout and fled for Persia in mid-272. She was captured on the banks of the Euphrates by a cavalry detachment sent in pursuit and brought before the emperor. He received the queen politely, and waited for Palmyra to open its gates, which it soon did. Aurelian forbade any plundering by the victorious troops, content with the capture of Zenobia, Vabalathus and the leaders of her independence faction. A court was convened at Emesa to try the Palmyrene rebels, and in a shameful act of cowardice Zenobia blamed her ministers for her actions. The ringleaders were executed and the remaining prisoners, together with Zenobia and Vabalathus, were sent to Rome.

Before he could hold a triumph, Aurelian was diverted in the autumn of 272 by another fierce campaign to drive invading Carpi from Moesia. He soon restored order and some Carpi were settled in plague-depopulated areas of Moesia and Thrace.

Sarcophagus sculpture thought to represent Queen Zenobia. It was when she issued coinage that styled her as Augusta and her young son Vabalathus (*below*) as Augustus that Aurelian prepared to end the empire of Palmyra.

Tetricus and his son Tetricus II.

1 Mausoleum of Augustus
2 Mausoleum of Hadrian
3 Solar clock of Augustus
4 Ara Pacis
5 Domitian's Circus (Piazza Navona)
6 Baths of Nero
7 Hadrineum (Temple of Neptune)
8 Pantheon
9 Odeion of Domitian
10 Saepta Julia
11 Temple of Isis
12 Baths of Agrippa
13 Theatre of Pompey
14 Porticoes of Pompey
   (site of Julius Caesar's murder)
15 Largo Agrentina
16 Theatre of Balbus
17 Portico of Ocatavia
18 Theatre of Marcellus
19 Trajan's Forum
20 Imperial Fora: i) Augustus;
   ii) Julius Caesar; iii) Nerva;
   iv) Templum Pax (Temple of Peace)
21 Capitol and Temple of Jupiter
22 Forum Romanum
23 Temple of Venus et Roma
24 Palace of Tiberius and
   Loggia of Septimius Severus
25 Forum Boarium
26 Palace of Domitian
27 Temple of Elegabalus
28 Palace of Septimius Severus
29 Septizonium
30 Amphitheatrum Flavium (Colosseum)
31 Baths of Titus
32 Portico of Livia
33 Baths of Trajan
34 Ludus Magnus
35 Temple of Claudius

As he was about to turn for Rome, dispatches alerted the emperor to renewed unrest in Palmyra where a revolutionary named Apsaeus had raised a small army, attacked and slain the small Roman garrison, and promoted Antiochus, a wealthy citizen, puppet king of Palmyra. With astonishing speed, the legions force-marched to the Bosphorus and across Anatolia to reach Palmyra at the start of 273. Since there had been insufficient time to reconstruct the fortifications, Palmyra was taken without much of a fight. This time Aurelian didn't hold back his troops and the city was thoroughly sacked. Because of his insignificance Antiochus was spared, but the other rebel leaders were executed.

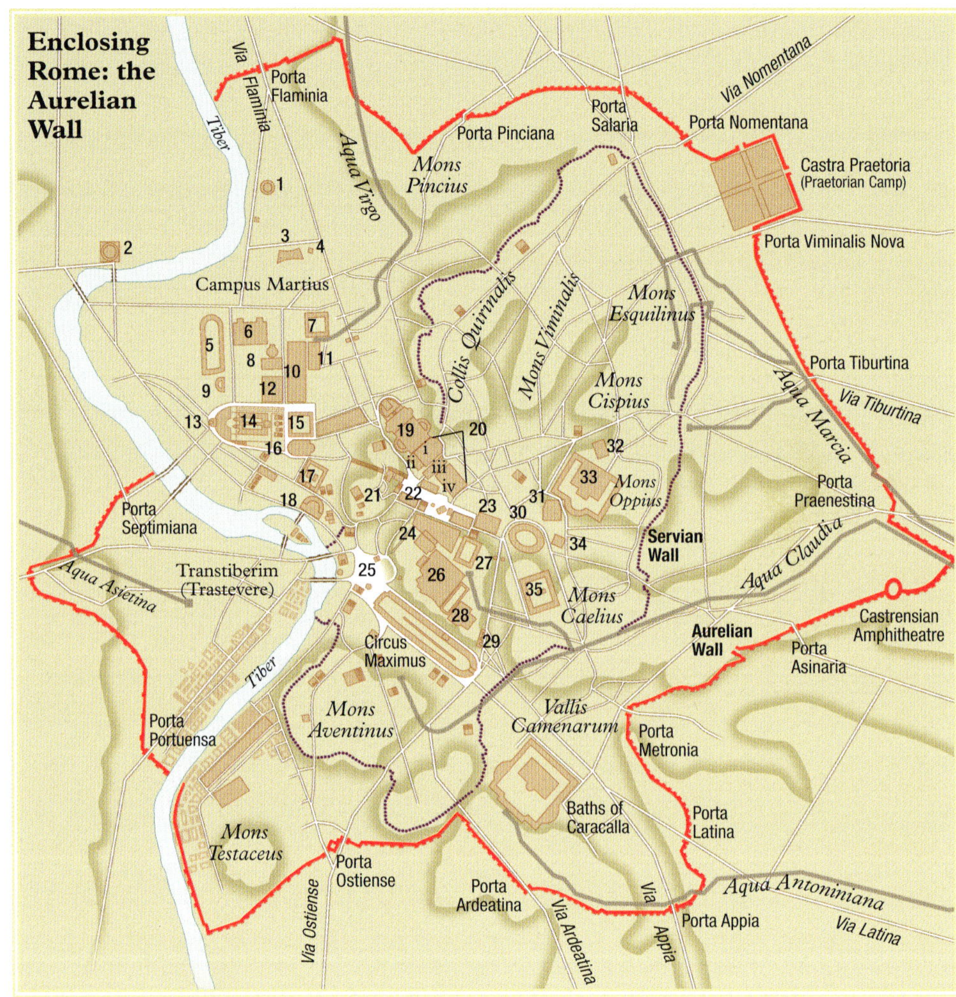



**WITH PEACE SECURED ALONG THE DANUBE** and – with the exception of Mesopotamia, still in Sassanian hands – the eastern provinces returned to Roman sovereignty, Aurelian was free at last to deal with the Imperium Gallorum. Tetricus had only maintained his position with difficulty. For one thing, Gaul and Britain were again prey to barbarian raids across the frontier rivers and pirate attacks from the sea; for another the governor of one province, a certain Faustinus, had rebelled with the support of soldiers opposed to Tetricus's passive policy. And the common people were disillusioned with an emperor who could no longer guarantee their security against barbarians or sedition. As Aurelian crossed the Alps, a reluctant Tetricus and his son took the field. The two armies faced off against each other in the early spring of 274 near Cavillonum (Châlons-sur-Marne) and Aurelian was, predictably, the victor.

In less than four years he had established peace along the frontiers and restored the eastern and western provinces lost under Gallienus; for his efforts the populace hailed Aurelian as *restitutor orbis* (restorer of the world). Aurelian's triumph in Rome surpassed any previous celebration within living memory. Zenobia and Tetricus were present as captives but neither was humiliated in the traditional way. Aurelian restored Tetricus to his senatorial rank and estates, while Zenobia (and presumably her son Vabalathus, of whom nothing more is recorded) was given her freedom and settled with a pension in a villa near Rome. Aurelian was hardly a merciful man, so this unexpected kindness was probably motivated by political expediency – an empire-healing gesture, perhaps.

Reform of the monetary system was urgent but Aurelian was unable to do much more than a cosmetic job by giving the Gallienic *billon* a slightly heavier coating of gold or silver. Nevertheless, he tackled commodities, fixing the price of bread but also increasing the Egyptian corn supply so that the *collegium pistorum* (millers' guild) should not lose out. He extended the dole to provisions such as meat, oil and salt, benefits which came at the price of freedom for the *collegia* of butchers, oil processors and bakers; previously voluntary associations were transformed into compulsory ones, subject to strict control, their members forced to live and work in military-style barracks, much as happened to the builders' constructing the new defensive wall. Aurelian's reforms extended the state's supremacy over the lives of all citizens, a hegemony that Diocletian and Constantine extended further in the fourth century.

Aurelian's religious reforms were no less radical. With unity restored, he demanded a common recognition of the empire's majesty and did so by focusing citizen's emotional needs through the widely spread worship of the sun, placing Sol Invictus at the head of the Roman pantheon. He ensured the puritanical rites, which encompassed all the Roman deities, had nothing in common with earlier Elagabaline excesses. The traditional imperial headwear of a circlet of oak leaves was now transformed into the 'rays' of the spiked gold diadem of Sol Invictus – forerunner of medieval crowns.

The improved fortification of Italian cities was not echoed along the northern frontiers. Material economies had to be made and, accepting the lack of frontier troops, Aurelian reluctantly gave up the Agri Decumates and Dacia in 275 to save the ruinous cost of garrisons. On the credit side, moving the Romanised population to the Danube's southern shore went a long way towards repopulating the provinces of Moesia, Pannonia and Thrace so ravaged by barbarian invasions and recurrent plague. On the other hand, Aurelian was determined to reoccupy Mesopotamia, and in the same year assigned Probus again to Egypt, while he gathered his Illyrian legions and headed for Byzantium – but he never reached the city. Encamped at Caenophrurium, outside Byzantium, a ridiculous plot devised by his secretary, Eros, which played on some officers' fear of Aurelian's notoriety as a disciplinarian, resulted in an alarmed and angry band marching to his tent where they killed him.

## Tacitus  Marcus Claudius Tacitus Pius Felix Invictus Augustus
[ c.November 275–April 276 ]

An *interregnum* of about a month followed, during which Aurelian's wife Ulpia Severina may have reigned, since some of her coins were issued after her husband's death. The emperor's murder created a unique situation, in which the Illyrian soldiers refrained from naming his successor, in part because they didn't want to appear part of the officers' conspiracy by profiting from naming their own choice, and partly because of their admiration for Probus. As Aurelian's most devoted supporter, the Illyrians wanted to discover Probus's wishes in the matter of the succession. Astonishingly, the soldiers referred the decision to the senate. In such a novel situation, their debate might have become protracted were it not for renewed

Tacitus was 75 years old when he was chosen for the purple.

109

unrest on the northern frontier that urged speed. Their choice was the seventy-five-year-old consular Marcus Claudius Tacitus.

At the time of his elevation he was in Interamna (Terni), from where he made his way to Rome to accept the instruments of power. It would be simple to interpret his accession as a revival of senatorial authority over the soldiers, but nothing in Tacitus's six months on the throne indicates any such thing. Indeed, the reigns of Tacitus and his successor Florian represent little more than an extension of the *interregnum*. Tacitus made his first business the seizure and execution of Aurelian's murderers, and his second the appointment of his half-brother Marcus Annius Florianus (Florian) as his praetorian prefect. Despite his advanced years, Tacitus proved to be extraordinarily energetic. A horde of Heruli Goths – apparently recruited by Aurelian for the Persian campaign – had overrun Asia Minor after the emperor's murder cancelled the expedition. Cheated of their opportunity for plunder, the barbarians ravaged through Pontus, Galatia, Cappadocia and as far south as Cilicia. Tacitus and Florian rounded up the barbarians and, by a mix of arms and persuasion, drove them back home. Tacitus had appointed another family member to be governor of Syria, but this Maximinus exercised such a harsh administration that a plot was formed to assassinate him. Having killed Maximinus, the angry conspirators, blaming Tacitus for their oppression, followed him as he made his way back to Europe and killed him.

Florian, half-brother of Tacitus, quickly became the victim of renewed civil war.

## Florian
### Marcus Annius Florianus Pius Felix Invictus
[ c.April 276–c.July 276 ]

Tacitus's death led to renewed civil war. Florian assumed the purple as a hereditary right without waiting for the soldiers' proclamation or the senate's recognition. However, within three weeks the eastern legions proclaimed Probus emperor. Believing he had the numerical advantage, Florian reversed his army's direction and marched south to engage Probus, but he had underestimated his opponent. Probus had not risen to his position under Aurelian without demonstrating an astute military ability. Aware of his disadvantage in numbers, he employed Fabian tactics and avoided a pitched battle at Tarsus, where the two sides met. Using the rugged terrain, Probus's experienced Egyptian troops kept drawing out Florian's Europeans, who became demoralised and then, when disease broke out among them, mutinous. Unwilling to face a prolonged campaign in adverse conditions, Florian's men chose the easy option and murdered him.

Dux Bonosus, Probus's commander of the Rhine fleet, made a doomed bid for the purple to avoid his master's retribution for losing a squadron of ships to marauding Germans.

## Probus
### Marcus Aurelius Probus
[ c.May 276–c.September 282]

Marcus Aurelius Probus, another native of Illyricum, was born in August 232 at Sirmium. During his reign he continued Aurelian's consolidation of the frontiers and the reconstruction of Gaul, which, as he had discovered during his tenure on the Rhine in 274, was still vulnerable to barbarian attack. He returned from Cilicia in order for the senate to ratify his imperial powers, and then immediately left Rome for Gaul, where separate bands of Longiones backed by Alamanni had crossed Germania Superior by way of the Neckar valley, and Franks in the north had crossed the Rhine. Probus split his force and sent his commanders to oppose the Franks while he tackled the Longiones. Both armies were victorious, and Probus captured the Longiones' chieftain, Semnon.

Another Germanic tribe, the Burgundi, had come to the Franks' aid, and Probus moved north to confront them across the Rhine. The enemy was by far the stronger numerically, and Probus again demonstrated his military shrewdness. He arranged for his troops to line the Roman bank and shout obscenities at the Germans. The easily insulted barbarians took the bait and began to cross the river to reach their sneering tormentors, but during their disorderly advance Roman archers picked them off as they waded waist-deep in the strong current. Those that made it to the left bank were not allowed time to organise before the legionaries fell on them. The Burgundi were offered terms and many enlisted in the legions; one contingent sent to serve in Britain proved effective and loyal.

Probus launched a concerted programme of strengthening the forts that had become dilapidated during the period of the Imperium Gallorum and erecting new defences. Some forts were constructed on the eastern bank of the Rhine to command all the major river crossings and provide protection for Roman towns in Germania Inferior, Superior and Gaul. Probus had a passionate belief in viticulture as a means of stabilising the economy and planted many vineyards throughout the western provinces. In 278 he repelled an invasion of Vandals in Illyricum (and planted more vineyards); in 279 he was in Lycia, dealing with Isaurian brigands; in 280 he was on the Nile where a desert tribe called the Blemmyes had advanced northwards as far as Coptos (Qift). While his generals dealt successfully with this incursion Probus occupied himself with the large-scale reconstruction of the dykes, canals and bridges along the Nile, work that led to a dramatic improvement in Rome's grain supply.

Indirectly, the emperor's devotion to growing grapes at every opportunity and the state of relative peace along the Danube contributed to his death. Mindful of the danger caused by under-employed soldiers, Probus put the legions stationed at Sirmium to reclaiming the marshy land around the city as part of his agrarian reforms. After celebrating a triumph in Rome, Probus set out for Illyricum in the summer of 282, intending to mobilise the army for a renewed attempt to recover Mesopotamia. While he was at Sirmium news arrived that the army in Raetia had proclaimed Probus's praetorian prefect Carus, who was in command there, as emperor. Angered by the labourers' work they had been subjected to in recovering the swamps for the planting of vineyards, the soldiers at Sirmium sided with their fellows in Raetia, rose up in mutiny and murdered Probus.

Probus had already enjoyed a long and successful military career by the time he became emperor.

## Carus  Marcus Numerius Carus / Marcus Aurelius Carus
[ c.September 282–c.August 283 ]

As soon as Carus heard of Probus's murder, he sent a dispatch to the senate to announce his elevation. He nominated first his elder son, Marcus Aurelius Carinus, and soon after his younger son, Marcus Aurelius Numerianus (Numerian), as joint rulers with himself, and gave them each the rank of Caesar. Carus was a break with the run of Illyrian emperors, since he appears to have been born in Narbo (Narbonne). He was probably in his early fifties at his accession in 282. Disdaining any senatorial approval, Carus spurned Rome and, leaving Carinus as Caesar of the European provinces, made for Syria with Numerian to complete Mesopotamia's reconquest. To further strengthen his dynastic ties he arranged the marriage of Numerian to the daughter of Arrius Aper, his praetorian prefect.

In a short reign, Carus accomplished much. Marching through Pannonia, his army defeated forces of Quadi and Sarmatae that had broken into the province. The Romans encountered little resistance from Sassanian border guards on the Euphrates, and once again Mesopotamia was returned to Roman sovereignty. Carus now invaded

In spite of his short reign, Carus achieved much.

Coin of Vahram II (276–93): his father, Vahram I, succeeded Shapur I to the Sassanian throne, but only ruled for three years.

Persia by way of Armenia and marched down the Tigris. Vahram II, who was still consolidating his reign after the death of Shapur I in 272, was unable to mount a concerted opposition. The Romans reached Ctesiphon and Carus added the title Parthicus Maximus to his titles. He was pressing further south when he suddenly died in late July or early August 283. The circumstances of his death are mysterious. Illness is the most plausible explanation, but several reports suggested that lightning struck him down. Of course, he may have been the victim of an assassination, but the smooth succession of Numerian points to death by natural causes.

**Numerian**  Marcus Aurelius Numerianus
[ c.August 283-c.November 284 ]
**Carinus**  Marcus Aurelius Carinus
[ c.August 283–July 285 ]

Unlike his father, Numerian shuddered at a soldiers' life – he much preferred studying literature and writing his own prose to the rigours of military campaigning. It's not known whether he concluded any treaty with Vahram, although subsequent events point to the fact that he just left Persia without making any diplomatic contact at all. By March 284 he was in Emesa and apparently in good health, but at some point after leaving his vision became impaired and he took to riding in a litter to protect his eyes from the sunlight. This seclusion provided his father-in-law Arrius Aper with the opportunity to kill his weakling emperor. For some days the prefect kept the crime secret, until the imperial bodyguard noticed the odour of decay issuing from the litter. The alternative explanation that Numerian died of an illness and his staff officers colluded in concealing his death from the troops until a suitable successor could be found is not supported by the consequences.

The discovery of the body led to an assembly in Nicomedia on 20 November 284, at which a senior officer named Valerius Diocles accused Aper of assassinating Numerian. Diocles personally executed the prefect for the crime and the troops proclaimed Diocles emperor in Numerian's place. Once again, the soldiers had followed the precedent of making an emperor, but in Diocles they had made one whose like Rome had not seen since Trajan.

The death of his father Carus had left Carinus, as the elder of the two Augusti, responsible for maintaining a semblance of order. There is evidence that he continued his father's campaigns against the Quadi, before spending the winter of 283–84 in Rome, where he also commenced his second consulship, with distant Numerian as his colleague. Soon after receiving news of Numerian's death, Carinus mobilised to confront Diocles. The rival emperors met in Moesia in the valley of the Margus in July 285. According to historical tradition, the army of Carinus was on the point of victory when the emperor

Coin depicting the brothers Carinus and Numerian as co-Augusti. Carinus (*left*) was made of sterner stuff than his younger brother.

was treacherously slain by a trusted officer (but whose wife he had allegedly seduced). The story of Carinus's murder is consistent with the negative literary tradition that referred to him as 'the evil emperor Carinus'. He is depicted as a bloodthirsty tyrant, executioner of senators, rapist of their wives and murderer of those who had teased him when they were together in school. The *Historiae Augustae* records that he had nine wives and ignored his real wife, Magnia Urbica. It's doubtful that Carinus had either the time or the energy for such excessive sexuality, and if he was – as the more warlike of the brothers – brutal, he was surely no better nor worse than any run-of-the-mill third-century emperor. The literary damnation of Carinus was almost certainly orchestrated by his successor in what was, by now, a time-honoured tradition of rewriting history; and the man who followed Carinus was certainly able to do that.

Marcus Aurelius Julianus, an Illyrian commander, seized the advantage over Carinus in Illyricum, but was defeated as the legitimate emperor advanced on his battle with Diocles.

**Above:** A view looking down to the Circus Maximus from the monumental ramparts of the Palatine palace; in the foreground the Domus Augustana of Domitian, beyond the remains of the additional palace of Septimius Severus.

**Right:** The Arch of Janus is a unique quadrilateral triumphal monument, which stands in the region of the Forum Boarium, at the foot of the Capitoline Hill in Rome. Erected at the time of Constantine, it later acted as the base of a medieval tower, now removed. The niches held statues.

**Above:** The Porta Ostiensis (Porta San Paolo), one of the massive twin-arched gates later narrowed by Maxentius to a single arch, and raised in height during the reign of Honorius.

**Left:** A section of the Aurelian wall, showing two of the regularly spaced mural towers. The broken section of cornice half way up indicates the wall's original height, while the piercings near the top of the tower mark the Maxentian height; the additional metres were added in the time of Honorius.

Bearded in his younger, military days, Diocletian went clean-shaven to his abdication more than 20 years later – the first and only emperor to do so of his own free will and wish.

# TEN
# The Tetrarchy

[AD 285–313]

**Diocletian**  Valerius Diocles / Gaius Aurelius Valerius Diocletianus
[ 20/11/284–1/5/305 abdicated; died 3/12/311 ]
**Maximian**  Marcus Aurelius Valerius Maximianus
[ Caesar summer 285, co-Augustus 1/4/286–1/5/305 abdicated;
 self-reinstated November 306–November 308; died July 310 ]

In a reign spanning more than twenty-one years, Diocletian altered the course of the Roman empire beyond recognition. Not only did he convincingly end the half century of Military Anarchy, his reforms laid foundations for the way the empire would be governed from this time on, and ultimately secured its continuity in the east for more than a thousand years. In this, there was no sentiment towards past tradition, indeed Diocletian completed the process begun by Augustus of consolidating absolute power.

Valerius Diocles was born in about 245 on the coast of Dalmatia. He and his wife Prisca had a daughter named Valeria. As an Illyrian Diocletian had easy access to a military life and, as he rose through the ranks, his prudent decisions as an officer appear to have been concerned with victory rather than personal glory. Under Carus he gained the rank of *comes domesticorum* (commander of the imperial bodyguard cavalry) and served as a consul in 283.

The forty-year-old who won the battle on the Margus emerged as a complex mix of attributes: wily politician, cunning manipulator, able administrator, passionate architect, by turns clement and harsh – a set of characteristics best summed up as 'cruel but fair'. Diocletian faced many problems in pursuing imperial unity and national security, chiefly the ever-present possibility of military rebellion. The best way to avoid military unrest was to deny generals victories that might induce their troops to proclaim them, which meant the emperor assuming command in all major campaigns. Two startling innovations emerged from this policy of imperial mobility: too far removed from the regions of military activity, Rome could no longer feature as the administrative centre; if the emperor was forever on the move, the court must be mobile too. The *palatium* or resident court officials situated in the Palatine palace were replaced by a 'travelling staff' of the emperor's companions (the *comitatus*). Pragmatic Diocletian understood that he alone could not deliver the level of action required to achieve his aims. With no son to delegate to, he followed Nerva's precedent of appointing a worthy colleague as his partner.

His choice fell on Marcus Aurelius Valerius Maximianus (Maximian), a fellow Illyrian born in about 249–50 at Sirmium and a close friend some five years his junior. In character Maximian was the opposite of Diocletian; while the latter was a shrewd statesman, the former was typical of his countrymen, uncultured, often brutal but a superb strategist. Diocletian appointed Maximian Caesar in the summer of 285 and to emphasise the nature of their relationship, Diocletian assumed the title *Jovius* and gave the title *Herculius* to Maximian, for Jove was the father of the gods, the supreme controller, while Hercules was the god of the earth. Diocletian now moved his peripatetic court to Nicomedia, while Maximian took command of the western provinces, making Mediolanum (Milan) his capital.

This happy state of affairs almost came unstuck in April 286 when his troops named him Augustus after successfully restoring peace to the Gallic provinces which had suffered barbarian raids following Carinus's depletion of troops in 284. This was exactly the kind of situation Diocletian had hoped to avoid, but he wisely acceded to the mens' claim and, by recognising Maximian as co-emperor, prevented any discord. Edicts were now issued in their joint names, but Maximian's reverence of his friend's intellect meant that Diocletian retained supreme power over the legislation. Between 286–88 Maximian and his praetorian prefect Constantius Chlorus (the Pale) brought order along the Rhine, operating from Treveri (as Augusta Treverorum was now known), including through the means of a novel treaty with a Frankish chieftain in 288. In return for being named king of the Franks and protected by Rome in his authority, he and his warriors would swear allegiance to the empire – the first ever barbarian client kingdom on the northern frontier.

Not everything went so smoothly. In the previous year Carausius, the commander of the naval fleet based at Gesoriacum (Boulogne), had turned pirate, invaded Britain and and set himself up as Augustus, from where he later launched a successful raid to capture his old base. For the time being Maximian and Diocletian were obliged to acknowledge Carausius's power, which – either as a snub or a peace offering – he proudly proclaimed on his coins that showed him as the third Augustus alongside his 'colleagues'. For Diocletian's part, he spent time hopping between the lower Danube fighting Sarmatae and the eastern provinces subjugating Saracens. While he was in Syria in 288, he took advantage of Vahram II's continuing internal strife and tidied up the situation left by Numerian's abrupt evacuation of Persia. He returned Armenia to Roman influence, placing an Arsacid, Tiridates III, on the throne and compelled Vahram to give up his claims on Mesopotamia.

**AFTER ABOUT EIGHT YEARS'** of warring in widely spaced theatres, Diocletian became convinced that his constitutional arrangements were inadequate to govern the modern empire. Two rulers couldn't be expected to meet all the demands made of them, and the failure to dislodge Carausius was a direct consequence of their lack of administrative resources. Accordingly he decided to double the number of rulers by each Augustus adopting a non-family member (Diocletian had no sons, and Maximian's son Maxentius, aged about ten, was far too young). In simultaneous ceremonies held in Milan and Nicomedia on 1 March 293, Diocletian nominated a staff officer, Gaius Galerius Valerius, as his Caesar, and Maximian nominated his prefect Constantius Chlorus as his Caesar.

Diocletian enforced the unity of the tetrarchy (rule by four) through inter-marriage as well as adoption. Constantius had to put aside his long-term mistress Helena, by whom he had a twenty-year-old son called Constantinus (Constantine), in order to marry Maximian's stepdaughter Theodora. Galerius was compelled to divorce his wife in order to marry Diocletian's daughter, Valeria. With this collegiate board of rulers, Diocletian had dissolved the problem of constitutional succession that had so plagued the principate. In theory, each Augustus would abdicate as he reached the appropriate retirement age, and his adoptive-nominate Caesar would take his place as Augustus, in turn immediately nominating his own Caesar. In theory it was a stable political system and it had the advantage that each new Augustus would first gain experience of government as a Caesar.

Each tetrarch was entrusted with approximately one quarter of the empire to rule. Diocletian assumed responsibility for the eastern provinces including Egypt, Maximian received Italy, Germania Inferior and Superior, and the provinces of Africa and Hispania. To the Caesars, Galerius was assigned the Balkans as far as the river Inn in the west, and Constantius received Gaul and Britain – which obviously meant he had to evict usurping Carausius to reclaim his patrimony. In 293 Gesoriacum was besieged and finally fell after the Romans constructed a barrage across the harbour

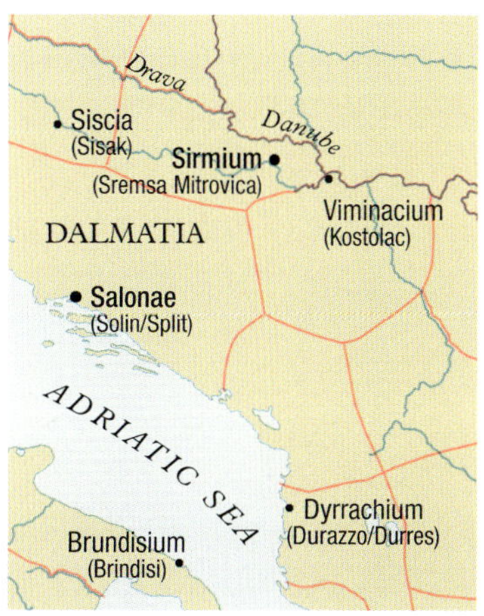

Coin of Maximian bearing the image of the fighting god Hercules on the reverse, embodiment of the House of Herculius, companion to Diocletian's House of Jovius.

British coin of the usurper Carausius (*top*) and his cheek in striking coins depicting him in the foreground with his 'junior co-Augusti' Diocletian and Maximian. Allectus (above) murdered Carausius and hung on to power in Britain for three years until destroyed by the tetrarchs, displaying their unity in this sculpture from Venice.

mouth to prevent any relief reaching it from Britain. For this failure, Carausius lost his authority and fell victim to an assassination plot orchestrated by his chief minister Allectus, who assumed the title of Augustus in his place. The restoration of Britain was delayed for a further three years while Constantius prepared an invasion, but when it came in 296, retribution against Allectus was swift – he was defeated and killed in battle to the south of London.

Between 293–96, Galerius was successful in his provinces along the Danube, developing the region's economic and agricultural life while engaging in several frontier wars with the Marcomanni and Sarmatae. And then in 297 Diocletian appointed him commander-in-chief of the army detailed for war with Persia, and Maximian took over from Galerius in Illyricum. Among his achievements he defeated that ancient foe the Carpi so thoroughly the tribe was erased from the list of barbarian invaders. In the following year Maximian campaigned in North Africa against a Berber confederation that had broken through the Numidian frontier. The war was swift and successful, and Maximian returned to Italy to visit Rome for the first time in his reign.

Meanwhile, the war in Persia opened disastrously for the Romans. Either through poor intelligence or because he underestimated the enemy, Galerius crossed the Euphrates in 297 with insufficient forces and in the region of Carrhae the Sassanians were the victors. Mesopotamia fell again into Sassanid hands. Ancient sources say that Diocletian was so angry at this defeat that he publicly humiliated Galerius by making him run beside his chariot for a mile. His own sense of failure was probably punishment enough for Galerius, who hastened to make good his reputation. In the following year, reinforced with detachments taken from Illyricum, he routed the Sassanians from Armenia, taking a huge booty that included the royal harem. The new Sassanian king, Narses, was so anxious to recover his possessions that he sued for peace. Galerius demurred, but Diocletian overrode the Caesar's wishes and made a treaty favourable to Rome. Not only was the province of Mesopotamia returned, it was extended north to the Tigris, and the client kingdom of Armenia was also extended to include the Caucasian Iberia. Further, merchants trading between the two empires were obliged to use the road that passed through the Roman garrison town of Nisibis, where they had to pay customs duties. The peace thus established was to last for forty years.

After years of uncontested rule, Diocletian started making good his aim of delivering sound government to the people. Under his direction undisguised absolutism came to the Roman empire, which made implementing his reforms a far simpler task than any of his predecessors had faced. Two of the most important reforms affected provincial organisation: the division of the old provinces into smaller administrative units (*see map, pages 120–21*), and the total separation of military and civilian power. Septimius Severus had already sub-divided the Augustan provinces, Diocletian now went further – only the smallest, such as Sicily, were left untouched, others were either halved or further divided into smaller fractions. Some provincial governors were still selected from among the senators, but all the appointments were in Diocletian's hands, and what had been a nominal control by the senate now disappeared entirely. A governor of equestrian rank was given the title of *praeses*.

This division had a twofold benefit in further reducing the power of individual governors, and making local administration more effective and efficient, particularly in view of Diocletian's tax reforms. Control of the *praesides* was organised by grouping the provinces into twelve dioceses: Oriens,

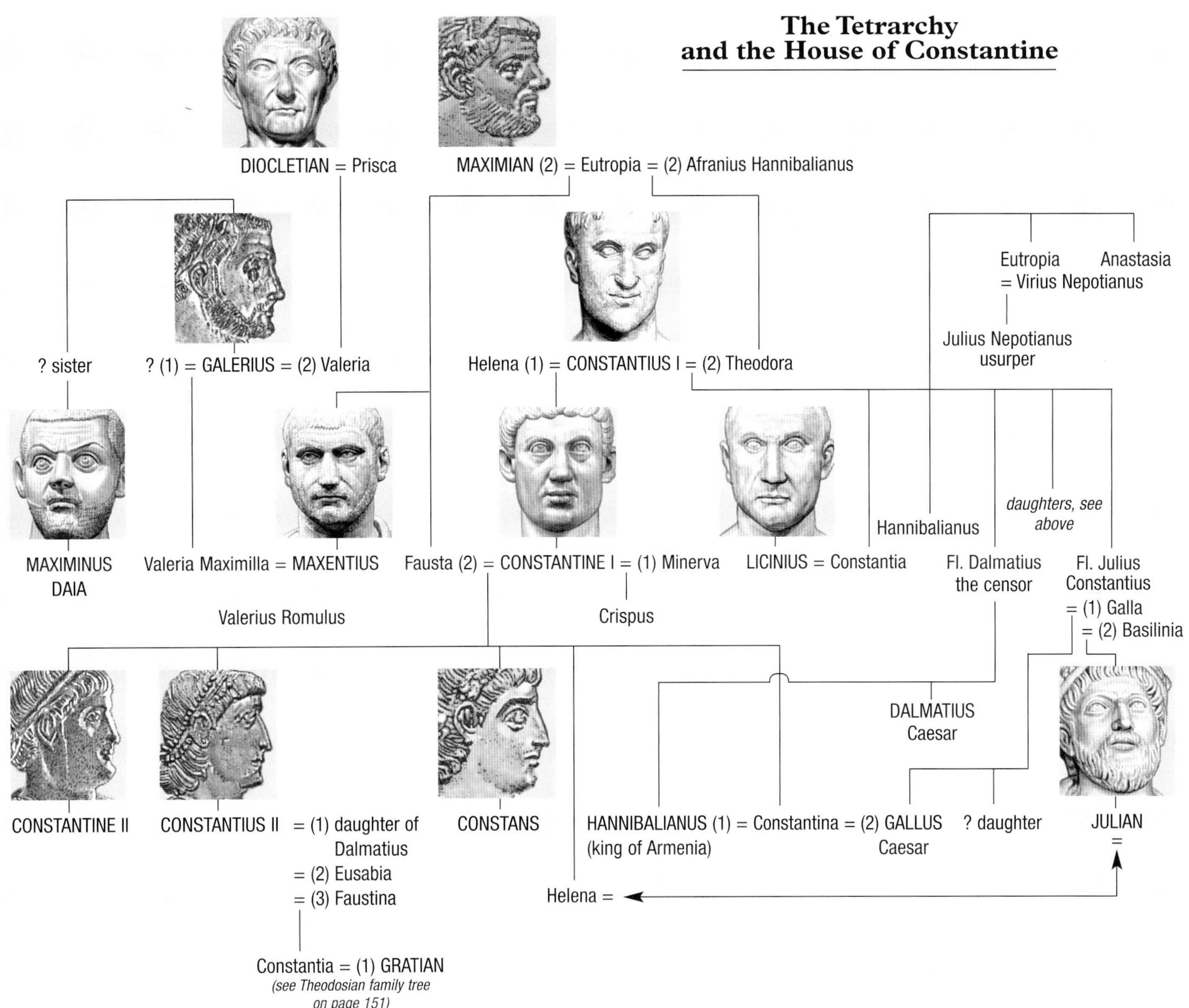


Pontica, Asiana, Thraciae, Moesiae, Pannoniae, Italia, Viennensis, Galliae (frequently also called Septem Provinciae), Britanniae, Hispaniae and Africa. Each diocese was placed under a new equestrian official, the *vicarius* (vicar), who acted as a representative of each tetrarch's praetorian prefect. The prefects, who had held no military command since Hadrian's reforms, retained judicial powers but were given supreme command of the armies of the empire. However, this praetorian power was regulated by giving the *vicari* direct access to the tetrarch to hear any appeals. Italy and the praetorian guard were the great losers in this restructuring. The proud heartland was broken up into 14 provinces of its own diocese and treated like any other region of the empire; eventually, even its traditional tax-exempt status would be removed. As for the praetorians, Diocletian reduced them to no more than the garrison of Rome.

In the army Diocletian made the separation of military and civilian administration absolute. From this point on, command of the frontier armies was in the hands of professional career soldiers styled *dux* (*duces* in the plural). The term had already gained common currency, but under the tetrarchy it became an official ranking.

**The reorganisation of the empire by Diocletian, showing the new dioceses and provincial boundaries**

**The twelve dioceses of Diocletian were numbered from the East**

| | | | | | | |
|---|---|---|---|---|---|---|
| I | Oriens | V | Moesiae | IX | Galliae | ▣ Severan boundary |
| II | Pontica | VI | Pannoniae | X | Britanniae | RAETIA Severan province |
| III | Asiana | VII | Italia | XI | Hispaniae | Diocletianic boundary |
| IV | Thraciae | VIII | Viennensis | XII | Africa | RAETIA I Diocletianic province |

Tetrarchic capital

Where the name did not change it is shown in Diocletianic style

In 296 Lucius Domitius Domitianus, coin above, had himself proclaimed Augustus at Alexandria. The short-lived revolt led Diocletian to a wide-ranging reorganisation of the provinces.

Under Augustus the legions were stationed in the imperial frontier provinces, with no provision made for reserves. To conduct a war meant denuding other sections of the frontier, leaving them open to barbarian attack – a situation continuously repeated throughout the chaos of the third century. The Roman army had also been deficient in cavalry, its relatively few units provided by allied auxiliaries. Gallienus had recognised the necessity of a larger, independent cavalry force, and Aurelian had expanded the notion. Further development now created a fully mobile field army to complement the increasingly stagnant *limitanei* (frontier garrisons), with an ever greater emphasis on cavalry. That the cavalry had gained in importance within the field army is highlighted by the name *vexillationes* used to describe the horsemen, the term that had once described infantry detachments of the Republican legions. The elite cavalry corps, which effectively replaced the praetorians as the imperial bodyguard and travelled wherever any of the tetrarchs went, was called the *scholae palatinae*.

**DIOCLETIAN'S PROGRESSIVELY INTRODUCED** tax reforms established a standard taxation system based on the workers and livestock employed on agricultural land, and on the area of land owned. This resulted in a calculated 'liability unit' which was subjected to a taxation rate applied uniformly throughout the empire, the rate altering depending on the annually predicted needs of the treasury. However, to avoid unrest it had to be an equitable system so allowances were made to take into account the land's fertility, available modes of cultivation and the cash-value of the crops that could be grown. For the first time, the Roman government was able to budget. After estimating the annual outlay and dividing the figure by the total number of tax-payer units, the tax rate could be calculated. These measures led to a hugely enlarged bureaucracy, causing the contemporary historian Lactantius to moan that the empire contained more tax-collectors than tax-payers.

The new system stratified the population into classes, each with an obligation to the state. Diocletian hardened Aurelian's state involvement in the labour market, bringing rigid control to what had once been a voluntary service among the nobility and a natural inclination among the lower classes for son to follow a father's trade. Now no one could leave his guild or change his trade, and sons were bound in law to their father's vocation. Although promotion was not made impossible, the privilege was jealously guarded. The policy created a caste system that stifled initiative, dampened ambition and reduced land workers to virtual slavery.

Fourth-century writers credit Diocletian with the adoption of many forms associated with an oriental monarchy. Layers of court officials, eunuchs and chamberlains restricted access to his presence, and he was rarely seen in public. He introduced the ceremony and etiquette of the Persian court, which included *adoratio* – prostration and the kissing of his hem – and was addressed as *dominus noster* (Our Lord), no longer *princeps*. It would be easy to see these developments as the self-aggrandisement of a power-crazed tyrant, but his abdication after twenty years suggests that these attributes of a glorified potentate were more to do with establishing the emperor's supreme authority than personal vainglory.

Diocletian was very conservative in his religious beliefs. He made offerings to numerous Roman and oriental gods, and his devotion to the old religion – especially Jupiter Optimus Maximus – meant that he was averse to any creed that might undermine the empire's unity. There was no official persecution of Christians during the early years, but this changed abruptly in 302. The blame is usually laid at the feet of Galerius, an uncompromising opponent of Christianity who after his Persian victories had gained considerable influence with Diocletian. Christians were expelled from the court and any soldiers who persisted openly in their faith were cashiered. On 23 February 303 Diocletian issued the first of three edicts that compelled Christians to worship the state's gods which led to mass arrests, executions and the closure of churches, their destruction and the burning of sacred books.

According to Lactantius, Diocletian was a mad builder with 'limitless passion for building'. Although Diocletian visited Rome once in his reign, he did not stint on its monuments. He made extensive repairs on a lavish scale and had a new *curia* built, the senate house which still stands today. Most extensive were his glorious baths, the largest in Rome, capable of holding 3,000 bathers at any one time. Most public works were undertaken in the provinces, especially at Nicomedia. For himself, Diocletian built a massive palace at Salonae on the Dalmatian coast overlooking the Adriatic. It was modelled on a Roman army camp, more a medieval castle than an open Roman palace.

Diocletian's only visit to Rome, together with Maximian, came towards the end of 303 to celebrate his *vicennalia*. He was about fifty-eight, suffering from some chronic complaint and wanted to order the moment of their joint abdication. A deeply reluctant Maximian finally agreed to step down also, and the abdication was set for

Constantius I Chlorus, father of Constantine the Great, was much loved but died early in his reign.

the spring of 305, after Maximian had also celebrated his *vicennalia*. The obvious choices to succeed Constantius and Galerius as their Caesars were Maximian's twenty-year-old son Maxentius and, his elder by some nine years, Constantius's son Constantine – but neither was selected. Lactantius describes the troops' bafflement on the first day of May 305 at Constantine being passed over and their bewilderment at hearing the names Flavius Valerius Severus (a friend of Galerius, but less popular with the troops) and Galerius's nephew Maximinus Daia read out. Constantine had already distinguished himself against the Persians and the Sarmatae, but Maxentius was passed over for military commands, probably reflecting Diocletian's doubts over his qualities as a future Caesar. This posed a dilemma – could he afford to pass over the legitimate son of Maximian, an emperor, in favour of the bastard of Constantius, a Caesar? Maximian's abdication promise would not withstand such a slight, and so neither was chosen.

Diocletian retired to his palace at Salonae, there to raise vegetables on the extensive roof-gardens, and Maximian retired to Lucania in the south of Italy. Unwell and worn-out, Diocletian was content to watch the outcome of his dynastic scheme from his cabbage patch, but Maximian was restless in his retirement. As a result of these arrangements, over the next eight years civil war boiled.

## Constantius I Chlorus
Gaius Flavius Valerius Constantius
(Caesar 1/3/293, co-Augustus 1/5/305–25/7/306)
## Galerius
Gaius Galerius Valerius Maximianus
(Caesar 1/3/293, co-Augustus 1/5/305–early May 311)

Galerius and his second wife Galeria Valeria, Diocletian's daughter.

The two new Augusti were wildly different people: Constantius Chlorus of noble Dardanian descent and traditional education, Galerius an unlettered peasant herdsman from near Serdica (Sofia) in Dacia Ripensis. Both, however, had made their fortunes in the army, Galerius thanks to Diocletian's patronage, rising to the rank of prefect as well. Later Christian writers place a negative spin on Galerius, the monster of Christian persecution, and a positive glow on Constantius, father of the first Christian emperor of Rome. Realisitcally, Galerius appears as direct and vigorous, a man of action, but also an unimaginative administrator, and frequently cruel, whereas Constantius gained the respect and affection among the provincials of Gaul and Britain. Had he survived longer than a year as Augustus, he might have grown into a worthy successor to Diocletian.

Nominally, Constantius became the senior tetrarch. However, Galerius's subordination meant little, for both the new Caesars were his men – Maximinus the son of his sister, Severus a long-time close friend – and neither seemed to possess the strength of character to counter his will. Thus, through Severus, he exercised considerable influence in Constantius's dominions, and effectively ruled three-quarters of the Roman empire. In addition, Constantius's son Constantine, residing with his mother Helena at Byzantium, was within Galerius's dominion – a useful hostage in any potential confrontation. However, when Constantius demanded Galerius send him his son to aid in the eviction of Pictish tribes from the north of Britain, Galerius complied. It was just in time. After a successful campaign, father and son retired to Eburacum (York) where Constantius died of some wasting disease on 25 July 306.

Constantine had ever been a popular figure with the eastern army, and in a short space of time achieved a similar level of affection among the western troops. The

Severus II – an unloved and unlucky Augustus.

British and Gallic armies had no hesitation in proclaiming him Augustus in his father's place and – wisely or not – he accepted. Galerius was caught on the hop. He wanted to raise Severus to the status of Augustus and nominate another of his own creatures as Caesar, but Constantine's popularity with the armies of west and east posed a danger. In the end he offered a compromise that recognised Constantine as Caesar to Severus as Augustus. Partly because he didn't yet feel strong enough to dispute Galerius, and partly out of respect for Diocletian's constitutional arrangements, he accepted this inferior status, and so the tetrarchy survived in its original structure.

### Severus II  Flavius Valerius Severus
[ Caesar 1/5/305; co-Augustus August 306–March/April 307, abdicated, died16/9/307 ]
### Maxentius  Marcus Aurelius Valerius Maxentius
[ 28/10/306–28/10/312 ]

Maximian's son Maxentius, who had remained in some obscurity within Rome's walls, now encountered fate at the hands of the disgruntled praetorian guard. Diocletian had reduced their number and affronted their dignity by downgrading them to lowly garrison status. Galerius went further, closing the *castra praetoria* and billeting them on civilians. Additionally, Galerius's decision to tax the citizens as part of the Italian diocese – something that had never happened in the city's history – drove the mob to demand a new emperor. Maxentius was the obvious candidate. With the tacit support of the urban prefect, Annius Anullinus, Maxentius assumed the purple on 28 October 306 without opposition except that of Abellinus, the *vicarius* and a supporter of Galerius, who was put to death for his resistance.

Amid the universal rejoicing for a legitimate son of an Augustus 'justly' succeeding his father Maximian, Maxentius must, nonetheless, have been worried. The depleted praetorian guards represented little in the way of an army, and while he could take comfort from his recognition by Africa, the Tyrrhenian island provinces, and southern and central Italy, he still had to proceed cautiously with northern Italy, loyal to Severus in Milan. Many of his father's veterans now served Severus, but if he could induce them to return to their old allegiance, his position would be safer, so he made overtures to his retired father in Lucania. Maximian had expressed his disapproval of an elevation made by the praetorian guard, but Maxentius seduced his father with an offer of the imperial insignia and told him it was his responsibility to resume his position as senior Augustus, which he hoped would legitimise his usurpation. Bored with inaction, Maximian consented.

Maxentius, son of Maximian, and his own son Valerius Romulus (below).

Pushed by Galerius, Severus left Milan early in 307, but Maxentius's trust in old loyalties proved well placed. Unwilling to fight the son of their old commander, the majority of men deserted, forcing Severus to flee back north with only a few remaining troops. Having resumed his position as co-Augustus, Maximian chased Severus to Ravenna, where peace terms were arranged. In return for his life Severus abdicated and was taken hostage. Son and father now controlled the African and Italian dioceses with the exception of Raetia, and the obvious next course of action was to make an alliance with Constantine to protect their position from Galerius. Through the marriage of his daughter Fausta – aged about fourteen – to Constantine, Maximian achieved this outcome in the spring of 307. He also legitimised his new son-in-law's rank of co-Augustus in return for Constantine acknowledging Maxentius as the senior emperor. Maximian stayed with Constantine at Treveri, while Maxentius looked after Rome.

Meanwhile Galerius had mobilised and advanced without opposition through Italy in the summer of 307, but at Rome he encountered problems. His forced march from the Balkans had prevented carrying siege engines and so his men were unable to storm the Aurelian Wall. Worse, his legions had ravaged the surrounding countryside in their progress, while Rome was well provisioned with supplies from Africa and Sicily. Galerius had no alternative but to beat a disorderly retreat. His army should have made easy pickings, but for some reason Maxentius remained firmly behind the city walls. When he learned of Galerius's escape, Maximian was furious with his son, and even more so when the news arrived that Maxentius had disobeyed his orders and put Severus to death on 16 September 307.

Galerius now appealed to Diocletian to intervene, but the result was divisive. In November 308 Diocletian – reluctantly dragged to a conference at Carnuntum – dashed Maximian's hopes for a favourable outcome by demanding his resignation and annulling all his imperial fiats. This, of course, included his legitimisation of Maxentius – who was declared a public enemy – and Constantine. To replace Severus Diocletian appointed another friend of Galerius, Licinianus Licinius, as Augustus, and gave him the administration of Italy, Africa and the Spanish provinces, although these were actually under the control of Maxentius (and Licinius was needed to help the ailing Galerius). Constantine was demoted to the rank of Caesar, and the position of Maximinus Daia was left untouched. Although Diocletian had re-established a tetrarchy, it was done in a manner inconsistent with his system because Licinius had achieved the rank of Augustus without ever having been a Caesar. Constantine resented the decision and Maxentius simply refused to accept the conference's outcome, effectively saying 'Come and get me!' Constantine followed suit and his defiance, marked by tumultuous cries of approval from the Gallic provincials and his legions, so alarmed Maximinus Daia that he had himself proclaimed Augustus by his Syrian army on the first day of May 310. Galerius was obliged to acknowledge the *fait accompli*. It was a busy year.

Maxentius mishandled the tense situation in Africa and the resulting rebellion led to the loss of his grain supply. His father Maximian was also stirring the pot at Treveri behind Constantine's back, but after overplaying his hand in his son-in-law's absence at the Rhine front, he was arrested, but escaped and fled to Massilia. Constantine spared his life, but soon afterwards he was found dead in his rooms. The official verdict was suicide, but it would not be hard to forgive Constantine if, exasperated by the sixty-year-old reprobate's continual scheming, he had ordered his execution.

Now Constantine acted. Falsely claiming that his father was the natural son of Claudius Gothicus, he legitimised his imperium on the principle of hereditary succession. He disassociated himself from the tetrarchic houses of *Jovius* and *Herculius*, replacing them with Sol Invictus, worshipped as Apollo in Gaul. At the end of the year he annexed the Spanish provinces, which loss was a disaster for Maxentius. Famine spread quickly in Rome, and street violence became endemic between the pampered praetorians and the starving mob. As many as 6,000 may have perished. Across the Mediterranean Galerius, who was in his mid-fifties, was in ill health by the spring of 311, suffering from a cancer that the Christians gleefully attributed to divine retribution for his hatred of their faith. Eusebius described his suffering with un-Christian relish:

> From [his suppurating wounds] came a teeming mass of worms, and a sickening smell was given off; for the whole of his hulking body, thanks to over-eating, had been transformed even before his illness into a huge lump of flabby fat, which then decomposed and presented those who came near with a revolting sight.

Perhaps Galerius believed that his sickness was a judgement of the gods because he issued an Edict of Tolerance on 30 April granting freedom of worship under certain conditions. But it did nothing to save him, and he died a few days later.

A coin struck in 308/9 depicts Constantine as *Filius Augustorum* – Son of Augustus – an 'honour' he loathed.

Lucius Domitius Alexander, *vicarius* of Africa, who opposed Maxentius and his policies, was proclaimed by his troops in late 308 and cut off the essential grain supply to Rome.

The empire was now in the hands of four emperors: Constantine held the western provinces, Maxentius Italy, Licinius the Balkans and much of Asia Minor, and Maximinus Daia – technically now the senior Augustus – Egypt up to eastern Cappadocia. On hearing of Galerius's death, Maximinus Daia increased his grip on the eastern provinces, annexing Pontica and Asiana, and forcing Licinius to a settlement that left him only the Illyrian dioceses, with the Bosphorus and Hellespont the boundary between them. Simply because he was the nearer, Constantine made an alliance with Licinius, since he never would with his rival Maxentius.

In December 311 Diocletian died at Salonae in his massive palace. Lactantius claimed he committed suicide from the disappointment at seeing the fruits of his constitutional labours ruined – perhaps he was right. With the death of the one man to whom Constantine most owed his allegiance he set out to make himself sole ruler of the Roman empire. In the early spring of 312 the war with Maxentius began. Constantine had no intention of leaving the Rhine frontier unguarded, so he set out from Gaul with only a quarter of his available force, an army of about 40,000 men. Maxentius could call on at least four times the number, although his inclination was to keep the bulk of his force behind the Aurelian Wall, which he began strengthening and transforming in the uncompromisingly tough manner of his buildings. In his six-year reign he contributed the largest vaulted building ever attempted by Roman civil engineers. The Basilica Nova of Maxentius, standing on the northeastern end of the Forum, was completed by Constantine, and is sometimes confusingly known by the latter's name as a result. Only four huge piers carried the monumental weight of its coffered ceiling. The basilica used innovative architecture that threw out most of the previous classical forms, and with its mix of groin- and barrel-vaults, is the forerunner of the great Romanesque religious basilicas of the medieval era. Maxentius laid out a large palace complex beside the Via Appia which included a circus to hold 15,000 spectators and a massive domed mausoleum. Maxentius never rested in his mausoleum, neither did his statue grace his basilica. After completing the building, Constantine set up the colossal statue of himself that can be seen today in pieces in the courtyard of the Palazzo dei Conservatori (Capitoline Museum) in Rome.

Constantine crossed the Alps, took Segusio (Susa) by surprise and captured Augusta Taurinorum (Turin). The Transpadene cities opened their gates, except Verona which soon fell after a fierce battle, followed by Mutina (Modena) after a short siege. At this point, Constantine's victories had come at a high price. Fatalities and injury had reduced his expeditionary force to about 25,000, nowhere near enough to confront Maxentius. Never a reckless commander, it looked as though he would have to retire, or beg reinforcements from Licinius. And yet this highly cautious man did neither: against all expectation he advanced towards Rome and what looked like certain defeat. Christian writers claimed that his confidence lay in the righteousness of his cause for – they wrote – Constantine was to all intents and purposes a Christian. This is putting it rather simply, however. His mother Helena *was* a professed Christian and this, in combination with his natural tolerance, had reduced his Roman immunity to the religion's mysteries. Eusebius tells of how, in later life, Constantine described to the chronicler of the vision he received while worshipping Gallic Apollo, in which a cross stood above the sun, accompanied by the words 'Conquer with this', followed by *XXX*, the years of the reign due to him.

A newfound religious fervour hardly explains Constantine's rash decision, however. There's more to the story. On his side he had the affection of his own troops and those of the eastern dioceses, and undoubtedly many in Rome admired his reputation, while Maxentius's soldiers were doubtful of their leader's abilities. The Christian histories also ignore Constantine's massive network of agents – many of them within the city. Thus he already knew the impact the recent famine had made on civilians and military alike, he knew about the severe division between regular

Bust of Helena, Constantine's mother, who as a professed Christian had a profound influence over her son, and a coin stamped with the Christian Chi-Rho symbol, the Greek letters symbolising the name of Christ.

soldiers and the praetorians, the sloppy discipline of the army and the disaffection in which Maxentius was held. Everything pointed to the fact that a determined march by a fiercely loyal army of highly trained and battle-hardened troops would – at the least – lead to a stream of desertions from the enemy's ranks. Nevertheless, he sought extra insurance and had his men paint the Christian Chi-Rho symbol on their shields. Close to Constantine as the tutor of his eldest son Crispus, Lactantius says that during the night before the final battle Constantine was commanded in a dream to do this. Under his new standard, the so-called *labarum*, his soldiers advanced as the first Christian army in history.

Constantine's aggressive tactics bore fruit. Maxentius altered his strategy and came out from behind his massive fortifications, a change probably forced on him by his soldiers' uncertain temper. After crossing the Pons Mulvius (Milvian Bridge) and a specially constructed pontoon bridge next to it, Maxentius's vanguard went upstream along the Tiber until the pass of the Saxa Rubra. Here, the column was blocked by advance units of Constantine's army and came to a standstill. Constantine seized the initiative. Leaving a sufficiently large force to hold the defile, he took his army across the ridges behind which the enemy was massed in the river valley. When he reached the Via Flaminia and the Milvian Bridge there was enough room to deploy into attack formation. The bridge was the objective, and the rocky ridges on either side protected his flank. Maxentius, hemmed in between the hills and the river, had no alternative but to convert the left flank of the strung out column into his centre. In one swift tactic, Constantine had reduced his foe's fighting capacity into a numerical inferiority.

Constantine's first assault broke the resistance of the enemy's front ranks and drove their supporting troops back in confusion towards the Tiber, swollen with winter run off from the Appenines. Thousands of Maxentius's panicking men drowned in the raging waters and many more, including Maxentius, were swept to their deaths when the pontoon bridge collapsed under their weight. It was 28 October 312, the very same day when, six years earlier, Maxentius had unilaterally assumed the purple. He was not yet thirty. Constantine entered Rome on the following day, carrying Maxentius's head, whose body had been recovered some way downstream. There was much rejoicing of the people and senate, who gratefully erected a statue of Constantine holding a cross in his right hand. Work began immediately on the magnificent arch by the Colosseum that to this day bears witness to his victory over the 'usurper' Maxentius. And by virtue of Constantine's shields, the battle of the Milvian Bridge became the first official Christian victory.

On a coin of c.313, a triumphant Constantine is depicted gazing heavenwards.

## Maximinus Daia
Gaius Galerius Valerius Maximinus Daia
[ Caesar 1/5/305; Augustus 1/5/310–July 313 ]
## Licinius
Gaius Valerius Licinianus Licinius
[ 11/11/308–19/12/324, abdicated, died early 325 ]

Constantine wasted little time in fulfilling the second part of his destiny. The day after entering Rome on 29 October 312 he formally recognised the nominal powers of the senate. Then he had the senators confer on himself the status of senior Augustus, which since the death of Galerius had been that of Maximinus Daia. In theory, this invested him with the constitutional right to nominate consuls, and he immediately sent a dispatch to Maximinus naming him his colleague for 313, together with an order to stop the continuing persecution of Christians. To this, Maximinus paid temporary lip service, presumably to prevent Constantine from

The struggle for supreme power between the tetrarchs, 308–13

OCEANUS GERMANICUS (North Sea)

Bust of Maximinus Daia and coin below. Diocletian's breaking of his own tetrarchic rules led directly to confrontation between all the parties, particularly between Maximinus and Licinius.

BRITANNIAE

Augusta (Londinium)

MARE BRITANNICUM (English Channel)

Germania II

Rhine

Germania I

Belgica II

Treveri (Trier)

Belgica I

Edict of Milan proclaimed, 313

Diocletian recalled to a conference of tetrarchs, 308

Danube

Norricum Ripense

Carnuntum

Lugdunensis II

Lutetia (Paris)

Raetia II

Norricum Mediterraneum

PANNONIA

Pannonia I

Valeria

Juliomagus (Angers)

G A L L I A E

Lugdunensis I

Sequania

Raetia I

Venetia

Sirmiu

Pannonia II

Aquatanica I

Augustodunum (Autun)

Alpes Graiae

Mediolanum (Milan)

Verona

Aquileia

Savia

Augustonemetum (Clermont-Ferrand)

Ludgunum (Lyons)

Segusio (Susa)

Augusta Taurinorum (Turin)

312

Mutina (Modena)

Flaminia

MARE ADRIATICUM (Adriatic Sea)

Dalmatia

Salonae

Aquatanica II

Brigantium (La Coruña)

Legio (León)

Gallaecia

Novem Populi

Tolosa (Toulouse)

Massilia

Tuscia et Umbria

ITALIA

Praevalitar

Constantine annexes, 310

Tarraconensis

Caesaraugusta (Zaragoza)

Corsica

Pons Mulvius October 28, 312

Rome

Campania

Epirus Nova

Tarraco (Tarragona)

Lusitania

Olisipo (Lisbon)

Augusta Emerita (Mérida)

Valentia (Valencia)

Carthaginiensis

Baleares

Sardinia

MARE TYRRHENUM (Tyrrhenian Sea)

Apulia et Calabria

Lucania et Bruttii

Epirus Vetus

Corduba

Baetica

Carthago Nova (Cartagena)

Rebellion, end of 308, declares Africa independent of Maxentius

311

Lilybaeum (Marsala)

Sicily

Tingi (Tangier)

Caesarea (Cherchell)

Hippo Regius

Carthage

HISPANIA

Mauretania Tingitana

Mauretania Caesariensis

Numidia Cirtensis

Proconsularis

Hadrumetum (Sousse)

Mauretania Tabia

Thamugadi (Timgad)

A

F

Numidia Militana

Byzacena

311, Maxentian forces regain Africa

R

I

Leptis Magna

Tripolitania

C

A

Division of the empire between the contenders

Constantine
Maxentius
Gallerius / Licinius
Maximinus Daia
held by Maxentius, annexed by Constantine
retained by Gallerius, disputed by Constantine and Licinius
territory of Licinius overrun by Maximinus Daia

Campaigns

Constantine
Maxentius
Licinius
Maximinus Daia

0  100  200  300  400  500  600  700 km

interfering in his sphere of influence – and countering his plans to conquer the dominions of Licinius.

During his stay in Rome Constantine ordered the complete disbandment of the praetorian guard because of its support for Maxentius, and began the process of returning to the Christian Church all the property that had belonged to it before the Diocletianic edicts. In the New Year he left Rome for Milan to celebrate the marriage of his half-sister Constantia to Licinius – part of the deal the two rulers had struck earlier. The political negotiations that followed the wedding were protracted, tough and uncompleted when they parted company. However, there was little disagreement from Licinius to Constantine's proposal of complete religious tolerance; the message of freedom to Christians in the eastern provinces was a useful weapon in the armoury against Maximinus Daia. The provisions of this new tolerance were compiled into what became known as the Edict of Milan, and were sent to all *praesides* in the western dioceses. Licinius was less happy to accept Constantine's assumed seniority, but eventually agreed to recognise it in return for the right to legislate within his own dominions. They had yet to agree on how to divide up Maxentius's army and no settlement on the future administration of Italy and its adjoining provinces had been reached when the conference was interrupted by Constantine's urgent recall to the Rhine. His absence provided

Maximinus Daia with his best opportunity to press home the attack on Licinius.

Beyond a birth date in the mid-260s in Dacia Ripensis, a peasant upbringing and an army career that brought him into contact with Galerius as a comrade-in-arms, nothing further is known about Licinius before his elevation to the purple on 11 November, 308. The tetrarchic enemy he now faced was of equally lowly origins. Maximinus Daia, son of a sister of Galerius, was born in Illyricum on 20 November 270. He married, but his wife and daughter's names remain unknown. Despite his lowly birth and lack of education, Maximinus encouraged the promotion of learning in his part of the empire, and seems to have had a statesman's grasp of politics and propaganda.

Like Galerius, Maximinus Daia was an ardent Christian persecutor. Although recusants were frequently sent to the mines, there were relatively few executions; but the propaganda was extreme. And it is clear that Maximinus understood the organisation of the Christian Church better than his colleagues, because he set up a pagan priesthood that was graded in a similar way to the Christian hierarchy. Naturally enough, the Christian writers excoriated him, and Lactantius claims that he could not keep his hands off Valeria, daughter of Diocletian and widow of Galerius, even while she was still in mourning. However, it should be noted that the dispossessed relatives of Galerius and Severus seem to have preferred to live under his protection rather than that of Licinius.

Early in 313, while the winter snow still lay thick on the ground, Maximinus besieged Byzantium with an army of some 70,000. The city capitulated after eleven days, leaving the way open into Thrace and a few days later his army was encamped around Heraclea. Licinius mobilised what army he could, probably only 30,000 men. He then marched towards Hadrianopolis (Adrianople) and joined battle with Maximinus on 30 April. By superior tactics and through the exhaustion of Maximinus Daia's men, Licinius was victorious. At Constantine's request, and no doubt because Licinius would not have turned his back on such a successful talisman, his men went into battle with the Christian symbol painted on their shields, so once again the army of the Christian god had prevailed over the forces of paganism.

Maximinus fled the battlefield disguised as a slave to be followed right across Anatolia by Licinius's army. By mid-summer Maximinus was surrounded by land and sea in the vicinity of Tarsus. There he died of his own hand by taking poison. Suitably for the great persecutor, it was a lingering death because the poison was slow-acting, and provided four days of agony before killing him. Thus, the entire eastern half of the empire fell into the hands of Licinius. With inhuman cruelty he ordered the deaths of all Maximinus's leading ministers and government officials. Then he turned on the family. Maximinus Daia's eight-year-old son and seven-year-old daughter were put to the sword, and their mother drowned by being thrown into the Orontes. As if to prove their wisdom in preferring the protection of Maximinus, Licinius executed Candidianus, the illegitimate son of Galerius, and Severianus, son of the former Augustus Severus. When she was later found hiding in Thessalonica, Galerius's wife Valeria too was put to death.

Bust and coin of Licinius and coin of his wife Constantia, half-sister of Constantine. The marital relationship did not prevent the final struggle for sole power over the empire.

# ELEVEN
## Constantine and Byzantium Supreme

[AD 313–364]

### Constantine I the Great  Flavius Valerius Constantinus
[ Caesar August 306; Augustus spring 307; sole emperor 19/12/324–22/5/337 ]

Constantine changed the course of first-millennium history. Because of his policies Christianity spread throughout the Roman empire and became the faith that fired the Western world. His conduct in later life didn't always appear appropriate for a servant of Christ, but by playing the religious card, Constantine united a fractured empire under one standard. He was born at Naissus (Nis) on 27 February in either 272–73 (later cited dates simply don't fit the facts). When his father Constantius married Theodora he accompanied his mother Helena to Byzantium. His first wife, Minervina, bore him a son, Flavius Julius Crispus, and his second, Fausta, the daughter of Maximian, gave him three more –Constantinus (Constantine II), Constantius (Constantius II) and Constans – and two daughters, Constantina and Helena the Younger.

The ten years of joint rule following the destruction of Maximinus Daia were stormy, the fate of Italy always in contention. Within three years Constantine and Licinius were at each other's throats after a series of subterfuges over the control of Pannonia flared into open hostility in the summer of 316. Both armies circled each other throughout the Balkans, fighting indecisive skirmishes before the principals came to terms at Serdica on 1 March 317. Except for Thrace all of Illyricum was ceded to Constantine. In return, Constantine retreated from the legislative powers of the senior Augustus and recognised the right of each to issue edicts within his own realm. Further, they agreed that neither emperor should enter his colleague's provinces except in the event of barbarian invasion.

The uneasy truce held for six years, its ending prompted by religion. Previous emperors had regarded Christianity as divisive to national unity; Constantine was determined to use its power as a unifying movement. Since most of the army and the upper classes were pagans, it was impractical to wed the Church to the state, but he wanted to utilise its moral and economic advantages for the state's benefit. In 318 he issued an edict that added up to a constitution. It recognised the jurisdiction of the episcopal courts and – where by mutual agreement the litigants brought a case before the bishops – accorded their decision the same validity as that of the civil magistrates.

Constantine began a massive programme of religious building, including a basilica for the pope on the site of what had been the camp of the mounted praetorian guard, and many other churches, among them the first St Peter's. To the people he presented himself as the champion of Christians everywhere. Licinius, while bowing to the Christian ethic, remained essentially pagan in his personal pursuits and beliefs. Nevertheless, at first the unity of the Church was important to him, if only to keep the peace with Constantine. What changed his mind was a schism caused by Arianism. A deacon and presbyter of Alexandria called Arius (c.250–336) had professed a heresy that had split the eastern arm of the Church in two. Under Bishop Alexander, the orthodox held that Christ was God, whereas Arius maintained that Christ was only 'His Creature'. The Arians held sway at Licinius's court because Arius – after his expulsion by Alexander in 318 – had become a confidant of the empress Constantia. Further, his follower the writer Eusebius of Nicomedia was favoured by Licinius. For these (hardly religious) reasons Licinius ordered that the teachings of Arius were

The purposeful, clean-cut Constantine and a coin of his mother, the Augusta Helena, and his second wife, Augustus Maximian's daughter Fausta.

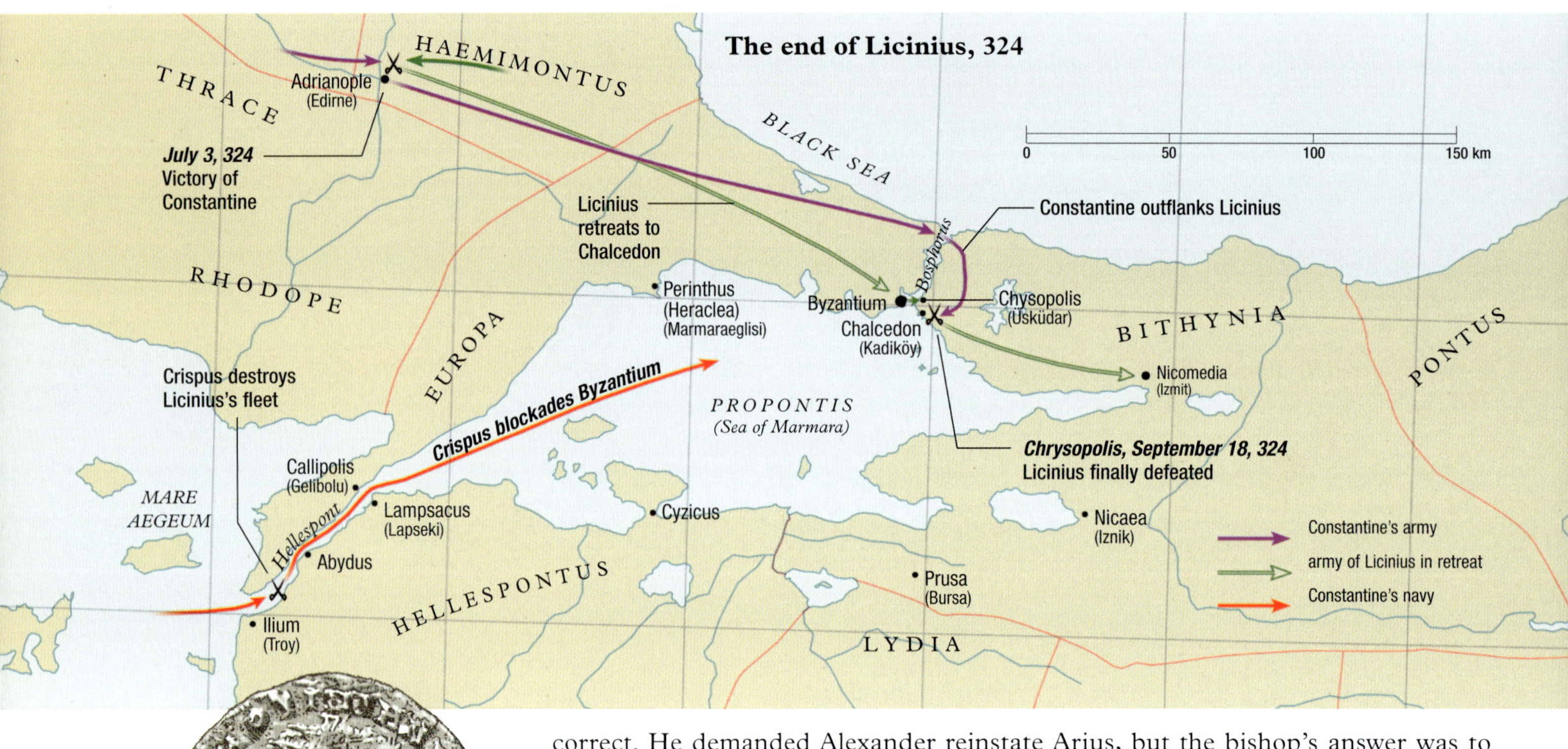

Licinius (above) and his young son Licinius II, who was spared but exiled as a slave-child and later executed on Constantine's orders in 336 to avoid any question of a succession contest.

correct. He demanded Alexander reinstate Arius, but the bishop's answer was to excommunicate Arius and his followers.

At this open defiance Licinius decided that he could no longer tolerate such a powerful organisation operating outside the state's control. In 320 he forbade any further synods and restriced clerical activities. He expelled Christians from the palace, army and the bureaucracy. Several were even condemned to death for failing to comply with his edict. There was a secondary advantage to the expulsions: Licinius was convinced that many Christians in his service were Constantine's spies; he was probably correct.

In 323, Goths entered Thrace. Constantine used the invasion as an excuse to enter his colleague's domain, as by agreement under such circumstances he was entitled to do. Licinius, however, called it aggression and declared war in the following spring. Constantine's army consisted of 120,000 infantry, 10,000 cavalry and a fleet under the command of his son Crispus of some 200 war-galleys and as many as 2,000 transports. Licinius was able to muster an even larger army drawn from all the eastern provinces: 150,000 infantry and 15,000 cavalry, together with a powerful Hellespont fleet. Sheer numbers, however, were not a guarantee of success and on 3 July at Hadrianopolis (Adrianople) he suffered a defeat, falling back on Byzantium. Meanwhile, Crispus sank most of Licinius's ships at the narrows of the Hellespont and sailed towards the Bosphorus. Licinius sued for peace and through the good offices of his wife and Constantine's sister, his life was spared. Licinius retired to Thessalonica, but caught engaging in intrigue shortly after, Constantine had him executed.

Constantine's ambition was fulfilled, at about the age of fifty-two he was the sole ruler of the Roman empire. But his enormous power failed to shield him from a domestic tragedy which occurred in 326. It involved Constantine's first son and his wife, and was to leave the emperor wracked by guilt. Crispus was a popular figure since his victory over Licinius's fleet, and high in his father's esteem. But he was also the son of Constantine's first wife and aroused the jealousy of Fausta on behalf of her own sons. When Crispus left for Treveri to take up his command of the western provinces, Fausta prepared a plot to bring him down. Constantine had issued an edict against sexual misconduct, and in this she saw her opportunity. One or two months later, when the family was reunited at Pola on the Histrian peninsula, Fausta accused Crispus of an adulterous attempt on her, and Constantine had his son executed. But Fausta's victory was short-lived. On the information of Constantine's mother Helena, Fausta was found guilty of a sexual affair with a slave, and condemned to death in accordance with the edict's suitable punishment by being thrust into a vat of boiling water.

It was, perhaps, an act of expiation for the executions that he donated all Fausta's property to the Church, and in penitence that Helena undertook her pilgrimage to the Holy Land shortly after. Her journey was remarkable in so far as few Christians to this point had taken much notice of Judaea as Christ's birthplace and the land of his mission. The very fact that the emperor's mother visited some sites endorsed their validity and established the Holy Land as the essential place of pilgrimage from then on. During her journey Helena acquired several pieces of the True Cross, and thus founded the passion for hunting down relics.

Constantine had spent almost no time in Rome and all of his impressionable youth in Byzantium and shortly after his victory over Licinius he began a massive rebuilding programme of the city. It's doubtful that that he set out to supersede Rome, but the west was now eclipsed in the imperial partnership with trade and culture buzzing in the east, as Asia grew in importance. More to the point, in contrast to pagan Rome, this was to be the Christian capital of the world. Constantine never dedicated the new city to his own name, it was styled Roma Nova and probably only became known as Constantinople after his death. He dedicated New Rome on 11 May 330. But even then it lacked a proper water supply, which was only provided by Valens in about 373 in the form of aqueducts, conduits and cisterns. Certainly Rome was snubbed and its prestige diminished, and as if to emphasise the point, the fragments of the True Cross brought back from Judaea by Helena were installed above the cupola of the triumphal arch known as the *millon* – the First Milestone. From here all distances in the empire were now to be measured; no longer did all roads lead to Rome, Constantinople was literally the centre of the world.

Religious toleration had been promised at Milan: 'Let no one molest another,' Constantine had written, and at first there was no suppression of pagan temples, although the erection of statues of idols was forbidden and pagan festivals were banned. Later, imperial *agentes* began a programme of confiscating the treasures of pagan temples and several, including that of Asclepius at Aegae, were closed. Nevertheless, Constantine continued to let pagans serve in the administration, even as Christian bishops began to predominate, and he styled himself *pontifex maximus* until his death. Finally, he banned gladiatorial games, although the city of Rome continued to defy the edict for the better part of a century.

In his administration Constantine extended and refined many of Diocletian's policies, rather than innovating. He formalised the division between infantry and cavalry under two new senior commanders, the *magistri peditum* (infantry) and *equitum* (cavalry) who reported to the emperor through the all-powerful commander-in-chief, the *magister militum*. Constantine also confirmed the lateral division of the army between the *ripenses* (the *limitanei* of former years, who manned the frontier forts) and *comitatenses*, the mobile field troops. The *comitatenses* received a higher pay than the *ripenses*, a factor that would contribute to a steady decline in frontier morale in the years to come. Rome's praetorian guards were replaced by units of the *scholae* cavalry. An important innovation was the creation of the *schola agentium in rebus*, an intelligence-gathering corps that replaced the numerous free-lance agents of previous regimes, such as the *delatores*. Henceforward spies, or *agentes*, were under military discipline.

Constantine established the base unit of gold currency, the *solidus*, at a lighter weight than the old *aureus* with a ratio of 72 coins to the pound, a value it retained

Popular Crispus (*coin above*), Constantine's son from his first marriage, fell foul of his step-mother Fausta in 326.

The empress Helena's visit established the Holy Land as the essential destination of pilgrimage.

Obverse and reverse of a coin celebrating the status of Costantinopolis as Roma Nova.

133

for centuries. To achieve what had eluded previous emperors Constantine required large amounts of the precious metal. This was acquired by melting down gold ornaments seized from pagan temples and from the Armenian mines that Diocletian's eastern campaigns had made accessible. Nevertheless, someone had to pay for Constantinople and the army's costs. The sixth-century Greek historian Zosimus noted that Constantine's taxes were so excessive that fathers were forced to hire out their daughters as prostitutes to pay their debts. And there was misery for the lower classes. Under Constantine, Aurelian's regulation of the workforce, tightened by Diocletian, was made absolute; the labourer became a virtual prisoner of his trade and workplace.

The elaborate court ceremonial exceeded that of Diocletian. Constantine wore a diadem encrusted with pearls and valuable gemstones over piled up false hair, often multi-hued, skillfully arranged by a team of stylists. He wore flowing robes of pure silk embroidered with flowers of gold, and where Diocletian's presumptions were to adorn the majesty of his position, Constantine's seemed more like an effeminacy so in contrast to his down-to-earth warrior youth. Despite this and his advancing years Constantine was still vigorous and undertook several military campaigns on the frontiers. In 328 he moved the imperial court to Treveri, from which, with young Constantine, he supervised operations against the Alamanni. Late in 332 the Sarmatae appealed for help against a threatening invasion of the Goths, and young Constantine was sent to take command, while his brother Constantius, who had been raised to the rank of Caesar in 324, followed him. The Roman army inflicted a crushing defeat on the Goths. In 333 Constantine's youngest son Constans was raised to the rank of Caesar at the age of ten, and in 335 the emperor made a fourth Caesar of the *magister militum*, his nephew Flavius Dalmatius

In 310 Shapur II had ascended the Sassanid throne and for twenty years he had consolidated his position. In 334 he kidnapped Tiran, the Arsacid king of Armenia, and in the following year annexed the country. Recognising the pointlessness of placing another Arsacid on the throne, Constantine appointed his nephew and son-in-law Hannibalianus king of Armenia; Hannibalianus was married to his eldest daughter Constantina. He immediately force-marched his army into Armenia, where he surprised and routed the Persians in 336.

Early in 337, Constantine established himself at Nicomedia in preparation to co-ordinate the follow up to Hannibalianus's success, and it was there in May that he fell ill. Sensing his death was near, the 'Servant of God' took the final step in his religious conversion and at the age of about sixty-four received the sacrament of baptism. Constantine died on 22 May, the Feast of the Pentecost, and was laid to rest in the Church of the Holy Apostles in Constantinople as the thirteenth of that illustrious number. However, the Roman senate – probably to appease the fury of the Roman mob that the emperor should be buried in the east – granted him divine honours, and so the first Christian emperor joined his pagan predecessors in the pantheon of Roman divinities.

His body was treated less kindly. Like any aspiring empire-builder Constantine had raised too many buildings too quickly with far too few skilled workers or decent

The young Caesars: Constantine II (*top*); Constantius II, obverse and reverse; Constans (*below*).

Constantine's nephews: Dalmatius (*above*) and Hannibalianus, the short-lived king of Armenia.

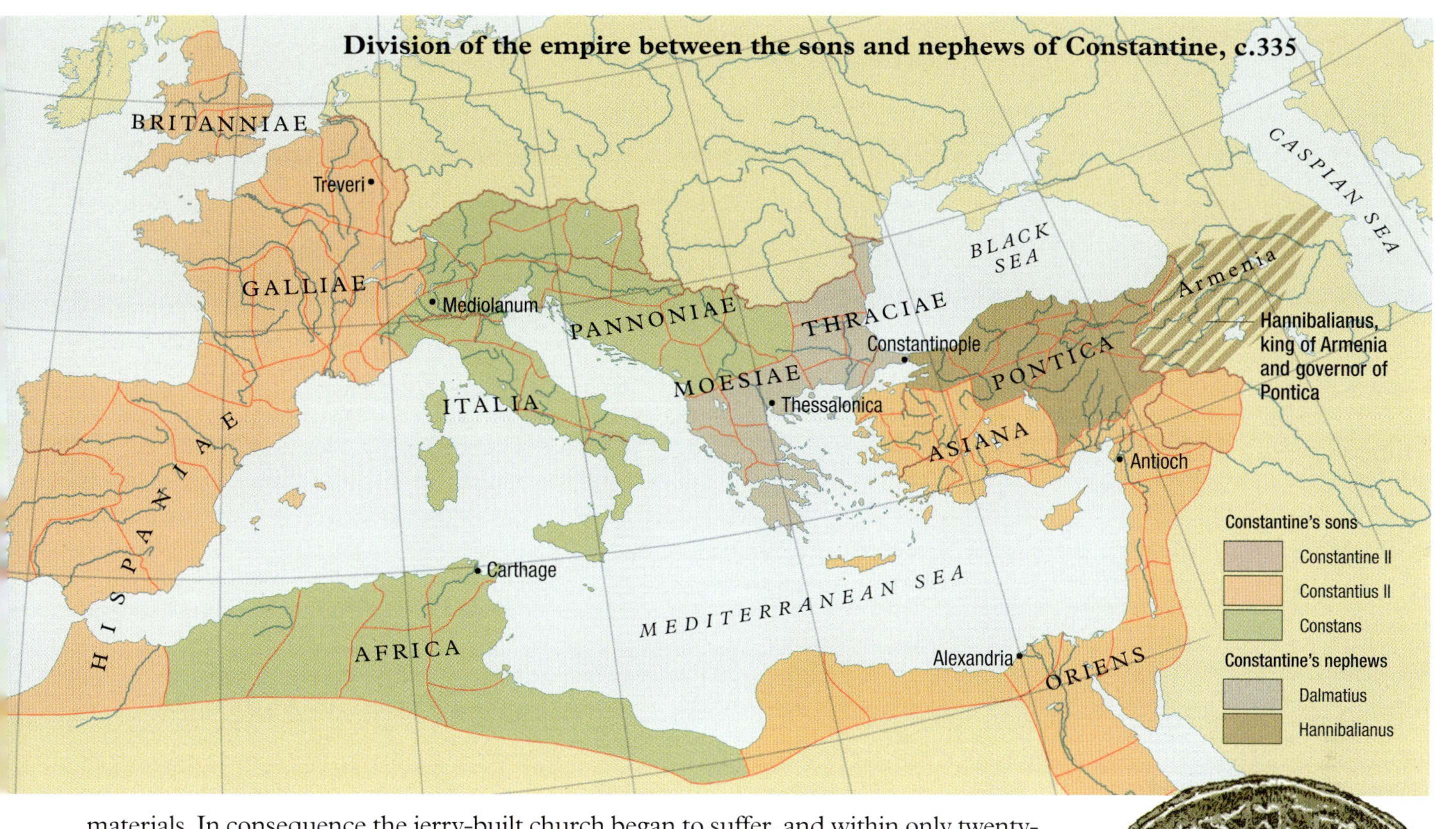



materials. In consequence the jerry-built church began to suffer, and within only twenty-five years had fallen so far into disrepair that the dome was in danger of collapse. Constantine's body was removed to the safety of St Acacius the Martyr. Despite its sad state, the Holy Apostles continued to stand until 550, when Justinian had it completely rebuilt; but by that time no trace could be found of the Apostolic sarcophagi or the great tomb of Constantine.

Constantine had unified the empire, secured the frontiers and safeguarded the provinces from civil war. On the debit side, most inhabitants of the empire were neither happy nor prosperous. Ground down by taxes and condemned to the unremitting drudgery of compulsory service, most were no better than slaves of the state. The massive weight of imperial bureaucracy that would characterise the late Roman empire had now come into being, together with the evils of corruption through the choice of imperial favourites for the many offices established. Rome had lost its pre-eminence and the old gods were almost gone. The theocratic state left by Constantine was still the Roman empire, but one that Augustus could not possibly have recognised.

Despite his professed Christianity, this coin proves that Constantine still accepted the pagan office of *pontifex maximus*.

### Constantine II  Flavius Claudius Constantinus
[ Caesar 1/3/317; Augustus 9/9/337–spring 340 ]
### Constantius II  Flavius Julius Constantius
[ Caesar 13/11/324; Augustus 9/9/337–3/11/361 ]
### Constans  Flavius Julius Constans
[ Caesar 25/12/333; Augustus 9/9/337–January 350 ]

All sons of the empress Fausta, Constantine II was born at Arelate in the summer of 316, Constantius II in Illyricum on 7 August 317, and Constans at some point between 320–23, either at Treveri or in Illyricum. They were, of course, also Maximian's grandsons and inherited some of the co-emperor's worst traits.

In Asiana, Constantius was closest to Constantinople and so presided over the funeral. The problem for the *comitatus* was that Constantine had not actually named

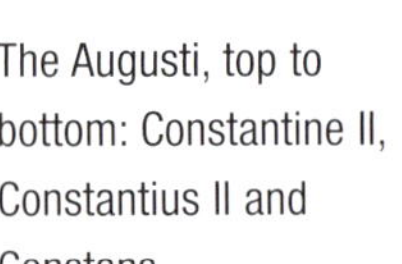

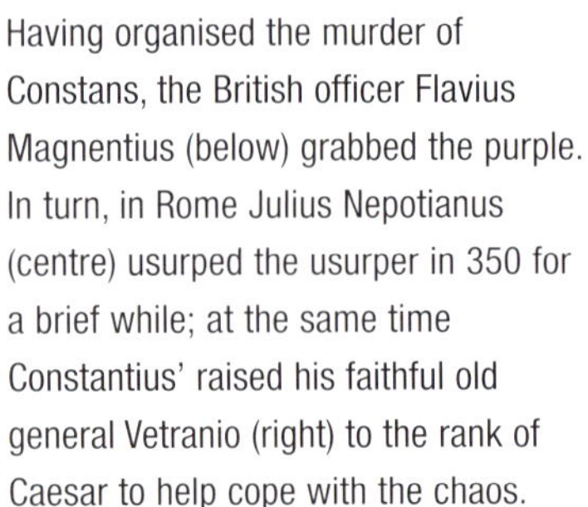

The Augusti, top to bottom: Constantine II, Constantius II and Constans.

Having organised the murder of Constans, the British officer Flavius Magnentius (below) grabbed the purple. In turn, in Rome Julius Nepotianus (centre) usurped the usurper in 350 for a brief while; at the same time Constantius' raised his faithful old general Vetranio (right) to the rank of Caesar to help cope with the chaos.

which Caesar should have *imperium* over the others. The soldiers everywhere proclaimed that they would only accept Constantine's sons, reigning jointly. In this uncertainty, the court ceremony continued in Constantine's name as though his death had not occurred. In the weeks before his father's funeral, Constantius's grace impressed Constantinople's aristocracy, but immediately after he discarded the polite mask and instigated a bloody cull of relatives. The flimsy pretext was a written message allegedly found clenched in the deceased Constantine's fist accusing his two half-brothers, Dalmatius and Julius Constantius, of having poisoned him.

However improbable this must have seemed, the people of Constantinople accepted it. Julius Constantius and his eldest son were cornered and both butchered a few feet from the palace steps, while Dalmatius was killed shortly after, together with his two sons, the Caesars Dalmatius and Hannibalianus king of Armenia. Constantine's two brothers-in-law, many of his closest friends, senators and the praetorian prefect Ablavius met similar fates, even though the latter's daughter was betrothed to Constans.

Although this massacre was co-ordinated by Constantius, it seems obvious enough that the other brothers supported the murders, except perhaps young Constans. And by its effects, when all three brothers met at Viminacium in the summer of 338 to divide the empire between them, they were the only living adult males of the immediate imperial family. The territorial distribution altered little and, with a few adjustments, they each retained the provinces they had held as Caesars: Constantine II held sway over Britain, Gaul and Spain; Constantius kept the eastern provinces and Egypt; while young Constans received the largest patrimony: Africa, Italy, the Illyrian dioceses, Macedonia and Thrace. This gave him the control of Constantinople, although in the event this was to be of little significance.

Unfortunately, none was the man his father had been. As the eldest, Constantine II attempted to exert his authority over the others, especially Constans, still little more than a youth. Constans refused to submit and late in 339 asked Constantius II for his help in return for giving him authority over Constantinople. The elder brother then invaded Italy but Constans proved a surprise – he laid an ambush near Aquileia and Constantine II was slain during the battle. Constans assumed command of the western and central dioceses. Some skill at soldiering was about the only quality Constans possessed. A campaign of 341–42 against the Franks was successful but with its conclusion he gave himself over to a life of depravity, neglecting his frontier legions in preference to indulging himself with homosexual orgies that involved selected numbers of his blond German captives.

The few duties he performed – including a visit to Britain in 343, the last legitimate Roman emperor to do so – were of little effect. For seven years the army put up with his antics until 18 January 350, when an officer of British extraction

named Magnentius claimed the purple at Augustodunum (Autun) with the backing of his fellow officers. Warned of the revolt, Constans fled, but was soon captured and killed on the spot where he was discovered. The chaos this murder caused spread rapidly throughout the western dioceses. In Illyria the venerable general Vetranio named himself Caesar and vowed revenge. At Rome Julius Nepotianus, the son of Constantine the Great's half-sister Eutropia, proclaimed himself emperor at the head of a band of gladiators. Magnentius quickly despatched a force sufficient to overwhelm Nepotianus, who was beheaded for his temerity.

Although Constantius had his hands full on the Persian front, he couldn't ignore the threat that Magnentius posed. He concluded a treaty with Shapur II, detached enough troops to form an army and marched west. On his way he met with Vetranio at Serdica and retired the old soldier on a pension for his remaining years. However, the unfolding events made it clear that he needed someone to look after the eastern dioceses, and while encamped at Sirmium he ordered his young cousin Gallus from Constantinople to join him, and there elevated him to the rank of Caesar.

## Gallus  Claudius Constantius Gallus

[ Caesar (East) 3/15/351–354 ]

Gallus, youngest of Julius Constantius and Galla's three children was born in 325–26 at Massa Veternensis in Etruria, northern Italy. His mother died at some point before 331, by which time Julius Constantius's second wife, Basilina, had also died giving birth to his half-brother Flavius Claudius Julianus (Julian). Gallus – blond-haired and handsome, but of an intemperate character – escaped the massacre of 337 instigated by Constantius that took both his father and elder brother Julian because he was thought to be suffering from a terminal illness. With his younger half-brother Claudius Julian, he was placed in the care of Bishop Eusebius of Nicomedia and the two boys were given a spiritual and classical education as befitted their status.

Gallus was about 25 in March 351 when he became Caesar and married the emperor's sister Constantina, to whom Constantine I had given the title Augusta when she married Hannibalianus. The marriage was meant to ensure Gallus's loyalty to Constantius, but it also removed his meddlesome sister from the volatile west; she could vent her political aspirations by controlling the young and inexperienced Gallus. Constantius made the choice of his ministers for him, and appointed his prefect, Thalassius, and *quaestor sacri palatii*, Montius Magnus.

Gallus Caesar married Constantina, the ambitious sister of Constantius, who ensured that their joint-rule of the east was a disaster.

As Gallus and Constantina travelled to Antioch, Constantius left Sirmium to face Magnentius, who had crossed into the Balkans. The armies met on 28 September 351 at Mursa (Osijek), where Constantius was the victor. Magnentius escaped and, with a part of his force, retreated to Gaul pursued by Constantius. Following several skirmishes, Magnentius was soundly defeated at Lugdunum in 353, after which the usurper fell on his own sword.

In the east, the reign of Gallus was going badly. He'd immediately earned the hatred of the Jews in Palaestina after his *magister peditum* Ursicinus had used a hammer to crush a nut of unrest, causing 'the murders of many thousands of men – even those too young to pose a threat' and putting many villages to the torch. Antioch's senatorial class hated him for rousing the mob's anger against them after Theophilus, the *corrector* of Syria, opposed his move to lower the price of grain. Theophilus was taken out and butchered, and street rioters burned down many houses of the wealthy. There followed trials against innocent victims of Gallus and Constantina's jealousy. Several senators were executed and their estates confiscated.

Thalassius did nothing to restrain Gallus's violence, but he kept Constantius informed of the Caesar's every move. When Thalassius died in 353, Constantius quickly appointed a successor before Gallus should take the matter into his own hands. The new praetorian prefect, Domitianus, acted in a tougher manner than his predecessor, aware that Constantius feared his cousin's excesses might precipitate open rebellion in Syria at a time when he was still facing threats along the Rhine following Constans' neglect and depletion of troops by Magnentius. But Gallus, enraged by haughty Domitianus, conspired to have him executed, along with the quaestor Montius Magnus who had reasonably pointed out that executing Domitianus would be exceeding his authority. Constantina, it was said, strode up and 'dragged down Montius from his judgement-seat with her own hands', and with the consent of Gallus the soldiers killed both men.

When Constantius heard of the treason trials and the execution of his appointee he determined on the removal of Gallus. After concluding a peace with the current threat – the Alamanni – he retired to Milan and requested Gallus and Constantina attend him. There is evidence that Claudius Julian, quietly residing at Athens, warned his half-brother of the emperor's real intentions, but Gallus was lured into journeying to meet Constantius for what he believed to be his elevation to co-Augustus. He may still have been saved had not Constantina died of a fever as they travelled through Bithynia, thus severing his legal connection to Constantius. When Gallus with his small contingent of bodyguards reached Poetovio near the border of Pannonia with Noricum, he was easily arrested. He was stripped of his imperial robes and dragged to Pola in Histria where he was interrogated about the treason trials and deaths of the officials. Unwisely, he laid all the blame for these events on the ambitions of his dead wife, which news so enraged Constantius that he condemned 29-year-old Gallus to summary execution.

### Julian the Apostate  Flavius Claudius Julianus
[ Caesar 6/11/355; Augustus spring 360–26/6/363 ]

Claudius Julian's father, Julius Constantius, was the younger of the two sons born to Constantius Chlorus by his second wife Theodora. The family had lived in exile due to Theodora's arch enemy, the Augusta Helena, Constantine's mother. However, after Helena's death, Constantine invited Julius Constantius to return to Constantinople and it was there in May or June 332 that his third son Julian was born to his second wife, Basilina. As an infant, Julian survived the destruction of his family by Constantius II. He was sent to Nicomedia to be tutored by Bishop Eusebius and brought up as a good Christian.

When Gallus became Caesar in 349, Julian was ignored, for which fact he was happy. Free to do as he pleased, he spent the next six years wandering the Greek world in search of every philosophical school, among them that of Libanius, a philosopher who had rejected Christianity and proclaimed himself a proud pagan. By the time Julian arrived at Athens early in 355, he'd become convinced that he must also reject Christianity and return to the ways of the old Roman gods. Nevertheless, he was too astute to avow his faith openly, especially with the uncertain temper of his cousin Constantius II all too evident. Julian lived in dread after his half-brother's execution, burying himself in his scholastic studies and hoping to remain ignored. But the removal of Gallus hadn't solved Constantius's problems. The empire was still too large for one man to rule, and Julian was the only surviving relative. So, in the summer of 355, when he was just into his twenty-fourth year, Julian received the imperial summons to attend Constantius in Milan.

Constantius held his young cousin in poor regard. A fellow-student of Julian's in Athens described him: '…*that oddly disjointed neck, those hunched and twitching shoulders, that wild, darting eye, that swaying walk, that haughty way of breathing down that prominent nose…*'. Lacking any company of his own age, bookish, shy and socially dysfunctional, Julian's speech was halting and his laughter when provoked was described as being 'nervous and uncontrolled'. Disdainful of his scholarship, Constantius had his student beard shaved, his long hair cut short in trooper style, his out-of-condition body stuffed into a military uniform and, on 6 November, paraded him before the troops as Caesar. Days later Julian married Constantius's second sister, Helena the Younger, in order to cement the alliance between them. Constantius felt he had little to fear from Julian, who had absolutely no military experience and would therefore behave perfectly as was intended – a figurehead. He was despatched rapidly to Gaul with, as Libanius put it, '*the authority to do nothing save wear the uniform.*' As he'd done with Gallus, Constantius appointed all Julian's ministers and generals, confident that they would defeat the Alamanni.

Coin of Julian Caesar: Constantius underestimated his bookish cousin's military abilities.

But Constantius had seriously underestimated the wandering scholar. Julian soon realised that his staff officers were reporting directly to Constantius and it irritated his typically Constantinian prickliness. He saw their orders as a deliberate attempt to diminish his authority rather than a perfectly sensible arrangement in view of his lack of civilian and military experience. As a conscientious student in all he undertook, Julian made it his business to learn soldiering fast. So the successful lightning campaigns of 356–57 resulted as much from his efforts as those of his cautious generals. From Vienna (Vienne), the army swept the Alamanni from Augustodunum (Autun), Tricasini (Troyes), Durocortorum (Reims) and Mediomatrici (Metz), pushing them through the Vosges, before sweeping north to retake Colonia Agrippina from the Franks. In the following year he defeated the Alamanni near Argentorate (Strasbourg), when 13,000 Romans faced 30,000 Alamanni and left over 6,000 dead on the field for a loss of only 247 legionaries. By 359 Julian had recovered the length of the Rhine frontier and spent time supervising the repair and extension of the fortifications. While this was being done, he made his new capital on the Seine at Lutetia Parisiorum (Paris).

On the eastern front Constantius was having a less happy time countering Shapur II. Fractious border skirmishes had escalated to the point that in 359 Sassanian forces had built a strong position in Mesopotamia and were threatening fortified Nisibis and the province of Osrhoene. Constantius desperately needed reinforcements and in January 360 ordered Julian to strip his army of 300 men for every unit under his command, plus four *auxilia* of Gallic and Frankish allies. Compliance meant reducing his strength by a half, but he had also promised his Gallic detachments that they would never have to abandon their homes, wives and families to the mercy of barbarians in order to serve in the east.

The troops vilified Constantius as unfit to rule them. Julian apparently retired to his chambers, but was disturbed in the night to be told the army was marching on the palace. According to his own words, he prayed to Jupiter who told him to accept the diadem. By this time Julian had enjoyed five years of military experience and grown into one of Rome's finest generals. His years of secretive worship had also convinced him that it was his destiny to restore the empire to the old Roman gods, and he was at the head of an army whose soldiers were still mostly pagans. There was no alternative. According to Ammianus Marcellinus – an officer in one of the *scholae* and one of the best sources for the period – since no suitable object to act as a crown could be found, the standard-bearer of a legion removed the great gold chain that was the insignia of his office from his shoulders and placed it on Julian's head. It was late February or early March of 360 and he was not yet twenty-eight.

For a year little happened. Julian was uncertain about how to proceed and negotiations between the two emperors became acrimonious. And then in 361 the stalemate broke. Some success against the Sassanians had led to a lull in the war and Constantius took the opportunity to detach units and head west. Because of his promise, and because of his unwillingness to denude the frontier garrisons, the army Julian could call on was pitifully small, only some 23,000 troops. Still, they set off and reached Naissus, where he decided to pass the winter. He'd been there for approximately four weeks when astonishing news arrived from Constantinople. Constantius was dead, and Julian had been proclaimed by the eastern armies.

Julian's bloodless victory came as a result of a fever which struck as Constantius prepared to cross Anatolia and he died at the small village of Mopuscrenae on 3 November 361. He was just forty-four. Julian ordered that Constantius's body should be taken in state to Constantinople and on 11 December he led the mourning for his cousin. Constantius was laid to rest beside his father Constantine I in the Church of the Holy Apostles; it was the last time that Julian set foot in a Christian church.

Julian was very different to his immediate predeccessors. After the recent death of his wife Helena the Younger he'd remained celibate, austere in comforts, and showed little interest in food or wine. His purge of the imperial court was swift and extraordinarily thorough. Libanius describes how the imperial cortège had grown exponentially since the time of Diocletian:

*There were a thousand cooks, as many barbers, and even more butlers. There were swarms of lackeys, the eunuchs were more in number than flies around the flocks in spring…*

When he was finished Julian's court consisted of little more than a skeleton staff. His reforms of religion and government were equally sweeping, oriented towards an older Republican tradition. He returned to the senate greater powers and attended meetings on foot as a sign of respect. He was assiduous in hearing judicial matters, and made steps to chastise the bureaucracy when he detected a decline in administrative or moral standards, for instance imposing penalties on governors who purposefully delayed appeals in court cases. With a non-existent imperial *comitatus*, Julian relied on the senate and consulars to act as intermediaries between himself and his subjects, which again gave more power and prestige to the old upper classes of Constantinople.

Julian's apostasy – the most striking feature of his reign – made him feared by the extensive Christian communities, although as a merciful man Julian never resorted to persecution – perhaps because he had learned that martyrs seemed to have an opposite effect on the Christian Church to that intended. He repealed the decrees that had closed the pagan temples and made sacrifices illegal, and issued an edict of religious tolerance. In a masterstroke he offered amnesty to all the orthodox churchmen who had been exiled under Constantius's pro-Arian government. Ammianus noted that Julian had found by experience 'that no wild beasts are so hostile to men as are Christian sects in general to one another'.

In the summer of 362 Julian moved his austere court to Antioch in preparation for war against Persia. In the six weeks he travelled across Anatolia he discovered to his dismay that the Christians were not tearing each other apart. Indeed, relaxing again after the initial fear of persecution had faded, the many communities he passed appeared to be flourishing, while those of the pagans seemed to be no stronger than in Constantine's day. So on 17 June 362 he promulgated an edict with far-ranging consequences. It banned any Christian from acting as a teacher of rhetoric or literature. His reasoning was that no Christian who professed to teach the classics – in those days, virtually the whole of the school curriculum – could be of the required moral standard, since he was teaching something he did not himself believe in. With the future of the empire's education in doubt, and with hot-headed young Christians willing to flirt with martyrdom, tensions ran high. Then the emperor reached Antioch, immersed himself in planning the imminent Persian campaign, and any further tightening of the screw was postponed until his return from the war. Fortunately for the Christians he did not.

Since the death of Constantius there had been a dangerous build up of Persian troops in Mesopotamia Superior. Julian knew he would have to act if the situation was not to worsen. The army set out from Antioch on 5 March 363. Using his trademark whirlwind strategy, Julian force-marched to Beroea (Aleppo) and on to Hieropolis (Membij), then slightly north to cross the Euphrates into Mesopotamia at Zeugma. By 27 March the army was all on the eastern side of the river, following its course southward, and Julian had constructed a flotilla to guard his supply line. His generals Procopius and Sebastianus were sent to help Arsaces, the client king of Armenia, to

As soon as became the sole emperor, Julian instituted radical reforms of court ceremony and brought back the worship of Rome's ancient gods.

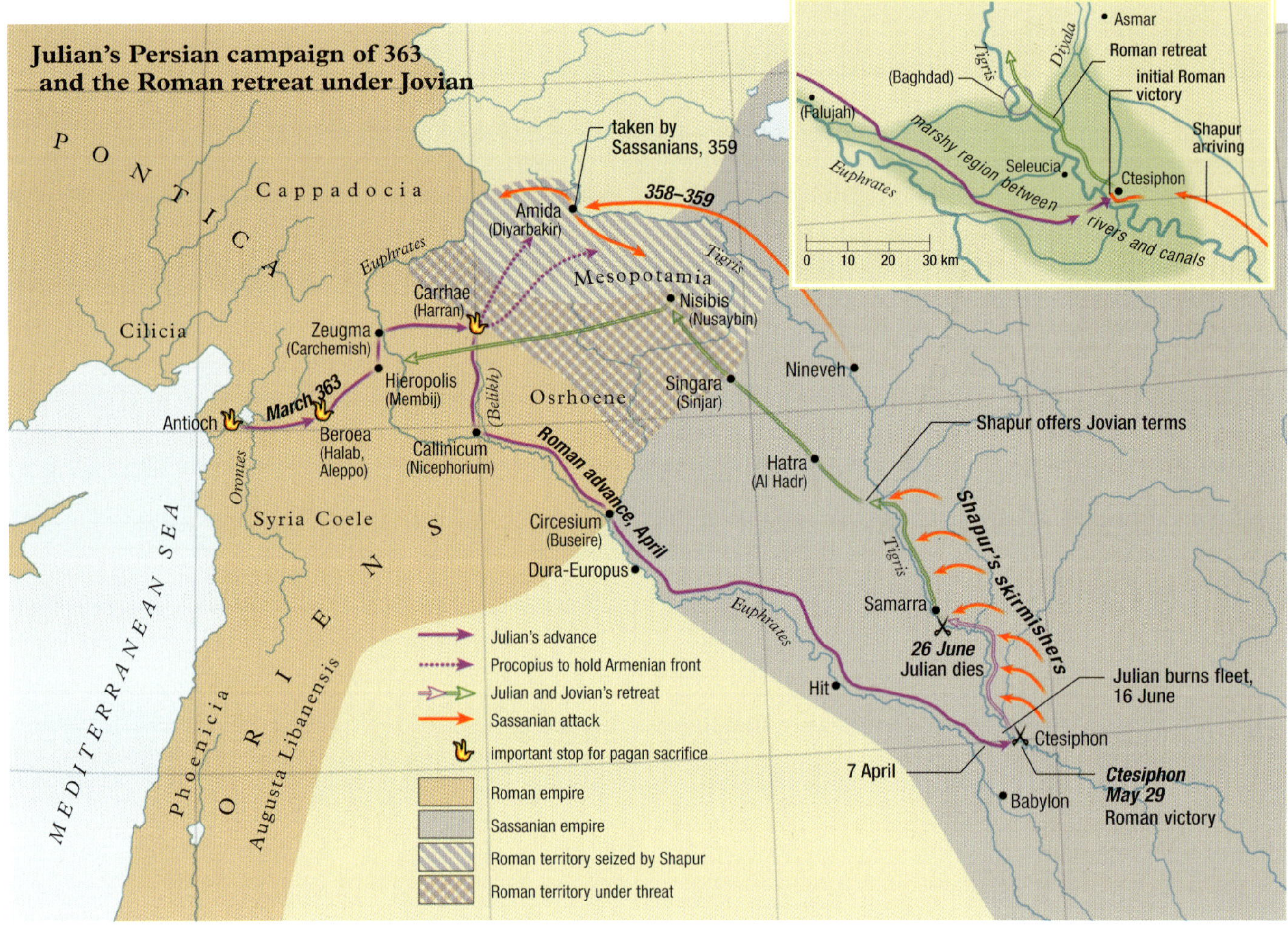



guard the northern Tigris line. By 7 April, after a few minor skirmishes and some sieges but without any serious trouble, the Roman army was on the west bank of the Tigris a short way north of Ctesiphon. Here, Sassanian resistance began to tell, and drawn up between the river and the city walls a Persian army stood ready for battle.

The Romans crossed the Tigris on 29 May and, despite having to fight their way across and form up on the opposite bank, were victorious. But it availed Julian nothing. His engineers advised that the siege would be drawn out and time was not on their side. The retreating Persians had scorched the earth to deny the Romans supplies, and the marshy ground, criss-crossed with canals and irrigation ditches between the two rivers, was badly flooded. The soldiers, close to starving, were further demoralised by squelching from one quagmire to another, while swarms of flies so thick that, according to Ammianus, they blocked out the sky, tormented them. Worse, scouts reported that a far larger army under Shapur's command was approaching. Julian's ambitions for glory were frustrated. He had the fleet burnt, for it would have struggled to sail upstream, and leaving it behind would only benefit the Sassanians. Julian ordered the retreat on 16 June. As the Romans trudged along the east bank of the Tigris they were harassed by horsemen. During a particularly heavy attack on 26 June the emperor dashed out without his armour to rally his men and was struck in the abdomen by a Persian spear. His officers carried him back to his tent, but he was too severely wounded to survive and died shortly after.

At his death Julian was only 31 and had been on the throne for a little over three years. In that time he achieved no legislation of any significance and wasted much of it attempting to revive a dying religion of confused parameters. It was, though, another case of an untimely death robbing the empire of a man who might well have become one of its finest rulers. His outstanding qualities – education, energy, an ability to inspire his soldiers, integrity and incorruptibility – were let down by his faults. His religious fanaticism blinded Julian to the priorities needed for good government, and his hesitancy – seen in continually asking the gods for guidance instead of making his own decisions – turned into inflexibility once the divine course had been laid out for him. And with his passing, the line of Constantius Chlorus came to an end. What followed was something of a joke, more of a comma in history than a full-stop.


## Jovian  Flavius Jovianus
[ 27/6/363–16/2/364 ]

The beleaguered Roman army commanders had little time for discussion, surrounded as they were by Sassanid forces the morning after Julian's death. Their first choice for emperor fell on Sallustius Secundus, prefect of the eastern provinces, but he declined on the grounds of his advanced age and growing infirmity. At that point, a small vociferous group of the *scholae* began to shout for their commander. Ammianus claims that the assembled army took up the acclamation, but by a dreadful mistake the men mistook the cry 'Jovianus!' to be 'Julianus!' because they thought their former emperor had recovered from his injury. The error became evident when the tall figure of Jovian was paraded before them, by which time it was too late to back down.

Jovian was born at some point in 331 at Singidunum (Belgrade). His father Varronianus had a distinguished career under Constantius II and his father-in-law Lucillianus had commanded the army against the Sassanians in 350. These factors more than his own abilities seem to have given him preferment, and Jovian had risen to become *primicerius domesticorum* of the imperial guard. He was a well-liked, genial soldier of bluff temperament, and a Christian. He had, however, no particular qualities to recommend him as a ruler. Terms were sought from Shapur and in return for being allowed an orderly retreat, Rome ceded five satrapies along the upper Tigris, five Roman frontier forts, including the two key strongholds Nisibis (Nusaybin) and Singara (Sinjar), and all the land to the east of them. Jovian also effectively renounced any claims over Armenia. The only benefit Jovian gained was a promise of peace for thirty years.

During the trek from the Tigris to Hatra and Nisibis, the desert almost finished Shapur's abandoned task. Only by killing all their camels did the troops survive to limp on to Nisibis and then to Antioch. There Julian's embalmed corpse was given to Procopius who, operating along the northern Tigris line, had avoided the debacle following Julian's withdrawal from Ctesiphon. Procopius, who was a distant kinsman of the deceased emperor, took the body for burial at Tarsus, where Julian had intended to establish his court. At Antioch Jovian issued an edict of religious tolerance, which was received by the Christians in great relief – they, at least, were happy with the pagan tyrant's removal.

Jovian left Antioch in mid-October, taking the army in easy stages through Anatolia, greeted at every stop by cheering Christian communities. On the first day of January 364 he assumed the consulship with his infant son Varronianus at Ancyra before moving on to the small town of Dadastana, half way to Nicaea. There, on the morning of 16 February, Jovian was found dead in his bedroom. The emperor was fond of his food and wine, and the mushrooms he had eaten the night before were suspected by some, while others blamed the fumes of an untended charcoal brazier in his bedchamber, from which he had suffocated. No one, however, suspected foul play. Jovian had been emperor for only eight months.

A bluff soldier, Jovian was ill-equipped for the role of imperial leader.

**Right:** Two of the circular panels borrowed from earlier monuments to decorate the triumphal arch of Constantine.

**Opposite above:** The Arch of Constantine straddles the route of the ancient roadway leading to the Colosseum (*right*) and the Via Sacra, leading to the Roman Forum.

**Below:** Coffered arches of the Basilica Nova of Maxentius are only one-third of the imense original building.

**Opposite below:** Detail of Theodosius I holding out the victor's wreath to a race winner in the Hippodrome; base of an obelisk in Constantinople (Istanbul). These late Roman carvings would hardly look out of place on the walls of a Gothic 14th-century church.

# TWELVE
## Valentinian and Theodosian Dynasty

[AD 364–455]

### Valentinian I  Flavius Valentinianus

[ 26/2/364–375 ]

Pondering on a choice of new emperor, the *consistorium* and army leaders agreed Flavius Valentinianus to be a suitable candidate at a conclave in Nicaea. A career officer stationed at Ancyra, he arrived in Nicaea on 24 February 364 and immediately announced that the army's welfare was his greatest priority. Further, to appease the eastern civilian administration he promised to appoint a colleague as co-Augustus and then surprised everybody by nominating his brother Valens, who assumed the title on 28 March.

Valentinian seems like a strange choice. He was of peasant origins, uncouth, illiterate and flew into uncontrollable rages when opposed. However, at forty-two he possessed a commanding, even forbidding presence, not at all like his brother Valens – seven years younger, pot-bellied, grotesque in appearance and possessed of neither courage nor ability. What the brothers had in common was a notorious brutality, and perhaps it was this quality that had been mistaken for stern discipline. Valentinian

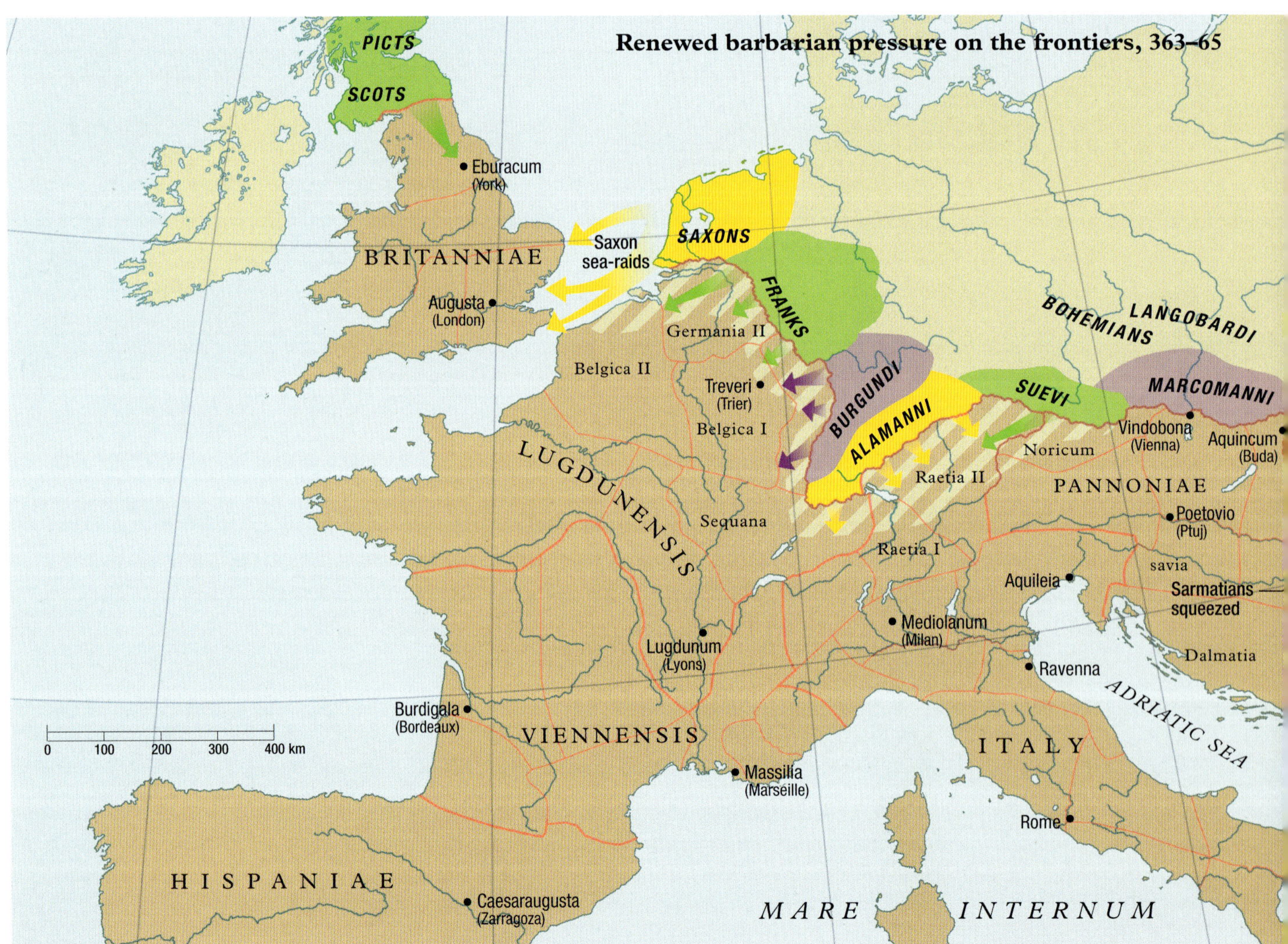

was born in 321 at Cibalae (Vincovci) in southern Pannonia, the son of Gratianus, a Pannonian rope-maker turned soldier renowned for his strength and wrestling skills. Valentinian married Marina Severa in 357, but she died some time after giving birth to a son Gratianus (Gratian) on 18 April 359 at Sirmium. He married again to Justina by whom he had a second son, Valentinianus (Valentinian II), and two daughters, Galla and Justa. Valens married Albia Domnica, but no children are known. Both brothers were fiercely Christian, with Valens championing the Arian creed. Valentinian – by contrast an orthodox Nicene – wisely refused to become embroiled in the religious controversies of the time. Towards the pagans he exercised remarkable tolerance, permitting the retention of the title *pontifex maximus* and passing legislation that confirmed the rights of pagan divination.

Over the winter months of 364–65 the brothers divided the empire into two spheres, with Valens ruling the eastern dioceses and the eastern Balkans, while Valentinian took the western dioceses including Italy, Africa and Illyricum. Valentinian then went to the Rhine to confront the renewed barbarian threat that had followed the departure of Julian in 361. A large-scale invasion by the Alamanni confederation took almost five years to bring under control and he pushed the Germans out of Gaul. In 367 a combined force of Picts, Attacotti and Scots overcame the British garrisons and pushed the province into anarchy. Valentinian was ill – seriously enough to consider the succession and elevate eight-year-old Gratian to co-Augustus – so he sent the *comes* (count)

Valentinian; a good soldier and a vigorous and thorough, if often brutal, administrator.

Theodosius to recover Britain, who landed in 368 with four legions. After restoring order to the south, he began a brilliant campaign of guerrilla tactics against the Caledonian invaders that hurled them beyond Hadrian's Wall. Theodosius restored the confidence and organisation of the garrison, installed a new *vicarius* and returned to Valentinian in 369 to be appointed *magister equitum.*

A flurry of activity over the next six years – military, diplomatic, intrigue and construction – brought an improved level of security all along the length of the Rhine. Valentinian's civil administration was generally rigorous, occasionally brutal and generally peaceful. The restoration of confidence in the army came at the expense of civilians and the ancient nobility; the army's plebeian commanders were the new elite. In Valentinian's world, the role of the senatorial class – whether in Rome, Milan (his capital) or Constantinople – was utterly diminished; military men made the important decisions, and the emperor delegated his authority to an ever longer chain of bureaucrats. The increasing tax burden crushed the people, and it's understandable that they resented paying for a security that they did not always receive.

In the end, Valentinian's ferocious temper tantrums were to literally be the death of him. The Quadi, who had been peaceful for several generations, began a two-pronged campaign of vengeance for the alleged murder of Gabinius, their king, by the officer in charge of building new forts along the Danube. The Quadi ravaged Pannonia but further to the east their allies the Sarmatae were driven back by legions under the command of an extraordinary young man, *dux Moesiae* Theodosius, son of Valentinian's *magister equitum* Theodosius, who was now governing Africa. In 375 Valentinian crossed the Danube at Aquincum (Buda[pest]) and pillaged Quadi lands without mercy, finally retiring to winter in Brigetio (Szöny). On 17 November a Quadi embassy arrived to persuade Valentinian to stop the raids, but he grew angry when the envoys insisted on an apology for the murder of their king. The emperor suddenly stood up in an apoplectic fit, paused, and collapsed to the floor in a faint. Realising his death was near and that Gratian was far away at Treveri and his brother Valens even further in Antioch, he raised four-year-old Valentinian to be co-Augustus with Gratian; after which, at the age of fifty-four, Valentinian expired. The empire was, therefore, in the hands of three rulers: an infant, an adolescent and a middle-aged sadist without merit.

Valens – illiterate and thuggish – brought Rome to its greatest military disaster since the battle of Cannae versus Hannibal in 216 BC.

## Valens  Flavius Valens
[ 28/2/364–9/8/378 ]

Ammianus writes that Valens was 'dilatory and sluggish; of a swarthy complexion; had a cast in one eye; his limbs were well set; his figure was neither tall nor short; he was knock-kneed, and rather pot-bellied.' He was also illiterate. Although there was little to recommend Valens as a ruler, the empire benefitted from his unswerving loyalty to Valentinian: 'He attended to his wishes as if he had been his orderly,' says Ammianus. This spared the empire the exhausting wars of Constantine's children. After a brief sojourn in Constantinople, Valens went to Syria where, despite Jovian's treaty, trouble was again brewing with the Sassanians. His absence prompted the uprising of Procopius – that distant kinsman of Julian – who claimed the Apostate had nominated him as his heir. Procopius caused Valens a deal of trouble before the emperor's forces defeated him in 366 and the usurper's head was taken by the treachery of his own men.

Some 3,000 Visigoths, or Tervingi branch of the Goths, who had offered their services to Procopius but arrived too late to help the usurper, now posed a problem – they were unwilling to return home empty-handed. Valens had them bound into captivity and dispersed among the cities south of the Danube, an act that aroused the

ire of Athanaric, the Tervingi chieftain. He demanded to know why some of his people, who had entered Roman territory at the wish of the 'emperor' Procopius, were being detained. Intemperately, Valens despatched an army in the spring of 367, from which the Visigoths fled into the fastness of the Carpathians. The Romans followed two years later, campaigning from the most northerly corner of Scythia, carrying the war right through Athanaric's Tervingi and into the lands of their kinsmen, the Greuthungi, or Ostrogoths, defeating them as well. Athanaric sued for peace and signed a ruinous treaty.

The satisfactory outcome of the Gothic war was well timed since it freed resources to turn on the Sassanians. Shapur, taking advantage of Procopius's usurpation to extend Sassanian power, had arrested the Armenian king and flung him into the grimly named Prison of Oblivion, an act which sparked a series of campaigns and counterattacks that occupied Valens in Armenian matters right up to 375. Even as Valentinian died in that evil-omened year, a vast pony-mounted horde of Huns, impelled westward by some unknown force, having subjugated the Scythian tribes between the Don and Volga rivers, had fallen without mercy on the Visigoths. Tribal groups withdrew to the Danube and sent embassies to Valens pleading for asylum within Roman borders.

Procopius, a distant cousin of Julian Apostate, made a desperate grab at the throne while Valens countered a Persian threat.

This was a tough problem – if a refusal led to a Gothic invasion there would be war on two fronts. Some advisors pointed out the advantages to be gained in granting the Visigoths their request. Not only would they strengthen the Roman army, in doing so they would also relieve local landowners of a duty to provide manpower (they could pay a tithe in much-needed gold instead), and the Visigoths would provide a bulwark on the borders against the Huns. Valens consented and negotiated with the chieftains of two groups, Fritigern and Alavivus, who had supported him against Athanaric's persecution of Gothic Christians. The deal's clinching point was Fritigern's promise to promote Arianism over orthodox Christianity. This exclusive deal did not, however, prevent other Goths from slipping across the Danube in the confusion that followed.

Valens left the supervision of the crossing and resettlement in the hands of the counts Lupicinus and Maximus. Alas, neither cared for efficiency – their principal aim was to make a fast profit out of the crisis. They underestimated the numbers of refugees and with insufficient forces available were unable to prevent another crossing lower down the river of equally terrified Ostrogoths. Instead of an orderly dispersal,

Lupicinus kept the refugees in appalling conditions on the river bank. Their valuables were taken as payment for inadequate supplies of food and, as hunger increased, so the exploitation worsened, as Ammianus witnessed: 'Slaves, money and furniture all being exhausted, they began – even the nobles – to sell their own children. Deep must have been the misery endured by those free German hearts before they yielded to the cruel logic of the situation.'

Lupicinus proved as incompetent as he was corrupt. Having failed to disarm the warriors, the barbarians annihilated his men outside Marcianopolis in 377. The Tervingi joined up with the Greuthungi, and the combined Gothic nation then rampaged through Thrace and Moesia. For Valens, it was the worst possible outcome. He abandoned the Persian campaign, returned to Constantinople on 30 May 378 and appealed to Gratian to send reinforcements. However, news that Gratian had secured a string of victories against barbarian enemies in the west aroused the fifty-year-old emperor's jealousy. Foolishly determined to win a victory in which his brilliant nephew should have no hand, Valens met the Goths at Adrianople, disdaining the advice of Gratian's recently arrived *comes domesticorum*, Richomeres, to wait and listening to intelligence reports that put the Gothic strength at 10,000 troops. Valens attacked on 9 August 378, and it was a disaster. The scouts had grossly underestimated the enemy's strength, and the Goths fell on the legions in fury. The Romans were crushed by the surprise arrival of Greuthungi cavalry, which split their ranks. According to Ammianus: 'In the great tumult the infantry, exhausted by the efforts and the perils of the fighting, no longer able to think or plan, their spears broken, rushed recklessly with drawn swords into the dense masses of the enemy, careless of their lives now that all escape was impossible.'

Valens was either killed by an arrow or, according to a different version, wounded in the battle but escaped to a nearby farmstead only to be burned to death by Gothic marauders. Two-thirds of the Roman army perished at Adrianople, in what Ammianus called 'the most destructive defeat since the battle of Cannae'.

Gratian, a studious young man with limited military skills, nevertheless presided over some lucky victories.

## Gratian Flavius Gratianus
[ co-Augustus 367–25/8/383 ]

There was concern over Gratian's elevation in 367. He was only eight and a studious boy who showed little interest in military matters. After it became clear that he wasn't up to the rigours of military life, Valentinian kept him behind the front lines. His tutor Ausonius, the leading rhetorician of the time, proudly described his student as possessing a golden mind. At fifteen he married Constantia, daughter of the late emperor Constantius II, but she died in 383.

After his father's death Gratian acquiesced to the army's demands on the teritorial division which gave him Gaul, Britain and Spain, while the regents of Valentinian II ordered the affairs of Illyricum, Africa and Italy. Reports of Gratian's victories along the Rhine were not exaggerated, but much was down to the quality of his senior staff. With the east in chaos, he wisely decided that his limited military skills were insufficient to the task of restoring order against so large a host. Besides, he was unwilling to denude the frontier of experienced officers and recalled to service his father's *dux moesiae*, Theodosius, who had distinguished himself in 373 in the campaign against the Sarmatae. When the call to duty arrived, Theodosius welcomed it, and on 19 January 379, Gratian raised him to be his co-Augustus.

Early in 383 Gratian countered another Alamanni incursion. This coincided with news of the proclamation by his troops of the *comes britannicae* Magnus Clemens Maximus as Augustus. A few days later Maximus landed in Gaul and confronted Gratian near Lutetia Parisiorum (Paris). Gratian may have won the day, but his

# The House of Valentinian and Theodosian Dynasty

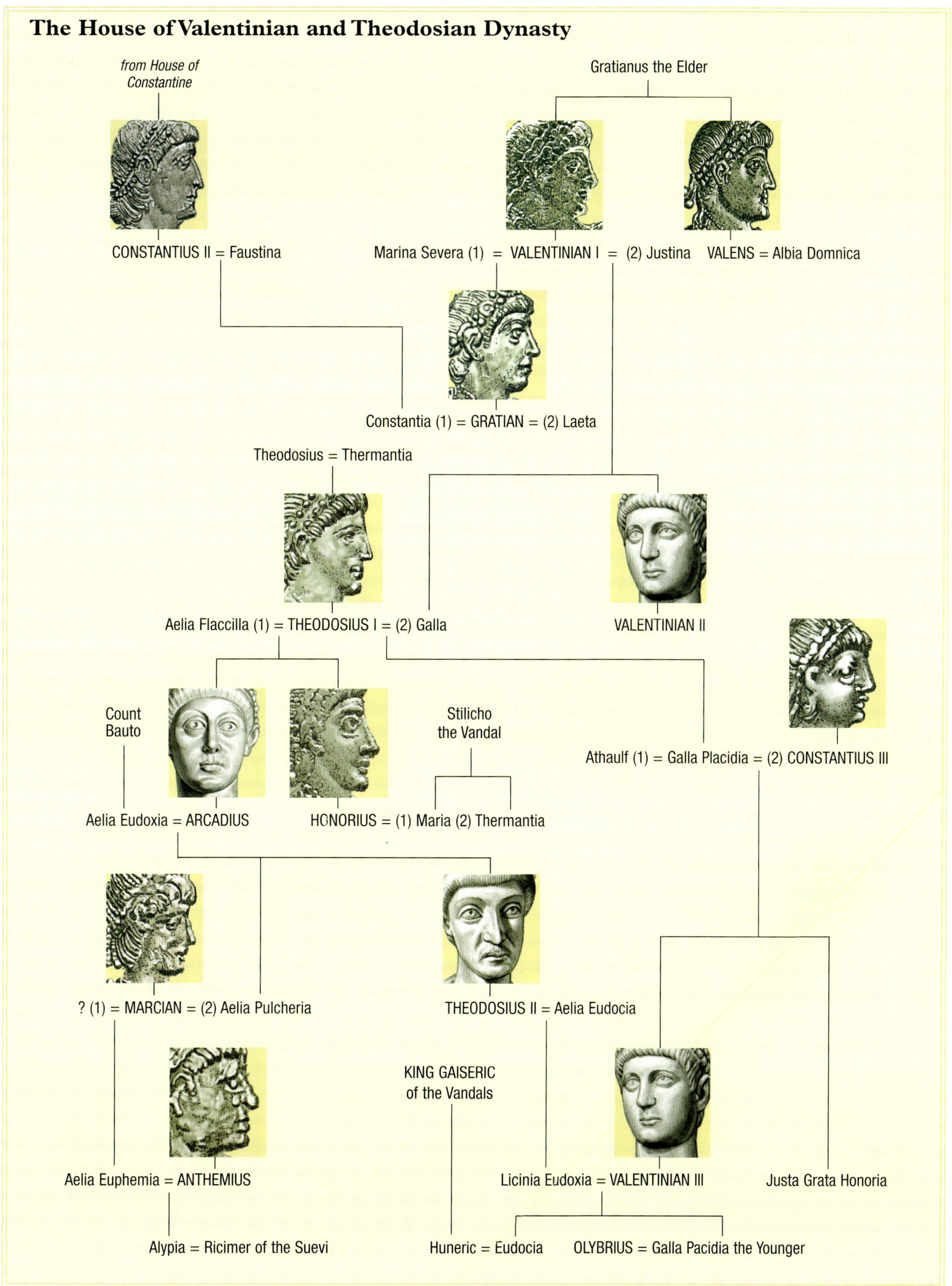

preference for barbarians in his household and guard had destroyed the soldier's affection for their young emperor, and when his Moorish cavalry unexpectedly defected, most of his troops followed suit. Gratian fled towards the Alps, but was caught at Lugdunum by Maximus's Gothic *magister equitum*, Andragathius, who killed him on 25 August 383.

The events of Gratian's reign highlight the continuing trend of assimilating barbarians and making many of them a part of the imperial court. Ammianus wryly observed that despite his 'golden mind', Gratian's talents lay in the opposite direction from what the empire needed. However, he had conferred on the empire one lasting benefit – the elevation of the younger Theodosius to supreme power.

## Theodosius I the Great  Flavius Theodosius
[ 19/1/379–17/1/395 ]

The story of the undivided empire's last great ruler began in approximately 346 when Theodosius was born at Cauca (Coca), a small town in the northwest of Hispania Carthaginensis, some 48km from modern Segovia. His father, the elder Theodosius, and mother Thermantia, were both from powerful provincial families, the real aristocracy of the mid-fourth-century Roman empire. Flavius Theodosius is described as being affable but with a noble, commanding presence, and a man of slender education – not surprising in one who spent all his youth in the military. He learned the military arts from an expert – his father; campaigning in Britain, Africa and Illyricum. His own abilities propelled him rapidly up the ranks until by 373 he was *dux moesiae* at the age of about twenty-seven. At some point, Theodosius married Aelia Flavia Flacilla, a Galician aristocrat, and they had three children: two sons, Arcadius and Honorius, and a daughter, Pulcheria. Arcadius was born either in 377 or 378, on the brink of Gratian's call to duty, Honorius on 9 September 384, and Pulcheria, who died in childhood, in 385.

It was fortunate for the empire in the months following the Adrianople disaster that the barbarians were always incapable of a cohesive policy. The Goths tried repeatedly to break into the shuttered city, but were driven back by the terrifying Roman catapults and ballistas. In not too many days, Constantinople found itself under siege, but again the stout defence bewildered the Goths and they retired to ravage in every direction, through Thrace, Dacia, Moesia and even into Pannonia at the very edges of Italy. Accepting his commission from Gratian at Sirmium, Theodosius moved south, skirting the largest concentrations of Gothic marauders, and came to Thessalonica which he made his headquarters.

The major headache after the terrible losses at Adrianople was manpower. Theodosius mitigated the disadvantage through surrounding himself with a large number of officers through a series of rapid promotions and directed them in guerrilla tactics learned in Britain. A continual stream of short, sharp hit and run attacks shook the Goths' confidence and at the same time raised Roman morale. His critics were uneasy at the increased numbers of higher ranks. While before it was customary to have two commanders-in-chief – the *magistri equitum* and *peditum*, now there were five, probably most with the cavalry. In keeping, Theodosius doubled the next ranks of *duces*, *tribuni* and centurions. This happened without an increase in total manpower, but in the war being

Theodosius would be called 'the Great' for his establishment of the Roman Catholic Church.

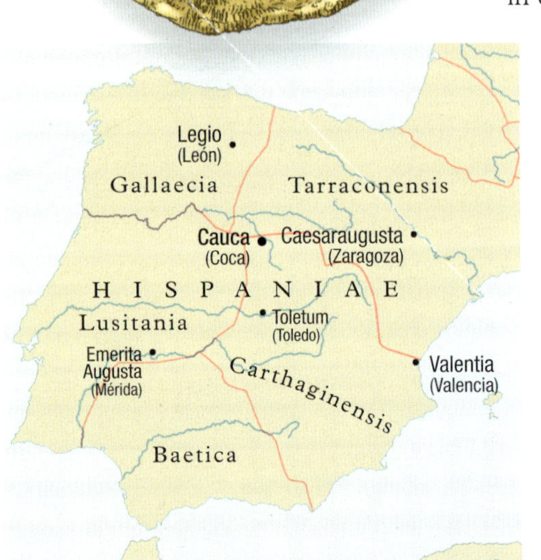

waged good leadership counted for more than sheer numbers. There was another good reason for filling his *consistorium* with many experienced officers. To bulk out the depleted ranks Theodosius engaged the services of captured Goths and for them to become a properly organised fighting machine in the Roman style these fierce but ill-disciplined warriors needed an officer they would obey because of his terrifying record on the battlefield.

No coherent account of Theodosius's tactics exists, but there is no doubt that his strategy was a triumph. On 17 November 379 he sent messengers to all the great cities announcing a victory over the Goths. It was not, however, entirely the end of the war. Parts of Greece were still overrun by Fritigern's Visigoths. At the beginning of 380, Theodosius fell seriously ill, and was forced to call on Gratian's help to evict the barbarians. He sent two Franks, the counts Bauto and Arbogast, who succeeded in clearing Macedonia and Thessaly, in the course of which Fritigern was slain. Gratian and Theodosius understood that they would never entirely expel the Goths. Instead, they proposed a treaty that granted land provided the Goths became Romanised and that the men should serve in the army and pledge their sons to the same; in effect the Gothic nation would become Roman confederates, *foederati*. The empire had again created a Republican-style *auxilia*, a military resource to be called on when required but with important differences to the ancient system: none were Roman citizens and they retained their own system of government and administration; more, *foederati* were not required to pay taxes, which did not endear them to the hard-pressed provincial Romans struggling to recover from the very devastation the Goths had caused.

On his sickbed, and fearing imminent death, Theodosius called on Thessalonica's saintly Bishop Acholius to baptise him. Restored to good health later in 380, Theodosius rose from his bed a convinced adherent of the orthodox faith. Finally, on 24 November 380, he made his way to Constantinople and entered his capital in all the state and glory due an *imperator*. Gratian's death three years later made him the senior Augustus over Valentinian II, and thanks to his experience and pragmatic approach, the empire was guided through tumultuous times.

The wife of Theodosius, Aelia Flavia Flacilla, appeared on coins dressed in the *paludamentum*, the clothing of an emperor and military leader, indicating her equal rank with her husband.

## Magnus Maximus  Magnus Clemens Maximus
[ usurper: spring 383–28/8/388 ]

Magnus Maximus was a fellow Galician of the elder Theodosius and may even have been a distant relative, but if not, certainly one of his clients. The reasons for his rebellion against Gratian remain unclear, but the British troops were thoroughly fed up with the emperor and his preferment of barbarians, and perhaps Maximus simply considered himself the better man for the job. He may have served in Britain under Theodosius during the campaign of 367–69 and he was in Africa in 373, when Valentinian I sent Theodosius to suppress a Moorish rebellion. In 380 he was made *comes britannicae*, and in the following year led the British legions to victory over invading Picts and Scots.

Following Gratian's defeat, Maximus established his court at Treveri, at first unopposed by Theodosius, who had to cope with Huns along the Danube. Reluctantly, he accepted that Maximus was in control of the western provinces, and it would have to stay that way until he was in a position to alter it. He agreed to leave the pretender alone as long as Maximus recognised Valentinian II's sovereignty over Italy and Illyricum. This accord of 383–84 was helped by the embassy to Treveri of Ambrose, the bishop of Milan. As a fellow Nicene, Ambrose pleaded with Maximus to leave young Valentinian – of Arian persuasion – alone. He also purchased time for Valentinian's Frankish *magister militum*, count Bauto, to fortify the Alpine passes against Maximus. However, almost immediately after Ambrose had departed, Maximus named his infant son Flavius Victor as co-Augustus and repudiated the rights of Valentinian II.

His illegitimate claim to the purple didn't make Maximus a poor ruler. While he would not allow any transgressions from the Alamanni, his friendly relations with several of their number eased the pressures on the frontier, and the Gallic economy prospered. He struck good coinage and issued new legislation to ease some of the previous tax burden on the populace and the provincial nobility. He reorganised the diocese by making new sub-divisions, creating Lugdunensis III and Lugdunensis Senonia and then invaded Italy in 387 – saving the empire from Valentinian's Arian heresy made an ideal excuse.

As Maximus crossed the Alps in force, Valentinian's domineering mother Justina fled with him to Thessalonica, where Theodosius met them and took the imperial fugitives under his protection. Theodosius was at first reluctant to take up arms but was persuaded to do so after Justina sent to him her daughter Galla to plead their cause because she knew that Theodosius was susceptible to the charms of attractive women. His wife, the Augusta Aelia Flavia Flacilla, had died recently, and apparently Theodosius became besotted with Galla and married her.

He retaliated in June 388, marching with great rapidity into Illyricum to meet Maximus's army, under the command of Andragathius, in battle at Siscia (Sisak) on the Sava, where he put the rebels to flight. Two more skirmishes at Emona (Ljubljana) and Poetovio (Ptuj) followed until Maximus was captured at Aquileia and brought before Theodosius. For a moment it looked as though the emperor would spare him, but knowing Theodosius's reputation for clemency, his soldiers whisked Maximus away and executed him instantly. His infant son Flavius Victor was captured by Arbogast, the *magister equitum*, and also killed. Maximus was just another usurper in Rome's long history, but his five-year reign marks a turning point. His cause, if

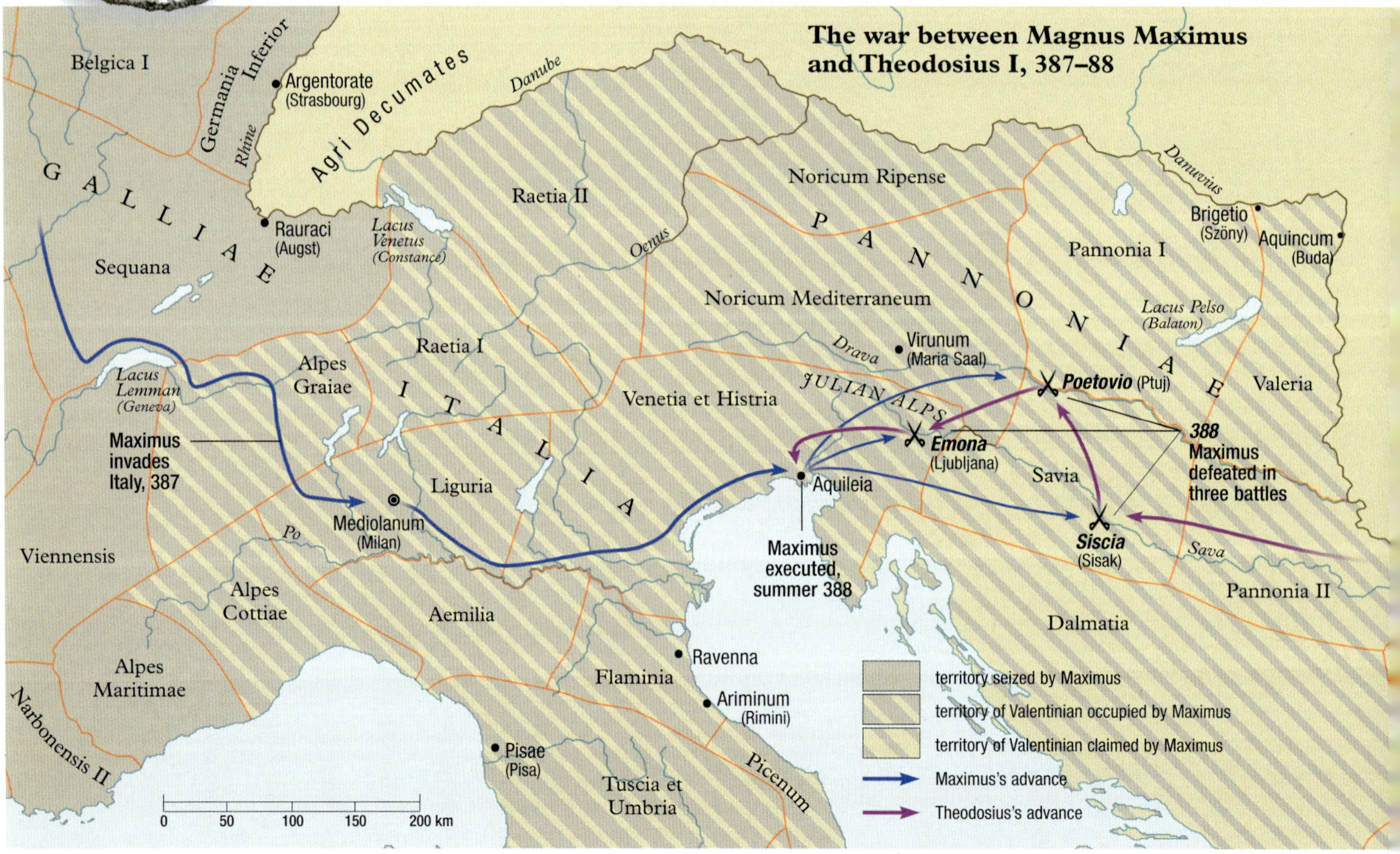

The usurper Magnus Maximus made his infant son Flavius Victor (below) his co-Augustus

misguided, was an earnest one; he intended to provide good government and he was the last really powerful emperor of the west; his defeat made Constantinople the *de facto* centre of the Roman empire.

One of the great boons of Theodosius's reign was peace with the Sassanian empire, a factor which allowed him to concentrate on the turmoil in the west. Shapur III, the new Persian king was an unknown quantity, so Theodosius sent an embassy led by an extraordinary man he had raised up, a full-blooded Vandal called Stilicho. Given the title *magister militum per orientem*, Stilicho travelled to Shapur's court and, after protracted negotiations, reached an accord in 387 that ensured a lasting peace between Rome and Ctesiphon. Since Armenia had always been the rose between two thorns, Stilicho's winning proposition divided it between the two empires. The Roman client king Arsaces retained possession of the western part of the country, while the Persians nominated a Sassanid called Khosro to rule over eastern Armenia. Thus, in the same year, Theodosius was prepared to deal with Maximus and save Valentinian's throne.

## Valentinian II  Flavius Valentinianus
[ co-Augustus 22/11/375–15/5/392 ]

The reign of Valentinian II was unremarkable other than it emphasised the subordination of the Roman west to that of the Roman east. Only four when he became co-Augustus with his half-brother Gratian and his uncle Valens, for the greater part of his reign he was a puppet under the thumb of his ministers and his mother Justina. And even when he achieved his majority he was expressly the junior partner to Theodosius.

Justina had prudently concealed her adherence to Arianism from her husband, Valentinian I, but now – abetted by a powerful Gothic (and therefore Arian) faction at the Milan court – she revealed her faith and determined to rear her infant son in the heresy. Her redoubtable enemy in this was Ambrose, the formidable bishop of Milan, who had extinguished the last embers of Arianism in his diocese and was determined to 'save' the young emperor. In the following years the struggle intensified, frequently putting Ambrose in danger of his life. Yet, despite a level of popularity among the people that bordered on devotion and would have made it possible for the bishop to depose Justina with one word, he never spoke it. Ironically, it was Ambrose who went on Justina's behalf to negotiate with Maximus in 383. Theodosius is supposed to have said in a letter to Valentinian that he deserved Maximus's enmity because he had deserted the true faith of his father.

Only four when made co-Augustus with Gratian and Valens, Valentinian II was always at the mercy of more poweful people.

After the defeat of Maximus, Theodosius remained in Milan for three years. At the beginning of this period Justina died and Theodosius finally disengaged Valentinian from his heretical Arianism. Valentinian was not allowed to enter into the administration, however, and Theodosius undertook all governmental matters, and appointed the ministers and military officers. The most important of these was the *magister militum* Arbogast, who Theodosius promoted to the rank of count of Gaul and charged with the protection of the western provinces in place of the recently deceased count Bauto.

A dreadful massacre at Thessalonica marred 390. Fuelled by resentment at having troops quartered in their homes – Roman soldiers had been bad enough in the past, but the barbarians were much worse – and sparked by an incident in which the *magister peditum*, himself a Goth called Botheric, imprisoned the city's most popular charioteer, the mob attacked the garrison headquarters and cut down Botheric. At Milan, Theodosius flew in to a rage when he heard of the insult. Ambrose's attempts to dissuade the emperor from taking vengeance failed and Theodosius ordered the *comitatenses* to show the city no mercy. The soldiers waited until a day of races when most of the citizens were gathered in the hippodrome and fell on them in a fury. By the evening 7,000 lay amid the gore and shambles; some sources double the figure. It seems that Theodosius, usually regretfully clement once a rage had subsided, sent another dispatch to countermand his original order, but it arrived too late for Thessalonica.

A crime on such a scale, a mass murder undertaken without even the semblance of Roman justice could not be overlooked, and Ambrose, who had already clashed with Theodosius over his rights to dispense justice in episcopal matters, would not. The bishop insisted on a public repentance and until such was forthcoming he refued Theodosius communion. Ambrose was unbending: the emperor must express his repentance publicly and pass an edict forbidding the execution of any citizen until after a period of thirty days, in which time either justice or natural mercy should prevail. Eventually Theodosius agreed both to this wise law and to his public humiliation.

On the following morning the emperor presented himself at the basilica dressed in sackcloth and unadorned by his imperial diadem, to prostrate himself before the high altar. When he was finished he turned to the bishop to receive communion, but Ambrose pointed out sternly that before Theodosius could receive the host he must remove himself beyond the altar railing and leave the sacred enclosure, which was reserved for priests. Although Theodosius was only following the procedure of Constantinople, where the emperor as the right of his august person celebrated communion at the altar apart from the mass of citizens, he obeyed Ambrose and accepted his words: 'The purple only makes emperors, not priests.'

It was a doctrinal turning point. A cleric had asserted the rights of the spiritual over the temporal power of the ruler, and in accepting the condemnation and punishment of a priest, the emperor had for the first time recognised an authority greater than his own. Ambrose was later to say of Theodosius: 'Stripping himself of every emblem of royalty he publicly in church bewailed his sin. That public penance, which private individuals shrink from, an emperor was not ashamed to perform; nor was there afterwards a day on which he did not grieve for his mistake.'

Before leaving for Constantinople on 16 June 391, Theodosius obliged Valentinian to accompany Arbogast to Gaul, and the unwilling junior Augustus removed his court to Vienna (Vienne). Arbogast was a Frank who counted among his relatives count Bauto, possibly his father, and his uncle Richomeres. There is little doubt that he was widely regarded as one of the finest soldiers of his time, and adored by his men for his 'flame-like' qualities of leadership and all-conquering energy. They especially saw in this gruff Frank an incorruptibility uncommon in officers of Roman extraction because he cared nothing for gold or the finer trappings of life. It goes without saying that Arbogast and Valentinian had nothing in common beyond a sneering contempt for the latter by the former and a resentful dread of too-powerful Arbogast by the young emperor.

Arbogast never shrank from laying hands on Valentinian's counsellors if he suspected them of any corruption – and several must have given him reason – and one intimate, a certain Harmonius, he ran through with his sword in front of the terrified emperor. Valentinian frequently complained to Theodosius, but his protestations fell on deaf ears. Matters came to a head when, determined to exert his authority, Valentinian issued a written order to Arbogast demanding his immediate resignation from all his offices. Arbogast stared at the note for a few moments, and then slowly ripped it into pieces before walking away. A few days later, on 15 May 392, Valentinian, now barely twenty-one, was found dead in his apartments. The official verdict was suicide, for which the only possible motive was despair that if he didn't

Ambrose, the bishop of Milan, clashed with Theodosius over the emperor's interference in episcopal affairs.

take his own life, someone else soon would. Since a suicide's soul was supposed to reside in purgatory, perhaps Ambrose's assurances to Valentinian's grieving sisters that he had been carried up to heaven indicated that the bishop suspected foul play. If so, for once he said nothing.

## Eugenius
[ usurper 22/8/392–6/9/394 ]

The reign of Eugenius was wholly the creation of Arbogast the 'king-maker'. Never a fool, he knew that being a barbarian it was unwise to assume the semblance as well as the substance of imperial power. More to the point, Arbogast was not even an Arian, he was a pagan. His choice of puppet fell on Eugenius, a middle-aged professor of rhetoric, a former head of the *fiscus* whom Richomeres had recommended to Arbogast as a clever and obedient subordinate. For his part, Eugenius was not anxious to receive this dangerous honour, but on reflection he realised it was an offer he could not refuse.

When the embassy from the west arrived in Constantinople to inform Theodosius of Valentinian's unfortunate death and the elevation of Eugenius Theodosius was furious – it was his right alone to designate a fellow-Augustus. Nevertheless, none was better acquainted with Arbogast's military skills, so he returned a diplomatic reply and began preparing for a difficult war. All through 393 those preparations continued, while Arbogast extended his power into Italy where Ambrose, vehemently opposed to Arbogast's protégé acclaimed in Gaul, cried out

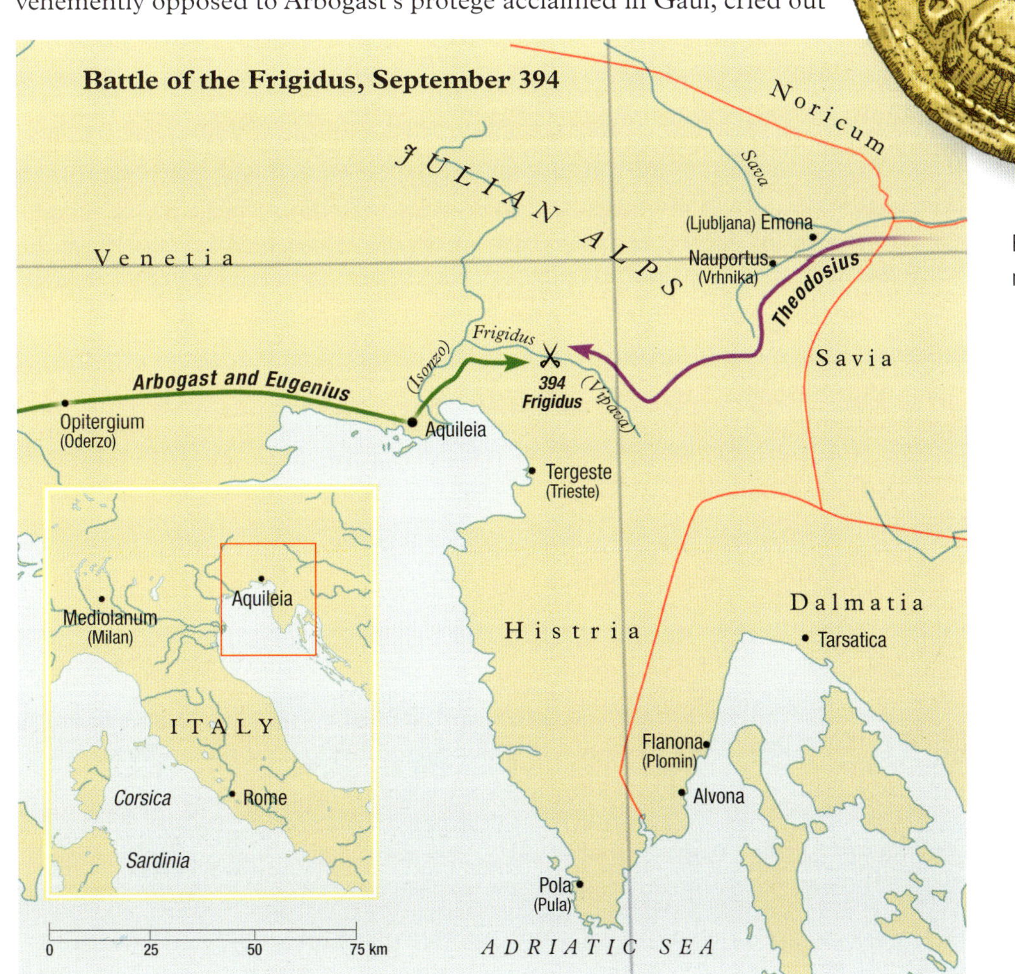


Eugenius, a professor of rhetoric, was no more than Arbogast's puppet.

The Roman empire at the
death of Theodosius I, 395
Valentia
Eburacum
(York)
Maxima
Caesariensis
Britannia II
Britannia I
Augusta
(London)
Flavia Caesariensis
OCEANICUS
GERMANICUS
(North Sea)
Rhenus
Colonia Agrippina
(Cologne)
Germania II
Moguntiacum
(Mainz)
Belgica II
Treveri
(Trier)
Germania I
Mare Britannicum
Lugdunensis II
Lutetia
(Paris)
Belgica I
Lugdunensis IV
Augusta
Vindelicorum
(Augsburg)
Brige
(Szó
Noricum
Ripense
Danube
Pannonia I
Lugdunensis III
Cenabum
(Orléans)
Lugdunensis I
Raetia II
Noricum
Mediterraneum
Liger
OCEANICUS ATLANTICUS
Maxima
Sequanorum
Raetia I
SAVENSIS
Alpes
Poeninae et
Graiae
Histria
Augustonemetum
(Clermont-Ferrand)
Lugdunum
(Lyons)
Venetia
Aquileia
Aquatanica II
Mediolanum
(Milan)
Liguria
Burdigala
(Bordeaux)
Aquatanica I
Rhone
Alpes
Cottiae
Aemilia
Ravenna
Dalmatia
Viennensis
Flaminia
Novem
Populi
Alpes
Maritimae
Picenum
ADRIATIC
SEA
Tolosa
(Toulouse)
Narbonensis I
Narbo
(Narbonne)
Massilia
(Marseilles)
Narbonensis II
Tuscia et
Umbria
Gallaecia
Tarraconensis
Corsica
Samnium
Rome
Campania
Portus Cale
(Oporto)
Caesaraugusta
(Zaragoza)
Apulia
et Ca
Cauca
(Coca)
Tarraco
(Tarragona)
Sardinia
MARE TYRRHENUM
(Tyrrhenian Sea)
Lucania
et
Bru
Lusitania
Augusta
Emerita
(Mérida)
Carthaginiensis
Valentia
(Valencia)
Baleares-Tarraconensis
Caralis
(Cagliari)
Corduba
Panormus
(Palermo)
Lilybaeum
(Marsala)
Sicilia
Baetica
Carthago Nova
(Cartagena)
Syrac
Gades
(Cadiz)
Hippo Regius
(Annaba)
Carthage
Tingi
(Tangier)
Septem
(Ceuta)
Caesarea
(Cherchell)
Numidia
Cirtensis
Africa
Proconsularis
Hadrumetum
(Sousse)
Mauretania
Caesariensis
Mauretania
Stifensis
Byzacena
Mauretania
Tingitana
Numidia
Militana
M A R E
Leptis Magna
Tripolitania
Britanniae
Macedoniae
Galliae
Thraciae
east-west division of the empire
Septem Provinciae
Asiana
Hispaniae
Pontica
Italia
Oriens
Pannoniae
Africa
Daciae
0    100    200    300    400 km

from the pulpit. Arbogast now played his trump card, appealing to the still largely pagan communities of Italy to support his puppet; even though Eugenius was Christian, he was also a classical rhetorician, willing to extend tolerance to gods whose classical names featured in many of his orations. By mid-393 Rome's temples had reopened, the smoke of sacrifices clouded the air, and conservatives were once again celebrating the ancient Roman festivals of Lupercalia and Saturnalia.

Reports of the pagan revival soon reached Theodosius's ears. In November 392 he issued an edict that outlawed every form of pagan worship throughout the empire, whether in public or in private, and made the practice of augury an act of treason. When, in late spring 394, Theodosius marched again for the west, he knew he was not only facing a usurper but also fighting for the faith. The two armies met on 5 September slightly to the north of Tergeste (Trieste), on a small tributary of the Isonzo called the Frigidus (Vipava). From the east, the host of Theodosius advanced under the holy Christian standard; from the west came Eugenius and Arbogast, their men

bearing banners of Sol Invictus. The battle lasted two days, with appalling losses on both sides. But on the second day a hurricane wind from the east blasted dust into the pagan army so that the soldiers could barely see in front of them. Christian chroniclers naturally attributed this good fortune to God's blessing. Eugenius was beheaded at the emperor's feet. Arbogast escaped into the hills, but after a few days' wandering decided not to test the famous Theodosian clemency again, and took his own life. Once more the empire was united under one ruler. In Rome the temples were hurriedly closed up and the idols were packed away, nevermore to be seen.

**FROM 390 – EXCEPTING THE BATTLE WITH EUGENIUS** – Theodosius devoted himself to administration for the next four years. A body of humanitarian legislation followed from the law Ambrose had obliged him to pass which greatly improved the lot of the common man. On religious matters he had already proclaimed in 380 that only those who professed the Nicene creed could be considered Catholic Christians, and all others were pronounced 'mad' and 'heretic'. Having banned paganism outright in 392, the Arian creed was outlawed. In spite of this Theodosius never sought to force his subjects to recant and he never caused persecution. The epithetical 'Great' had previously been awarded to Constantine as the establisher of frontier security and the expander of Roman territory. Theodosius had accomplished the former but added nothing to the empire, even halved Armenia's client status. So it is for his establishment of the Roman Catholic Church that he is known today as Theodosius the Great.

Since in 394 he was approaching his fiftieth year, Theodosius turned his attention to the succession. Valentinian II had died childless, so there was no other male heir to complicate matters, and he decided to divide the empire between his sons, both of whom were in Constantinople, sixteen-year-old Arcadius to rule the east and ten-year-old Honorius to rule the west from Milan. Having made his decision and appointed Stilicho regent, Theodosius immediately sent for his younger son to attend him. It was mid-January that Honorius arrived at Milan, in the company of his cousin Serena, Stilicho's wife, to discover that his father had fallen dangerously ill. Theodosius recovered at the sight of his young son sufficiently to attend the games held to celebrate the boy's safe arrival, but collapsed during the racing and was taken to his bedchamber. On the following night of 17 January 395 Rome's last great emperor passed away, and his death was the 'beginning of the end of all things'.

Young Arcadius, bust and silver coin above, was slothful and weak in intellect and character, hardly any better than his younger brother Honorius, gold coin above, whose one passion was raising chickens.

## Arcadius  Flavius Arcadius
[ co-Augustus (east) January 383; Augustus 18/1/395–1/5/408 ]
## Honorius  Flavius Honorius
[ co-Augustus (west) 393, Augustus 18/1/395–26/8/423 ]

When Theodosius left Constantinople in 394 to confront Eugenius and Arbogast, he'd left his sons under the regency of his praetorian prefect, the ruthless and ambitious Rufinus, a low-born Gaul who had wormed his way into the emperor's affections through well-placed flattery. In Milan, Honorius was better blessed in his regent. The Vandal Stilicho's star had risen rapidly after his successful embassy to Persia in 387. In the following year, he had married Serena – the emperor's favourite niece and adopted daughter. Stilicho maintained that Theodosius had given the care of both his sons to him, but Rufinus scorned this alleged seniority – he was too busy using his office to accumulate wealth in preparation for a grab at the purple. Arcadius might have been expected to put Rufinus in his place, but the boy was slothful and stupid. Small of stature and swarthy of complexion, Arcadius's character was as weak as his intellect.

Only too well aware of his rival's character, Stilicho arranged for his assassination. After the battle of the Frigidus, the armies had remained massed on the Italian border, including a large contingent of *foederati* Visigoths under their leader Alaric. Furious that they had never received the promised pay, the Visigoths went on the rampage across unguarded Thrace to besiege Constantinople where they demanded their gold. Rufinus offered Alaric a small bribe to return to Italy and sent dispatches to Stilicho demanding the return of Arcadius's legions for the city's protection. In this, the Vandal saw his opportunity and complied, returning the men under the command of a Goth called Gainas. As the eastern legions halted outside the Golden Gate on 27 November 395 for their traditional welcome by the emperor, Rufinus appeared with Arcadius. Imperious and arrogant, the prefect walked among the soldiers not noticing that they were closing in around him. A moment later a sword flashed, followed by others, and he fell dead. According to the historian Claudian, the man who struck the first blow cried out: 'With this sword, Stilicho strikes you!' Gainas carried out this assassination partly as a tribute to his friendship with Stilicho and almost certainly to place himself in an advantageous position at Arcadius's court. With Rufinus dead, feeble Arcadius was ruled by three persons: his Frankish empress Aelia Eudoxia, possibly Bauto's daughter, who he'd married in April, the eunuch Eutropius, *praepositus sacri cubiculi* (superintendent of the sacred bedchamber), and now Gainas the Goth who assumed the office of praetorian prefect by the right of arms. Within weeks, Stilicho appointed Gainas as *magister militum per orientem*.

While these events transpired in Constantinople, Stilicho chased and encountered the Visigoths in several inconclusive skirmishes all over Thessaly, Boetia and Attica. This confrontation of brave Stilicho and wily Alaric remains one of Roman history's great mysteries. Stilicho deliberately let the Visigoths escape. The sources are patchy, and where they exist, downright improbable as to the reasons for what happened. The most sensible conclusion is that Stilicho wanted to keep Alaric strong as a counterpoise to Constantinople and use the Visigoths as a recruiting resource. Concluding some sort of agreement with Alaric, Stilicho took his legions back to Italy.

In Constantinople, Eutropius emerged as the power behind the throne, taking advantage of the prefect's absences as he organised his military commands. Elderly, bald-headed and wrinkled, he'd formerly enjoyed much success as a catamite and a pimp before working his way up through the imperial household. Under the eunuch government became more corrupt than ever, with the open selling of offices throughout the east. But he was also a cunning politician and capitalised on Stlicho's stalemate by getting Arcadius to award Alaric the title *magister militum per illyricum*, effectively confirming him in a prefecture the Visigoth had already taken by force. This smart move created a buffer state intended to keep Stilicho out of eastern affairs.

Since gaining full control of Arcadius, Eutropius had pursued a vigorous policy of excluding military men from the emperor, particularly the numerous German officers, and it was Gainas who decided to eliminate the eunuch. Arcadius was not happy with

One half of a carved ivory diptych depicts the Vandal general Stilicho; the other half showed his wife Serena.

Eudoxia, Arcadius's Frankish wife, who moulded her feeble husband to her own ends.

Primitive likeness of Alaric from a coin.

this suggestion, but Eudoxia urged him to agree. Eutropius's continual reminders that it was through his machinations that she sat on the throne beside Arcadius had become irksome; she wanted him dead too. Eutropius fled but was finally tried and executed in the autumn of 399. Gainas fared little better. For six months he tried to initiate his own primacy, including a failed attempt to seize the imperial palace, after which he was forced to withdraw from the city. The mob, thoroughly fed up with the barbarians, slaughtered 7,000 of his German troops before they could retreat through the gates. Somewhere on the northern border Gainas fell into the hands of Uldin of the Huns, who took off his head and sent it to Arcadius as a grisly goodwill present.

Despite his relatively lengthy reign, there is little to say about Honorius. Morally destitute and otherwise incapable of any real emotion, he remained a remote figure securely wrapped up by Stilicho in the palace. In his later years, he engaged in the only activity that interested him: raising chickens. In 398 he married Stilicho's daughter Maria, which clearly placed Stilicho at the peak of his influence and power. However, the beginning of the fifth century – the year 1153 by Roman reckoning – marked the beginning of the end. In the summer of 401 Alaric attacked Italy from Illyricum in concert with an invasion through Raetia by the pagan Ostrogoth Radagaisius. Stilicho seems to have countered Radagaisius with comparative ease – Alaric was another matter. Had the senate and Honorius known the secret of his heart, disaster might have been avoided. Born probably in about 370 at Peucé, an island in the Danube mouth, Alaric was of the noble Visigothic family of the Balthi and, like so many invaders who came after him, he did not seek the destruction of the Roman empire. He wanted to be adopted by it, to form his own nation within its boundaries and thereby become like one of the old Latin states, offering civic obligations and military service in return for his own *imperium* within the state.

A huge army of Visigoth warriors and their families poured through the passes of the Julian Alps, Bypassing Aquileia and Ravenna, they turned west towards Milan and short of the capital, at the small village of Pollentia (Pollenzo), met Stilicho's army on Easter Sunday, 402. The battle was bloody and indecisive, but Stilicho turned the Visigoths and they retreated eastwards. Stilicho was technically the victor, but he allowed Alaric to retire over the passes and into Illyricum without pursuit; the third occasion on which he had let the Visigothic king escape. The reason appears to be an agreement to hire Alaric's army for a planned attack on Constantinople in order to extend Milan's control over Arcadius. There were two consequences of this raid. First, Stilicho moved the imperial palace from vulnerable Milan to defensible Ravenna, surrounded by marshy ground and adjacent to the Adriatic naval base, which made provisioning – as well as a quick escape – possible. Second, Alaric's avowed intent had been to reach Rome and the panicked citizens clamoured for a further reinforcement of the city gates and the raising of the Aurelian Wall where needed. This was done but ironically the strength of Rome's fortifications would ultimately count for less than its citizens' weak fortitude.

Stilicho declared war on Constantinople in 406. Alaric was ready in support but in the event the only hostile action was the blockading of Arcadius's shipping from Italian ports, because Stilicho received alarming news that changed everything. Increasing pressure from Huns on their own eastern borders forced the massed tribes of Vandals, Alani, Suevi and Burgundi to take advantage of the particularly harsh winter of 406–07 to cross the frozen Rhine on a wide front. At Moguntiacum the severely weakened Roman garrison was overwhelmed and all Gaul lay open for the taking. A few weeks later Constantine, count of Britain, crossed to Gaul, ostensibly to deal with the barbarian invasion. Instead, he proclaimed himself Augustus Constantine III.

The situation was desperate. Stilicho simply did not have the forces to deal with either threat. But then events at Constantinople and in Italy overtook him. On the first of May 408 Arcadius died of unknown causes at the age of thirty-one, leaving the eastern empire in the hands of his seven-year-old son Theodosius II. Shortly after, the Visigoths encamped on the Italian border, Alaric demanding recompense for his costs. Stilicho's counsel prevailed and gold sufficient for Alaric's immediate needs was handed over. And in further compensation for the campaign's cancellation Stilicho dispatched the Visigoths to deal with Constantine in Gaul. This freed him to go to Constantinople to take up the regency of Theodosius II in accordance, he reminded the court, with his pledge to Theodosius the Great.

But Stilicho had overstepped the mark, Ravenna seethed with jealousy. The Christians were righteously appalled by the haste with which he'd married his second daughter, Thermantia, to Honorius earlier in the year after her sister, the empress Maria, had died. The Italians resented his presumption, arguing that a barbarian Vandal should know his place and not set himself up above two emperors. The troops were restless at Stilicho's natural preferment of barbarians and at his increasingly harsh discipline. The apparent abandonment of Gaul to the barbarian invaders had lost him the people's faith.

Rumours were put about that Stilicho's real intention was to place his son Eucherius on the eastern throne in place of Theodosius II. While this hardly fits the character of the man, there's no denying that as the descendant of Theodosius the Great by Stilicho's marriage to Serena, Eucherius had an imperial pedigree that his Vandal father did not. At this point even Stilicho's best officers abandoned his doomed cause. Stilicho was arrested in Ravenna by an officer called Heraclianus, tried, found guilty and executed on 23 August 408.

## Constantine III  Flavius Claudius Constantinus
[ usurper early spring 407; co-Augustus (west) 408–18/9/411 ]

Recent events in Gaul cut off Roman Britain from the empire and the citizenry felt that they would have to fend for themselves. It is understandable, then, that Britain had become a 'province fertile in usurpers', the instability a symptom of fear. During 406 no less than three officers were raised and thrown down until the garrisons chose a 'common soldier' of ability – he was probably a centurion – by the name of Constantinus and raised him to the purple with the appellation Constantine III in the spring of 407. If the civilians hoped he would provide security, they were sorely mistaken. Constantine moved quickly, crossing to Gaul with virtually all the remaining mobile army of Britain.

The disaster at Moguntiacum spelled the end of the Roman hegemony in Gaul. The great host that crossed the frozen river on the last day of 406 consisted of Vandals, Suevi and Alani, with the Burgundi soon following the initial crossings. The German tribes fanned out across Gaul, took Aquitania by 409 and crossed the Pyrenees into urbanised Spain, where they soon set up competing kingdoms. Over the next few years the old Gallo-Hispanic provinces brought to heel by Julius Caesar were awash with different competing tribes whose long envy of Rome made them want the mantle of Roman civilisation more than plunder. Plunder, however, they also took as they dodged between the ambitions of competing Roman usurpers and the occasional armies sent against them from Italy. The confusion was incomprehensible.

Into this maelstrom came Constantine, bent on taking the throne from Honorius. His Gallic troops fought their way across the country and into the Rhône valley. In May 408 Constantine reached Arelate and made it his capital. In this position, he was sandwiched between Italy and a chunk of Spain still in the hands of Theodosian cousins of Honorius, where a rag-tag army was gathering. Constantine sent his son Constans to scatter the Theodosians. Two cousins, Didymus and Theodosiolus, were

Constantine III, raised to the purple in Britain, took the last remaining Roman troops from the island in his bid for real power in Gaul.

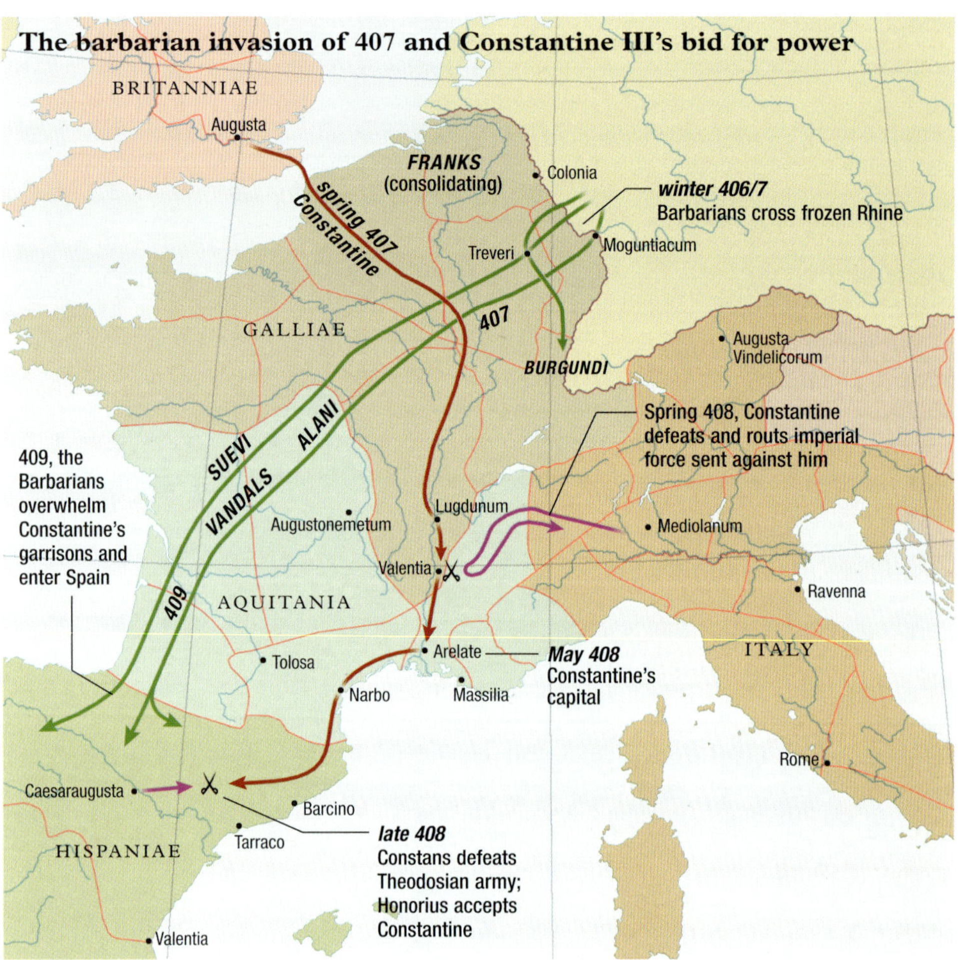

Sad pawn in the power game, the cultured urban prefect of Rome, Priscus Attalus, found himself elevated by the senate to appease Alaric in 409. He was captured in 414, paraded before Honorius and then exiled to die on the Lipari Islands.

captured, while two others, Lagodius and Verianus, escaped by ship and fled to Constantinople. Meanwhile, any organised threat from Italy melted away with Stilicho's execution and the chaotic events that followed as a consequence. In Rome the Italian troops, their distrust of the *foederati* spilling over, began slaughtering the families of their German colleagues who had served in Stilicho's army. These men saw the Visigoths as their only hope of protection. An estimated 30,000 flocked to Alaric's standard.

The Visigoths had returned from a desultory swing into Gaul and were roaming unchecked through Etruria. On hearing of the massacre, Alaric marched on Rome in September 408. Alaric had no siege engines, but he was content to blockade the city and wait. Shortly before Christmas he accepted a bribe to go away: 5,000 pounds of gold, 30,000 pounds of silver, 3,000 pounds of pepper and thousands more of hides and silk clothing. Constantine seized this opportunity and offered Ravenna his support. Feeble Honorius eagerly recognised Constantine as his distant colleague and co-Augustus, and the two were joint consuls for 409. Little good it did Honorius. Alaric hadn't gone far, only to Ariminum (Rimini), close enough to bully Honorius into an outrageous grant of land, but the emperor's counselors, buoyed up by Constantine's offer, refused him. Alaric's response was to return to Rome next spring and, while he was kept outside the walls, he was successful in setting up the urban prefect, a Greek named Priscus Attalus, as a puppet Augustus..

Negotiations continued to no avail, and with his patience exhausted, in the early summer of 410, having publicly stripped Attalus of his purple, Alaric again enclosed the city. This time, there was little delay, and towards the end of August sympathisers within the walls opened the Salarian Gate at the foot of the Pincian hill, and for three days Rome was sacked: a foreign foe had taken the city for the first time in eight centuries, although the disaster hardly impinged on the emperor. One anecdote tells of how he received the news of Rome's sacking. A chamberlain rushed into his presence crying out, 'Roma has perished!' The distraught emperor looked up and replied, 'Roma perished? It is not an hour since she was feeding out of my hand.' When it was explained that it was the city that had been destroyed, the relieved Honorius said, 'I thought you meant that I had lost my chicken Roma.' Alaric enforced his ruling that no church was to be harmed and no citizen who freely surrendered was to be harmed, which restricted the damage, and after three days, taking Honorius's half-sister Galla Placidia with him, Alaric moved to the south of Italy to prepare an invasion of Sicily, prior to taking Africa. But he got no further than Cosentius (Cosenza) where, stricken with a fever, the Visigothic king died.

The year 409, when he shared the consulship with Honorius, was Constantine III's high-water mark. In September the barbarians reached the Pyrenees, where they overwhelmed his garrisons and poured into Spain. In the midst of this disaster his *magister militum* Gerontius revolted to place his own son on Constantine's rocky throne and Britain defected. The abandoned island diocese, suffering Saxon sea-raids in the south and invasions of Scots and Picts in the north, expelled Constantine's tax collectors and officials. At this point the island passed entirely from any form of Roman control and became, in the words of one contemporary, 'an island ruled by tyrants'.

In 410 Constantine found himself besieged in Arelate by Gerontius, who had already executed Constantine's son Constans. In turn Gerontius found himself facing a newly reorganised Roman army which descended from the Alps and fell on the besieging troops. Under the command of a general worthy of Stilicho, Flavius Constantius, the Romans quickly routed Gerontius's army and demanded Constantine III's surrender. Before complying, Constantine took holy orders, and then on receiving promises of safe conduct for himself and his youngest son Julianus, opened the gates. Constantius honoured his pledge to spare Arelate and its inhabitants, but Constantine and Julianus were sent under escort to Ravenna. Before reaching the city, soldiers met the party, bearing orders to execute the 'usurper', and the late Augustus was beheaded on the spot, together with Julianus, on 18 September 411.

## Constantius III  Flavius Constantius

[ co-Augustus (west) 8/2/421– 2/9/421 ]

Despite all the setbacks Honorius survived on the western throne longer than an emperor of his meagre talents at that time had any right. But the last years of his reign did not really belong to him, but to his general Constantius, and the amazing woman who Constantius finally married, the emperor's half-sister. Galla Placidia inherited all those Theodosian attributes that had clearly bypassed his two sons. Her

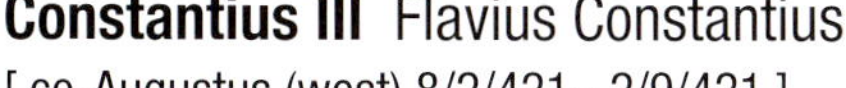

The *magister militum* Gerontius promoted his own son Maximus (*above*) to be Augustus in place of his master Constantine, only to fall foul of a Roman army under Constantius III.

In another Gallic revolt, the noble Jovinus (*top*) seized power in Moguntiacum in 411, and made his brother Sebastianus (*above*) his colleague. Two years later, their heads lay at Honorius's feet.

Constantius III (*coin below*) married Galla Placidia, who assured him the position of co-Augustus.

mother Galla died in 394 when she was about four, so she was placed in the care of Stilicho's household and raised by his wife Serena, her cousin, and she was with Serena in Rome at the time of Alaric's capture of the city. Although Alaric treated her with all respct, she was nonetheless a royal hostage and a prisoner for ransom. After Alaric's death his brother-in-law Athaulf was proclaimed king in his place. Athaulf, who was a far milder character than Alaric, ambitiously wanted to 'restore the empire to its former splendour'. He also fell in love with Galla Placidia and stopped badgering Honorius for her ransom when it became obvious that she was returning his affections. Meanwhile, there was another suitor for her hand.

Constantius was a native of Illyricum, born at Naissus (Nis). He'd served in many campaigns under Theodosius I and came into his own when Honorius most needed a strong arm. He is described as having a sulky look, with a broad head set on a thick neck, with large, full eyes that darted about as he scowled – the complete tyrant in appearance, perhaps not unlike Mark Antony. Appearances apart, he was a polite man, and good company at suppertime. And for the decade after Stilicho's death Constantius was the dominant Roman military leader.

Probably the most powerful of all Roman women since Livia Drusilla, Galla Placidia later ruled the western empire through her son Valentinian III.

After defeating Gerontius and capturing Constantine III, Honorius allowed him to keep the spoils, which provided sufficient funds to celebrate an ovation and, more importantly, secure the release of Galla Placidia, with whom he was madly in love. Unfortunately, negotiations had not resulted in Placidia's return. He pressed for her restitution, and Athaulf demanded concessions of land, money and corn in ever-greater amounts. At the end of 413 they reached Narbo, and there, in January, Athaulf and Galla Placidia were wed. Placidia took her Christian vows as a Roman matron befitting her imperial status; Athaulf was garbed not as a German chieftain but in the raiment of a Roman senator. Amid the splendour of the nuptials, presided over by the Arian bishop Sigesarius, something unique had taken place – the union of barbarous Gothia with civilised Rome.

Shortly after the wedding of his beloved to another, Constantius received in Arelate an embassy seeking tax concessions headed by a young Gallic noble called Avitus. But the distractions of administration did not deter Constantius from his hatred of Athaulf; however, fate soon took a hand. The Visigoths had settled for a while at Barcino (Barcelona), where a servant who bore him some ancient grudge assassinated Athaulf in 415. His brother Walia honoured the dying Athaulf's last wish and restored Placidia to the Romans in return for the right to settle on land spanning southern Aquitania and the western half of Narbonensis Primus. The treaty, concluded in 418, gave the Visigoths a nation with Tolosa (Toulouse) its capital under nominal imperial authority.

Constantius met his bride-to-be – the betrothal had been commanded by Honorius – at the foot of the Alps to escort her to Ravenna and they married in 417. Within two years Placidia bore Constantius a daughter, Justa Grata Honoria, followed by a son, Valentinian. On 8 February 421, Constantius became Constantius III, co-Augustus with Honorius, and Placidia became styled Augusta. In keeping with the custom, statues of Constantius were sent to Constantinople for erection in the eastern capital. However, news of the unilateral addition to the Augusti did not sit well with Theodosius II – or rather with his sister Aelia Pulcheria, who effectively ruled in his name. The statues were returned and Theodosius refused to recognise Constantius, who in consequence began somewhat petulant preparations for a war. Conflict was only avoided because Constantius developed pleurisy and, depressed by the curtailment of his freedom through the tedious court ceremonial, he continued to sicken and died on the second day of September 421.

Widowed for a second time, Placidia now found herself faced with her half-brother's incestuous passion. Honorius started kissing her at public functions and acting jealously in the presence of her ministers. Placidia quarrelled with Honorius and the conflict became so bitter that in the spring of 423 she withdrew to the court of her nephew Theodosius II in Constantinople, taking her two children with her. Her absence from Ravenna contributed directly to events when Honorius, aged 39 suddenly died of 'dropsy' (probably a disease of the lungs) on 26 August 423. Into the imperial vacuum stepped another usurper.



## Joannes  Also Johannes

[ usurper September (West) 423–c.March 425 ]

How an obscure clerk like Joannes became the emperor in Ravenna is hard to understand, and the ancient histories offer little in explanation. The office of *primicerius notariorum* – a chief clerk and diarist – was a useful one, but hardly at the forefront of the imperial bureaucratic hierarchy. The only explanation that fits the

The usurper Joannes was probably the puppet of Honorius's *magister militum,* but they both lost the gamble to Theodosius.

Ivory disc celebrating the patrician Flavius Aspar, son of the Alan barbarian general Ardaburius. After the death of Theodosius, Aspar became the most powerful figure in Constantinople,

politics of the period is that Honorius's *magister militum* Castinus supported the pretension of Joannes, predictably because he expected to enjoy the real power without the pain that any experienced general knew attended imperial failure; much as had Arbogast supported Eugenius.

As befitted his position, Joannes was an intelligent man, and the historian Procopius praised his mild manner and also his general abilities as an administrator. However, all the ills that a pretender to the throne might be expected to attract beset his eighteen-month reign. Theodosius II refused to recognise him and went so far as to elevate the infant Valentinian III to the rank of Caesar, clearly indicating a war ahead. Joannes, looking to recruit a Hunnish army in his support, sent a young man named Aëtius on an embassy to Rugila, their king. The son of a mixed marriage of an Italian mother and Gaudentius, a Visigoth in the service of the empire who had risen to become count of Africa, Aëtius had been given in his youth first as a hostage to Alaric, who taught him the military arts, and then to the Hunnish king Rugila. In his mission Aëtius was successful, receiving a detachment of some 60,000 Huns to come to Joannes' aid. However, Theodosius II reacted too quickly for Aëtius to save his master.

Under the command of the *magister militum,* an Alan called Ardaburius, and his son Aspar, the Theodosian army took Ravenna with hardly any casualties. Joannes was captured and dragged into the circus and his right hand was cut off, after which, in a mockery of a triumph, soldiers led him around the city mounted on an ass to the jeers of the mob before executing him. To punish Ravenna for supporting a pretender, the city was sacked for three days, which loss proved Rome's gift as it regained the temporary status of capital. Valentinian III – now six – was taken there to be crowned with the diadem and become co-Augustus with Theodosius.

Only three days after Joannes' death, Aëtius belatedly returned at the head of his army of Huns. This sudden and frightening influx of Rome's occasional ally but usually deadliest foe forced Ardaburius and Aspar to rally the troops, from their pillaging, and take to the field. But the initial skirmishes were hollow – neither side was keen to spill blood. The Huns rattled their swords in order to raise the price of their quietly going home, and this was agreed between the Augusta Placidia and Aëtius. In receipt of a handsome sum of gold, the Huns retired peacefully, and Placidia gave Aëtius the title of count of Italy, from which position he became her chief adviser.

## Theodosius II  Flavius Theodosius
[ co-Augustus (east) 402; Augustus (east) May 408–28/7/450 ]

Theodosius, son of Arcadius and Aelia Eudoxia, was born in April 401. He was the fourth child but the first boy, so his arrival was received with great joy, both by his family and by the populace of Constantinople. When his father died in 408, the seven-year-old was fortunate in his prefect, Anthemius. This able and high-principled man had dominated the last years of Arcadius's reign, in welcome contrast to the feckless emperor's previous counsellors. Anthemius was the real architect in 413 of the great new land walls to protect Constantinople, known as the Theodosian Walls, parts of which still stand today. Anthemius died at some time after 414, at which point Theodosius fell under his sister Aelia Pulcheria's domination. Only two years his senior but already named Augusta, she represented the real power on the throne.

Weak and easily led, Theodosius didn't look as though he would be much of an improvement on his father. However, he possessed the charm Arcadius had lacked, was an earnest student in Latin and Greek classics, mathematics, natural sciences and in art. His Greek nickname Kalligraphos honoured his skill at manuscript illumination. Nevertheless, his reign was characterised by the squabbling women who largely ran his affairs. His dominating and exactingly devout and pious sister Pulcheria demanded the same of her two other sisters, Arcadia and Marina. In 420 Theodosius decided to take a wife, and asked Pulcheria to find one. She settled on a beautiful young pagan Greek girl named Athenaïs, who was speedily baptised with the name Aelia Eudocia, and the couple were married on 7 June 421.

When she delivered a daughter in the following year, named Licinia Eudoxia, Theodosius antagonised Pulcheria by awarding his wife the title Augusta. And then in the same summer the empire's third Augusta arrived, Galla Placidia, with her children Justa Grata Honoria and Valentinian. The marriage fourteen years later of Licinia Eudoxia to Valentinian III only reinforced the struggle. Athenaïs-Eudocia had vowed that if her daughter married Valentinian she would make a pilgrimage to Jerusalem. She did, and returned in 439 with such important relics – including the original chains with which Herod had bound St Peter – that she put Pulcheria's saintly reputation in the shade. Pulcheria swiftly engineered Athenaïs' fall from favour, when eunuchs in her camp fabricated a charge of adultery. Protesting her innocence, the empress was exiled and returned to Jerusalem in 443, where she remained until her death in 460.

Theodosius's magnificent legacy is the first great pandect of Roman law. The principal concern was to rationalise the extensive legislation compiled since the last comprehensive law code issued in the time of Diocletian and harmonise those laws of the eastern and western halves of the empire. A commission of nine scholars started work in March 429 and after six years completed a first edition. A second commission improved the language and created a system by which the code could be further emended and enlarged as necessary in the future. The *Codex Theodosianus* was finally promulgated on 15 February 438 jointly in the senates of Rome (still the centre of western jurisprudence) and Constantinople. The code exercised enormous influence both in itself and in future legal history. Together with the work of those great third-century jurists Ulpian, Papinian and Julius Paulus, it became the basis for Justinian's much more ambitious judicial reforms in the following century. It is also possible to trace considerable portions of King Alaric II's *Lex Romana Visigothorum* of 507 to the *Codex Theodosianus*.

**BY THE TURN OF THE FIFTH CENTURY,** the Huns had settled north and east of the Danube, particularly along the plains of what is now Hungary. While they caused the empire occasional problems they also served under Roman arms when it suited them. An annual tribute payment of some 350 pounds of gold helped to maintain the peace. However, the situation changed dramatically when Attila succeeded as the Huns' warlord. The terror of the Christian world was described in contemporary sources – no proven images of him exist – as being short, with small, beady eyes, a snub-nose, swarthy like his race and with a head too large for his body, his chin adorned with a straggly beard. Surprisingly for the destruction he caused, Attila was no great general – the only pitched battle he fought against disciplined troops, he lost.

Attacks against the eastern empire began escalating after 441, until in 447 Attila demanded double the tribute and Theodosius refused to pay. The Huns stormed across the river, sacking cities and razing many, including Philippopolis, Sirmium,

Studious and weak, Theodosius II pursued a religious life in his secluded palace, dominated by his sister Aelia Pulcheria (*below*).

Coin of Aelia Eudocia, pagan Athenaïs before marrying Theodosius.

No known portrait exists of Attila the Hun, this is derived from a Christian imagining of the scourge of Christianity, creature of Satan.

Naissus and Serdica. The cruelties Attila inflicted in this campaign earned him the title 'Scourge of God' by Christians. The Huns then swept south into Thessaly and eastwards to Constantinople, destroying everything between the Adriatic and the Aegean, as far south as Thermopylae, and as far east as the Hellespont, where they inflicted a defeat on Roman forces at Gallipoli. Only the capital's massive new walls completed by Theodosius in the nick of time saved the empire from total disaster. That and the old enemy of the barbarian ravager – the land laid so much to waste could no longer support the horde, and the Huns drifted back towards the Danube. Negotiations for peace commenced, aided by the fact that with so much devastation in Thrace, Attila turned his eyes towards Italy and Gaul.

At this critical moment, a fall from his horse while out hunting killed Theodosius on 28 July 450. Since he had produced no male heir, it was down to Pulcheria to direct the succession, which she did by contracting a marriage with a Thracian ex-soldier and senator called Marcianus (Marcian), and placing him on the throne beside her. Marcian's first act was to confirm the refusal to pay any further tribute. Whether bravado or a calculated gamble, Marcian's spies had informed him that Attila's plans for an operation against the west were too far advanced to delay them for a punitive attack on Constantinople, which in any case would only have the unsatisfactory outcome of the earlier raid. Rejoicing broke out some days later when news arrived that the Huns were riding away.

## Valentinian III  Placidius Valentinianus
[ Caesar c.October 423; co-Augustus (west) 424–3/15/455 ]

Because he was barely seven at his coronation in 419, his mother Galla Placidia utterly dominated Valentinian's reign, and she was to precede him to the grave by only five years. Ineffectual, spoiled, devoted to religion and astrology in equal measure, Valentinian III was unfit to rule, and showed neither the aptitude nor inclination to do so. The only effective measure he seems to have taken was to grant greater ecclesiastical power to the bishop of Rome, especially Pope Leo I the Great. The story of his reign, then, is really that of the Augusta Galla Placidia.

Intellectually challenged, weak-willed, Valentinian III was utterly dominated by his mother, Galla Placidia.

The two great calamities of Placidia's reign were the loss of Africa to the Vandals, and the invasion of the Huns under Attila. In 420 the Vandal king Gunderic defeated a Romano-Visigothic army in southern Spain and became ruler of a Vandal kingdom centred on Baetica. The Visigoths, however, continued to push southwards and in 428 Gunderic's successor and half-brother, the shrewd and militarily outstanding Gaiseric, led all 80,000 of his people across the narrow strait to begin an assault on Mauretania. From the African bridgehead, the Vandals rapidly advanced eastwards towards Numidia and Africa Proconsularis, delayed by the spirited defence of a certain Bonifacius, who commanded the Roman militias even though he only held the rank of military tribune.

In early skirmishes, Bonifacius won some victories, but it was clear he could not hold on for long, and Placidia had no reinforcements to send. Bonifacius was defeated in a great battle in 431, and compelled to flee with his forces to Italy, leaving Mauretania and Numidia in Vandal hands. Gaiseric had remained out of Africa Proconsularis in return for *foederati* status, and so grain for bread in Rome – albeit in reduced quantities – still came, and some nominal Roman presence was maintained at Carthage. But at his capital in Hippo Regius (Annaba), Gaiseric had no intention of abiding by this agreement, and in 439 he attacked Proconsularis. The loss of Carthage was a shock to the Romans, but their hands were full elsewhere.

During this period Aëtius had campaigned tirelessly throughout the mire that was now Gaul, principally against the ever expanding Frankish kingdoms, against whom he was mostly successful. On his return to Italy he was displeased to find Bonifacius currying favour with Placidia in Ravenna. Fearing for his position, Aëtius challenged his rival to single combat and, in this somewhat Teutonic conflict, Bonifacius received a mortal wound. Placidia was furious with Aëtius, but Attila's arrival tempered her anger. His huge army of Huns and allied German tribes crossed the Rhine in 451 and swept south, sacking first Colonia Agrippina, then in succession Moguntiacum, Argentorate, Remi (formerly Durocortorum), and were on the verge of taking Cenabum Aureliani (Orléans) when Aëtius at the head of an alliance of Romans, Visigoths, Salian Franks and some Burgundi met them in June in what was perhaps the greatest single engagement western Europe was to witness before 1914. The battle of the Catalaunian Plain near Durocatalauni (Châlons-sur-Marne) resulted in Attila suffering his first reversal and, according to contemporary accounts, left more than 200,000 dead, among them Theodoric, king of the Visigoths. Military strategists have since criticised Aëtius for allowing Attila to retreat across the Rhine, but the Romans had also taken massive losses and were in no position to pursue the enemy. Perhaps Aëtius also felt a continued threat from the Huns would hold his Gallic alliance together.

Galla Placidia didn't witness her general's success. Approaching her sixtieth year, she died on 27 November 450. The imperial court had been in Rome for twenty-five years, but her body was returned in state to her beloved Ravenna. She was, therefore, also spared the horrors to come. When he returned in 452, Attila wreaked a terrible revenge on Italy. Descending the Frigidus, he put Aquileia to the torch, rapidly followed by Concordia, Altinum (Altino) and Patavium (Padua). Others opened their gates and were saved from burning but not from pillage, and the citizens were taken into slavery. In the end Italy was saved by the intervention of Pope Leo I, already raised high by Valentinian, who went to meet Attila where the Mincio meets the Po. Here, by means unrecorded Leo convinced the Hun to return to his lands on the Danube.

Attila was contemplating a further attack against Constantinople, when he died in his sleep in 453, and Christian Europe gave a great collective sigh of relief. In the following year the Ostrogoths won a great victory over the demoralised Huns, after which most of the nation drifted away to regions around the Caspian Sea. In an interesting footnote, during the attacks the thousands who fled from the Huns' wrath hid out among the uninhabited marshes and lagoons of the Adriatic coast north of Ravenna, and there built a village on stilts. Over time the settlement grew and became named after the region, Venetia, and developed into the city we know today as Venice.

With Placidia in her mausoleum, Aëtius was clearly the most powerful person in the empire, and the emperor's youngest daughter, Galla Placidia the Younger, was promised to him in marriage. In the palace in Rome, where Valentinian had resided during the invasion, wily eunuchs poisoned his vacant mind against Aëtius. Since Valentinian had no son the marriage to his sister would place Aëtius in line for the succession. The whisperings of chamberlains had their effect, so much so that Valentinian was driven himself to strike the killing blow with his own dagger. Asking a palace official after the murder whether he had performed a good deed or not, the courtier replied: 'I am scarcely able to say. One thing, however, I do know, that you

Bonifacius, *comes Africae*, was an able warrior who met his match when his Roman forces were overwhelmed by the advancing Vandal horde of Gaiseric.

The parlous state of the western empire at the death of Valentinian III, 455

A coin of Gaiseric issued from the Carthage mint, actually portrays Honorius – an indication that the barbarian kings still considered the real authority to be Roman in the mid-fifth century.

JUTES
ANGLES
SAXONS
FRIESIANS
c.450
c.450
c.450
c.450
SAXONS
Lundene
Colonia (Köln)
SALIAN FRANKS
Rhine
Treveri (Trier)
Moguntiacum (Mainz)
Remi (Reims)
RIPURIAN FRANKS
Castra Regina (Regensburg)
ARMORICANI
Lutetia (Paris)
Durocatalauni (Châlons-sur-Marne)
451
Catalaunian Plain
Argentorate (Strasbourg)
ALAMANNI
Danube
THURINGII
Cenabum Aureliani (Orléans)
Juliomagus (Angers)
Loire
Aventicum (Avenches)
BURGUNDIAN KINGDOM
Raetia
Virunum (Maria Saal)
Venetia
Aquilea
Avernum (Auvergne)
Alpes Graiae
Mediolanum (Milan)
Verona
Augustonemetum (Clermont)
Lugdunum
Vienna (Vienne)
ALANI
Augusta Taurinorum (Turin)
Liguria
Aemilia
Burdigala (Bordeaux)
Rhône
Alpes Cottiae
Flaminia
Ravenna
GOTHIA
Arelate (Arles)
Alpes Maratime
Tuscia et Umbria
Tolosa (Toulouse)
Massilia (Marseilles)
Brigantium (La Coruä)
VASCONI (Basques)
Narbo (Narbonne)
Corsica
Aleria
Rome
Legio (León)
Ebro
Tarraconensis
Sa
Portus Cale (Oporto)
Douro
Caesaraugusta (Zaragoza)
nominal Roman control with occasional aid from the Visigoths
Sardinia
455 sack of Rome
Ca
Cauca (Coca)
Tarraco (Taragona)
SUEVIC KINGDOM
Toletum (Toledo)
Tagus
Caralis (Cagliari)
Olisipo (Lisbon)
Valentia (Valencia)
Balearic Islands to Vandal Kingdom
439 Carthage captured, ending Roman rule in Africa
Lilybaeum (Marsala)
Augusta Emerita (Mérida)
Guadiana
first Vandal capital
Cordoba
Guadalquvir
Carthago Nova (Cartagena)
Hippo Regius (Annaba)
Carthage
Hispalis (Seville)
Gades (Cadiz)
Malaca (Málaga)
Cartenae (Ténès)
Caesarea (Cherchell)
431 Gaiseric defeats Bonfacius
Hadrumetum (Sousse)
Tingis (Tangier)
Septem (Ceuta)
VANDAL KINGDOM
Siga (Takembrit)
Tacape (Gabes)
0  100  200  300  400 km
Sabrata
Italy and territory owing allegiance to Ravenna
nominal Roman allegiance
Visigothic kingdom
Frankish kingdoms
Burgundian kingdom
Suevic kingdom
Vandal kingdom
eastern Roman empire
campaign of Attila, 451–52
initial Vandal sea-raids on Italy
German raids on southern England, c.450

have chopped off your right hand with your left.' In the middle of March 455 while he watched training athletes, Optila and Traustila, two henchmen of Aëtius, sprang out from behind a bush and stabbed the emperor to death. With Theodosius II in his grave five years, his sister Pulcheria for three and now Valentinian III gone, the dynasty of Theodosius the Great had ended.

# THIRTEEN

# Fall of the West

[AD 455–467]

### Petronius Maximus  Flavius Anicius Petronius Maximus
[ 17/3/455–31/5/455 ]

The army's choice fell on sixty-year-old Petronius Maximus, quite simply because he was the highest-ranking senator in Rome and promised to make a good emperor. The grandson of usurping Magnus Maximus, he had attained the exalted rank of Patrician at the age of about fifty. By the fifth century, the term meant something very different to its Republican usage, when it referred to the first families of Rome. Constantine the Great revived the title in the fourth century, but only as a personal honorific, not a hereditary dignity. In this way, Aëtius wore this rare distinction for the last twenty years of his life, and to the common folk the title Patrician came to be associated wth the head of government and real power in the state, the first minister.

Sexagenerian Petronius Maximus demanded the hand of Valentinian's widow, the young Licinia Eudoxia (*right*). It's said she appealed to Gaiseric to rescue her. He did.

The rapid downfall of Petronius Maximus is attributable to his own surprising ineptitude that lost him the affection of the senate and people, and his attempts to ally himself by marriage to Valentinian's widow. He failed to prosecute Valentinian's murderers and, worse, received them into the circle of his friends – his suspicious subjects detected his hand in the assassination. But Rome was even more appalled when he demanded Valentinian's widow, the beautiful Licinia Eudoxia, marry him. With no one around to protect her, it's said that she called on Gaiseric to save her, but the Vandal assault on Rome probably had more to do with taking advantage of Valentinian's recent death. The fleet arrived off Ostia in May and instead of mounting a defence Maximus prepared to flee north, issuing a proclamation that anyone who wished was free to leave Rome.

He needn't have bothered. The wealthy had already packed up and left. But the common people had nowhere to go, and in their fear and fury, rose up with the garrison soldiers on 31 May – only two days before Gaiseric arrived – and tore Maximus limb from limb, throwing the dismembered parts into the Tiber. For fourteen days the city was subjected to 'a leisurely and unhindered' extraction of its wealth. If Eudoxia really had appealed to Gaiseric, she received more than she had wished for. As the Vandals left, they took the empress with them, together with her daughters, the princesses Eudocia and Galla Placidia the Younger. Only the year before, Galla the Younger had married the senator Olybrius. He was a scion of the powerful Anician family of Italy, originally from Praeneste (Palestrina), whose living members could trace their noble ancestry back to at least 168 BC. However, since he is not mentioned in connection with his wife's kidnapping by the Vandals, it must be assumed that he was absent from Rome, perhaps at court in Ravenna or, more likely given the following history, in Constantinople on business.

The *magister militum* Marcellinus, commanding Dalmatia, had written of the death of his friend Aëtius: 'With him died the western empire, nor since then has it been able to recover.' And the Theodosian ambassador and historian Priscus didn't even mention Petronius Maximus; he summed up the remaining inheritors of the western purple disdainfully: '…although I know their names, I shall not mention them. For it so fell out that they lived only a short time after attaining the office, and as a result of this accomplished nothing worthy of mention.' Harsh, and not always fair.

## Avitus  Marcus Maecilius Flavius Eparchius Avitus
[ 10/7/455–17/10/456 ]

For two months the throne remained vacant until the nobles of battered Gaul raised up a nobleman of Avernum (the Auvergne region) at Arelate on 10 July 455. The Roman senate accepted Eparchius Avitus without a murmur since he was from a distinguished Gallic senatorial family, probably about sixty at his accession. Educated, eloquent and a lifelong friend of Theodoric I of the Visigoths, he had three children, Agricola, Ecdicius, who later became *magister militum* under Julius Nepos in 475, and a daughter Papianilla. He had successfully won tax concessions from Constantius III and served under Aëtius eventually rising to the rank of *magister peditum per galliae*. Between 439–45 he served as the praetorian prefect for Gaul before retiring to his estate near Augustonemetum, in the heart of Avernum.

It was Theodoric's son, Theodoric II, who urged Avitus to assume the purple, although he had a personal agenda in suggesting the move. Avitus was, at best, a reluctant ruler, and his sixteen-month reign was preoccupied with establishing his authority over various parties; particularly his senior military commanders, Majorian and a count of the Suevi nation named Ricimer – who barely concealed his barbarian contempt for the emperor. Constantinople refused him recognition and the Vandals continued blockading the ports. Theodoric's eyes were set on conquering Suevic Spain, while ostensibly making it appear he was acting in the emperor's name. Early in 456, a massive Visigothic army descended into what had been Roman Gallaecia and over the summer months destroyed the Suevi kingdom. In the same year Ricimer destroyed a Vandal fleet off Corsica and then defeated a Vandal army near Agrigentum in Sicily, which recovered all of the island apart from a small enclave centred on Lilybaeum (Marsala).

Ricimer's victories should have reflected well on Avitus, but a famine in Rome soured any joy and he had alienated the senatorial order through exclusively appointing Gauls to office at junior and senior levels. Ricimer suddenly publicly declared Avitus unfit to rule. There was a personal angle here – his father was a Suevi and he blamed Avitus for the nation's destruction. Avitus fled towards Avernum, but was taken prisoner on 17 October at Placentia (Piacenza) by Ricimer, who now styled himself *magister utriusque militae* and called himself Patrician. Ricimer felt unable to execute Avitus, other than his assumption of the purple an innocent old man, but he stripped him of his insignia and consecrated him as bishop at Placentia, where he died about a year later.

Gallic Avitus filled the imperial vacuum caused by Italian dithering.

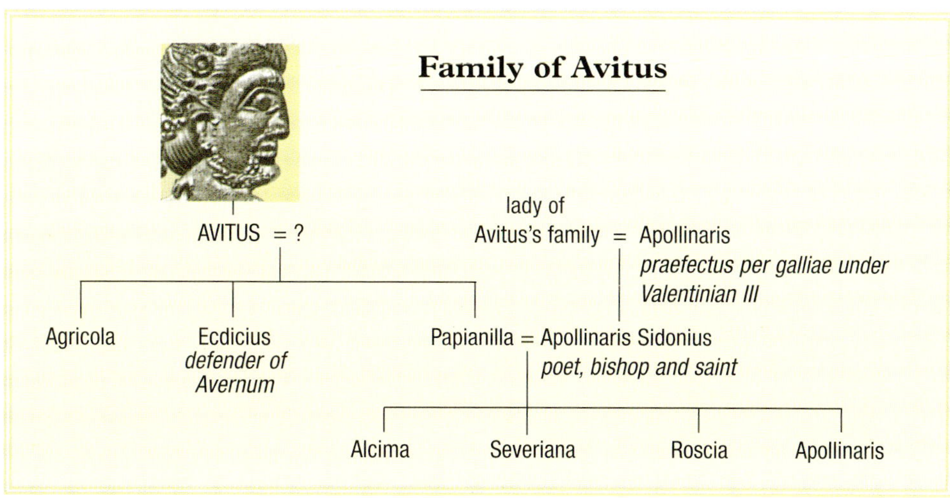

## **Majorian**  Julius Valerius Maiorianus
[ 1/4/457–2/8/461 ]

Majorian was the first military man to rule for 70 years, but his sound administration worked against him – Ricimer wanted a more amenable puppet.

Bust and coin of Leo I, a military man raised to power by Apsar the Patrician.

For the next sixteen years, Ricimer was virtually head of the western Roman empire. Born in about 405, he was an Arian Christian, son of a prince of the Suevi and the daughter of Walia, king of the Visigoths, successor to Athaulf. His sister was married to Gundiok, king of the Burgundi. Such connections concentrated in his hands the kind of power denied to those earlier Teutonic knights who had come to the failing empire's rescue, men like Stilicho, Arbogast, Gainas or Aëtius. As a German, he knew there would only be unrest if he assumed the title of Augustus, which left him alternatives: dissolve the western court and govern legitimately as a *dux* or duke of the emperor in Constantinople or set up his own puppet emperors and rule through them. He chose the latter, of course.

The first of Ricimer's shadow-rulers, Majorian, commanded the elite unit of the imperial guard. There was a four-month wait while Ricimer corresponded with Constantinople before he elevated Majorian on 1 April 457 at the Columellae army camp outside Ravenna. In Constantinople the new emperor Leo approved Ricimer's choice – only two months previously, on 7 February, he had succeeded Marcian as the result of machinations by Aspar, whose position in the east corresponded with Ricimer's in the west. Under the circumstances Leo was hardly in a position to cavil at Majorian's similar elevation. As a result the two courts were in more harmony than had been the case for some years.

Of all the shadow emperors, Majorian was the best. He came of warrior stock and proved it: he sent troops to eject an Alamanni force that had broken through the Raetian Alps and himself led an army to the rescue of the Campania from ravaging Vandal raiders. The enemy was driven off with some loss on their side and little to the Romans. A two-year war with Theodoric II, angered at the deposition of 'his' emperor Avitus, ended with a treaty favourable to Majorian in that it included rights for the Romans to use Gothic bases in Spain for a reconquest of Vandal Africa. Majorian's administration also displayed great wisdom. To counter a dangerous fall in the birthrate he forbade women to become nuns until their fortieth year, and made widows remarry a second husband five years after the death of the first (despite the Church's disapproval). He banned the practice of families burdened with too many children to force younger sons into the clergy to keep down the cost of raising them. He created the position of ombudsman to protect the poor against abuses committed by rapacious imperial officers in his name. And he legislated to prevent building contractors from knocking down Rome's greatest ancient monuments to use in new construction.

Majorian's only real failure was the African campaign. A fleet of 300 ships, which had been gathered in the harbour of Carthago Nova (Cartagena), were captured or destroyed in May 460. Gaiseric it seems had got wind of the plan, laid waste the provinces of Mauretania that Majorian intended as his beach-head and then arranged his own fleet to sneak into the harbour. No doubt Majorian's failure to retake Africa detracted from his reputation, but his real downfall came about because of the very qualities the empire so desperately needed: a zealous military nature and the hands of sound administration. These were proving far too spirited for the great Patrician, and Ricimer dethroned him on 2 August 461 and had him put to death near Dertona (Tortona).

## Severus III  Libius Severus
[ 19/11/461–15/8/465 ]

To say that Libius Severus was a Lucanian from the south of Italy, that he 'lived religiously', and to give the dates of his reign is the sum of knowledge about Ricimer's second shadow emperor. His death in Rome may have been the result of natural causes or it may have been because he drank from a cup poisoned by the Patrician's hand. When – almost unnoticed – Libius Severus slipped away on 15 August 465 Ricimer nominated no successor, and for the next twenty months acted as the sole source of government in the west.

However, in Constantinople Leo – who was proving, like Majorian, to be a great deal more independent of his puppet master Aspar – pressured Ricimer to accept his own choice of imperial colleague. This raised the consideration of whether a better benefit was to be obtained by an alliance with Constantinople or Carthage, for Gaiseric was also insistently championing his candidate, no less than the Anician senator Olybrius. When Gaiseric had carried off the Augusta Eudoxia from Rome in 455, he had also taken her two daughters. The elder of the two, Eudocia, had been married to Gaiseric's son Huneric, which made him brother-in-law to Galla Placidia the Younger and her husband Olybrius, who was absent in Constantinople. Gaiseric eventually sent her with her mother to Constantinople, where she was reunited with Olybrius. Gaiseric now argued that Olybrius was a suitable candidate for the west's emperor – but the marriage ties offered the Vandal king potential advantages in the future. Eventually, to Gaiseric's towering rage, the decision went to Constantinople, and Ricimer agreed to Leo's choice of Anthemius.

Coin of Severus III.

## Anthemius  Procopius Anthemius
[ 12/4/467–11/7/472 ]

In the spring of 467 Anthemius and his wife Euphemia, daughter of an emperor, his sons Marcian, Romulus and Procopius, and his daughter Alypia arrived at Ostia to be greeted by Ricimer. At some point along the Via Ostiensis, on 12 April, Anthemius received the imperial powers of the western Roman empire – in reality only Italy and a precarious toehold down the Rhône valley and in Avernum.

Anthemius was the previous eastern emperor Marcian's son-in-law. He descended on his father's side from Procopius, the kinsman of Julian Apostate who revolted against Valens. On his mother's side his grandfather Anthemius had been the prefect and regent to Theodosius II, the real architect of Constantinople's land walls. He himself had risen to become count of Illyria, *magister peditum* and a consul. One important part of the compact between Ricimer and Leo was to invade Africa and rid the world of Gaiseric and his Vandal kingdom. This vast undertaking was largely financed and fitted out by Leo, with limited material support from Italy, but due to complex politics in Constantinople the amphibious invasion was placed in the hands of the emperor's incompetent brother-in-law, Basiliscus, which doomed it.

Anthemius suffered from the disaster in Africa which Ricimer rightly blamed on Constantinople's blundering.

For much of his reign, Anthemius warred against the aggressive Euric, who had recently succeeded Theodoric II. Seeing how divided Rome had become the new Gothic king decided that he could take over all of Gaul without opposition. There were several Roman offensives but all of them disasters which marked the end of any Roman influence in the Gallic provinces. Now everything except Italy was lost beyond small, short-lived pockets around Arelate, Massilia and in Avernum, heartland of that valorous Gallic tribe whose most famous son Vercingetorix bravely resisted Julius

Euphemia (*right*), wife of Anthemius, was the daughter of the previous eastern emperor Marcian (*below*).

Caesar before the dawn of empire. Here Ecdicius, son of the late emperor Avitus, now led Roman resistance against new barbarians.

The honeymoon period – if there had ever really been one – for Anthemius and Ricimer was over. The great joint enterprise against Gaiseric that might have united Patrician and Augustus failed, thanks to the bungling of Basiliscus, and failure only emphasised that Ricimer had humbled Rome before the east to no avail.

The almost complete loss of everything beyond the Alps contributed to a sense of despair, and hot-headed Anthemius fretted increasingly at his puppet status. A state of internecine warfare existed between Patrician and puppet, hostilities that broke out in early 472. Having learned what was happening, Leo dispatched the senator Olybrius to Italy to arbitrate between Ricimer and Anthemius, or perhaps to wrest the crown from Anthemius. At this point – about April – Ricimer proclaimed Olybrius emperor, thereby conciliating Gaiseric. Anthemius barricaded himself in Rome but eventually Ricimer's force broke in, found the emperor and slew him. Anthemius perished on 11 July 472,

This coin of Basiliscus shows the distinct difference between the classic profile portraits of the west and the recent development of full-face portraits of Constantinople.

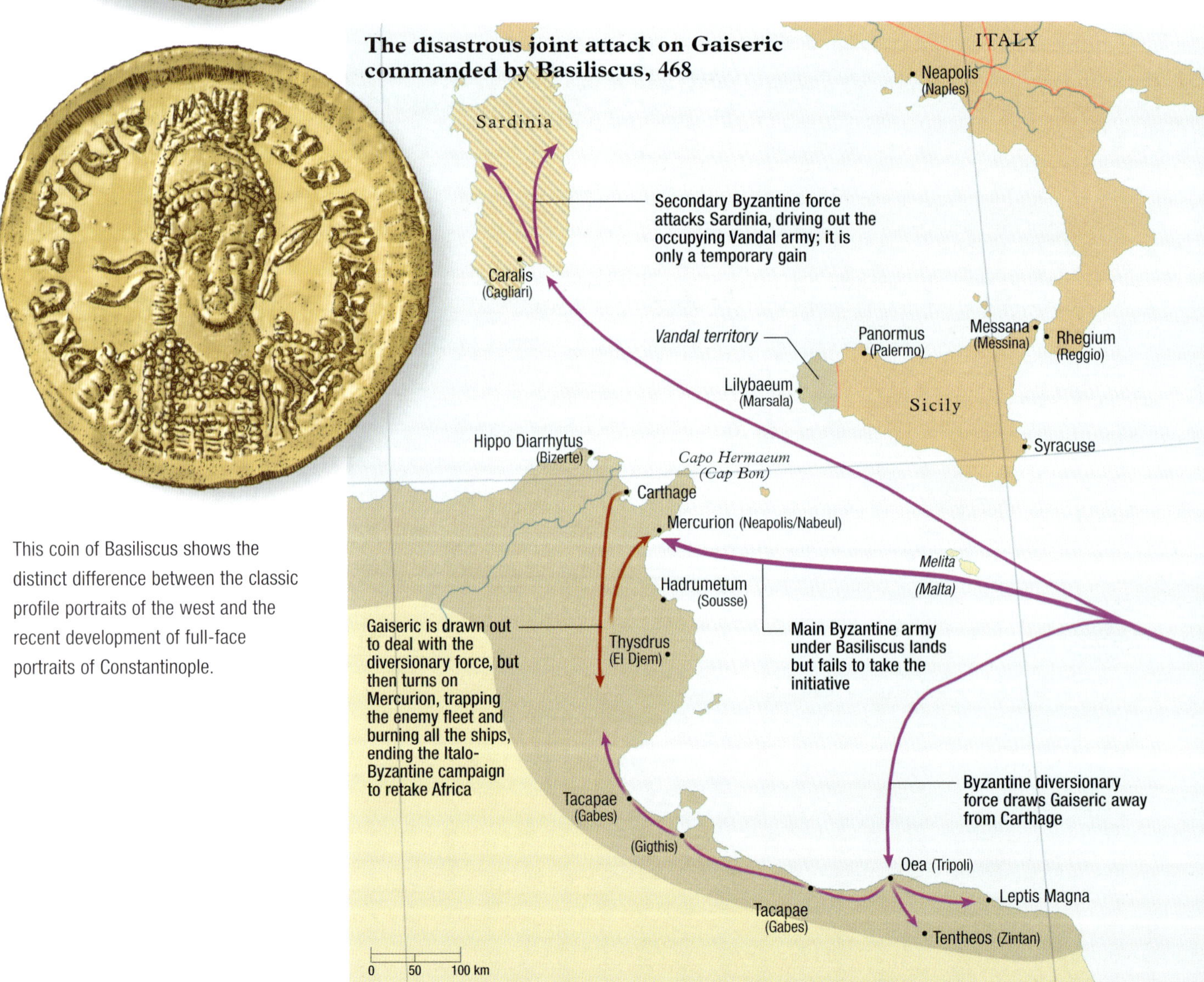

leaving Olybrius, Gaiseric's unexpected prize candidate, on the throne. He might have worried that his fate would be similar to his immediate predecessor's, but the great Patrician suffered a haemorrhage a few days later and died on 18 August.

## Genealogy of eastern and western emperors, 467–91

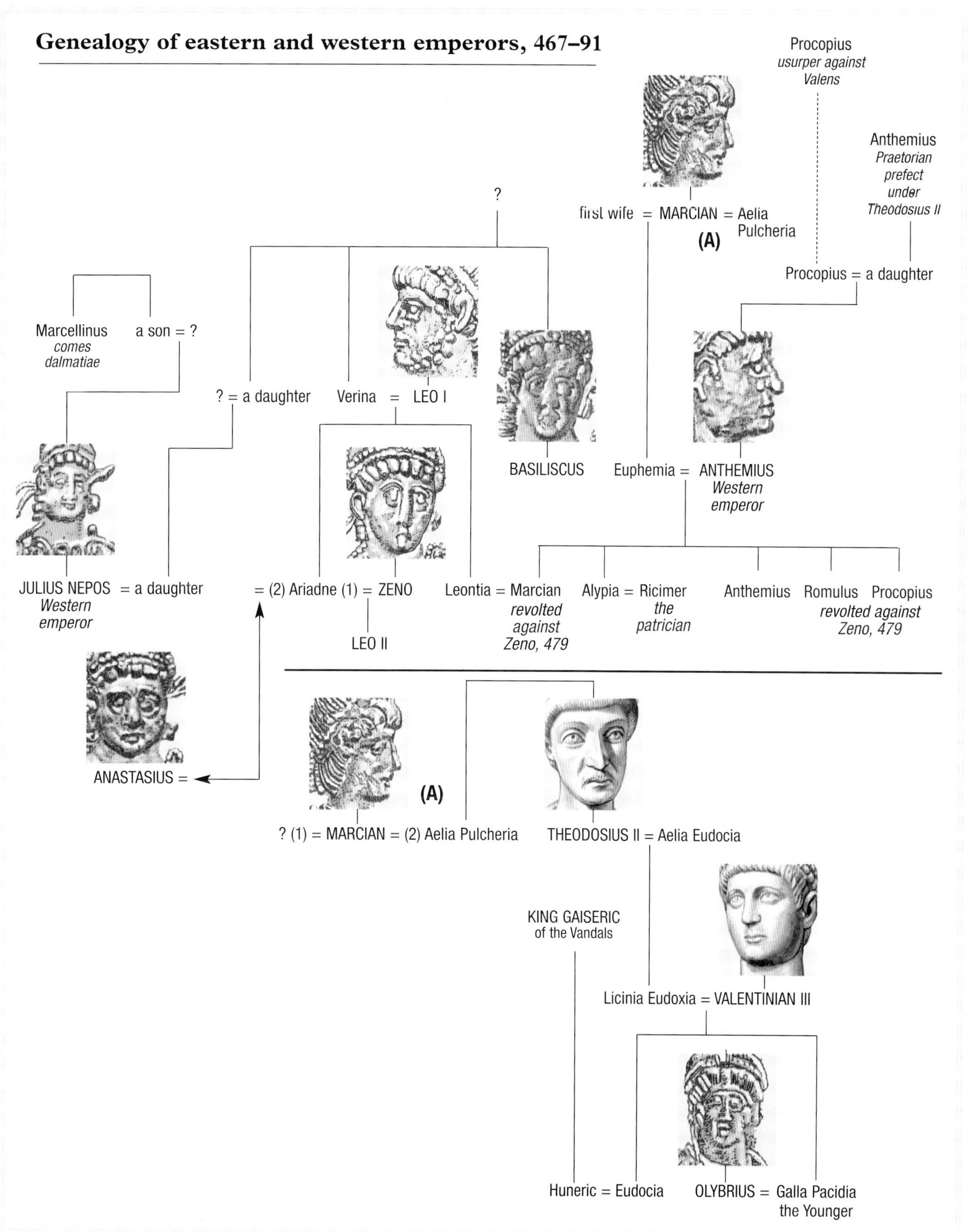

Olybrius had always been Gaiseric's choice for the western throne, but he died before becoming useful.

## Olybrius  Anicius Olybrius

[ April 472–23/10/472 ]

In spite of his family's powerful political legacy, Olybrius was not to add any lustre to his gens Anicii despite being raised to a higher positon than any before him. Owing to his marriage in 454 to Valentinian III's daughter Galla Placidia the Younger and her sister's to Huneric, he was effectively a vassal kinsman to the Vandal king. His reign lasted barely eight months, and of the first five nothing is known except for his coinage struck in Milan. As to his fitness to rule, abilities in legislation, or fiscal policies, Olybrius's own death of 'dropsy' little more than three months after his predecessor's precludes any conjecture. From a political perspective, Ricimer's choice had been wise. Not only would Olybrius's Italian aristocratic heritage have recommended him to the senate, but he would have been a more palatable candidate than the Greek Anthemius.

Only one item of his administration is clear: after Ricimer's death he conferred the title of Patrician on the young Burgundian prince Gundobad, whose mother was Ricimer's sister. Gundobad had come to Italy to seek his fortune with his powerful uncle and found his desires fulfilled somewhat sooner than he could have hoped for. With the title came the loyalty of the majority barbarian element of the Roman army and so, when Olybrius dropped dead on 23 October 472, the remnants of the western Roman empire fell into young Gundobad's hands.

## Glycerius

[ 5/3/473–24/6/474 ]

Another *interregnum* followed of five months, doubtless while Gundobad consolidated his power. Then, on 5 March 473, he raised the *comes domesticorum* Glycerius to the throne at Ravenna. It seems as though the new emperor reigned only in the north because none of his coinage was struck in Rome. Not surprisingly, the Byzantine court of ageing Leo refused to accept Glycerius – an Augustus made 'more by presumption than by constitutional selection'. Leo appointed Julius Nepos, *magister peditum* of Dalmatia, to command an army and reclaim Italy from the usurper. Leo died in January of 474 to be succeeded by his grandson, the infant Leo II, with his father Zeno as regent and co-Augustus. Incongruously, these events meant that Glycerius was the most senior of the three reigning emperors.

His handling of the Ostrogoths was typical of his ignominious administration. When Theudemir and Widemir, brother-kings of the Pannonian Ostrogoths, split their tribe to seek better land, Theudemir headed for Thrace and Widemir for Italy. Glycerius sent an embassy to Widemir and shamelessly suggested the Ostrogoths bypass Italy and raid in Gaul. The blandishments and bribery worked, and Widemir led his Ostrogoths across the Alps and down into the valleys of the Rhône and Loire, where they soon made cause with their kinsmen the Visigoths, and removed from Rome those few remaining outposts of imperial resistance in the south: Arelate and Massilia; Avernum and a tiny enclave north of Reims alone held out.

Glycerius was distant from his subjects and, when they could be bothered, they hated him. No one, therefore, was greatly perturbed to hear that Julius Nepos was coming, and Glycerius was left on his own. Even the puppet-master Gundobad deserted in the hour of his emperor's need, for his father Gundiok had died, and the Patrician decided that his future was better served by taking up the Burgundian mantle rather than face hostilities with a large Byzantine army.

Glycerius (*above*), abandoned by his patron Gundobad, abdicated under pressure from Leo and the new co-emperors, his grandson Leo II and his father Zeno, celebrated on this coin.

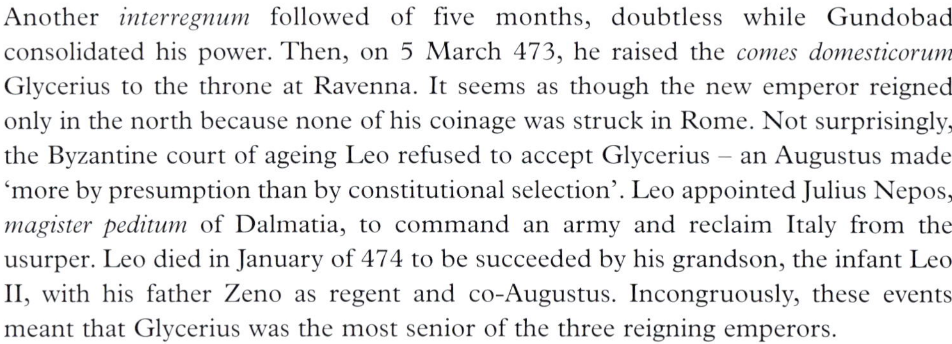

Glycerius must have perceived the outcome. Without the support of senate, people or army, his cause was lost, and he made his way to Rome to throw himself on the mercy of the invader. So on 24 June 474 Julius Nepos was raised to the purple where he landed and granted the deposed Glycerius his life and retirement to obscurity as a consecrated bishop in Dalmatia. His kindly fate recalls that of Avitus, but unlike the former bishop of Placentia, Glycerius survived for a considerable time. And, in the following year, he enjoyed sweet revenge of a kind, when Nepos was forced out of Italy and returned to Dalmatia whence he had come, only to discover that Glycerius was to be his bishop.

## Julius Nepos
[ 24/6/474–28/8/475 abdicated]

Julius Nepos, son of Nepotianus, *magister peditum* in Thrace between 458–61 had married a niece of the emperor Leo. The major events of his fourteen-month reign took place in what was left of Roman Gaul, as the Visigoths attempted to wrest Avernum from imperial control. Unlike Theodoric II, his brother Euric was a bitter Arian and strongly anti-Roman. Euric's fury fell on the walls of Augustonemetum in 474, stoutly defended by Ecdicius, son of the emperor Avitus. Nepos bestowed on Ecdicius the title of Patrician and made him *magister militum* of the Roman army; an empty gesture considering his isolation on the other side of the Alps and the fact that Nepos had no reinforcements to send. At the end of the campaigning season, Euric withdrew, leaving the city untaken but with half its walls lying in ruins.

In the following year Euric changed strategy and prepared to invade Italy by way of the Alpes Maritimae, along the coastal road – once the route by which Julius Caesar had invaded Gaul. On hearing the alarming news, a council of Ligurian bishops turned to Epiphanius, bishop of Ticinum and the peacemaker of his age. The bishop went forward, met Euric and persuaded him to abandon the invasion. But his success in this mission came at a cost: Nepos had to hand Avernum to the Visigoths. The fate of brave Ecdicius is unknown, thrown to the enemy through treacherous Roman diplomacy.

Appointed by Constantinople. Julius Nepos lasted for just over a year before being exiled to Dalmatia.

Nepos now needed a replacement for the offices of Patrician and *magister militum* and appointed a certain Orestes, who promptly took his army from Rome to Ravenna, and there proclaimed his son Romulus emperor. Like his predecessor, Nepos had little alternative but flight, and left Italy for Salonae in Dalmatia on 28 August 475. Romulus came to the throne on 31 October. Nepos outlived the western empire by four years, dying on 15 May 480 at the hands of assassins, whose motives are unknown.

## Romulus Augustulus
[ 31/10/475–4/9/476, abdicated ]

Orestes' was a curious career. An Illyrian provincial born in Pannonia, he had made his way to Attila's court as a young man, where the king employed him as his personal *notarius*. After Attila's death he entered imperial service, and commanded the household troops under the short-reigning emperor Anthemius. At the time of his revolt against Nepos, his son Romulus was aged about fourteen, so it remains a mystery as to why Orestes placed the purple on his slender shoulders. Orestes was as full-blooded a Roman as Trajan or Diocletian, and therefore did not suffer the drawback of barbarian prospects like Arbogast, Stilicho or Ricimer. Perhaps it's an indication of how low the prestige of the title Augustus had fallen in

Bearing the name of Rome's founder and that of its first princeps, Romulus Augustulus was no more than a child.

mens' minds that real power should be more identified with the title Patrician.

At his accession the boy became Romulus Augustus, but everyone knew him as Augustulus, the 'little emperor'. The short reign of this, the last Roman emperor in the west, so poignantly bearing the name of the nation's founder and wearing the title bestowed on its first great *princeps*, was marked only by one significant event, a peace treaty with Gaiseric. Orestes concluded this, probably in return for Rome confirming the Vandals' toehold on Sicily at Lilybaeum.

By this time the Roman army contained few men of Roman extraction, let alone even any Italians or at the very least Gallic troops. It was composed of the many Teutonic tribesmen that had taken service with the eagles of the ancient legions more and more over the past century, and they wanted what Rome had granted the Visigoths, a land of their own. However, unlike the settlement given to Walia, the barbarian legionaries wanted one-third of Italy, and this outrageous demand a Roman like Orestes could never accede to. He probably believed the demand was open to negotiation, but he misjudged. Under the leadership of Orestes' own standard-bearer – the Herulian Goth Odoacer – the soldiers mutinied.

Orestes retreated with his loyal retainers and Romulus to the dubious sanctuary of Ticinum, pursued by the mutineers, hoping that their discipline would dissolve without his leadership and their resolve fail. But Odoacer proved a resilient general, and the town was surrounded and quickly taken. For two terrible days Ticinum was sacked, but the quarry had fled, this time to Placentia (Piacenza). And it was there, only five days after the elevation of Odoacer, that Orestes was taken and at once beheaded. When Romulus was dragged before the victorious Odoacer at Ravenna, the Herul was moved to mercy by the boy's innocent beauty and his pitiful state. Instead of having him executed, Odoacer granted the little Augustus a palace and a generous pension for life. And so on 4 September 476 Romulus Augustulus retired to the splendid villa near Neapolis that had originally been built by Lucius Lucullus, the great Republican general who had defeated Mithridates. Not even a fragment of history exists to reveal further the fate of the last Roman emperor of the west.

A coin of Odoacer shows that the Herulian king had learned from the Romans the importance of coinage as a means of stamping his imperium on his subjects – Roman and barbarian alike.

The Western Roman empire at the accession of Romulus Augustulus, 475

western Roman empire
'Roman' kingdom of Aegidius and Syagrius 462–86
Visigothic kingdom and Ostrogoths in the East
Frankish kingdoms
Burgundian kingdom
Suevic kingdom (under Visigothic domination)
Vandal kingdom
eastern Roman empire
east-west division of empire
capital city

Colonia
(Köln)
Rhine
Moguntiacum
(Mainz)
Treveri
(Trier)
RIPURARIAN
FRANKS
Durocatalauni
(Châlons-sur-Marne)
Argentorate
(Strabourg)
ALAMANNI
BOHEMIANS
Danuvius
(Danube)
THURINGII
ALAMANNI
only nominal Roman control
LANGOBARDI
(Lombards)
Vindobona
(Vienna)
Brigetio
(Szöny)
OSTROGOTHIC
KINGDOM
GEPIDAE
OSTROGOTHS
Aventicum
(Avenches)
BURGUNDY
Raetia
Virinum
(Maria Saal)
Poetovio
(Ptuj)
Dravus
Histria
Liguria
Venetia
Aquileia
Pannonia
Siscia
(Sisak)
Savus
Milan
Verona
Po
Singidunum
(Beograd,
Belgrade)
Danuvius
Moesia II
Augusta
Taurinorum
(Turin)
Ticinum
(Pavia)
Placentia
(Piacenza)
Aemilia
Ravenna
Dalmatia
effective control to
Eastern empire
OSTROGOTHS
Naissus
(Nis)
only nominal
Roman control
Thracia
Alpes
Cottiae
Flaminia
GEPIDAE
Dacia
ALANI
Nicaea
(Nice)
Sinus
Ligusticus
(Ligurian Sea)
Tuscia et
Umbria
Tiberis
Picenum
Salonae
(Solin)
Praevalitana
Rhodope
assilia
arseilles)
Corsica
to Vandal
kingdom
Aleria (Aléria)
Rome
Samnium
MARE ADRIATICUM
(ADRIATIC SEA)
Dyrrachium
(Durres)
Macedonia
Thessalonica
456
Ricimer's fleet destroys
the Vandal navy.
Campania
Apulia et
Calabria
Brundisium
(Brindisi)
Apollonia
(Pojan)
Epirus
Thessalia
MARE
AEGEUM
(AEGEAN SEA)
Neapolis
(Naples)
Tarentum
(Taranto)
Lucania et
Brutti
Sardinia
to Vandal
kingdom
MARE TYRRHENUM
(Tyrrhenian sea)
Nicopolis
Caralis
(Cagliari)
Achaea
Athens
to Vandal
kingdom
Panormus
(Palermo)
Messana
(Massina)
Rhegium
(Reggio)
MARE
IONIUM
(IONIAN SEA)
Lilybaeum
(Marsala)
Sicily
Agrigentum
(Agrigento)
Syracuse
456
Ricimer regains
most of Sicily
Hippo Regius
(Annaba)
Carthage
Creta
VANDALS
Hadrumetum
(Sousse)
Melita
(Malta)
MARE INTERNUM
(MEDITERRANEAN SEA)
Cyrene
(Shahhat)
Oea
(Tripoli)
Leptis Magna
Berenice
(Banghazi)
Libya
Superior
Libya
Inferior
0   100   200   300   400 km

# Into Byzantium

## [AD 476–565]

Some scholars start the chronicle of the Byzantine empire with the birth of Constantine's Nova Roma – Constantinople. Others prefer to wait until the death of Justinian I in 565, arguably the last emperor of the classical period and the last Latin-speaking ruler. Before him came a series of rulers of greater or lesser ability and fitness. The death of Theodosius II left something of a constitutional crisis, since there were no sons. His sister Aelia Pulcheria solved the problem in tandem with the Patrician Aspar by marrying his choice of military man, and Marcian – while nonetheless something of a puppet, proved a sensible organiser, recovering the empire's finances after Hunnish ruination. Marcian also died without male issue and Aspar turned to another officer, Flavius Valerius Leo I, who proved to be a tougher nut for the Patrician to crack. Leo oversaw Aspar's downfall through the offices of his son-in-law Zeno, who looked to succeed when the time came. So did the emperor's brother-in-law, the supremely ambitious Basiliscus, whose incompetence led to the disaster in Africa in 468.

In the event, Leo I passed over both his marital relatives in favour of Zeno's son, Leo II, and died in 474. The provision was pointless, since Leo's daughter Ariadne made her infant son raise his father Zeno to be co-Augustus, a role he filled reasonably for a year until Basiliscus launched a coup and overthrew him. The two-year reign of Basiliscus is best forgotten, other than it ended in ignominy when Zeno made a successful bid to return in 477. Zeno was followed by Flavius Anastasius, who married the widowed Ariadne in 491 and died childless in 518, passing the diadem to his commander of the *excubitori*, the imperial bodyguard, a tough Thracian called Justin. But it was Justin's clever young nephew Justinian who is best remembered for his extraordinary reign which started in 527 and included a magnificent revision of Greek and Latin law, the rebuilding and gilding of Constantinople – at a ruinous cost to the tax-payer which resulted in riots – and the

Despite the apparent adult age of the coin portrait, Leo II was only an infant at his accession, and died soon after.

Leo I's wife, the meddlesome Aelia Verina (*above*), backed her brother Basiliscus in his coup against Zeno (*above right*), her son-in-law. Zeno made a comeback two years later.

Anastasius brought common sense to the government and a sometimes too-careful hand on the purse strings.

reconquest of Vandal Africa and Ostrogothic Italy, the last actually devastating a land that had happily accommodated to its new Gothic order.

After deposing Romulus Augustulus, Odoacer had assumed the kingship of Italy and Dalmatia with the tacit recognition of Zeno in Constantinople, but Zeno was also dealing with the king of the Pannonian Ostrogoths, Theodoric, who was in theory a vassal of the emperor. Theodoric took the comission to lead his people into Italy and destroy Odoacer's kingdom, which he managed after a bitter war, executing the Herulian in March 493. Theodoric ruled his new multi-national kingdom with great wisdom, returning Italy to a land of prosperity. Sadly, few of his successors were so great and the Ostrogoths were in a poor position to resist when Belisarius, Justinian's general, invaded in 536. Nevertheless, the initial stages of the reconquest were bitterly contested by the king, Witigis, who was eventually trapped in Ravenna.

Belisarius returned to Constantinople a hero, but those who administered Italy after him brought it to ruin and rebellion. In only a few months, a resurgent Gothic army wiped out all the gains Belisarius had made, and his return to the peninsula was less than successful. In the end Justinian recalled him and sent a eunuch called Narses to clear up the mess. Narses achieved this in 552 by reducing Italy and its population to pauperdom using an army that was almost entirely barbarian in composition, predominantly Lombard. Narses restored Ravenna to its former glory as the Byzantine capital of the new exarchate or military government. Justinian died in November 565, satisfied that the extent of the Roman empire was at its greatest since the early fifth century. But it was at a cost. Italy had been laid waste, the senatorial class that had survived and even flourished under Theodoric was obliterated, and within three years of the emperor's death the Lombards returned in force and took the north of Italy for their own kingdom and the south became a scattering of Lombard duchies. The gains in Spain were also soon lost and, except for a tenuous hold on the Exarchate of Ravenna, the former western Roman empire was split away from Constantinople and plunged into the darkness of the early medieval period.

The empress Theodora, seen here from a contemporary mosaic, was a powerful influence on Justinian, another coin below.

The only known portraits of Belisarius are a mosaic in San Vitale, Ravenna, in which he stands next to Justinian, and on the reverse of a coin of Justinian (*below right*) which shows the general mounted, riding to war.

Justin (*above*) – an illiterate soldier from Thrace – was a good ruler, but it was his clever nephew Justinian (*right*) who would return stability to the eastern empire.

**The recovered Roman empire at the death of Justinian, 565**

Under the Ostrogothic king Theodoric, Italians enjoyed the peace and prosperity they had missed for decades.

Totila was the last Ostrogothic king of Italy who, despite his youth, reunited the peninsula against Constantinople. When he was killed in battle in 552, all effective resistance crumbled.

Theodoric's daughter, Amalasuntha (*right*) assumed the regency of her dysfunctional son Athalaric, (*centre*) after her father's death, but fought with Theodahad (*far right*), Theodoric's nephew. Theodahad proved a poor and greedy ruler, and his murder of Amalasuntha provided Justinian with the excuse to invade Italy.

SLAVS
SLAVS
AVARS
AVARS
GEPID KINGDOM
Kerch
Chersonesus (Sevastopol)
ALANI
Lazica
Sirmium (Sremska)
Avars conquer both Gepid and Lombard kingdoms by 568
BLACK SEA
ALANI
Viminacium (Kostolac)
Novae (Svishtov)
Odessus (Varna)
Sinope
Trapezus (Trebizond)
ICUM
Naissus (Nis)
Serdica (Sofia)
Armenia
Philippopolis (Plovdiv)
SASSANIAN EMPIRE
Dyrrachium (Durazzo/Durres)
Constantinople
Nicomedia (Izmit)
Thessalonica
Nicaea (Iznik)
Ancyra (Ankara)
Caesarea (Kayseri)
Melitene (Malatya)
AEGEAN SEA
Pergamum (Bergama)
Edessa (Urfa)
IONIAN SEA
ACHAEA
Smyrna (Izmir)
Iconium (Konya)
Ephesus (Selçuk)
Halicarnassus (Bodrum)
Antioch
Rhodes
Rhodes
Cyprus
Palmyra
LAKHMIDS
Gortyn
Crete
GHASSANIDS
Sidon
Tyre
MEDITERRANEAN SEA
Cyrene
Aelia Capitolina (Jerusalem)
Alexandria
ORIENTIS
LIBYA
EGYPT
Heliopolis
0   100   200   300   400 km
Roman empire
Lombard conquest, 572
Visigothic kingdom
Frankish kingdoms
Suevi
Lombard kingdom
Gepid kingdom
Sassanian empire

# Table of emperors

## Julio–Claudian dynasty

Augustus 27 BC–AD 14
14–37 Tiberius
37–41 Gaius Caligula
41–54 Claudius
54–68 Nero

## Year of the Four Emperors

68–69 Galba
69 Otho
69 Vitellius

## Flavian dynasty

69–79 Vespasian
79–81 Titus
81–96 Domitian

## Nervo–Trajanic and Antonine dynasties

96–98 Nerva
97–117 Trajan (97–98 with Nerva)
117–38 Hadrian
139–61 Antoninus Pius
161–69 Marcus Aurelius (with Lucius Verus)
161–80 Marcus Aurelius (sole ruler)
180–92 Commodus

## Civil war and the Severan dynasty

193 Pertinax
193 Didius Julianus
193–211 Septimius Severus
211–12 Caracalla (with Geta)
211–17 Caracalla (sole ruler)
217–18 Macrinus (with Diadumenian, 218)
218–22 Elagabalus
222–35 Severus Alexander

## Period of Military Anarchy

235–38 Maximinus Thrax
238 Gordian I and II (Africa); Balbinus & Pupienus (Italy)
238–44 Gordian III
244–49 Philip the Arab (with Philip II, 247–49)
249–51 Decius
251–53 Trebonianus Gallus (with Volusian) (with Hostilian, 251)
253 Aemilian
253–60 Valerian (with Gallienus)
260–68 Gallienus (sole ruler)

### Imperium Gallorum

259–69 Postumus
268 Laelianus
268 Marius
269–71 Victorinus
271–74 Tetricus

## Restoration of Empire

268–70 Claudius II Gothicus
270 Quintillus
270–75 Aurelian
275–76 Tacitus
276–82 Probus
282–83 Carus
283–84 Carinus and Numerian

## The Tetrarchy and House of Constantine

| WEST | | EAST | |
|---|---|---|---|
| 287–305 | Maximian Aug. | 284–305 | Diocletian Aug. |
| 293–305 | Constantius Caes. | 293–305 | Galerius Caes. |
| 305–06 | Constantius Aug. | 305–11 | Galerius Aug. |
| 305–06 | Severus II Caes. | 305–09 | Maximinus Daia Caes. |
| 306–07 | Severus II Aug. | 309–13 | Maximinus Daia Aug. |
| 306–12 | Maxentius (*in Italy with Maxentius reinstated 307–08*) | | |
| 306 07 | Constantine I Caes | | |
| 307–24 | Constantine I Aug. | 308–324 | Licinus Aug. |
| | 324–37 Constantine I Aug. (sole ruler) | | |
| 337–40 | Constantine II Aug. | 337–61 | Constantius II Aug. |
| | 337–40 Constans Aug. (Italy) | | |
| 340–50 | Constans Aug. | | |
| | | 351–54 | Gallus Caes. (with Constantius II) |

## House of Constantine continued

| WEST | | EAST | |
|---|---|---|---|
| 355–61 | Julian Caes. (with Constantius II, Aug. from 360) | | |
| | 361–63 Julian Aug. (sole ruler) | | |
| | 363–64 Jovian Aug. (sole ruler) | | |

## Valentinian and Theodosian dynasties

| WEST | | EAST | |
|---|---|---|---|
| 364–75 | Valentinian Aug. | 364–78 | Valens Aug. |
| 375–83 | Gratian Aug. | 365–66 | Procopius (usurper) |
| 375–92 | Valentinian II Aug. | 379–92 | Theodosius Aug. |
| | 392–95 Theodosius Aug. (sole ruler) | | |
| 392–94 | Eugenius (usurper) | | |
| 395–423 | Honorius | 395–408 | Arcadius |
| 409–11 | Constantine III | 408–50 | Theodosius II |
| 421 | Constantius III (with Honorius) | | |
| 423–25 | Joannes (usurper) | | |
| 425–55 | Valentinian III | 450–57 | Marcian |

## Fall of the west

| WEST | | EAST | |
|---|---|---|---|
| 455 | Petronius Maximus | | |
| 455–56 | Avitus | 457–74 | Leo I |
| 457–61 | Majorian | | |
| 461–65 | Libius Severus III | | |
| 467–72 | Anthemius | | |
| 472 | Olybrius | 474 | Leo II |
| 473 | Glycerius | 474–75 | Zeno (deposed) |
| 473–75 | Julius Nepos | 475–77 | Basiliscus |
| 475–76 | Romulus Augustulus | 477–91 | Zeno (restored) |

---

| **POPES OF ROME** | | | |
|---|---|---|---|
| d.AD 64 | St. Peter | 399–401 | St. Anastasius I |
| c.66–c.68 | St. Linus | 401–17 | St. Innocent I |
| c.79–c.91 | St. Anacetus | 417–18 | St. Zosimus |
| c.91–c.101 | St. Clement I | 418–22 | St. Boniface I |
| c.100–c.101 | St. Evaristus I | 422–32 | St. Celestine I |
| c.109–c.116 | St. Alexander I | 432–40 | St. Sixtus III |
| c.116–c.25 | St. Sixtus I | 440–61 | St. Leo I |
| c.125–36 | St. Telesphorus | 461–68 | St. Hilarius I |
| c.138–c.42 | St. Hyginus | 468–83 | St. Smplicius I |
| c.142–c.55 | St. Pius I | | |
| c.155–66 | St. Anicetus | **PARTHIAN KINGS** | |
| c.166–74 | St. Soter | c.77–80 | Vologaeses II |
| c.174–89 | St. Eleutherius | 78–105 | Pacorus II |
| 189–98 | St. Victor I | 80–90 | Artabanus III |
| 198/9–217 | St. Zephyrinus | 105–47 | Vologaeses III |
| 217–22 | St. Callistus I | 109–29 | Chosroes I |
| 222–30 | St. Urban I | 129–40 | Mithridates IV |
| 230–35 | St. Pontian I | 147–91 | Vologaeses IV |
| 235–36 | St. Anterus | 191–208 | Vologaeses V |
| 236–50 | St. Fabian | 208–28 | Vologasees VI |
| 251–53 | St. Cornelius | 216–224 | Artabanus IV |
| 253–54 | St. Lucius I | **SASSANIAN KINGS** | |
| 254–57 | St. Stephen I | 224–41 | Ardashir I |
| 257–58 | St. Sixtus II | 241–72 | Shapur I |
| 260–68 | St. Dionysius | 272 –73 | Hormizd I |
| 269–74 | St. Felix I | 273–76 | Vahram I |
| 275–83 | St. Eutychian | 276–93 | Vahram II |
| 283–96 | St. Gaius | 293 | Vahram III |
| 296–?304 | St. Marcellinus | 293–303 | Narses |
| 306–08 | St. Marcellus I | 303–09 | Hormizd II |
| 310 | St. Eusebius | 309–79 | Shapur II |
| 311–14 | St. Miltiades | 379–83 | Ardashir II |
| 314–35 | St. Silvester I | 383–88 | Shapur III |
| 336 | St. Mark | 388–99 | Vahram IV |
| 337–52 | St. Julius I | 399–420 | Yazdgerd I |
| 352–66 | Liberius | 420–38 | Vahram V |
| 366–84 | St. Damasus I | 438–57 | Yazdgard II |
| 384–99 | St. Siricius | 457–59 | Hormizd III |
| | | 457–84 | Peroz |

### Colouring a Roman

The 'noble' white marble busts seen in museums today were actually covered in paint. This added to the realism of the sculptor's vision, and would have been particularly evident in details like the eyes – alive with colour and, perhaps, intelligence, rather than the disconcertingly blank gaze we see today. This example shows how Lucius Verus – so proud of his gold-dusted blond hair – might have appeared when the bust was spanking new.

### Getting it right

The problems encountered when authenticating the likeness of an historical figure are demonstrated by the bust on the left. Its owner, the Museum of Antalya in Turkey, claims it shows the co-Augustus Balbinus (AD 238), but if it is compared to the portrait on the coin struck by him (*right below*), a distinctly closer semblance can be found with the Balbinus bust in the Vatican Museums (*right*).

### Comparison of coin sizes

The coins depicted in this book are used as portraiture. As a result, they are shown considerably larger than their real size. This can be seen from the comparison of Trajan's coin, shown left, as it appears on page 50, and its real size (11mm), to be found in the Museo Nazionale di Roma, Rome.

# Index

141, 149, 155
Army reforms
  Augustus 17, 18
  Constantine I 133
  Diocletian 119, 120
  Gallienus 103
  Marius 6
  Septimius Severus 79
  Theodosius I 152-153
Arsaces, joint-king of Armenia 155
Arsaces, king of Armenia 141
Artabanus V, king of Parthia 82-83, 88
Aspar, the Patrician 168, 176-177, 184
Athanaric, Visigoth chieftain 149
Athaulf, king of the Visigoths 166-167, 176
Athenaïs, Theodosius II's wife 169
Attacotti, tribe 147
Attalus, Priscus puppet Augustus 164
Attianus, Acilius 53, 54
Attila 169, 170-171
Augusta Treverorum, battle of 75
**Augustus**, Gaius Octavianus **12-21**, 29
    the early years 12-15
    rise to power 15-17
    administration 18
Aurelian Wall 106-107, 109, 125, 126, 162
**Aurelian**, Lucius Domitius 101, 104-105, **106-109**, 122, 134
Aureolus, cavalry commander 101, 104, 106
aureus, gold weight 133
Avernum (Auvergne) 175, 177, 180-181
Avitus, Julius 83
**Avitus**, Marcus Flavius Eparchius, emperor **175**, 176, 178, 181
    Meets Constantius III 167

**B** _______________________
bakers *see collegia*
**Balbinus**, Decimus Caelius **91, 92**
Ballista, Macriani praetorian prefect 100
Balthi, noble Visigothic family 162
Bar Kokhba, prince Simon 59
barbarian invasion (AD 407) 162, 163, 165
Basilica Nova 126
Basilina, mother of Julian Apostate 137, 138
Basiliscus 177, 178
    as eastern emperor 184
Bassianus, Julius 83
Bassianus, Septimius *see* Caracalla
Bassianus, Varius Avitus *see* Elagabalus
Baths of Caracalla *see thermae antoninianae*
battles
  Actium 15
  Augusta Treverorum 75
  Bedriacum 37
  Cannae (reference) 150
  Catalaunian Plain 171
  Cavillonum 108
  Cremona 39
  Cyzicus 74
  Emesa 107
  Frigidus 159, 160, 161
  Gallipoli 170
  Imperial mint 106
  Issus 74
  Lugdunum (AD 197) 75
  Lugdunum (AD 353) 137
  Marcianopolis 150
  Margus 113, 116
  Milvian Bridge 127
  Munda 9, 12
  Mursa 137
  Naissus (Nis) battle of 104
  Naulochos 14
  Pharsalus 8, 40
  Philippi 13
  Pollentia 162
  Siscia 154

Tapae 50
Tinurtium 75
Verona (AD 249) 95
Verona (AD 312) 126
Bauto, count 153, 155
Bedriacum, battle of 37
Belisarius 185
*billon* 103, 109
Blemmyes, tribe 111
Bonifacius 170-171
Borani, tribe 98
Botheric, *magister peditum* 155
Brenner Pass 98, 104
Britannicus, son of Claudius 31, 33, 43
Brutus, Caesar's assassin 12
Brutus, Junius Decimus 12-13
building programmes
    Antoninus Pius 64; Augustus 18; Claudius 30-31; Diocletian 122; Domitian 45; Hadrian 57; Maxentius 126; Nero 34; Septimius Severus 77, 78; Tiberius 25, 26; Titus 43; Trajan 50-51; Vespasian 42
Burgundi, tribe 111, 162, 163, 171, 176
Burrus, Sextus Afranius 31, 32-33
butchers *see collegia*
Byzantium Hippodrome 78
    destruction by Severus 76
    rebuilding by Severus 78
    siege of (AD 313) 130
    support for Niger 73-74

**C** _______________________
Caenis, Vespasian's mistress 40
Caesar, Julius 7, 8, 15, 17, 21, 181
Caesarion, Ptolemy XV 9, 15
**Caligula**, Gaius Julius Caesar **25-28**, 31, 59, 86
    invasion of Britain 28
Callistus, freedman of Claudius 30
Cannae, battle of (reference) 150
Capellianus, governor of Numidia 91
Capito, Fonteius, proconsul 36
Capri 25, 26
**Caracalla** 75, 76-77, 78-79, **80-81**, **82-83**, 84, 87
Carausius, usurper 117, 118
**Carinus**, Marcus Aurelius 111, **112-113**
Carnuntum, conference of 125
Carpi, tribe 94, 98, 107, 118
Carrhae (Harran) 8, 82, 92, 98, 118
**Carus**, Marcus Numerius **111, 112**, 116
Cassius Chaerea 28
Cassius Dio, historian 17, 76, 79, 85
Cassius Longinus, Caesar's assassin 12
Cassius, Gaius Avidius 66-67, 68-69, 74
Castinus, *magister militum* 168
Catalaunian Plain, battle of 171
cavalry, importance of 101, 121
Cavillonum, battle of 108
Ceionia Fabia 65
Chatti, tribe 45
Chi-Rho Christian symbol 127
*chortes urbanae, see* urban cohorts
Chosroes I, king of Parthia 53
Christians 31, 34, 47, 64, 95, 122-123, 126-127, 129, 130-132, 141, 149, 163
Cicero, Marcus Tullius 9, 12
Cilo, Lucius Fabius, legate 74
Circus Maximus 29, 45, 51
Civilis, Julius, rebel 41
Claudian, historian 161
Claudians, the gens 21
**Claudius Caesar** 19, 29, **29-32, 34,** 52, 81
**Claudius II Gothicus** 101, **104-105**
Cleander, praetorian prefect, 70, 76
Clemens, Flavius 47
Cleopatra Ptolemy VII 9, 10, 15
**Clodius Albinus** 70, 72-73, **74-75**
Clodius Macer, legate 34

*Codex Theodosianus* 169
Codification of the Praetor's Edict 58
*collegia*, military organisation 109
Colosseum 42, 45, 51, 64
Column of Marcus Aurelius 68
Comazon, Publius Valerius 84-85
*comes domesticorum* 116
*comitatenses* 133, 156
*comitatus* 116, 135
Commission of Twenty 91, 92
**Commodus** 67, **68-70**, 71
Commodus, Lucius Ceionius *see* Lucius Verus 59
*concilium* 17, 27, 58, 77, 87
**Constans** 131, 134-**135-137**
Constans, Constantine III's son 163, 165
Constantia, Constantine I's half-sister, marriage to Licinius 129, 131
Constantia, Constantius II's daughter 150
Constantina, Constantine I's daughter 131, 134, 137, 138
**Constantine I the Great** 109, 117, 123, **124-135**, 174
    passed over for promotion 123
    and Christianity 126
    alliance with Licinius 126
    war with Maxentius 126-127
    domestic tragedy 132-133
**Constantine II** 131, 134-**135**
**Constantine III**, usurper 162, **163-165**, 167
Constantinople 133, 184
**Constantius I** Chlorus 117, 118, **123**, 131, 138, 143
**Constantius II** 131, 134-**135-140**
**Constantius III 165-167**
Constantius, Julius Constantine I's half-brother 136-137, 138
*constitutio antoniniana* 81
Constitutional Settlement 15
*contubernium* 79
Corbulo, Domitius 35, 44, 49
court ceremony 122, 134, 141
crafts *see* trades
Crassus, Marcus first triumvir 7, 8, 22
Cremona, battle of 39
Crispus, Flavius Julius 131, 132-133
Ctesiphon, Persian capital 52, 64, 77, 93, 112, 142, 155
*curia*, Rome's senate house 122
*cursus honorum* 19, 40, 48, 54, 58, 79
Cyzicus, battle of 74

**D** _______________________
Dabel, king of Nabataea 50
Dacia, conquest of 50
    abandoned 109
Dacian Wars 46
Dacians, tribe 45, 46, 50
Dalmatius, Flavius, Constantine I's half-brother 136
Dalmatius, Flavius, Constantine I's nephew 134, 136
Decebalus, Dacian king 50
*decennalia, see also vicennalia*
    Gallienus 103
    Septimius Severus 77, 78
**Decius**, Gaius Messius 94, **95-96**, 99
*delatores* 24, 26, 45, 46, 81
**Diadumenian 82-83**
Didius Julianus *see* Julianus
Didymus, cousin to Honorius 163, 164
*dioceses* 118-119
**Diocletian** 109, 112-113, **116-123**, 125, 134
    administration reform 116, 118-120
    court ceremony 122
    death of 126
Domitia Lepida, Nero's aunt 33
Domitia Longina, Domitian's wife 44, 47
Domitia Lucilla, mother of Marcus Aurelius 72
Domitia Paulina, Hadrian's mother

54
**Domitian** 39, **44-47,** 48
Domitianus, praetorian prefect 137
Domus Augustana, palace of Domitian 45, 48
Domus Aurea, palace of Nero 34, 51
Domus Flavia, Flavian palace 45
Domus Populi 48
Drusilla, Caligula's sister 27
Drusus Caesar, son of Germanicus 25
Drusus the Elder, brother of Tiberius 14, 19, 20, 22
Drusus the Younger, son of Tiberius 21, 23
*dux/duces* 119

**E** _______________________
Ecdicius, son of Avitus 175, 178, 181
Edict of Milan 129, 133
*edictum perpetuum* 58
Edirne *see* Adrianople
Egnatia Mariniana, Valerian's wife 97
**Elagabalus** 80, 83, **84-86**, 87
El-Gabal, god 83-85
Emesa, battle of 107
epidemics 66, 96, 101
Epiphanius, bishop of Ticinum 181
*equites*/equestrian 14, 19–26, 30, 44–45, 58, 79, 83, 87, 101, 118
Etruscus, Herennius, son of Decius 95, 96
Eucherius, Stilicho's son 163
Eudocia, Valentinian III's daughter 174, 177
**Eugenius**, usurper **157-160,** 168
Euphemia, wife of Anthemius 177
Euric, king of the Visigoths 177, 181
Eusebius, Christian historian 125, 126, 131, 137
Eutropius, historian 105
Eutropius, *praepositus sacri cubiculi* 161, 162
Exarchate of Ravenna 185
Exedares, king of Armenia 53

**F** _______________________
Fausta, daughter of Maximian, second wife of Constantine I 124, 131, 132, 135
Faustina the Younger 65, 68
Faustina, wife of Antoninus Pius 64
Felicissimus, mint procurator 106
First Triumvirate 8
*fiscus* or imperial treasury 30, 34, 45, 46, 48, 67, 78-79 157
Flavia Domitilla 40
**Florian**, Marcus Annius **110**
*foederati* 153, 161, 164, 170
Franks, tribe 98, 110-111, 117, 135, 140, 171
Frigidus, battle of 159, 160, 161
Fritigern, Visigoth chieftain 149, 153
Fronto, Marcus Claudius 66
Fulvia, Mark Antony's first wife 13, 14
Furia Sabinia Tranquillina, Gordian III's wife 92
Fuscus, Cornelius, legate 46

**G** _______________________
Gainas, *magister militum* 161, 162, 176
Gaiseric, king of the Vandals 170, 174, 176, 178, 182
Gaius Caesar, grandson of Augustus 19
Gaius Marius 6
**Galba**, Servius Sulpicius 24, 27, 34, *36-38*
**Galerius**, Gaius Valerius 117, 118, 122-**123-125**
Galla Placidia the Younger, Valentinian III's daughter 171, 174, 176, 180
Galla Placidia, half-sister to Honorius 165-169, 170-171
Galla, Valentinian I's daughter 147, 166
    marriage to Theodosius I 154